ONWARD TO THE OLYMPICS

ONWARD TO THE OLYMPICS

Historical Perspectives on the Olympic Games

Edited by Gerald P. Schaus
and Stephen R. Wenn

2007
Publications of the Canadian Institute in Greece
Publications de l'Institut canadien en Grèce
No. 5

Wilfrid Laurier University Press ·

We acknowledge the financial support of the Government of Canada through the Book Publishing Industry Development Program for our publishing activities.

Library and Archives Canada Cataloguing in Publication

Onward to the Olympics : historical perspectives on the Olympic Games / Gerald P. Schaus and Stephen R. Wenn, editors.

Proceedings of a conference held in Waterloo, Ont., Oct. 3, 2003.
Includes bibliographical references and index.
ISBN-13: 978-0-88920-505-5
ISBN-10: 0-88920-505-1

1. Olympic games (Ancient)—History. 2. Olympics—History. I. Schaus, Gerald P., 1950–
II. Wenn, Stephen R. (Stephen Robert), 1964–

GV721.5.069 2007   798.4809   C2007-900303-6

© 2007 Wilfrid Laurier University Press and
The Canadian Institute in Greece/L'Institut canadien en Grèce

Cover design by David Drummond. Text design by C. Bonas-Taylor.

⊚
This book is printed on Ancient Forest Friendly paper
(100% post-consumer recycled).

Printed in Canada

In memoriam
Victor Matthews

CONTENTS

PART II: THE MODERN OLYMPICS

LIST OF ILLUSTRATIONS

PREFACE

This collection of essays is the result of a conference entitled *Onward to the Olympics: Historical Perspectives on the Olympic Games*, sponsored by Wilfrid Laurier University (WLU) and the Canadian Academic Institute in Athens (now the Canadian Institute in Greece) and held in Waterloo, Ontario, on 3–4 October 2003. The idea behind the conference was to explore and in some small way reinforce the connection between the Olympic Games of the ancient Greek world—held for a thousand years at Olympia, 250 km west of Athens—and the modern Olympic Games, which were about to return to Athens in the summer of 2004 after a 108-year absence. It was expected that Greece, as host country of the Games of the 28th Olympiad, would engage the attention of both students of history and the curious public at large, who would watch the Olympics in their "place of origin" for the first time in a century. A strong interest in the history of the Olympic Games by the co-chairs of the conference organizing committee, both of whom teach the subject at WLU, as well as the considerable research strengths of colleagues at nearby universities, gave further impetus to the idea, and led to the formation of an organizing committee representing both ancient and modern sides of the Olympic history divide.

A small but serious concern was how to bridge this divide effectively so that scholars of quite different historical periods could learn from each other and offer insights into the forces of change governing the Games, whether ancient or modern. We hoped that by organizing joint sessions and encouraging exchange, especially on topics of mutual interest, we might break down any natural reticence to step across the divide. In the end, we probably need not have worried, since our common interests in history and in sport were enough in and of themselves to bring participants together. Nonetheless, the process was encouraged through inspiring addresses from His Excellency the Ambassador of Greece to Canada, Leonidas Chrysanthopoulos, and Paul Henderson, member of the International Olympic Committee to Canada, reminding us of the incredible tradition of the Olympics in Greece and alerting us to the herculean efforts being exerted by Greece to host the Games successfully once again. The "icing" on the cake, if you will, for conference participants was a night out together at the local hockey rink to watch the defending Canadian junior champions, the Kitchener Rangers, play one of their provincial rivals in front of a full house of passionately cheering spectators. Such occasions evoke universally felt emotions.

It is fitting that this volume is dedicated to the memory of Victor Matthews, a member of the conference organizing committee and strong supporter of the idea for the conference from its inception. Sadly, Professor Matthews passed away while preparing for his last week of classes before retirement. He was a fine scholar in the field of epic poetry, Hellenistic literature, and ancient sport. He was also a wonderful colleague. His love of sport and his enthusiasm for teaching were deep and genuine, and it is hoped that these papers in some small way reflect that love and enthusiasm.

A brief comment on the spelling of ancient names and terms is in order. In a collection of papers such as this, authors have their own preferences for Greek or Latin spellings, but it is left to the editors to impose consistency. We have opted for Latin spelling with a few exceptions where the Greek spelling was simply more familiar—for example, pankration, kourotrophic, klepshydra, pentathlon. We hope that readers will understand.

It is left to offer a brief but very warm thanks to those whose efforts on behalf of the conference, and this volume, made both possible. First, we wish to thank the members of the organizing committee (listed below), and secondly the sponsoring institutions; besides WLU and the Canadian Institute in Greece, these include the University of Windsor, the University of Guelph, and the University of Western Ontario. Next, special mention should be made of Cheryl Lemmens for her careful copy editing of the typescript. Finally, very warm thanks go out to many individual helpers, including Faith McCord, Debbie Currie, Pam Schaus, Jo-Anne Horton, Trevor Osborne, John Hergel, Karen Sotiriou, Donald Welch of Golder Associates, and the people at WLU Printing Services. A silent cheer in your honour should rise from the stadium of Olympia.

Gerald P. Schaus, *Co-Chair*
Stephen Wenn, *Co-Chair*

Members, Organizing Committee
Robert Barney, University of Western Ontario
Nigel Crowther, University of Western Ontario
Scott Martyn, University of Windsor
†Victor Matthews, University of Guelph
Kevin Wamsley, University of Western Ontario
Robert Weir, University of Windsor

INTRODUCTION

◈

Gerald P. Schaus

Mark Dyreson, president of the North American Society for Sport History and one of two keynote speakers at the conference entitled *Onward to the Olympics*, held in Waterloo in October 2003, asked his audience to consider which of two prominent views of the Olympic Games was more appropriate. When Baron Pierre de Coubertin launched the Olympic movement 110 years ago, his vision, noted Dyreson, was "to construct a better and more peaceful world" through sport. Peace, however, was a fragile concept—both in the world and on the playing field—by the time George Orwell issued his famous denunciation of sport as "war minus the shooting."

In 2004, the IOC-sponsored Olympic Games returned to Greece for the second time[1] with security precautions at an unprecedented level from fear of global terrorism, and with competition so fierce that some athletes were willing to cheat to the point of jeopardizing their careers, their reputations, and their personal health. Equally troubling was the fact that many nations spent immense amounts of scarce national resources for the sake of Olympic victory and the reflected glory that would come with it. Even so, the olive branch symbol of the 2004 Athens Games, and the friendly intermingling of athletic contingents from every corner of the globe at the close of the Games, reflected Coubertin's hopes. So Dyreson posed the question, and in the concluding paper of this collection of essays from the conference, he attempts to elucidate the future direction of the Olympics, suggesting that the Games will continue to thrive only if the movement itself adapts to the changing world around it. About what that change is, at least in the short term, Dyreson offers some visionary thoughts of his own, but he allows readers to exercise their own powers of prediction. This collection of essays provides plenty of food for thought so that, arriving at Dyreson's paper, the reader is richly prepared to offer his or her own prediction of the future direction of the Games. The present volume provides an historical overview of the Games, not from a 110-year perspective, but from more than a millennium of celebration, beginning in the mists of early Greek history. The ancient Olympic festival was terminated by the Roman emperor Theodosius when it failed to adapt to the change from paganism to Christianity. So, what are the changes facing the modern Olympic festival? Will it adapt to them in time, or will it decline and even face extinction again?

There is much to learn from considering the entire history of the Olympic Games, as the two days of conference papers, and now decades of scholarship on both the ancient and modern Games, have made clear. The celebration of *Athens 2004* was an excellent occasion to bring together historians of the Olympics, both ancient and modern, in order to consider similarities and differences between the two eras and the two normally separate disciplines. Greece, as the birthplace of the Games and now their most recent summer host nation, provides both source and impetus for each of us to consider the role that athletic competition has played, is playing, and will continue to play in human society across the globe.

The director of the German excavations at ancient Olympia in the mid-1980s, Helmut Kyrieleis, once accepted an invitation to visit Waterloo and speak to a class at Wilfrid Laurier University on ancient Greek sport. The main message he delivered that day eighteen years ago was not that Olympia stood for unity among the Greeks, nor for any sort of brotherhood, and certainly not for peace. The so-called "sacred truce" was put in place simply to allow the Olympics to be celebrated regularly amidst a world of bitter political rivalries and danger; it was not to promote peace. Kyrieleis stressed that Olympia ultimately stood for victory and the defeat of fierce rivals, and that it demonstrated the power of the gods, and the power given to men. On display throughout the grounds of the Sanctuary at Olympia were the memorials of winners, in athletics and in war. This is reflected in the essay by Nigel Crowther, who examines the question of ancient Olympic ideals and notes the strong emphasis on victory in the "athlos" or "contest," whether in the stadium or on the battlefield. Crowther also recognizes, however, that a by-product of the Games was an opportunity to create a feeling of unity among Greeks (Panhellenism), and to resolve disputes between Greek states.

In studying ancient Greek athletics, specifically the contests staged at Olympia, we only learn about losers by chance, because of who defeated them, how they had once themselves been winners, or how they had won or lost in strange circumstances. Otherwise, it was only in prize games, not in the great crown games like the Olympics, that second place was at all rewarded, much less recalled—unlike the Games of today, with their gold, silver, and even bronze medals. The paper in this volume that addresses the issue of Olympic losers was authored by Victor Matthews, himself a winner—as his first name foreshadowed—in long-distance running and as a long-time coach of national champion runners at his university. He had the heart of a champion, but it was mortal. So he is remembered here with warmth and respect, just as the Greeks long ago recognized that it is the memory of one's "victories" that lives on.

Study of the ancient Olympic festival, covering a much longer interval than the modern Games, has faced a very great obstacle—a paucity of evidence. Besides the German excavations at the Sanctuary of Zeus, Olympia, begun 130 years ago, and a rather lengthy description of the Sanctuary by Pausanias in the mid-second century AD, well after the Games had passed their "Golden Age," our evidence is very scrappy indeed. This quickly becomes evident when reading a few of the papers proffered here on the Games in antiquity. Scholars search for the minutest of references, evaluate their worth, balance them against often contradictory evidence separated in date by centuries at times, and then try to create a picture from these few pieces of the puzzle. This may discourage even the most patient readers who are not familiar with the ancient sources or specialized vocabulary. For this reason, an overview of the history of the ancient Games is offered, as well as a glossary of terms. The reward for those who persevere is a much greater understanding of our sporting past. As once noted by Erich Segal, a Classics professor at Yale University and author of the best-selling 1970s tearful romance *Love Story*, the ancient stadium is an entranceway to the world of the classical Greeks.[2] With this volume, it is hoped that the reader, by being exposed to one part of the ancient "stadium," will not only learn something about the Classical world but also gain a new perspective on the arena of modern athletics.

Two major themes emerge from among the studies on the ancient Games. The first is the origins of the festival and its earliest development. Four papers tackle aspects of this theme. Senta German contends that public athletic events were practised regularly during the Aegean Bronze Age, more than a half millennium before the Olympics even began. These events were attended by large audiences, giving youth of the aristocratic class an opportunity to display their prowess, in a manner similar to the Olympic Games in their early history. Even if a direct connection between the Bronze Age and Early Iron Age practices cannot be demonstrated, it is difficult to ignore the possibility of cultural inheritance in the later era.

Thomas Hubbard examines the complex web of evidence surrounding the mythical attribution of the Olympic Games to Heracles, and tries to explain why there are two separate threads, one attributing the Games to Heracles of Thebes, and the other to Heracles the Cretan dactyl from the age of Cronus, father of Zeus. Equally difficult and just as puzzling is the issue of the date, 776 BC, proposed for the first occasion of the historic Olympic Games. Max Nelson examines the tradition of this date, and why it is now generally regarded with great skepticism as a reliable foundation date for the Games. Finally, Paul Christesen attempts to explain why athletic festivals blossomed suddenly in the first half of the sixth century, so that a circuit of four great Panhellenic Games appeared. This, he argues, was caused by a fundamental shift in the practice and purpose of public athletic endeavours, as non-elites adopted features of elite athletic activity, including nudity.

The second major theme is the workings of the ancient athletic festival itself. Four papers cover a rather diverse range of topics within this general theme, but all attempt to solve specific problems posed by the disparate evidence. In the first of these, David Romano provides a broad overview of the judges at the Olympic Games and the problems they faced in carrying out their duties. Not only were they judges, but they had to organize the Games, supervise the training of the athletes, weed out the poorer quality participants, and ensure that cheaters were found out and punished. A similar role is seen for the Sixteen Women who organized the foot races for girls at the festival in honour of Hera which was also held at Olympia but at a different time from the Olympics.

The second paper, by Aileen Ajootian, describes how and where the Olympic organizers scheduled draws for opponents in paired competitions such as boxing, wrestling, and *pankration* (a combat event like "extreme fighting"). Not only does she point to the exact place in the

Sanctuary where this took place, but she recreates the setting, surrounded by bronze statues of Trojan War heroes.

The third paper addresses a somewhat sensitive question: Were women involved at Olympia and in Greek sport generally, and if so, in what way? This paper—by Donald Kyle, the second keynote speaker at the conference—should be especially interesting to a modern audience, since both the Olympics and the sporting world in general have undergone profound changes in the past century. Although Kyle's firm conclusion may disappoint some at first, it should not, since it serves to highlight the accomplishment of our own world in striving for inclusion and equality, thus aspiring to a goal never dreamed of in antiquity.

The fourth paper on this theme is by Hugh Lee, who looks at the question of how athletes competed in the jumping event of the ancient pentathlon. This may seem like a minor topic, but it typifies the search for answers for which the evidence offered is so troublesome. Was it a running long jump, or a standing jump, remarkably using heavy hand-held weights? The evidence at first seems very clear, with many examples of the actual weights (*halteres*) preserved for us to examine, and just as many depictions of their use on Greek vases. Ancient authors, however, are totally silent on the matter, or so it has seemed until now.

My own paper takes a very different approach to the Olympic Games. Instead of viewing them from within and concentrating on details of their history and competition, this paper looks at them from an outside perspective—that of the tiny city state of Stymphalus in Arcadia, which enjoyed a brief period of glory at Olympia and then virtually disappeared from the national stage of sport spectacle, as much as it hoped for more.

As a bridge between the ancient and modern worlds of Olympic history, Robert Weir focuses his thoughts on coinage issued in association with Olympic celebrations in antiquity, and those in modern contexts since 1952. The reasons for such commemorative coinage are easy for us to understand in light of present needs to finance the increasingly expensive, nationally rotating Games, but what was the motivation for issuing special coins associated with Olympia in antiquity? Again, the evidence from the ancient world is much more difficult to interpret than that of the modern.

Weir's paper not only shows the contrast in availability of evidence to historians of ancient and modern sport but allows us to judge better the value of studies illuminating the earlier Olympics. On the other hand, we can appreciate the efforts by historians of the modern Olympics in locating available sources and evaluating their worth. The papers that examine the Games of today can also be neatly divided into two main groups—those considering topics prior to the Second World War and those after the War. One paper in particular not only bridges the divide but also provides a wonderful foil for Donald Kyle's examination of women's sport in the ancient world. This is Kevin Wamsley's study of the great change in women's Olympic participation during the twentieth century, especially the role that Avery Brundage, head of the International Olympic Committee from 1952 to 1972, played in that change. It is clear from Wamsley's overview that in the early years of the modern Olympics, female athletes were given about as much place as on the very best occasions of ancient sporting events. This fact alone highlights the astounding advances made to the present.

Three papers bring to light features of the Olympics prior to the Second World War. Jim Nendel describes the accomplishments of Duke Kahanamoku, a larger-than-life Hawaiian swimmer of royal blood whose success led to his participation in the Olympics of 1912 and 1920. Aristocratic influences of the early eurocentric Olympic Movement, together with American nationalism and native Hawaiian ambition, came together around this "duke" to create something of a media sensation.

The story of another link to ancient Olympia is explored in the paper by Robert Barney and Anthony Bijkerk. The torch relay from Olympia to light the flame for each new Games is a product of Adolf Hitler's Berlin Games in 1936, but the story began eight years earlier in the design of the stadium for the Olympics in Amsterdam. The history of this poignant reminder of Greece's past, so much anticipated in every opening ceremony today, is therefore very recent, and begins with a Dutch architect named Jan Wils.

The third pre-War vignette is provided by Jonathan Paul. Analyzing local newspaper coverage of the 1932 Summer and Winter Olympics, both held in the United States, Paul notes the unexpectedly positive attitude to them, despite the severe economic hardships of the Depression. This is all the more striking when compared with the mixed attitudes found in media coverage of more recent Olympics, despite the much more pronounced prosperity of today's host nations. Has the shine worn off the role of host? Has the size and complexity of hosting become too great for an educated, socially conscious public to bear? This change is yet another one worth pondering.

After the Second World War, the Olympics were marked by change, controversy, and issues of social responsibility; at the same time, they have become larger, more expensive, and vulnerable to political manipulation.

This section of our volume begins with Wamsley's look at the increased participation in the Games by women and continues with two movements that made headlines in Canada in 1976: the anti-apartheid boycott by African nations at the Montreal Summer Olympics, and the place of the Paralympics, brought to the fore by the Fifth Paralympic Games, held in Toronto that same year. These two subjects, considered by Courtney Mason and David Greig, respectively, demonstrate a profound change in attitudes towards the Olympic festival. Clearly, the celebration of sport can also be used to promote serious social and political change rather than to serve only as a display of national aspirations or political ideologies on the world stage.

Possibly the greatest change in the running of the Games has been the advent of television. This new medium has had a great impact in a number of ways, not the least of them the funding of the Games. The selling of television rights along with a world corporate sponsorship program has allowed the IOC to focus on other pressing problems, from doping to bribery scandals to the involvement of athletes in the highest levels of decision-making, both under the leadership of former IOC President Juan Antonio Samaranch and current President Jacques Rogge. These matters all come within the scope of the paper by Stephen Wenn and Scott Martyn.

Mark Dyreson's vision of the future of the Olympic Games has already been mentioned, and it is a fitting close to this retrospective examination of a truly great sporting festival. There is, however, one other paper which touches on future developments of the Games, although from quite another perspective. Baron Pierre de Coubertin revived the Olympic Games based on his view of ancient Olympic ideals, hoping that the new Games would be an inspiration to the youth of his time, and reinforcing Victorian, aristocratic outlooks. More than a century later, Tim Elcombe proposes a different set of ideals, pragmatic ones, which change, which are not fixed; rather, they adapt to changing needs, perceived and expressed by the voices of a new society. The Olympic Movement need not seek a single fixed goal, such as "peace" or "equality"; rather, the Games may continue to be relevant for another century or more by identifying social and political divides, and by acting as a vehicle or a voice for change. The call at the close of each Olympics for the youth of the world to gather in four years' time—to celebrate the Olympic festival once more in the spirit of peace, harmony, and brotherhood—has begun to wear thin. Only a tiny fraction of the world's youth gathers for each Olympiad, and this fraction is viewed by some as a pampered elite, recognized as much for its self-seeking nature as its self-sacrificing extremes. A fair portion of the Olympic athletes have included, within and among their sacrifices for sport, the loss of time from a formal education. To be frank, how many of society's real leaders and decision-makers have actually competed in the Olympics? No, the Olympics inspired ancient Greek youth to work hard, to seek glory in order to honour their family, their city state, and their gods. What higher goals should the modern Olympics inspire our youth to strive for, whether in their daily lives, their education, or their sporting endeavours? Not just youth, of course, but also we ourselves, each one of us, might be guided by the ideals promoted by the Olympic Movement. Here is something of which history can make us more conscious, even if it must necessarily leave the definition of those ideals to others.

Notes

1 "Olympic Games" were organized in Greece in 1859, 1870, 1875, and 1889 with mixed success, but without the necessary support internationally to continue them on a regular basis. Coubertin's first IOC-organized Olympic Games were held in Athens in 1896. Greeks again organized Games in 1906, but these were not recognized as an official Olympiad by the IOC.
2 Foreword to Waldo E. Sweet, *Sport and Recreation in Ancient Greece: A Sourcebook with Translations* (Oxford: Oxford University Press, 1988), p. vii.

ABBREVIATIONS

Part I: The Olympics in Antiquity

Abbreviations for ancient authors and sources in the Notes and Works Cited are those found in Simon Hornblower and Antony Spawforth, eds., *The Oxford Classical Dictionary*, 3rd ed. (Oxford: Oxford University Press, 1996). The more commonly used abbreviations, as well as those used in the captions to illustrations, are listed below.

ABSA	*Annual of the British School of Athens*
Agora X	Lang, Mabel, and Margaret Crosby. *Weights, Measures and Tokens. Athenian Agora* 10. Princeton, NJ: American School of Classical Studies at Athens, 1964.
Agora XXVIII	Boegehold, Alan L., et al. *The Lawcourts at Athens: Sites, Buildings, Equipment, Procedure, and Testimonia. Athenian Agora* 28. Princeton, NJ: American School of Classical Studies at Athens, 1995.
AION	*Annali, Istituto universitario orientale, Napoli*
AJA	*American Journal of Archaeology*
AJP	*American Journal of Philology*
AR	*Archaeological Reports* (British School at Athens)
*ARV*²	Beazley, J.D. *Attic Red-Figure Vase-Painters.* 2nd ed. Oxford: Clarendon Press, 1963.

BCH	*Bulletin de correspondence héllenique*
BICS	*Bulletin of the Institute of Classical Studies* (University of London)
*CAH*²	*Cambridge Ancient History,* 2nd ed. (1961–)
CQ	*Classical Quarterly*
DAI	Deutsches Archäologisches Institut
Etym. Magn.	*Etymologicum Magnum*
FHG	Müller, Karl. *Fragmenta Historicorum Graecorum.* Paris, 1841–70.
FGrH	Jacoby, Felix. *Fragmente der griechischen Historiker.* Berlin and Leiden, 1923–.
GRBS	*Greek, Roman, and Byzantine Studies*
HSCP	*Harvard Studies in Classical Philology*
IC	Paton, W.R., and Edward Lee Hicks. *The Inscriptions of Cos.* Oxford: Clarendon, 1891.
IG	*Inscriptiones graecae*
IvO	Dittenberger, Wilhelm, and Karl Purgold. *Die Inschriften von Olympia.* Berlin, 1896.
JDAI	*Jahrbuch des Deutschen Archäologischen Instituts*
JHS	*Journal of Hellenic Studies*
JWI	*Journal of the Warburg and Courtauld Institutes*
JSH	*Journal of Sport History*
LCL	Loeb Classical Library
LCM	Loeb Classical Monographs
MDAI	*Mitteilungen des Deutschen Archäologischen Instituts*
MDAI(A)	*Mitteilungen des Deutschen Archäologischen Instituts. Athenische Abteilung*
OJA	*Oxford Journal of Archaeology*
PCPS	*Proceedings of the Cambridge Philological Society*
RE	Pauly, August F., Georg Wissowa, Wilhelm Kroll, et al., eds. *Paulys Realencyclopädie der klassischen Altertumswissenschaft, neue Bearbeitung.* Stuttgart: Metzler, 1893–1980.
RhM	*Rheinisches Museum für Philologie*
RHR	*Revue de l'histoire des religions*
Rose³	Rose, H.J. *Handbook of Greek Mythology,* 3rd ed.
SEG	*Supplementum Epigraphicum Graecum*
SIG	*Sylloge Inscriptionum Graecarum.*
SNG	*Sylloge Nummorum Graecorum*
Suda	Greek Lexicon formerly known as *Suidas*
TAPA	*Transactions of the American Philological Association*
ZPE	*Zeitschrift für Papyrologie und Epigraphik*

Part II: The Modern Olympics

ABC	American Broadcasting Corporation
ABC	Avery Brundage Collection
CBS	Columbia Broadcasting System
EBU	European Broadcasting Union
FSFI	Fédération Sportive Féminine Internationale
IAAF	International Amateur Athletic Federation
ICOS	International Centre for Olympic Studies (London, Ontario)
IOC	International Olympic Committee
ISL	International Sports and Leisure Marketing
ISMG	International Stoke Mandeville Games
ISOD	International Sports Organization for the Disabled
NBC	National Broadcasting Company
NOC	National Olympic Committee
NZRFU	New Zealand Rugby and Football Union
OCOG	Olympic Games Organizing Committee
SANOC	South African National Olympic Committee
SANROC	South African Non-Racial Olympic Committee
SCSA	Supreme Council for Sports in Africa
USOC	United States Olympic Committee

PART I

THE OLYMPICS IN ANTIQUITY

༟

The Ancient Olympic Games through the Centuries

Nigel B. Crowther

Despite their importance, or perhaps because of it, the ancient Olympic Games have not always been well served by historians. One of the German archaeologists working at Olympia, Ulrich Sinn, recently lamented the absence of current, scholarly works in English on the ancient Games.[1] Although almost all histories contain much useful information, for a long time many were permeated by Victorian concepts of the gentleman athlete, the evils of professionalism, imaginary times of innocence, non-existent images of fair play, and even the triumph of Christianity over pagan Olympia.[2] In the late nineteenth century, Baron Pierre de Coubertin, although a visionary for the modern Olympic Movement, interpreted the ancient Games to fit his own sporting and political conceptions. He believed that Greek athletics had remained "pure and magnificent" for centuries, and that competition was a "dangerous canker," even though the *agon* was the very essence of Greek sport.[3]

Many of these misapprehensions have at last been laid to rest, although modern scholars are still not in full agreement, nor perhaps will they ever be, given the paucity of sources. Several misconceptions, however, still remain, which this volume should help to redress. In this introduction, I intend to comment on the mythological and historical origins, the

Panhellenism, the democratization, the development, the decline, and the popularity of the ancient Games.

Myth, Cult, and Ritual

According to Pausanias (5.14.4–10), there were more than seventy altars at Olympia, but most of these were only indirectly associated with the Games, and few can be located today with any accuracy. Numerous myths are associated with Olympia, but their connection with the origins of the Games is flimsy.[4] The legends of Zeus, Pelops, Heracles, and others are contradictory,[5] and even the ancients found them confusing. According to Strabo (8.355), "one should disregard the ancient stories both of the founding of the temple [Sanctuary] and of the establishment of the Games... for such stories are told in many ways, and no faith at all is to be put in them."[6] Perhaps over the centuries the Greeks updated the myths, as the character of the cult changed.[7] Indeed, scholars have associated the gods and heroes of Olympia with various phases of the Games. This is especially true of Pelops, whom Burkert considers to be a central figure in the cult.[8]

If we follow the view of Rose,[9] sport at Olympia began spontaneously, rather than directly from funeral contests. Sinn suggests that the local inhabitants probably met regularly on the site to pay homage to the gods.[10] He further proposes that these ritual gatherings were festive, with competitions in foot races, which were associated in Greece not only with Olympia but with cults in general. Early games at Olympia such as these, however, were not necessarily the same as the Olympic Games themselves, as Lee has observed.[11]

According to Philostratus (*De Gymnastica* 5), the origin of the first running event (the *stade*) was a race to the altar of Zeus, where the victor lit the sacred fire for a sacrifice to the god.[12] Robertson even speculates that early contests were a sort of initiation rite, in which boys were taken from their community, with the priestess of Demeter Chamyne, the only married woman at the festival, representing the "domestic milieu."[13] Yet it is still uncertain whether it was religion, or other factors, that provided the impetus for sport at Olympia.

Ritual remained much in evidence at Olympia over the centuries. Oaths were taken, for example, by athletes beside the image of Zeus (Paus. 5.24.9–10). Expensive statues (*Zans* or *Zanes*) were dedicated to Zeus at the foot of the Hill of Cronus by those athletes who were convicted of cheating. The Olympic "truce" (*ekecheiria*) was sacred to Zeus. The prize of the olive wreath was traditionally made from the wild olive tree near the temple of Zeus.[14] Yet not every facet of the Games was oriented to religion. Siewert believes that neither the *Hellanodikai,* the judges at the Games, nor their predecessors, the *diaitetai,* had religious associations.[15] Although the Greeks regularly practised sport in sacred places, the Games were not especially religious in a society where religion was ingrained in every aspect of life.[16]

776 BC and All That

Even such well-established Olympic dates as 776 BC and AD 393 have been questioned by scholars. The very reckoning by specific Olympiads and by the victory list of Hippias is now considered questionable by Shaw, who believes that 776 BC "is...a fixed point that may be, and probably is, spurious."[17] Recent excavations at Olympia which have concentrated on the southwest area of the *Altis* (especially on the clubhouse and the Roman mosaics) have been fruitful in establishing new dates for victors at the Games. In 1994, Sinn discovered a bronze plaque, which lists victors at Olympia as late as AD 385.[18] Not only does the honour of being the last known Olympian no longer belong to Varazdat(es) of Armenia in AD 369, but it is significant for our understanding of the "end" of the Games that these latest Olympians came from Athens, not from distant parts of the ancient world.

It was long believed that as early as 1500 BC there were Mycenaean remains at Olympia, but Mallwitz has argued that there is no convincing evidence for Mycenaean shrines and suggests that Olympia first became a sanctuary in the ninth or eighth century BC.[19] In its early days, the Olympic festival was probably one of the numerous competitions that arose in Greece on an informal basis, which would have had little in common with the illustrious Games that they were to become. If one follows the traditional account (which is now considered to be far from certain), there was only one event in the first Olympiad, the *stade.* Since this race of less than 200 metres would have lasted for under thirty seconds, it is unlikely that at this time athletics were a major part of the festival. Sport, however, gradually became more prominent as two other foot races (the *diaulus* and *dolichus*) were added. Eventually the Olympic program consisted of twenty-three contests, although there were never more than twenty at any one Olympiad.

The year 776 BC used to be considered a firm date for the Olympic Games, and "one of the few absolute dates available for the Iron Age."[20]

The year seemed to fit with what is known of the history of the period, for it coincided approximately with the introduction of the alphabetic script into Greece. Yet even in the ancient world, Olympic chronology was challenged by Plutarch (*Numa* 1.4) and others. Pausanias (5.8.5) states that the Games lapsed in the time of Oxylus and were refounded in the reign of Iphitus. Eusebius says that Coroebus of Elis was not the first victor but the first *recorded* victor, and that there had previously been twenty-seven [unrecorded] victors. Some ancients believed that the Games began in the ninth century, and indeed, circa 1000 BC, offerings of tripods and figurines of charioteers began to appear in the *Altis*. Lee proposes that these dedications at Olympia, which became more numerous in the eighth century, may have been connected with sport.[21] In contrast, Morgan believes that such figurines do not necessarily imply the existence of chariot racing at this time, but may show the importance of horse rearing and horsemanship as aristocratic values.[22] Even though dedications of tripods are associated with funeral games in Homer and are represented on later Greek vases, she argues that they are also linked with offerings other than those at funeral games.[23] Hence, she concludes that there are no archaeological reasons to move back the festival earlier than 776 BC.

Was the date for the first Games later than 776 BC? Siewert believes that no written regulations for the Games existed at this time, observing that there are no inscriptions from the Sanctuary before ca. 600 BC, although dedications from previous times have been discovered, as we have seen.[24] Some scholars have suggested that the Games began ca. 700 BC, when the number of wells at Olympia increased.[25] Others, however, have argued that the evidence of the wells merely reflects the growing popularity of the Games, as new contests were added.[26] Yet we should still bear in mind the warning of Shaw that 776 BC is not an absolute date, and that Olympiad chronology can be problematic.

Participants, Panhellenism, and Democratization

The first participants in sport at Olympia were probably those who lived in the area, or were visitors to the Sanctuary. Gradually this changed, when athletes journeyed to Olympia specifically for the purpose of taking part in the contests.[27] For almost two hundred years—if we accept the traditional dating—the Olympics were the only "Panhellenic" festival until Games were founded (or re-established) at Delphi (586 or 582 BC), at Isthmia (582 or 580 BC), and at Nemea (573 BC). Hence, in the sixth century we find an athletic circuit in Greece (*periodos*) with potential "grand slam" winners (*periodonikai*).[28] In the fifth century, victors in the crown games could be immortalized in the verses of Pindar and Bacchylides, but only those athletes who could afford the poets' fee. Ostensibly, to compete at Olympia, contestants had to be Greek, but the festival attracted competitors and visitors from ever-distant parts of the Mediterranean world.[29] As the Games became more popular, the stadium increased in size, and more facilities were added.[30] The festival gradually became more democratic and more accessible to athletes, but this did not lead to a moral decline at Olympia, as sometimes thought.[31] According to Farrington, however, over the centuries the attraction of Olympia as a Panhellenic centre did not remain constant.[32] He notes from epigraphical sources that in the late Hellenistic period interest in the Games and shrine decreased; although thereafter the prestige of the Games revived, the shrine itself never regained its former importance as a Panhellenic cult. Perhaps "the backwardness and relative inaccessibility of Elis" now counted against Olympia.[33] We should remember, too, that the Eleans strictly controlled all access to the festival and Sanctuary.[34]

The terms "amateur" and "professional" have long since been abandoned by most scholars in reference to the ancient Games, for these have been shown to be modern conceptions that would have had little meaning to the ancients. Young clearly demonstrated that "the decadent era of professionalism" was not preceded by "the glorious age of amateurism."[35] Even in the earliest recorded Games, he believes that lower-class athletes were present, and in large numbers, noting that a cook and a goatherd were among the first victors. The social status of athletes, however, is a complex problem, and other scholars have modified the views of Young somewhat.[36] Pleket, for example, proposes that lower-class "professionalism" arose only after the time of Pindar.[37] Kyle doubts that "lower-class" athletes had the same opportunities as the privileged,[38] and notes that the aristocracy always dominated in equestrian events. One wonders, too, whether the poorer athletes would be able to afford the time away from home to attend the thirty-day training period at Elis and the five days of the Games, with the added cost of travel.[39]

From the sixth century BC onward (and perhaps before), even though the prize at Olympia was merely symbolic, cities like Athens handsomely rewarded Olympic victors.[40] These payments helped to make athletics a "profession," and no doubt contributed to the Panhellenic nature of the Games and to the quality of competition. At least from the time of the great boxer Theagenes, in the fifth century BC, athletes had become increasingly specialized and were able to make a living out of the numerous

Greek festivals.[41] This growing commercialization of the Games, however, should be no reason per se for believing that Olympia was now corrupt and facing decline.

Olympia in the Roman Period

With the Roman conquest of Greece in 146 BC, Olympia entered a more uncertain stage, which extended for over five hundred years. The city states of Greece, including Elis, were now incorporated into the power of Rome and were no longer independent entities. Victors in the Games came in greater numbers from outside mainland Greece, notably from the cities of Asia Minor and Egypt, which had benefited much from the wealth of Rome.[42] In times of economic decline, however, the host city of Elis was still prominent among Olympic victors. Sometimes Olympia received favourable treatment from the Romans, who were interested in Greek culture, but on other occasions it experienced periods of neglect and even humiliation. In 146 BC, the Roman general Mummius showed his interest in the Sanctuary by dedicating a bronze statue of Zeus and adorning the temples. Yet in 86 BC, Sulla plundered the sacred treasures in the *Altis*, and six years later for political reasons transferred most of the Games to Rome, albeit only for one Olympiad. By the time of the Empire, cult statues of Roman emperors and generals were found in the Sanctuary next to those of the Greek gods. Now the success of the festival depended not only on Elis, but also on external support: Augustus, Agrippa, Herod I of Judaea, and others all made significant improvements to the athletic facilities. Although Nero's antics in the Games of the 211th Olympiad (postponed by him to AD 67 and annulled after his death) showed how powerless Elis had become, not all emperors were as contemptuous of the traditions of Olympia. Domitian, for example, undertook a general rebuilding program and became the benefactor of the guild of athletes. Hadrian especially assisted the Games, and, by issuing coins that bore the image of Zeus, symbolically linked Greek and Roman ideals. He renovated Stadium III, on which is based the stadium seen by visitors today.[43] Also in the second century AD, the aqueduct of the wealthy Athenian Herodes Atticus brought water for visitors and athletes, which was stored in the monumental fountain known as the *nymphaion*. After Hadrian, however, few emperors appear to have supported the Games actively.[44]

The Decline of the Ancient Games

The Olympic festival had suffered in the aftermath of the Peloponnesian War, with the rise of Macedon in the third century BC, and on several other occasions. In the third century AD, the site was partly destroyed by the invasion of the Heruli, and later by the incursions of the Germanic tribes and others. Earthquakes, beginning in AD 290, and several severe floods also damaged Olympia. Yet towards the end of the fourth century AD, as we have seen from the recently discovered bronze plaque, the Games appear to have been flourishing still. The reasons for the decline of Olympia were external rather than internal. According to Scanlon, there was no moral or inner decay.[45] It is evident, as Weiler says, that the demise was not linear: "physical degeneration," "collapsing national strength," "corruption and brutality" and other factors all existed at Olympia, but these alone were not reasons for the decline.[46] Mystery religions and the philosophical movements of Neopythagoreanism and Neoplatonism, with their belief in an afterlife, conflicted with the cults of the Sanctuary. Yet despite the popular view that pagan cults and Christianity could not coexist, Christianity seems not to have been a major cause of the demise of the Olympic festival.[47] There were, however, several events that precipitated the end of the Games: in AD 393, Theodosius I issued an edict that all pagan cults be banned, although this decree makes no reference to Olympia and its athletic events.[48] In AD 426, Theodosius II ordered that all Greek temples be demolished. According to the scholiast on Lucian, in this year fire destroyed the temple of Zeus and brought an end to the Games.[49] Archaeology has shown, however, as Scanlon observes, that it was not flames but an earthquake (in the sixth century) that destroyed the temple.[50] Weiler, therefore, rightly rejects the single-cause theory for the end of the Games and proposes that the decline is associated with the "socio-economic" conditions of the times and with the transference of power away from the Greek city state.[51] Olympic Games of a sort, however, still continued to be held at Antioch (Daphne) long after the edicts of the two Roman emperors.[52]

The Popularity and Prestige of Olympia

It is beyond debate that throughout the centuries the ancient Olympics were considered to be the foremost games in Greece. Pindar (*Olympian* 1.3–7), for instance, proclaims that no contests were greater than those of Olympia. Sometimes, however, the Games did face competition from other festivals, even though, as Cairns remarks, there was a considerable gap in status between Olympia and the other crown games.[53]

Many reasons have been offered for the great prestige of Olympia in the ancient world. Even in the early days, Olympia seems to have been an important meeting place for trade and diplomatic exchanges. According to Finley and Pleket, its very insignificance as a place and the relative unimportance of Elis as a *polis* might account for some of its success.[54] Certainly the Elean supervisors of Olympia were outstanding and considered to be irreplaceable, as the Spartans discovered in 399 BC after their conquest of Elis (Xenophon *Hell.* 3.2.31). Perhaps the Greeks appreciated the conservatism of Olympia, since it remained relatively unchanged for over a millennium. According to Sinn, the pre-eminence of Olympia may have resulted from its origins as an outstanding agricultural festival; he remarks that vegetation gods, including Artemis, Aphrodite, Demeter, and Gaia, all had altars in the Sanctuary and were predominantly worshipped in the area.[55] On the other hand, Morgan points out that the Olympic festival "was timed to miss all major harvests, and possibly may never have been an annual event."[56] The oracle of Olympian Zeus, small as it was, had great fame in antiquity (Strabo 8.355), and may have contributed to the high status of the festival.[57] For Kyle, "the success of the ancient Olympics owed much to aristocratic display, the addition of equestrian events, intra- and interstate competition, colonization, and state rewards, as well as to the power of the Olympic ideal."[58] Morgan too, noting that Olympia faced towards the west, sees Greek colonization of Sicily and southern Italy as an important element.[59] These western colonists may have viewed Olympia as a kind of home away from home. Olympia was the preferred meeting place for the successful Greek émigrés and for those they had left behind.[60] An important link between Olympia and the colonists is the Olympian seers, who escorted the Greeks as they set out for the west.[61] The success of these emigrants and the seers must have added to the fame of Olympia.[62] Whatever the reasons for its success, Olympia received the supreme compliment of having Isolympic imitators throughout the Mediterranean, where many Games, especially in Asia Minor, took the title of "Olympic."[63] The Elean controllers of Olympia treated this as a commercial transaction, since aspiring festivals had to pay a "franchise" fee to gain the rights to the name.[64]

Athletics in Greece existed before the Olympic Games and would have existed without the Games. Yet it was Olympia that provided "the ultimate stage on which athletes could compete and triumph."[65]

Notes

1 Sinn 2000, 136. This absence has been substantially filled through books published in the past several years, notably by David Phillips and David Pritchard (eds.), *Sport and Festival in the Ancient Greek World* (2003); Nigel Crowther, *Athletika* (2004); John Hermann, Jr., and Christine Kondoleon, *Games for the Gods* (2004); Stephen Miller, *Ancient Greek Athletics* (2004a); Nigel Spivey, *The Ancient Olympics* (2004); William Blake Tyrrell, *The Smell of Sweat* (2004); Panos Valavanis, *Games and Sanctuaries in Ancient Greece* (2004); and David C. Young, *A Brief History of the Olympic Games* (2004). This article first appeared in Crowther 2004, 1–10, with update, p. 51.

2 The subjectivity of scholars towards the ancient Games can also be seen in references to the "Golden Age" of Olympia, where a wide variety of dates have been suggested, ranging from the eighth to the late fourth centuries BC. See Golden 1998, 20, and Weiler 1985–86, 256.

3 Coubertin 2000, 543. Coubertin might have been surprised to know that the oracle at Olympia (note 57) was used to predict the results of contests. See Morgan 1990, 136, on this aspect of the oracle.

4 For a fuller account of these myths, see Drees 1968 [1962], although some of his conclusions on Pelops should be treated with caution.

5 On Heracles and Elis, see the essay by Thomas Hubbard in this volume.

6 See Golden 1998, 12–14. I quote here the Loeb translation.

7 One should consult on this point Ulf 1997, who attempts to bring the myths into the context of Greek history. For detailed comments on cults, ritual, and initiation, with a useful survey of literature, see Ulf and Weiler 1980. Despite the original date of publication, the article by Rose (1985 [1922]) contains useful observations on the origins of Greek athletic festivals.

8 Burkert 1983, 93–103. See also Sansone 1988, passim, who comments on Burkert's views regarding the association of Greek athletics and religion.

9 Rose 1985 [1922].

10 Sinn 2000, 12.

11 Lee 1988b, 113.

12 See Sansone 1988, 82–83, on the connection between the race and the sacrifice to Zeus, and the comments of Golden 1998, 18–19, on Sansone.

13 Robertson 1988, 23. This is a general work, but has useful observations and references.

14 For more (speculative) comments on sport and ritual, see Sansone 1988.

15 Siewert 1992, 116. He sees a distinction between "the ritual and the agonistic functions" at Olympia.

16 As Golden 1998, 23, has noted.

17 Shaw 2003, 242.

18 For the text of this inscription and insightful comments, see Ebert 1997.

19 Mallwitz 1988, 81–89.

20 Morgan 1990, 47. It was originally believed that the date 776 BC was derived from Hippias of Elis, who compiled his victory list in the mid-fifth century; but see now Shaw 2003 and the essay by Max Nelson in this volume, as well as Möller 2005 and the forthcoming book by Paul Christesen on Olympic chronology.

21 Lee 1988b, 111.

22 Morgan 1990, 90.

23 Morgan 1990, 43–47.

24 Siewert 1992, 114.

25 These wells were dug about four to six metres underground. See Mallwitz 1988, 98–99. Peiser (1990) dates the Games even later than this, to the first part of the sixth century. See also Ulf and Weiler (1980) on the early Games.

26 Lee 1988a, 133.
27 Sinn 2000, 29, and see n. 11 above. In the early days, individual worshippers undertook religious pilgrimages to Olympia, but later the Greek city states took a growing interest (Morgan 1990, 44).
28 For the *periodos*, see the essay by Paul Christesen in this volume.
29 On this complex problem of eligibility and Panhellenism, see my later essay in this volume.
30 For details on Stadium I, Stadium II, and Stadium III, see Romano 1993, 17–24. See also below on Stadium III.
31 See the well-argued discussion in Kyle 1997.
32 Farrington 1997.
33 Finley and Pleket 1976, 112.
34 For more on Elis and Olympia, see my later essay in this volume.
35 Young 1984, 76–82.
36 We should be aware that by using the term "lower class" we might be introducing modern connotations. Some scholars have questioned the accuracy of the ancient sources on early athletes, since they may show later prejudices.
37 See Kyle 1998, 121–25, for the numerous articles written by Pleket on this topic. To these we can now add Pleket 2001, an updated version of his 1974 article in *Mededelingen Nederlands Instituut te Rome*, 36, 57–87.
38 Kyle (1998, 124) asks whether the first recorded victor, Coroebus of Elis, was the "cook" of Young or the "priest" of Pleket, since he believes that the term *mageiros* can be interpreted either way.
39 Stephen Brunet, however, in a paper delivered at the conference, believes there may have been more "subsidies" available than is commonly believed.
40 There is less evidence that cities (or patrons) supported athletes *before* they were successful, as Brunet argues in his conference paper.
41 For an argument against the idea that athletes became more specialized, see Young 1996a.
42 Scanlon 2002, 49.
43 Romano 1993, 24.
44 For more on Olympia under the Romans, see the excellent chapter by Scanlon (2002, 40–63), who notes that in the second century AD, we find several major Greek literary sources for Olympia.
45 Scanlon 2002, 59–60.
46 See the thoughtful article by Weiler (1985–86), on which much of this section is based. He convincingly sifts through arguments put forward by scholars over the years on the reasons for the decline of Olympia.
47 In fact, after it ceased to be a place for athletic competition, Olympia—with its abundant supply of water—became a settlement for Christians. See Sinn 2000, 122–26.
48 As Weiler (1985–86, 257) observes.
49 Scholiast on Lucian (*Rhetorum praeceptor* [ed. Rabe] 176, 3–6; 178, 2–7).
50 Scanlon 2002, 59.
51 Weiler 1985–86, 259.
52 See also below, nn. 63–64, for cities other than Olympia that celebrated Olympic Games.
53 Cairns 1991. See also Pleket 1992, 147, for the Olympics as the most prestigious festival in Greece. On differences between the ancient and modern Games, see Kyle 1998, 110 n. 22. For the rise of the modern Olympic movement with references to the ancient, see Young 1996a. The modern Olympics are different from the ancient, since by comparison as a whole they have no serious competitors to their pre-eminence.
54 Finley and Pleket 1976, 22–23.
55 Sinn 2000, 11. See also Swaddling 1980, 12.

56 Morgan 1990, 43.
57 See Pausanias (5.14.10) for the oracle of Gaia. For more on the oracle, see Hönle 1972,
    15–24.
58 Kyle 1998, 114.
59 Morgan 1990, 105. For Olympia and the western colonies, see Hönle 1972, 68–119.
60 Sinn 2000, 25. Sinn also notes that eight of the treasure houses in the *Altis* were dedi-
    cated by colonial cities, and that many Etruscan artifacts have been found at Olympia.
61 See Hönle 1972, 68–70, and Siewert 1992, 116.
62 See Sinn 2000, 19, for further comments.
63 Farrington (1997, 35–43) lists the more than thirty known Isolympic festivals.
64 At the time of Claudius, for example, Antioch was granted an Olympic festival after pay-
    ing an appropriate fee to Elis; see Malalas 249 and 286.
65 Lee 1988a, 139.

Politics and the Bronze Age Origins of Olympic Practices

Senta C. German

Introduction*

It did not take long after the discovery of the cultures of the Aegean Bronze Age to find evidence of a prehistory of public athletic competition not unlike the Olympic Games. Schliemann's excavations at Mycenae in the 1870s included the discovery of images of chariot racing.[1] Among Sir Arthur Evans's discoveries at Cnossus in the first decade of the twentieth century were representations of bull leaping.[2] From the following decade, LaRosa's excavations at the villa of Hagia Triada yielded a stone vessel on which images of wrestling were carved.[3] Later excavations at Mycenaean sites in Cyprus yielded images of foot races.[4]

In E. Norman Gardiner's book *Athletics of the Ancient World*, published in 1930, the Minoan and Mycenaean evidence was included in discussions of the origins of the Games. Gardiner himself did not think that Bronze Age sport was Olympic, and he concluded instead that the evidence seemed to illustrate merely common fighting and performance of extraordinary feats.[5] Since Gardiner, however, a handful of authors have argued that these images and other evidence do indicate an origin in the Bronze Age for Olympic practice.[6]

It is important to note here that "Olympic practice" is not meant to refer to the specific celebrations beginning in the eighth century at the site of Olympia (since this would be chronologically and geographically impossible), but rather to the essential character of the games, formalized athletic proceedings with political patrons, celebrated by a large audience with a religious component. These earlier practices, then, would be the precursors to the athletic events which arose in later Iron Age Greece, of which the Olympic festival is a primary example.

In a 1988 article on the origins of the Olympics, Colin Renfrew opines that despite a considerable array of evidence, there still is little reason to think that Bronze Age athletic activities were nascently Olympic. Renfrew sees the Classical Olympics as serving two functions: first, as a venue for peer group interaction between Greek city states, and, secondly, as a great religious celebration.[7] The Bronze Age evidence, in his opinion, does not bear this out. I would argue, however, that the evidence is sufficient on both counts.

Bronze Age Olympia

The first logical place to look for a connection between the Iron Age Olympics and any Bronze Age antecedent is the site of Olympia itself. Such an investigation, however, ends in frustration, since there are only a very few Bronze Age remains. In 1907, Wilhelm Dörpfeld, one of the original excavators of Olympia, found prehistoric remains in a trench between the *Heraion* and the *Metroon*. Specifically, he found six houses; five were apsidal in shape, and one lay beneath the northeast wall of the *Pelopion*. There were some other remains of buildings near the Altar of Zeus. The masonry appears pre-Mycenaean,[8] indeed more typical of the Early to Middle Helladic period, and the apsidal aspect connects the structures to other pre-Mycenaean levels at Tiryns (at the earliest strata) and Orchomenus, as well as Middle Helladic Corinth.[9] Finds in and around these structures included smoothed and chipped stone implements, some of obsidian, terracotta spindle-whorls, hand-made monochrome incised pottery, and a very few fragments of painted pottery. The pottery is certainly of local manufacture and of typical pre-Mycenaean type.[10] One late Mycenaean sherd was found in these early excavations, under the wall of House Four, although there is some doubt whether House Four is prehistoric, according to Herrmann's re-study of the finds.[11] Furthermore, two clay Mycenaean "idol" fragments were found.[12] One is the fragment of a head and body, the other the body and "Psi" type arms. Also, some pieces of bronze Mycenaean jewellery were discovered.[13]

The settlement appears to have been somewhat long-term, since one of the houses, number Five under the *Pelopion* wall, had at least two distinct occupation levels. Stratigraphically, this period comes to an end with a layer of gravel, which Fritz Weege,[14] one of the later excavators at the site, argues was a levelling or foundation course put down by the builders of the first *Pelopion*. Excavations by the Greek archaeological service in the mid-1960s discovered a Late Mycenaean cemetery of twelve chamber tombs on the Kalosaka hill, 100 metres north of the Hill of Cronus, which might have been associated with a Late Mycenaean settlement destroyed in the later constructions at the site of Olympia.[15]

From secondary contexts, Emil Kunze, another excavator of Olympia, found Early Helladic to Late Helladic pottery at the Olympic Stadium, although he suspected that it might have rolled down the Hill of Cronus.[16] Alfred Mallwitz interpreted the remains of a stone wall discovered in well 14 of the Stadium as prehistoric.[17]

In the vicinity of Olympia, due north, at a site called Maghira, a small group of later Mycenaean pithos burials was found, as well as some clay figurines of a typical early "Phi"-shaped Mycenaean type.[18] Minoan-looking figurines have been found at Epitalion, due west of Olympia.[19]

One last piece of evidence of prehistoric Olympia comes from the Mycenaean Linear B texts. Among a group of tablets from Pylos, the Mycenaean palace site closest to Olympia, there are those which appear to describe the military arrangements for an attack from the sea—specifically, listing units and where they are stationed.[20] One tablet lists towns along the coast north of Pylos. L.R. Palmer argues that *Pi-jai* indicates a town in the location of the port of Olympia, Φεάς, which is on the route taken by Telemachus on his voyage back from Pylos to Ithaca (Hom. *Od.*15.295). This location is also mentioned by later authors, namely Thucydides and Strabo (Thuc. 2.25.3, Strabo 8.342).[21]

We can conclude, then, that the archaeological evidence for any sort of Bronze Age athletic practice (or, indeed, activity of any sort) at the site of Olympia is glaringly lacking. This, however, need not be the end of an investigation into Bronze Age origins of the Olympics. That is to say, if we concentrate not on cultural continuity at the site of Olympia but instead focus on continuity of Olympic practice itself, there are still avenues to explore. Let us begin with a review of some evidence from the Bronze Age for athletic competition.

Evidence of Athletic Competition in the Bronze Age—The Example of Bull Leaping

Evidence for athletic competition in the Bronze Age Aegean is of considerable variety and seems to indicate that athletic events were well-organized occasions and attended by large audiences at the Minoan and later Mycenaean palaces. The evidence for bull leaping is particularly rich, and so will be used to exemplify Bronze Age Aegean practice.

Evidence for bull leaping in the Aegean Bronze Age is very early indeed, first appearing in the form of small-scale terracotta sculpture found at the Prepalatial cemeteries at Koumasa and Porti in the Mesara Plain on Crete, ca. 2500 BC.[22] The only evidence of bull leaping in the following First Palace period on Crete, ca. 2100–1700 BC, is in the form of a venue for such activity, the so-called "theatrical areas" and central courts of the Minoan palaces, built at this time.[23] Later wall painting indicates that these areas were used for performances.[24] Beginning in the Second Palace period, ca. 1700–1450 BC, several representations of bull leaping are found in the archaeological record; including the famous ivory leapers from Cnossus, found in the Temple Treasury. These, presumably, would have been placed in association with a small model of a bull, a fragment of which was found with the figures.[25] Equally famous and dating to this period is the boxer *rhyton* from Hagia Triada.[26] This steatite vessel is divided into four horizontal registers; the second one from the top illustrates two charging bulls, one of which has gored and tosses a man, presumably a less talented bull leaper. In the other three registers, combat sports are illustrated, suggesting a kind of athletic program of events.[27]

Many representations of bull leaping come from the glyptic arts during the Second Palace period, most of which are sealings. Examples from Hagia Triada include men doing backflips over bulls in mid-leap over a strong ground line, evoking the built environments in which performances at palaces are depicted in wall painting.[28] The only representation of bull leaping from the Mainland at this time is a small fragment of an ivory plaque which shows only the hoof of a charging bull and the leg of a leaping person, which comes from Grave Circle B at Mycenae.[29]

From the following Third Palace period, the time of Mycenaean domination of the Aegean region, ca. 1450–1375 BC, several representations of bull leaping come from both the Mainland and Crete. It is from this period that the familiar "toreador" wall paintings belong, found in the Court of the Stone Spout at Cnossus.[30] From the Mainland at the same time, there are now many examples of bull leaping, which is regarded as an example of the extent of Minoan influence on Mycenaean culture. Indeed, images of bull leaping have been found among the wall paintings at three Mycenaean palaces: Tiryns,[31] Pylos,[32] and the Ramp House at Mycenae.[33] The example from the Ramp House offers specific evidence that there was an audience for bull leaping.[34] Examples of bull leaping on seals and sealings are known from both Crete and the Mainland at this time, including one gold ring from a Mycenaean chamber tomb in Anthia, not far from Olympia, which again includes the representation of a paved surface beneath the feet of the bull.[35]

Finally, from the very end of the Third Palace period on the Mainland, a *larnax*, or ceramic coffin, found in the cemetery at Tanagra, exhibits a particularly dynamic example of the motif. A scene on one side of the sarcophagus illustrates three bulls in a row, each with a leaper in flight above them. The fact that this scene is on a *larnax* suggests that it is an illustration of funeral games.[36]

What is revealed by this brief review of one athletic activity practised in Bronze Age Greece is its consistency of form and frequency throughout the history of the period. The evidence indicates that this activity was performed in a built environment, and that an audience witnessing the bull leaping event was an important aspect of the activity. Furthermore, the majority of the evidence for bull leaping is firmly associated with Bronze Age palaces, the political focal point of the period.[37] Therefore, insofar as the athletic practice of bull leaping in the Aegean Bronze Age was a formalized practice, associated with important political entities and attended by audiences, they appear not dissimilar to the Olympic practices at Iron Age Olympia.

Or is this just slim evidence for a mere coincidence of social practice between the Bronze and Iron Ages? If indeed there is a genuine similarity between these two athletic practices, then we would expect to find a similarity between their two meanings. We are familiar with the social meanings of the Iron Age Olympics; let us now turn towards an exploration of the possible meanings of Bronze Age athletic practice.

Meanings of Bronze Age Athletic Practice

Aegean Bronze Age scholars generally agree that a variety of social practices, as well as their visual representation, were adopted by Mycenaeans from the Minoans. Given the evidence cited above, we can see that bull leaping was one of those social practices. The question is, how have

Aegean scholars interpreted bull leaping? Since the event appears to have been performed overwhelmingly by male youths and is clearly a physically dangerous feat, it has been suggested that bull leaping was part of a rite of passage.[38] Such rites initiate members of a younger age group into an older age cohort. Anthropologists studying these surprisingly common rites of passage ceremonies note that they function as a critical step in building group identity, not only of the group experiencing the initiation but the group sponsoring it.

Furthermore, since evidence for bull leaping and other athletic activities can be found in a number of media across palatial Minoan and later Mycenaean sites, it might be seen as evidence of the building of inter-palatial group identity. Indeed, if this is the case, it is not the only example of inter-palatial contact which could have served this purpose. For instance, there is evidence for close economic ties between the Minoan Palaces in the Second Palace period in the form of "look alike" or replica rings or gems.[39] These rings and stones look identical to one another, presumably having all been made from the same mould or by the same artist or workshop. They are typically known only from the sealings made by their impression. The most interesting examples of the "look-alike" or replica phenomenon are the ten Cnossus replica rings, all presumably manufactured at Cnossus during the LMIB period. The decorations on these rings include a chariot drawn by two horses, two running lions in front of a palm tree, two combat scenes, and six different bull leaping scenes. Fifty-three impressions found at six different sites on Crete—Gournia, Hagia Triada, Cnossus, Sklavokampos, Zakros, and Chania—were identified as having been made from these rings, thirty-six of which illustrate bull leaping; all were made from local clay.[40] This evidence from the "look-alike" or replica rings indicates not only inter-palatial contact but the currency among the palaces of the images of athletic practice.

During the Third Palace period, there is increasing evidence for luxury gift exchange among the Mycenaean palaces. Indeed, recent research into the Mycenaean palaces defines them as wealth-financed political systems, where the palaces paid for state-sponsored activities with high-value prestige goods. These prestige goods, such as perfumed oil, bronze tripods, and woven cloth, would have circulated between regional elites in a system of reciprocal gift exchange, further strengthening group identity.[41]

To what extent, however, does any of this evidence help us understand the meaning of athletic practice in the Aegean Bronze Age? An interesting circumstance of elite gift exchange within a pointedly athletic context is found in Book 23 of Homer's *Iliad*, in which the funeral games of Patroclus are described. After Patroclus is buried, Achilles brings from his ships a variety of valuable items, such as cauldrons, tripods, iron, horses, mules, oxen, and even women to offer to the winners of athletic competitions staged in honour of his fallen friend (Hom. *Il.* 23.257–261). Important Greeks, namely Diomedes, Antilochus (the son of Nestor), Menelaus, and Meriones, compete for these prizes in a chariot race, placing in order. At the end of the contentious awarding of the prizes, Achilles offers a two-handled vessel to Nestor as a kindness, recalling his past days of athletic accomplishments. This encourages Nestor to recount "the day when the Epeians were burying lord Amarynceus at Buprasium.... In boxing I overcame Clytomedes, son of Enops, and in wrestling Ancaeus of Pleuron... Iphiclus I outran in the foot-race... and in casting the spear I outthrew Phyleus and Polydorus" (Hom. *Il.* 23.629–637, Loeb transl.). Nestor, the legendary Mycenaean king of Pylos, describes games in which he has participated together with other important regional Greek leaders. These games were also occasions of gift exchange. Both of these activities work to build group identity.

Indeed, although we must always treat any evidence of the Bronze Age found in Homer with great caution, it is worth keeping in mind that many of the myths connected with the founding of games at Olympia involve presumable Bronze Age heroes, such as Pelops and Heracles. Comparable heroic figures from this earlier age may well have sponsored games at the palace sites, perhaps many of which were connected with funerals, such as we read about in *Iliad* 23, and the likes of which seem to be illustrated on the sarcophagus from Tanagra. These events would foster group identity among the palaces.

The building of group identity sounds surprisingly similar to the way in which the later Olympic Games were regarded. Mark Golden, in his excellent study *Sport and Society in Ancient Greece*, discusses three critical differentiations that institutionalized Greek athletics advanced. First, he argues that they created boundaries between groups and solidified group identity—specifically, between Greeks and non-Greeks, between male competitors and female non-competitors, and between different ages of competitors. Secondly, and very importantly, these events created winners and losers. Lastly, Golden argues that athletic competition in the ancient Greek world provided a forum in which to debate the relative value of types of competition, the types themselves being class-specific.[42] Although the veneration of the Olympian gods was a critical component of the Olympic festival, this work of social definition might also be seen as the essential political aspect of the Games.

If one then focuses on this essential aspect of social definition through differentiation, the strengthening of group identity, in association with competitive athletic practice, perhaps the origins of the Olympics, in a sense, can be found in the Bronze Age. Questions, of course, abound. For example, to what level of specificity can connections be made? At what point are apparent connections merely coincidences and not fundamentally issues of cultural continuity? Is there more evidence that might illuminate the matter further?

Again, the Linear B documents offer some information here. For example, on tablets found at Pylos, we find warrior names that stress physical prowess common in all strata of Mycenaean society.[43] For instance, Po-to-re-ma-ta means "strong warrior" or "fighter"; Da-i-to-ra-ro, "he who is swift in battle"; Wi-su-ro, "he who plunders with force."[44] The same sort of evidence is found in Homer; for instance, Orsilochus, a man from Crete whom we meet in the *Odyssey* (13: 258–70), is described as "fleet of foot." Could the names of these men, mentioned in the Linear B documents and echoed in the *Odyssey*, reflect individuals who had trained at competitive athletic events, not unlike the Olympics, perhaps one of them being bull leaping? These names at the very least seem to imply a competitive spirit.

Yet even if we knew that members of Mycenaean society, and perhaps Minoan society before it, prepared for military combat by engaging in competitive athletic activities, does that make them Olympic practice? Perhaps the most conspicuously missing, or overlooked, element in the Bronze Age evidence is religious ritual in connection with games. On the other hand, a number of the religious elements that come together at Olympia and later at Delphi can indeed be traced back to Mycenaean origins. Indeed, Martin Nilsson has convincingly argued for the roots of later Classical religion in Minoan and Mycenaean cult practice.[45] New finds, again from the Mycenaean palace at Pylos, offer evidence for strongly similar cult practice, specifically of animal sacrifice, between the Bronze and later Iron Age.

In the excavation of the final destruction levels at Pylos (or possibly before), six discrete groups of discarded animal bones stood out.[46] All consisted only of mandibles, humeri, and femurs from both left and right sides. These bones derive primarily from cattle (at least five to eleven cattle in each group) and secondarily from red deer (parts of at least one deer in each of two groups); all were young to mature adults, and, where sex could be determined, were male. The extent of burning was variable. This specific group of mega-fauna is not readily explainable in terms of taphonomic (fossilizing) processes or the practicalities of carcass processing. Examination of the incisions on the bones and the effect of burning on breaks indicated that they had been stripped of meat prior to being burned, but the marrow was not removed. Further, the stratigraphical find-spots for these groups of bones (one inside the entrance to the palace) indicate that they were carefully deposited, as opposed to treated as common refuse.[47] Were these the remains of sacrifices at festivities at which bull leaping and other athletic activities took place?

We cannot know, of course, but it seems a possibility. Certainly, sacrifices were a common occurrence at festivals, and such festivals commonly included a performance of some sort. One type of performance which was common among the Minoans and Mycenaeans was athletic practice, as we have seen above.

Conclusions

Do Late Bronze Age finds offer enough evidence to posit a Mycenaean site at Olympia? The notion seems plausible, given the location of a Mycenean cemetery to the north of the Hill of Cronus and a few finds in the Sanctuary and Stadium area, although any idea of its size and function is impossible to determine without more excavation. Remains of such a site were very likely affected by later building projects around the Sanctuary of Zeus. Were there athletic competitions at a presumed Mycenaean site at Olympia, as have been found at other Mycenaean sites? Speculation here will not yield any positive results.

What can we say for certain, then, about the Classical Olympics and Bronze Age athletic competition? Clearly, the examples of Bronze Age sport do not look exactly like later Olympic competition, but one can see a relationship between the two which might very well indicate continuity of Bronze Age practice into the Iron Age. The question remains: Were the meanings of these activities shared between the Bronze and Iron Ages? In so far as the later Classical Olympics were an exercise in the building of group identities among different political entities, a similar practice in the Bronze Age may be evident. The Classical Olympics were a preoccupation of male youth; the same is evident in the Bronze Age. Furthermore, there is evidence which indicates continuity between Bronze Age and Iron Age religious practice, in the sacrifice of animals, at one Mycenaean palace (Pylos)—in the same venue as athletic competitions are thought to have occurred.

In the end, nothing will ever look just like the Classical Olympics, even what we have witnessed in Athens in summer 2004, and any argument for Bronze Age origins for the Olympics must be circumstantial unless, for instance, a very different sort of Linear B archive is discovered. If, however, one regards the earlier Bronze Age period as one in which social, political, and religious memories were originally created in the minds of Greeks, we can see the performances of activities like bull leaping at special occasions within palatial centres as a precursor to the Olympics, or at least to Olympic practices of later antiquity.

*I would like to thank Gerald Schaus and Stephen Wenn for the opportunity to participate in the conference *Onward to the Olympics: Historical Perspectives on the Olympic Games*, and especially Gerald Schaus for his helpful comments.

Notes

1 Schliemann 1880, 81, fig. 140.
2 Evans 1930, fig. 144.
3 Halbherr et al. 1977, 83–86, figs. 51–52.
4 Rystedt 1986.
5 Gardiner 1930, 9–14.
6 For instance, see Evjen 1986, 51–52; Evjen 1992, 97–100; Ridington 1935, chaps. 3 and 4; Putnam 1967, 184–93; Mouratidis 1989, 43–45; Guttmann 1992, 57.
7 Renfew 1988, 22.
8 Dörpfeld 1935, 73–96. The construction was characterized by rubble masonry without ashlar footings. Present signage at Olympia identifies the apsidal houses as Early Helladic III, dating ca. 2150–2000 BC, and the associated pottery is said to bear a resemblance to the Cetina culture from the Dalmation coast to the north. Kyrieleis 2006, 27, concludes that there is no evidence of cult continuity at Olympia from the Mycenean to the early Iron Age based on excavation results. (This book appeared too late to be considered here.)
9 Herrmann 1987, 427–28.
10 Gardiner 1973 [1925], 32, but see n. 8.
11 Herrmann 1987, 428–30.
12 Heilmeyer 1972, 8–9, pl. 2.1–2.
13 Herrmann 1987, 434–36, pl. 113.
14 Weege 1911, 163–65. Prehistoric remains below the *Pelopion*, including a tumulus surrounded by a rubble enclosure wall, are now dated to the Early Helladic II period, according to signage at the site.
15 For the settlement, see Themelis 1969, figs. 1–3. For the cemetery, which was dated to LHIIIA-B, see Yalouris 1965.
16 Kunze 1967, 13.
17 Mallwitz 1967, 22.
18 Themelis 1969, figs. 1–4.
19 Themelis 1968, 202, fig 3.1.
20 Palmer 1956, 120–130.
21 Ibid., 132.
22 Xanthoudides 1921, 32–40, pls. 27–28.
23 That the central courts were the location for bull sports is generally accepted. See Graham 1957, which has since been supported by Thompson 1986 and 1989.
24 Davis 1987.

25 Evans 1930, 428–35. Evans reports that at least three figures were discovered, but only one was sufficiently well preserved to be sure that it represents a leaper of some sort. The head of a bull at the same scale found together with it (apparently in a wooden box) makes the association between the two figures likely.

26 Halbherr et al. 1977, 83–86, figs. 51–52.

27 Younger (1995) provides a complete listing of all known representations of bull sports from the Bronze Age Aegean.

28 Müller and Pini 1999, nos. 43–44. Representations of dance in glyptic art during this period are illustrated with the same ground line, and in wall painting include more detail of the built environment in which the performance takes place. See German 1999.

29 Poursat 1977, 68, pl. 19.

30 Evans 1930, 208–17.

31 Schliemann 1885, 303–307, pl. 13.

32 Lang 1968, 77, pl. 24.

33 Rodenwaldt 1911, 230–34; Lamb 1919–21, 192–94, pl. 7; Shaw 1996, 167–90.

34 Shaw (1996) offers a new reconstruction of the fragments of the Ramp House fresco, which places the fragments of assembled groups of spectators within the same composition as the bull leaping scene.

35 Pini 1993, no. 135.

36 Spyropoulos 1970, fig. 16.

37 Marinatos (1994) even argues that images of bulls functioned as potent symbols of Minoan palatial authority overseas, specifically in Egypt.

38 Koehl 1986, 109–10, n. 66; Scanlon 1999. Koehl sees bull sports as a male rite of passage; Scanlon sees them as a rite of passage in which both males and females participated. Scanlon accepts the use of Egyptian colour conventions, white skin for female and brown for male, and therefore identifies two bull-leaping images at Knossos, the famous Toreador Fresco (see n. 30 above) and the miniature fresco from the Queen's Megaron (Evans 1930, fig. 143), as acts of women. The use of this colour convention has often been questioned (see Hitchcock 2000 for the most recent and interesting challenge); however, if it is true, the two wall paintings from Knossos are the only representations of women participating in bull sports, compared to thirty-one examples of men in various media. For a breakdown of the full catalogue, see German 1999.

39 The primary research on the Cnossus replica rings was accomplished in Betts 1967. Some additions to the original sealing count, as well as some corrections, were made by Hallager (1996, 207–209).

40 Hallager and Hallager 1995, 551.

41 Galaty and Parkinson 1999, 6–8; Galaty 1999, 83ff.; Killen 1994.

42 Golden 1998, 176–78.

43 Lindgren 1973, 18, 23, 50–51, 58, 83, 90, 97, 102, 121, 161. See also Chadwick 1973, 160, for a text from Pylos in which musicians are mentioned; 183–85, for military arrangements; 361–63, about chariots. Furthermore, see Palmer (1957) for a discussion of an inventory of furniture which he supposes was burned during burial feasting.

44 Deger-Jalkotzy 1999, 122–23.

45 Nilsson 1968, 447–84.

46 Isaakidou et al. 2002, 86–92.

47 Isaakidou et al. 2002, 88.

Pindar, Heracles the Idaean Dactyl, and the Foundation of the Olympic Games

Thomas K. Hubbard

Pindar's *Olympian Odes* consistently attribute the foundation of the Olympic Games to the Theban Heracles,[1] and Heracles' importance at Olympia is given programmatic emphasis in the metopes of his twelve labours in the Temple of Zeus. Several passages in Pausanias and other writers,[2] however, preserve an alternate tradition claiming to be older: that the "Heracles" who founded the Games was actually one of the Cretan dactyls, metalworkers with magical powers who lived in the age of Cronus and are often conflated with the Curetes as guards present at the birth of Zeus on Mount Ida. According to this tradition, the Games were attributed to the more famous Heracles only as a result of later confusion. My present inquiry aims to explore the antiquity and sources of these competing accounts, to relate them to the interaction of Panhellenic and epichoric claims surrounding Olympia and its cults, and to frame these claims in turn within the historical and political factors that engendered them.

At first glance, the tradition about the dactyl may appear to be a late revisionist fabrication, as both Lobeck and Farnell have argued;[3] however, Lobeck's argument that Pindar would never have made his claims if another tradition were current is surely naive, in light of Pindar's well-known penchant for mythological revision and reconciliation of competing variants.[4] Plutarch's statement (*De Malign. Hdt.* 857F) that the ancient poets (of whom he names Homer, Hesiod, Archilochus, Peisander, Stesichorus, Alcman, and Pindar) knew only one Heracles, the Theban, is merely an *argumentum ex silentio,* coloured by Boeotian pride, and is certainly of no probative value concerning details of local cult; Cicero (*Nat. D.* 3.16) had already catalogued no fewer than six.

Many signs point to the Idaean Heracles as more than merely a literary creation of late mythographers: Strabo (8.354–55) explicitly refers to his role in Olympic foundation as an "old story" like that concerning the other Heracles. The Idaean dactyls as a group were certainly well known by Pindar's time, having been the subject of a work in the Hesiodic corpus (the Ἰδαῖοι Δάκτυλοι: fr. 282 MW specifically locates them in Crete),[5] and they were also mentioned by fifth-century historians, including Pherecydes of Athens (3F47 *FGrH*), Hellanicus (4F89 *FGrH*), and Stesimbrotus (107F12 *FGrH*). They also played a role as primeval figures in the *Phoronis,* an archaic Tirynthian epic concerning the hero Phoroneus, supposedly the first human being.[6] Heracles was specifically named as one of them by Onomacritus, an oracle-forger of Peisistratid date who appears to have had Orphic connections (Paus. 8.31.1).[7] This Heracles' connection with the Orphics may also be suggested by Ephorus (70F104 *FGrH* = Diod. Sic. 5.64.4), who reconciles the competing traditions associating the dactyls with either Phrygian Ida or Cretan Ida by relating their migration from Phrygia to Crete and noting that they made many stops on the way, teaching their magic to both Orpheus and the Samothracians.[8] Orphic sources place the birth of Dionysus Zagreus on Crete and refer to the Curetes (another name for the dactyls) as his protectors.[9] When discussing the six different heroes known under the name "Heracles," of whom the Theban was the sixth and last, Cicero (*Nat. D.* 3.42) attributes his information to *interiores et reconditas litteras* [more profound and mysterious writings], a phrase that may refer to Pythagorean writings.[10] Cicero's source refers not only to multiple Heracles figures, but also to at least three Jupiters; some of these figures are divinities or heroes from other traditions (the Egyptian Heracles, the Tyrian Heracles, the Indian Heracles), but the first and oldest that Cicero names was the one who fought Apollo for the tripod. The influence of syncretistic and allegorical traditions is clear. That these were already operational in the fifth century is suggested by Herodotus' knowledge of both Egyptian and Phoenician divinities whom he identifies with Heracles (Hdt. 2.43–45).

Heracles the Idaean dactyl, however, was clearly more than just an iconoclastic bi-formation of mystery religions, even if those Panhellenic movements may have contributed to his diffusion. Pausanias makes it clear that he was also a physical presence in the cults of Elis and other localities. His representations were part of the artistic program in temples of Demeter in both Boeotian Mycalessus (9.19.4) and Arcadian Megalopolis (8.31.1), suggesting continuity with the dactyls' original associations with Phrygian Cybele and Cretan Rhea.[11] One of the altars of Heracles the dactyl in Olympia may have been near the *Gaion*, a shrine where Gaia had an ash altar and formerly an oracle; the two were described contiguously in Pausanias' tour of the site (5.14.9–10). Altars of both Heracles the dactyl and Demeter and Kore were present in the old gymnasium in Elis (6.23.1–3), along with Eros and Anteros, gods that one would normally expect in a gymnasium.[12] Even Pindar (*Ol.* 5.18) refers to a "holy Idaean cave" in the territory of Elis, a site also attested by the Alexandrian geographer Demetrius of Skepsis (fr. 54 Gaede = Σ Pind., *Ol.* 5.42a Drachmann).[13] Although not specifically mentioning the dactyls, Pindar's allusion does suggest one more cultic space belonging to the Idaean Mother, where the Idaean dactyls may very well have also gained a presence.

The Arcadian connection, rather than Cretan or Orphic influence, was probably the direct source for the introduction of these figures into Elis and Olympia. The cult of Rhea was particularly strong in Arcadia, perhaps due to Pelasgian connections with Minoan Crete, and several accounts posit Arcadia as an alternative birthplace of Zeus:[14] Callimachus (*Hymn to Zeus* 4–41), although acknowledging Cretan claims, deems those of Arcadia superior and locates his birth on Mount Lycaeum. Pausanias (8.36.2–3) identifies a sacred cave of Rhea on the mountain near Zeus' birthplace; the same passage says that she assembled allies (the dactyls/Curetes?) for any struggle against Cronus on nearby Mount Thaumasias. The river Lymax near Phigalia obtained its name from Rhea's cleansing herself in its waters after giving birth (Paus. 8.41.2). A parallel story (Paus. 8.8.2) holds that at an Arcadian well named Arne, Rhea gave birth to Poseidon and concealed him among a flock of lambs, telling Cronus that she had given birth to a foal and giving him one to eat. The temple of Athena Alea at Tegea included an image of Rhea and a nymph holding the infant Zeus, surrounded by other nymphs (Paus. 8.47.3). The Mother had a shrine at the source of the Alpheus (Paus. 8.44.3). Further along the Alpheus on the border between Arcadia and Elis, Dio Chrysostom (*Or.* 1.52–56) attests to a sacred grove and ruined shrine of Heracles inhabited by a prophetess of the Mother of the Gods. Although he does not specifically identify this Heracles as the dactyl, it may originally have been, since the Theban Heracles has absolutely no mythological connection with

Rhea or Cybele. In the vicinity of Arcadian Acacesium (Lykosoura) was a shrine of Despoina including images of Demeter, the Mother of the Gods, and the Curetes (Paus. 8.37.1–6).[15] Both an altar (Paus. 5.14.9) and shrine of the Mother (Paus. 5.20.9) were present at Olympia; Herodotus (31F34a *FGrH*) says that Heracles founded altars to the twelve gods at Olympia, among them a joint altar of Cronus and Rhea. Athena's cult is also brought into this ritual complex at a location in the Elean *chôra* some distance from Olympia,[16] where a temple of Cydonian Athena was supposedly founded by Clymenus, a descendant of the Idaean Heracles, who came from Cretan Cydonia (Paus. 6.21.6).[17]

There was without question a strain of pre-Olympian religion at Olympia, as suggested most conspicuously by the Hill of Cronus, repeatedly invoked by Pindar (*Ol.* 1.111, *Ol.* 5.17, *Ol.* 6.64, *Nem.* 6.61).[18] Pausanias (5.7.6) says that there was once a temple of Cronus as well, when the Golden Race of men dwelt upon the earth. Strabo (8.353) speaks of an Olympian oracle, and Pausanias (5.14.10) refers to an ash altar of Gaia, where she once had an oracle; many scholars argue that this oracle, like the early association of Delphi with Gaia, predated the Olympic Games and the Zeus cult, since it appears to have become obscure by Classical times, when its reputation would have been overshadowed by that of the Games.[19] Jeanmaire believed that the story of Demeter's eating of Pelops' shoulder reflected the primacy of an Earth cult with elements of human sacrifice prior to the Zeus cult at Olympia.[20]

Two passages in Pausanias attribute the origin of the Olympic Games to the Titanomachy between Zeus and Cronus. Paus. 5.7.10 says that Zeus wrestled Cronus for the throne, but records the variant that the first Games were held to celebrate Zeus' victory, with Apollo defeating Hermes in the foot race and Ares in boxing. Paus. 8.2.2 repeats the idea that Zeus and Cronus wrestled, but has the Curetes running the first foot race; it is interesting that this last reference comes in the Arcadian section of Pausanias' geography, suggesting that its source may well have been Arcadian, like so much material connected with the birth of Zeus. While this particular version of Olympic foundation may be late,[21] it does reflect a perception that Olympia was host to an ancient conflict between Pelasgian and Olympian traditions, with the latter displacing the former in a violent contest analogous to Apollo's slaying the Python and thus displacing the forces of Gaia at Delphi. Particularly suggestive is the detail about the Curetes running the first foot race, since the Curetes and dactyls are often conflated. This would then coincide with the information of Pausanias 5.7.6–9 about the first foot race being run by the four brothers of Heracles the Idaean dactyl. The information of 8.2.2 may therefore be an attempt to situate the Curetes/dactyls within this larger story of conflict between Cronus and Zeus, older deities and newer, Pelasgian and Olympian. Indeed, Kaibel argued that the dactyls were another name for the Titans.[22]

This evidence from a variety of related local cult sites in both Elis and Arcadia is simply too plentiful for Heracles the Idaean dactyl to be merely a late mythographic invention: not all of these cults can have been late foundations, and anything connected with cults and stories of Rhea and Cronus seems to presume great antiquity even in the eyes of Greeks of the Classical period. Could it then be the case that the story of Heracles the Idaean dactyl really was older than the official myth of the Games' foundation by the great Heracles? Kaibel, Cornford, Harrison, Vallois, and Jeanmaire were all of this view.[23] Cornford, contributing a chapter on the Olympic Games to Jane Harrison's *Themis*, laid great stress on the various indications of Earth Mother religion in Olympia, and endorsed Robert's view that the "Idaean cave" mentioned by Pindar was equivalent to a small shrine of Eileithyia and Sosipolis embedded in the Hill of Cronus (mentioned in Paus. 6.20.2). He viewed Eileithyia as merely another manifestation of the mother goddess, and speculated that Sosipolis was a cult title of the infant Zeus.[24] Vallois argued more convincingly that the association of Theban Heracles with the Games could not have been early because it appears to have had no reflection in Olympic ritual; Pindar's references to Heracles establishing a τεθμὸν μέγιστον [very great custom] (*Ol.* 6.116–17) and a version of the Games with multiple events (*Ol.* 10.55–75) rather than a single foot race suggested to Vallois a reorganization of an earlier institution.[25] At the very least, they must indicate a seventh-century date for the myth, since some of these events were not introduced until 680 BC.[26] Cornford and Vallois both called attention to the olive as a tree more likely to have come to Olympia either from Crete or the cult of the Earth Mother than in connection with Theban Heracles and the Hyperboreans (see below).[27]

While all of these considerations may point to Theban Heracles as a later presence at Olympia than the Idaean dactyls, they do not necessarily guarantee the originary status of "Heracles the Idaean dactyl." There was in fact no consistency among ancient sources about either the names or number of the Idaean dactyls, and the question seems to have been one on which considerable innovation was possible.[28] The four names that Pausanias (5.7.6, 5.14.7) gives for the brothers of Heracles—Paeonaeus, Epimedes, Iasius, and Idas—are nowhere else attested, and mostly seem to be modelled on words associated with healing.[29] Could this have been a cultic function which they came to have at Olympia? On the other hand, Hesiod appears to have named one of the dactyls either Delas the Scythian, or Scythes (fr. 282 MW = Clement, *Strom.* 1.16.75). Apollonius of Rhodes (1.1126) names two of them Titias and Cyllenus. The dactyl with the widest attestation in a range of sources is Celmis, of whom an elaborate story is narrated as early as Sophocles (fr. 365 Radt); almost as well attested are Damnameneus and Acmon.[30] The mystery religions, which we have seen to be a source for Heracles as a dactyl, also knew a Cretan dactyl named Morgus, whose initiates purified Pythagoras (Porphyry, *Vita Pyth.* 17). Lucian (*De Salt.* 21) even names Priapus as one of the dactyls.

Our first evidence for a dactyl named "Heracles" is late sixth century (Onomacritus). Interestingly, this is also the period in which the myth of the Theban Heracles receives its clearest canonization and maximum diffusion in the epic of Peisander of Rhodes, and becomes most widely attested in iconographic representations.[31] While Archilochus' victory song celebrating Heracles and Iolaus (fr. 324 w) seems to have been traditional at Olympia by Pindar's time (*Ol.* 9.1–4), there is no certainty that it was originally meant for Olympia or gives us any real evidence about the date of Heracles' presence in Olympic mythology. I would argue that the identification of one of the dactyls as "Heracles" was probably a reaction to the growth of the more famous Heracles' myth as an Olympic etiology; adherents of the older cultic strain at Olympia, consisting of the interrelated cults of Cronus, the Mother of the Gods, Demeter Chamyne, and the Idaean dactyls, invented this figure as a way of discrediting the newer etiological dispensation by reclaiming the figure of "Heracles" as their own. As I will proceed to show, this mythological controversy makes sense if embedded in the local politics of the Peloponnese in the late Archaic and Classical periods, whereas one is at a loss to explain why the story would have been invented closer to Pausanias' and Strabo's own times.

It may be no accident that the two areas where we find the most cultic evidence for the alternate Heracles are Arcadia and Elis, the two principal non-Dorian states of the Peloponnese. While the Theban Heracles is not specifically a Dorian hero,[32] his cult at Olympia is said to have been introduced by Iphitus, a descendant of Oxylus, the Aetolian leader of the Heracleidae when they returned to the Peloponnese (Paus. 5.4.5–6); Oxylus himself came to rule over Elis as his reward for helping the Heracleidae (Paus. 5.3.5–5.4.5). Pausanias tells us that Iphitus renewed the celebration of the Olympic Games after a long pause (cf. 5.8.5); Strabo (8.354–55) demythologizes the first Games by claiming that they were founded not by Heracles, but by the Eleans themselves after having been strengthened by the kingship of Oxylus. The involvement of the Heracleidae and their allies in this legend suggests that the Dorian influence must have had something to do both with the Heracles cult and with some stories about how the Games were founded or refounded. That this claim of influence was not without challenge is suggested by Phlegon of Tralles' narrative (257FI.5–6 *FGrH*), which adds that Iphitus' refoundation of the Games met initial resistance throughout the Peloponnese, overcome only after a plague and multiple pronouncements of the Delphic oracle.[33] The tendency of that account is to dissociate the games from Elis's neighbours, just as Pausanias' account suggests that the Eleans' own negligence had been responsible for the Games ceasing to be celebrated, and external influences were paramount in motivating their renewal, as well as their initial celebration.

I suspect that the story of Heracles the dactyl at Olympia evolved out of such a contest of mythological claims and counterclaims between Dorian and local Elean sources, or perhaps, to put it more accurately, between pro-Spartan and anti-Spartan elements within Elean politics. The history of Elis during the Archaic and early Classical periods is known through only the most fragmentary indications, but the one constant that seems to characterize almost everything we know about the history of Elis is the paramount importance of Sparta as a presence in their affairs, whether as an ally or enemy. Several sources (Paus. 6.22.2, Hdt. 6.127, Strabo 8.358) tell us that Pheidon of Argos attacked Elis and took over leadership of the Olympic Games during one Olympiad, and that the Spartans assisted the Eleans in driving him out; this event has, with some plausibility, been dated to 652 BC.[34] Pisa had apparently done the same in 676 BC or shortly thereafter (see Strabo 8.355), with Sparta again coming to the Eleans' rescue and with the Eleans, for their part, helping Sparta in the Second Messenian War; Pausanias (6.22.2) dates this event to 644, but that date may be another instance of Pisa doing the same thing.[35] About Elis in the sixth century we know only that a pre-emptive attack was made against Pisa in 588, and that state's independence ended not long afterwards (Paus. 6.22.3–4). By the time of the Persian Wars, the Eleans were at best an unreliable ally of Sparta: they were not at Thermopylae (Hdt. 7.207), and although they were one of the states planning to blockade the Persians at the Isthmus (Hdt. 8.72), they showed up late for the Battle of Plataea (Hdt. 9.77). As one historian has put it, Plataea, "with its lengthy preliminaries, was eminently a battle for which it was difficult to be late by accident."[36]

In 471–470, a few years after the Persian Wars, Elis moved towards synoecism (see Diod. Sic. 11.54.1, Strabo 8.366) and possibly a shift towards
a more democratic constitution, as may be suggested by epigraphical evidence from the period;[37] Aristotle (*Pol.* 1306a, 16–25), however, speaks
only of a more moderate oligarchy. What Strabo does tell us is that Elis's
synoecism, like that of Mantinea at the same period, was brought about
through Argive influence, which suggests that both were anti-Spartan
moves: the principal reasons for previously independent towns to unify
themselves was the perception of a common threat, particularly from a close
neighbour.

Thucydides (1.121.3, 1.143.1) shows that Elis was part of the Peloponnesian League at the outbreak of the Peloponnesian War, but as in the
earlier conflict with the Persians, Elean participation seems to have been
meagre and unenthusiastic.[38] They soon quarrelled with the Spartans over
Lepreon, an Elean dependency which, with Spartan support, refused to pay
tribute during the war (Thuc. 5.31); Pausanias (5.4.7) says that the Man-
tineans and Argives encouraged their revolt from the Peloponnesian League.
Because of this conflict and other charges, the Spartans were even banned
from participation in the Olympics of 420 (Thuc. 5.43). Thucydides (5.50),
Xenophon (*Hell.* 3.2.21), and Pausanias (6.2.1–3) all relate an incident
involving a prominent Spartan named Lichas, who, since the Spartans
were banned from participation, entered a chariot team in the name of the
Thebans. When he took the occasion to bind a ribbon around the head of
his victorious charioteer with his own hands, the Eleans interpreted the act
as an offence against their role as umpires and judges and whipped Lichas;
in Thucydides' version, Lichas' offence was merely to reveal after his victory that he was actually a Spartan. Sparta used this incident as a pretext
for declaring war against Elis almost twenty years later, in 401/400; the temporal distance suggests that it cannot have been the true cause of that conflict, which must have been motivated by many years of building tension
and distrust, of which this incident was a particularly colourful and provoca-
tive illustration.[39]

For the fourth century, we are better informed about Elean politics
thanks to Xenophon's *Hellenica*. For the period 370–367, Elis was allied
with the Argives and Arcadians against Sparta; Arcadia was at the time
largely democratic and federated (6.5.6–10). By 365, however, Elis had
realigned itself with the Spartans and against the Boeotian-Argive-Arcadian
alliance, with a view to recovering territory that had been lost earlier to
Arcadia (7.4.12–36). This realignment was motivated by a change in regime
in Elis, when the oligarchs took power and expelled the pro-Arcadian

democrats. After its victory in the ensuing war, Arcadia created independent states in Pisatis and Acrorea out of territory captured from the Eleans; Pausanias (6.22.3) records that the Arcadians managed the Olympic Games of 364.

The question for us to consider is how much these tensions attested in Elean politics of the late fifth and early fourth centuries can be retrojected to Pindar's time. Could there have also been, in that period, a struggle between a pro-Spartan oligarchy and a more democratic faction oriented towards the Peloponnesian democracies of Argos and Arcadia? If so, could that political factionalism have been reflected in cultic allegiances, with the pro-Spartan group associating the Olympic Games with Heracles, the coming of the Heracleidae, Oxylus, and Iphitus, while the pro-Arcadian group promoted local cults and myths common to both Elis and Arcadia, such as those connected with the Mother of the Gods and the birth of Zeus? We enter here into the realm of speculation, but this reconstruction would certainly make sense of the evidence as we have it. Just because our sources are silent about factional conflict in this rather marginal part of mainland Greece does not mean that it did not occur in this earlier period: our sources of evidence for most Greek cities are deficient for the same time. Under this scenario, we can understand the ambiguity of Elean policy during the Persian Wars, the shift in alliance during the Peloponnesian War, and especially the Argive-inspired movement towards synoecism at the same time as in Arcadia.

Let us now focus with some precision on how these issues may be reflected in the text of Pindar's *epinicia*. *Ol.* 10.24–77 is Pindar's most detailed exposition of Heracles' role in Olympic foundation, specifically situating it in the aftermath of his labour for Augeas, the king of Elis, and his military defeat of Augeas' allies, the Moliones; the same events are alluded to more elliptically in *Ol.* 2.3–4, a poem written for Theron of Acragas in the same year. Heracles is the one who founded the altars of the twelve gods and named the "Hill of Cronus," which was previously anonymous (*Ol.* 10.48–51). The Olympics were, from the beginning, a festival with multiple contests, and the first victors listed in *Ol.* 10.60–73 were all among Heracles' military allies, coming from either Arcadia or the Argolid; none came from Elis itself.[40] Another poem written for Theron in the same year, *Ol.* 3, gives more details: the Olympic judges, the *Hellanodikai*, were of Aetolian descent (*Ol.* 3.11–13), a detail in accordance with the story about the Games being connected with the Aetolian Oxylus, the patron of the Heracleidae, and his descendant Iphitus (Paus. 5.4.5–6).[41] We are further told that when Heracles became a god and ascended to Olympus, he handed over to the Dioscuri supervision of the chariot race (*Ol.* 3.34–38). Since this last association is nowhere else attested, many scholars have assumed that it must be an innovation arising from the performance of this ode at the Theoxenia festival, but this context is not at all certain.[42] The prominence accorded the Dioscuri may have more to do with what is evident in all of Pindar's poems having to do with Olympic foundation: an insistence upon the Panhellenic, or, more accurately, the pan-Peloponnesian status of the Games from the very beginning, established by a Theban/Tirynthian hero, with the first victors from Arcadia and the Argolid, the judges from Aetolia, and supervision of the chariot race in the hands of the Spartan heroes Castor and Pollux. That their Spartan identity is at issue in *Ol.* 3 may be implied by their being invoked together with their sister Helen in the poem's first line and the song's self-characterization as a "Dorian tune" in v. 5.

What Pindar seems at pains to exclude are versions which seem too epichoric or local in their inspiration; hence, he dismisses the possibility of pre-Olympian religion at Olympia by insisting that the Hill of Cronus, far from being a cultic remnant from the Age of Cronus, was anonymous before Heracles. Similarly, *Ol.* 1 aims to minimize the importance of the old ritual inaugurating the foot race with the sacrifice and dismemberment of a black ram at the precinct of Pelops by denying the etiological myth of Pelops' dismemberment that lay behind that ritual; this was too close to the traditions of human sacrifice that were part of the old religions which still lurked in parts of Arcadia, with remnants in the cults of Lycaean Zeus and Demeter.[43] Instead, the emphasis is placed on the chariot race, which was a more recent historical introduction, but is treated by Pindar as if it had been present at Olympia from the very beginning.[44]

The importance of the chariot race relative to the foot race may also be asserted in the principal myth of *Ol.* 3, according to which Heracles brings the olive tree to Olympia to provide crowns for the victors and shade around the course of the hippodrome (see especially vv. 33–34). Heracles' bringing the olive to Olympia from the Hyperboreans has long been assumed to be Pindar's innovation, based on the lack of parallel texts,[45] but Pausanias' account of Heracles the Idaean dactyl may give us some additional insight into the significance of Pindar's claim. Pausanias (5.7.6–9) says that the Olympic Games originated with a foot race staged by Heracles the Idaean dactyl among his four brothers, during the age of Cronus, and that the olive was brought to Olympia from the Hyperboreans by this Heracles, who used its branch to crown the victor. One might at first suppose that this detail was a direct response to Pindar on the part of the Cretan's cultic devotees, and indeed the mention of the Hyperboreans may well have ultimately gone back to Pindar, but Pausanias relates one other detail about the olive which is not Pindaric: namely, that the olive existed in such a profuse supply that the four brothers of Heracles slept on beds of green olive leaves. This sounds like a ritual etiology.[46] Pausanias' testimony is also confirmed by a late notice in Proclus' commentary on Plato's *Republic,* which says that according to Orpheus (i.e., Orphic poems), the Curetes (= dactyls) were the first to be crowned with the olive branch.[47]

Other considerations also suggest that the Cretan dactyls may have been associated with the olive long before Pindar attributed this story to the Theban: the olive was in fact especially common on Crete, where its cultivation may reach back to Early Minoan times,[48] and had ritual significance in some rites of passage on the island. Particularly interesting is a ceremony at Dreros, wherein each youth competing in a foot race was required to plant an olive tree.[49] The foot race seems also to have had initiatory significance at Gortyn, since the Gortyn Code identifies fully initiated youths with the term *dromeus* [runner], the not yet initiated as *apodromos* [almost at or without the race course].[50] Eveline Krummen has put these indications together with the abundant evidence for *dendrophoria* [tree bearing] rituals in connection with a powerful goddess to suggest that the story which Pausanias records concerning the Idaean dactyls did indeed precede and influence Pindar.[51] To her masterful treatment I would add that this motif may have had its origins in Bronze Age Crete, as suggested by the iconography on at least two Minoan signet rings and possibly also on the so-called "Ring of Minos": what we see is a goddess and a tree-shrine in a boat.[52] One possible interpretation is that Crete saw itself as exporting this tree to other parts of Greece, either under the goddess's patronage or in connection with diffusion of her cult. While the tree on these rings cannot be identified with certainty, a male figure on the Ring of Minos holds a rhyton beneath the tree as if to imply that a precious liquid was derived from the tree; this would suggest that the sacred tree is indeed intended to be an olive. Given Crete's prominence as an early centre of olive oil exportation and the sacral uses of oil,[53] stories about a Cretan origin of the sacred olive tree at Olympia are entirely comprehensible, and likely to be of great antiquity.

As in other accounts regarding Olympic foundation, multiple variants circulated. According to a version preserved by Phlegon of Tralles (257F1 *FGrH*), the olive crown was not the original Olympic victory prize, but was awarded only beginning in the seventh Olympiad, after Iphitus consulted the Delphic oracle. Pausanias (5.15.3) identifies a location in the Olympic complex where the sacred tree from which the branches were cut was surrounded by a fence; many scholars have speculated that this tree had its origins in a pre-Greek tree cult,[54] similar to what is attested on the Minoan signet rings. According to an Athenian tradition preserved among the works of Aristotle, the mother tree from which Heracles brought the first olive branches was not located among the Hyperboreans, but in the Attic Pantheion in the vicinity of the river Ilissus; this tree was also sacred and could not be touched.[55] Athens naturally wanted to maintain its claims to being a centre and source of Greek olive culture. This variation in traditions concerning the olive suggests that there was never any one canonical version of this story, but it was an arena for competing cultic claims and literary invention.

By attributing the Olympic olive's origins to neither Crete nor Attica, but to the elusive Hyperboreans, Pindar formulates a Panhellenic version which transcends the claims of any one locality. Pindar's program of placing the Theban Heracles at the centre of myths concerning Olympic foundation was surely motivated by more than just Theban nationalism, or even by a desire to glorify a hero whose importance at Olympia was maintained by the neighbouring Spartans. Pindar's perspective in this regard, as elsewhere in his odes, is pre-eminently Panhellenic, but with a Dorian bias. It is interesting to note that there were also competing foundation myths with internal and external constituencies at both Nemea and Isthmia. Bacchylides (13.46–57) clearly associates the Nemean Games with commemoration of Heracles' defeat of the Nemean lion.[56] On the other hand, Pindar's *Nem.* 10.28, from an ode for an Argive victor in local Argive games, highlights a version in which the Games were founded to commemorate the death of the infant Opheltes, killed by a snake while his nurse Hypsipyle helped the Seven Against Thebes find a spring; this would be the account that an Argive audience would expect. *Nem.* 8.51–52, however, ambiguously suggests that "the song of victory" existed even before Adrastus made war against Thebes, as if to acknowledge that athletic games, perhaps even the Nemean Games, existed before this time;[57] Pindar may here hint at an alternate version of their foundation, without overtly discrediting the Argive account. If so, his rhetorical strategy in this case is implicitly to acknowledge competing versions, which may have arisen out of the complex interrelations between Cleonae, the state with formal powers of supervision, and Argos, its most powerful neighbour.[58] Nevertheless, Pindar never offends the Argives by explicitly alluding to Heracles as Nemean founder, even though he plays a central role in the myth of *Nem.* 1 and is invoked in a prayer near the end of *Nem.* 7; in Pindar, Heracles is instead given recognition as the founder of the more important Olympic Games.

Similarly, there were two competing versions of the foundation myth to the Isthmian Games, one commemorating the hero Theseus' defeat of the Isthmian robber Sinis, the other representing the games as funeral celebrations organized by Sisyphus for the infant Melicertes, killed when his mother Ino jumped off an Isthmian cliff.[59] It may be that as Theseus became a more specifically Athenian hero rather than a local Isthmian figure, he seemed less palatable to the Corinthians as a patron of the Games, who as a result proffered a version emphasizing the role of their legendary king Sisyphus and local heroes.[60] In a fragment of a lost Isthmian ode (fr. 5 s-м), Pindar emphatically favours this Corinthian version. One of the most interesting ways he supports Corinthian claims is by insisting that the Isthmian crown was made of celery, and specifically identifying the celery crown as "Dorian" (*Isthm.* 2.16, *Isthm.* 8.63–64); Plutarch (*Quaest. conv.* 672D), basing his remarks on specific Hellenistic authorities, including Callimachus and Euphorion, says that the change from a pine crown to a celery crown was motivated out of emulation for Nemea and Heracles. A long papyrus fragment of Aeschylus' *Isthmiastae* (fr. 78c, Radt, especially vv. 39–40) alludes to pine crowns as the Isthmian garland, but also implies that "innovations" (frr. 78a.34, 78c.49–50) have recently taken place in the festival. Pine may have been a remnant of the festival's earlier association with the victory of Theseus over Sinis the pine-bender, which would explain the interest of Aeschylus and his Athenian audience in seeing it maintained at Isthmia. To the extent that the Corinthians chose to adopt celery in emulation of Heracles and the Nemean Games, they were discounting any Athenian associations, and instead valorizing their connection with their Dorian neighbors to the south.[61] Pindar reinforces this reorientation by alluding to it as if it were always the custom, and specifically labelling it "Dorian."

We therefore see Pindar adopting three slightly different strategies in regard to the mythological controversies surrounding the etiology of each festival, but in each case claims which can be seen as "Dorian" are respected: in regard to Olympia, he clearly, repeatedly, and in detail narrates the Games' foundation by Theban/Tirynthian Heracles after conquest of the local power, and appropriates for the Heracles myth the olive crown which may originally have been associated with a competing local version. In Isthmia, he confirms the reorientation of the games away from the Athenian hero Theseus and the pine crown, instead valorizing the myth of Ino and Melicertes and the Dorian celery crown. As with Heracles at Olympia, the etiology that Pindar favours is one that links Theban heroes with Dorian states. Most complex is the challenge of dealing with Nemea, where he implicitly acknowledges the existence of two competing accounts, each with Dorian credentials, valorizing the Argive position when addressing Argives, ambiguating the matter when addressing non-Argives. That Pindar takes these matters up even in poems addressed to faraway states like Aegina or Sicily suggests a broader agenda of Theban and pan-Dorian realignment, particularly in the wake of the Persian Wars and the tremendous shifts in the politics of the Greek world that emerged as a result.[62]

*In addition to presentation at Waterloo, a longer version of this paper was delivered at Cambridge University in June 2003. Both audiences are thanked for their insights. The author owes particular acknowledgement to Nicolle Hirschfeld and Senta German for their advice on Bronze Age matters. All errors remain the author's alone.

Notes

1 *Ol.* 2.3–4, *Ol.* 3.11–38, *Ol.* 6.67–70, *Ol.* 10.24–77. See also *Nem.* 10.32–3, *Nem.* 11.25–8.

2 Paus. 5.7.6–9, 5.8.1–5, 5.13.8, 5.14.6–9. Cf. Strabo 8.355, Diod. Sic. 5.64.6. Dinon (690F2 *FGrH*) says it was Heracles the dactyl who was defeated by the twin Moliones, not the Theban Heracles; for the connection of this story with Olympic foundation, see Pindar, *Ol.* 10.24–77.

3 Lobeck 1829, II, 1168–79; Farnell 1921, 129–31. See also Adshead 1986, 52.

4 For various instances thereof, see van der Kolf 1923; Dornseiff 1921, 126–27; Pini 1967; Köhnken 1974; Hubbard 1986, 1987b.

5 Schwartz (1960, 246–48) expresses doubts about the authenticity or even the independent existence of this work, thinking it may have been confused with the *Phoronis.* Pohlenz (1916, 569–72) speculates that the Curetes/dactyls and their interrelation with the Greek mainland may have formed part of Epimenides' *Cretica.*

6 At least two of the six fragments—fr. 2 and fr. 2A—seem to be connected with the dactyls. Fragment 2, Davies (1988), says they were the first metalworkers (cf. Paus. 2.19.5, who says that the dactyls owed the discovery of fire to Phoroneus). Fragment 2A, Davies, refers to the Curetes, who may here, as elsewhere, just be an alternate name for the dactyls (Hesiod, fr. 123 MW, says the Curetes were connected to Phoroneus genealogically). On the likely date of this epic ca. 600 BC, see Jacoby 1922, 366, and Kleingünther 1933, 26–28.

7 Herodotus (7.6.3–4) attests his date and falsification of oracles that he attributed to Musaeus. Pausanias (8.37.5) assigns to him the story of Dionysus' dismemberment and eating by the Titans. Many ancient sources also connect him with the composition of the Orphic poems: see Graf 1974, 146–49, for a careful review of the evidence. Linforth (1941, 350–53) adopts a position of complete skepticism that Onomacritus had written anything, but this forms part of his general program to deny any early evidence of Orphism; more recent discoveries have confirmed the movement's existence in this period. For his connection with other epic forgeries, including texts related to Heracles, see Schwartz 1960, 495–98. It is hardly likely that Pausanias is here invoking Onomacritus as a sham authority: he was too notorious as a forger to serve that function.

8 Strabo (10.466) relates that some sources viewed the Telchines, Idaean dactyls, Cory-
   bantes, and Samothracian Cabiri as all being identical with the Curetes, whereas other
   sources present them as distinct, but related. Kaibel (1901, 502, 512–14) and Hemberg
   (1950) argue against dismissing this catalogue as merely the fruit of Hellenistic syncretism, but see the interrelations between these figures as more fundamental. Jeanmaire (1939, 604–10) argues that Strabo is here drawing on specific fifth-century
   historiographical sources interested in Cretan ritual.
9 For Dionysus' birth on Crete, see frr. 210, 214, 303, Kern. For the Curetes as Dionysus'
   protectors, see frr. 34 and 210 K; that this motif is fairly early is confirmed by Euripides, *Cretans*, fr. 472.9–15 N, where a connection between Dionysus Zagreus and the
   Curetes is clearly implied. Crete and the Curetes are frequently mentioned in the Orphic
   fragments: see, in addition to the above, frr. 19, 31.7, 150, 156, 185, 186, 191, 314 K.
10 See van den Bruwaene 1981, 70 n. 98. See the parallels catalogued by Pease in Cicero
    1955–58, 1051–52.
11 On the syncretism of these three figures, along with that of Gaia, see Farnell 1921,
    128–29; Farnell 1909, III, 30–32, 291–95; and Burkert 1985, 178. At Olympia, Deme-
    ter was worshipped with the epithet Chamyne (= "making her bed on the ground"),
    which seems especially to emphasize her associations with the Earth: see Vegas-Sansal-
    vador 1991, 145–50. On the syncretism of Demeter and other female goddesses espe-
    cially in Arcadia, see Immerwahr 1891, 112–27, and Jost 1985, 297–355.
12 See Paus. 1.30.1 on the altar at the entrance to the Academy. See Ps.-Theocr. 23.56–60
    and Athen. 13.561 D-E for statues of Eros in other gymnasia.
13 Farnell (1932, II, 39) attempts to discredit the existence of this cave on archaeological
    grounds (i.e., that no such cave can be found in the Hill of Cronus or was mentioned
    by Pausanias and other sources), but nothing either in Pindar or the scholium says any-
    thing about the cave being located in the Hill of Cronus. Demetrius of Skepsis merely
    says it is in Elis, and Pindar merely lists it together with the Hill of Cronus and river
    Alpheus as characteristic geographical features of the area around Olympia that Zeus hon-
    ours. For the same mistake, see the sources in n. 23 below.
14 Jost (1985, 241–49) surveys the legends of Zeus' birth in Arcadia. She notes numerous
    toponyms in common between Arcadia and Crete, but deems the question of priority
    ultimately insoluble: it may have been a syncretism of originally independent myths
    and divinities. Although Paus. 8.53.4 suggests the presence of Arcadian colonies in
    Crete, this story may have been developed as support for Arcadia's claims to be the
    original source.
15 Jost (1985, 523) notes that the archaeological remains of this complex include a mosaic
    of late fourth-century date, suggesting some antiquity to the site.
16 Frazer (1965 [1898], IV, 94) identifies the spot as being 35 furlongs from Olympia to
    the south of the Alpheus. See also Pausanias (trans. Levi), 1971, 350 n. 186.
17 See Paus. 5.3.2, where Athena is surnamed a "Mother" goddess in Elis, thus bringing her
    into the same interrelated group of female divinities we have been discussing.
18 See Pohlenz 1916, 550–51, 559–62. Herrmann (1962, 3–34) surveys the evidence for
    pre-Olympian religion, and notes that the cult places of various pre-Olympian god-
    desses are all in the vicinity of each other and the Hill of Cronus; he connects the ori-
    entation of these cult places with evidence for Mycenaean settlement at Olympia.
19 See Cornford 1963, 236–37; Herrmann 1962, 10–11; and Hönle 1972, 15–20, with fur-
    ther references.
20 Jeanmaire 1939, 413–15. He also points to Demeter's kourotrophic character as an
    element appropriate to her sponsorship of athletic games involving young men.
21 For instance, the presence of boxing as an event in 5.7.10 points to a period long after
    the Games' historical foundation, since boxing and other events were not introduced until
    later. See Golden 1998, 40–41, for a useful list of dates.

22   Kaibel 1901, 490–96.

23   Kaibel 1901, 505–10; Cornford 1963, 236–41; Harrison 1963, 370–72; Vallois 1926, 307–18; Jeanmaire 1939, 413–15.

24   Cornford 1963, 239–40, citing Robert 1893. See also Herrmann 1962, 6–8.

25   Vallois 1926, 307–308.

26   See above, n. 21.

27   Cornford 1963, 236–37; Vallois 1926, 308–309.

28   *Schol.* Ap. Rhod. 1.1126b Wendel, assembles several accounts concerning the dactyls: the first gives their total number as ten, with five male, all of them right-handed, five female, all left-handed; Strabo (10.473) attributes this version to Sophocles (= fr. 366 Radt), but specifically says that sources disagree about the names and number. Pherecydes (3F47) says there were twenty right-handed ones, all metalworkers, and 32 left-handed ones, who were the magicians. Hellanicus (4F89) says that they derived their name from hosting Rhea by taking hold of her fingers (*daktyloi*), whereas Mnaseas derives their name from a father named Dactylus and a mother named Ida.

29   See Lobeck 1829, 1174–75, Kaibel 1901, 506, and Hoeck 1823, I, 338–39. In 5.14.7, Pausanias acknowledges an alternate name of "Acesidas" for Idas, likely an emendation to fit this thesis, but surely unnecessary given the dactyls' connection with Mount Ida, from which Idas would be an entirely appropriate name. Hoeck 1823, 330–35, also identifies Iasius with the Iasion of the Demeter myth; cf. Cornford 1963, 237 n. 2.

30   These three names are all in the *Phoronis* (F2 Davies) and Strabo 10.473; the latter includes Heracles in the same list. Clement of Alexandria (*Strom.* 1.74) mentions Celmis and Damnameneus; at the end of the section he names Scamo of Mytilene, a fourth-century historian, Theophrastus, Aristotle, and a number of other authorities, but it is uncertain which bits of information he derives from each of these. The *Marmor Parium* (= *CIG* 2374.22) names "Kelmios" as one of the dactyls and appears to list others, but their names are missing. Nonnus 14.39 names "Skelmis" and Damnameneus as Telchines, comparable figures from Rhodes. For the name Damnameneus in magical formulae and on amulets, see Fröhner 1865, 544–46. For etymological derivation of these names as appropriate epithets for metalworkers, see Hoeck 1823, I, 308–10; cf. Kaibel 1901, 502–503.

31   On Peisander and other early Heracles epics, see Huxley 1969, 99–112; the fragments and testimonia are collected in Davies 1988, 129–35. On Heracles' presence in Archaic lyric, see Philipp 1984, 334–39. For pictorial representations, which begin after 650 BC, but become especially common in the late sixth century, see Brommer 1986. The cycle of his labours does not appear to become canonical until this later period.

32   See Farnell 1921, 103–25. On the other hand, the Heracleidae were fundamental to self-conceptualizations of Dorian identity, as Pindar makes clear in *Pyth.* 1.62–66 and *Pyth.* 5.69–73; even before him, see Tyrtaeus, fr. 2.12–15 and 11.1 w. It is of course recognized in the Dorian tribe name of the Hylleis, derived from Heracles' son Hyllus.

33   Pausanias (5.4.5–6) narrates the sequence of events surrounding Iphitus' consultation of the Delphic oracle a bit differently. In his version, Greece was overrun with plague and civil strife before Iphitus' consultation of the oracle and renewal of the Games, not as a result of anyone resisting the command to reinstitute them.

34   See the arguments of Hönle 1972, 36–40; Pausanias' mistaken information (6.22.2) that this event dated to the eighth Olympiad, long before the likely period of Pheidon's rule, was probably a retrospective Elean attempt to put this humiliation as far back in its history as possible.

35   See Hönle 1972, 37–40, for the history of Elis' problems with Pisa during this period.

36   D.M. Lewis, "Mainland Greece, 479–451 B.C." *CAH*² 5:104.

37   See Andrewes 1952, 2–3; Forrest 1960, 229–32; Adshead 1986, 95–96; and Lewis (above, n. 36), 103. Some of the epigraphic evidence is compiled in Jeffery 1990,

218–20, especially no. 15, a rhetra from the early fifth century assuring due process for an official accused of abuse of office. Further bibliography is listed in Hönle 1972, 162–64, who takes a more skeptical view of Elean democracy at this period. See Roy 2002, 249–64, for the most recent treatment of Elean synoecism in light of the archaeological record.

38 Pausanias (5.4.7) says that they participated in the Spartan invasion of Attica unwillingly.

39 See Hönle 1972, 154–56. Falkner (1996, 17–25) points to Sparta's desire to open up trade access to the north and west. Hornblower (2000, 212–25) reviews the question whether Sparta had been banned from the Games for the entire twenty-year period. On the Lichas episode, see also Hornblower 2004, 274–86.

40 Interestingly, Pausanias (5.8.3–4) gives a different list of victors and contests, but this list also excludes Eleans in favor of a Theban (Iolaus), Arcadian (Iasius), and the Spartan Dioscuri, as well as Heracles himself winning in wrestling and *pankration*. It may be worth noting that Iasius was the name of one of the brothers of Heracles the Idaean dactyl, who competed in the first foot race; if this is the source of this otherwise obscure name's appearance in Pausanias' list, it may be an attempt at syncretism. It also confirms an Arcadian origin for the story of the dactyls.

41 As Pausanias also relates, it was Iphitus who instituted the divine cult of Heracles in Elis, since Heracles was previously regarded as an enemy to the Eleans because of his defeat of Augeas.

42 The association of this poem with the Theoxenia goes back to the Alexandrian scholars, who gave it the title εἰς Θεοξένια in the manuscripts; see also Schol. *Ol.* 3. inscr. et fin., 1c, 10c, Drachmann. For doubts about the alleged Theoxenian context, see Fränkel 1961, 394–97, and Shelmerdine 1987, 65–81. The positive case is best made by Krummen 1990, 223–36, but even she admits the matter is uncertain.

43 See Jost 1985, 258–67.

44 On the significance of Pindar's challenge to traditional Olympic ritual, see my discussion in Hubbard 1987a, 3–21. For Pindar's version of the Pelops myth as a shift from emphasis on the footrace to the newer chariot contest, see Nagy 1990, 116–35, although he is more prone than I am to see this as an official shift in Olympic ideology rather than a poetic innovation by Pindar. I do not believe that there ever was such a thing as an "official Olympic ideology" amid the welter of cults and conflicting stories that were present at Olympia. I believe that Nagy is also mistaken in asserting (pp. 119–20) that Pelops was viewed as the "founder" of the Olympic Games; nowhere does Pindar make this claim, and its sole attestation is in the work of Phlegon of Tralles (257F1 *FGrH*), a historian of Hadrianic date. Herrmann 1962, 18–22, drawing on Dörpfeld, assembles evidence for the Mycenaean date of the Pelops cult at Olympia, but argues that its origins were in the northeast Peloponnese.

45 See the review of evidence by Fehr 1936, 38–39; Devereux 1966, 289–94; Köhnken 1983, 55–8; and Krummen 1990, 255–57. Robbins (1982, 299–303) assembles iconographical material that may suggest the story was earlier, but see the objections of Krummen 1990, 236 n.1. Interestingly, Pindar's one other allusion to a trip to the Hyperboreans, that of Perseus in *Pyth.*10.31–46, also appears to have been his invention; see my remarks in Hubbard 1986, 32–33.

46 Cornford (1963, 236–37) cites the parallel of the Selloi at Dodona, sleeping on the ground to draw oracular wisdom from Gaia in their dreams. Note also the epithet with which Demeter is honoured at Olympia: *Chamyne*, "she who makes her bed on the ground" (see n. 11 above).

47 Proclus, *Comment. Plato. Rem Publ.* I, 138.12 = Orph. fr. 186, Kern.

48 Hoops (1944, 44–60) believes that olive cultivation was spread from Crete to the rest of the Greek world in Mycenaean times. See also Renfrew 1972, 285–87. Runnels and Hansen (1986, 302–304) review the evidence of pollen studies, suggesting that olives

were not cultivated in most areas of mainland Greece (except Boeotia) until the Late Bronze Age; however, in Crete olive pollen has been detected at a core level ca. 3900 BC Blitzer (1993, 163–75) makes an even stronger case for Early Minoan cultivation and oil production. Hamilakis (1996, 1–32) is more skeptical of the evidence for Early Minoan olive culture, but sees systematic production of olive oil starting in the Second Palace period. Even in the Late Bronze Age, Crete does appear to have been the major exporter of olive oil to the Mainland, since the inscriptions and clay type of most stirrup jars are Cretan; see Haskell 1984, 99–100.

49 See Willetts 1957, 381–84, and 1962, 201; Detienne 1970, 21–23.

50 See Jeanmaire 1939, 426, and Willetts 1955, 119–23.

51 Krummen 1990, 239–47.

52 Heraklion 259, a gold signet ring from Mochlos dated ca. 1450 BC (see Warren 1987, pl. 11), and Ashmolean 1938, no. 1129. On the Mochlos ring, see Sourvinou-Inwood 1973, 149–58, and Platon 1978, 438. The Ring of Minos (see Warren 1987, pls. 1–10) differs from these in that the tree and its surrounding shrine are not directly in the boat, but hover above it in the air, although the tree's presence may be implied by the conveyance of a similarly shaped shrine in the boat; see Warren 1987, 488. That the boat is at the very least a symbol of Cretan naval power and its protection by the goddess was argued by Platon 1984, 67. Doubts about the authenticity of the Ring of Minos persist in some quarters, but recent chemical analysis by the Archaeological Museum of Herakleion (as yet unpublished) claims to confirm its antiquity.

53 On Crete's centrality in the olive trade, see Haskell 1984, 99–100. For the primary use of olive oil in perfume and other sacral contexts, see Bennett, Jr., 1958, 37–38; Shelmerdine 1985, 123–28; and Hamilakis 1996, 19–20.

54 Weniger 1895; Herrmann 1962, 17. See de Visser 1903, 117–56, for a catalogue of evidence of tree cults throughout the Greek world. On this practice in Minoan Crete especially, see Evans, 1901, 99–204, and Willetts 1957, 67–71.

55 See Aristotle, *Mirab.* 51.834a = Schol. Aristoph., *Plut.* 586 and *Suda*, s.v. κοτίνου στέφανος. On this variant tradition, see Weniger 1919, 32–40. Hemsterhuis proposed emending Ilissus to Elissus, in which case the reference would be to an area on the border between Elis and Pisa; various sources also attest an Elean Pantheion. See L. Ziehen, "Pantheion," in *RE* 18.2: 720–22, and Blech 1982, 130. In this case, the variant tradition would be Elean, not Attic.

56 See *Hyp. Nem.* d,e Drachmann, which suggests that Heracles was just a refounder of earlier games that had fallen into neglect. Aeschylus' *Nemea*, probably coeval with Pindar, reflects the Adrastus-Archemorus version: see fr. 149a Radt = *Hyp. Nem.* c Drachmann; the same scholium mentions a third version, in which Adrastus celebrates the first Nemean Games at the funeral of his brother Pronax.

57 This seems to be the way that the passage is interpreted by *Hyp. Nem.* c Drachmann, which after listing versions of Nemean foundation related to Adrastus, then adds, εἰσὶ δέ τινες οἳ καὶ παλαιότερον εἶναί φασι τὸν ἀγῶνα τοῦ Θηβαικοῦ πολέμου [some say that the games are older than the Theban War]. See also L. Dissen, ap. Boeckh 1821, 11:2, 451.

58 Adshead 1986, 59–60, speculates that the Heracles version was in fact the older of the two, but was displaced by the Argive account as a conscious reaction against the anti-Argive policies of Nemea's other close neighbor, Cleisthenes of Sicyon.

59 See *Hyp. Isthm.* b,c Drachmann, and Plutarch, *Thes.* 25. Similar to the speculations about Heracles as a "refounder" of the Olympic and Nemean Games, *Hyp. Isthm.* d Drachmann attempts to reconcile the two competing versions by saying that the original Isthmian Games established by Sisyphus ceased to be celebrated because of robbers infesting the roads to the Isthmus, and Theseus re-established the games after purifying the area.

60 See Adshead 1986, 61–63.

61 See Adshead 1986, 76–82, who argues that this change in crowns was part of an unsuccessful Corinthian campaign to assert hegemony over Nemea and the Dorians of the northeast Peloponnese. For further sources on the change of crowns and an attempt to specify the date, see Blech 1982, 131–34.

62 On Pindar's general relation to the politics of this period, see my survey in Hubbard 2001, 387–400.

The First Olympic Games

Max Nelson

There are certainly many ways in which the ancient Olympic Games, the oldest and greatest of the Panhellenic athletic festivals, can be considered of prime importance in the ancient Greek world. They were a vivid manifestation of such Hellenic ideals as "excellence" (ἀρετή) and "beauty and nobility" (καλὸς κ'ἀγαθός), and further reinforced the pervasive pursuits of competition and display, all the while being set in a religious context. While all these aspects have been much studied, another important aspect of the Olympic Games will be discussed here, that is, the Olympic Games as the basis for a proper chronological framework among ancient historians. This too is well-trodden ground, but I hope to show that re-examining the evidence is well rewarded.

To begin, let me present what tends to be the *communis opinio* concerning the ancient chronological works based on victors at the Olympic Games, as laid out succinctly by E. Norman Gardiner over eighty years ago:

> The growth of the festival can be traced in the Olympic Register even in the imperfect form in which we possess it. It was first compiled by the Sophist Hippias at the close of the fifth century. It consisted originally of a historical introduction, and a list of victors in the different events, with notes on athletes of special importance. It was revised by Aristotle and

continued and expanded by various eminent scholars, Eratosthenes, Timaios, Philochoros, and at a later period Phlegon of Tralles and Sextus Julius Africanus.... The list of Africanus exists in full. It is a complete list of the winners of the stade race down to Ol[ympiad] 249.[1]

Most recent work tends to accept the notion that there was one tradition of Olympiad reckoning which was passed down throughout antiquity,[2] though Paul Christesen has recently provided a more careful and nuanced analysis: Hippias compiled and published the first cumulative list of Olympic victors, while Aristotle, following Hippias, was the first to number the Olympiads sequentially, and later Timaeus was the first to use Olympiads chronographically, that is, as a means of historical reckoning.[3] This paper will dispute the idea of a very simple handing down of a single list which was revised and emended over time, and instead will follow the position of a minority of scholars who have challenged this idea, attempting rather to show that there were in fact many, in a sense competing, lists, or rather accounts of Olympic Games and victors, with various starting points.[4] Julius Africanus' list, although it is the product of centuries of work, is just one more such list, which begins in 776 BC and which just happens to survive complete. An argument can be made that neither Hippias nor Eratosthenes should be credited with fixing the date of the first Games at 776 BC (in our terms), as is so often accepted,[5] but rather it was Aristotle.

In the second century AD Plutarch noted in his life of the legendary Roman king Numa: "And so it is difficult to determine precisely the era [when Numa lived], especially [the era] reckoned from the Olympic victors, the register of whom, they say, Hippias of Elis published at a later time, starting from nothing certain to prompt belief."[6] Aside from this one passage in Plutarch, we have no other evidence for Hippias' work; no fragments survive, and no one else mentions it. In our earliest references to Hippias, in Plato and Xenophon, he is spoken of as an ambassador for Elis, a wide traveller, an educator, and a great memorizer and orator.[7] In the *Hippias Major*, Plato has Hippias tell Socrates that when visiting the Spartans he recounted genealogies of heroes, men, and the foundation of cities, but no mention is made of a work on the Olympic victors.[8] Plato does have Hippias note in the *Hippias Minor* that he often recites speeches at the Olympic Games,[9] and also that once when he participated he had on himself only things which he had made himself (from his clothes and sandals to his ring, comb, and perfume flask).[10] Philostratus's short biography of Hippias, evidently highly indebted to Plato, speaks of Hippias' skills in memorizing and public speaking, his knowledge of geometry, astronomy, music, rhythm, painting and sculpture, his work on Spartan history, and his work on Nestor, but no mention is made of a *Register of Olympic Victors*.[11] Philostratus also adds: "He enchanted Greece in Olympia with ornate and well thought-out speeches."[12] Finally, Pausanias notes that Hippias composed elegiac verses for bronze statues dedicated in Olympia to a chorus of boys that had drowned at sea.[13] Other ancient sources add little else of interest.

Despite Plutarch being our sole source for Hippias having written on Olympic victors, scholars unanimously accept this testimony, finding it only appropriate for a resident of Elis, the location of the Olympic Games, especially one with historical interests and a compiler of historical anecdotes, to write on its winners. Scholars also further tend to presume that, as a local, Hippias had ready access to written records, as well as oral tales, to compile the list.[14] It is important to observe, however, that Plutarch couches his statement with φασιν [they say that], thus distancing himself from the attribution of Hippias as author of the *Register*. It is quite noteworthy that not long after Plutarch, Pausanias often cites what he calls the ancient writings on the Olympic victors, without attributing them to any author.[15] Similarly, Eusebius simply speaks of the *Olympic Registers among Greeks* without naming a specific author.[16] If any early compilations had been transmitted without an author's name attached, it could readily be seen why some considered Hippias, the great polymath of Elis and reciter at the Olympic festival, to be a good candidate as author. Without stating that he certainly did not write a *Register*, we should at least entertain the possibility that he did not.

It is well known that the early Greek historians did not use numbered Olympiads as a standard chronological marker, relying instead on local lists of holders of political offices or religious appointments. Some scholars have wished to consider the historian Philistus of Syracuse (late fifth or early fourth century BC, and thus a contemporary of Hippias) as the first to do so.[17] Stephanus of Byzantium, in his entry on the city of Dyme, quotes from him as follows: "and Philistus [in the] first [book] of his *Sicelicai*: 'in the Olympiad in which Oebotas of Dyme won the *stadion* footrace.'"[18] No numeral preceding the notice of an Olympiad is found in the text, and thus we cannot assume that Philistus reckoned by the sequence of Olympiads; nevertheless, scholars tend to restore without hesitation the numeral for six in the text, since Oebotas is found to be the winner of the sixth Olympiad *stadion* race in some much later sources.[19] We should certainly not assume that Philistus counted the first Olympiad from 776 BC or even used numbered Olympiads, nor can we assume that he had a full list of victors at his disposal.

The ancients certainly did not believe that athletic competitions at Olympia were first put on in 776 BC (moderns too, we could add, have marshalled much archaeological evidence against it).[20] As Thomas K. Hubbard discusses in detail elsewhere in this volume, Pindar ascribes the establishment of the Games much earlier to the Theban Heracles. Pindar in fact considers these original Olympic Games to have been an event held every four years and already involving the *stadion* foot race, wrestling, boxing, chariot racing, the javelin throw, and the discus throw, as well as the presentation of olive wreaths for the victors.[21] That an early connection with Heracles was approved of in Olympia itself seems further confirmed by the appearance of Heracles' labours on the metopes of the Temple of Zeus at Olympia (built in the early fifth century BC), and by the fact that in a speech given by Lysias at Olympia, and thus unlikely to be providing a foundation story not approved by the Olympians, Heracles is made out to be the founder of the Games.[22] Pausanias much later attributes the foundation of the Olympic Games to a Cretan Heracles, saying that they were held every four years and involved (at the very least) a foot race and boxing, and an olive wreath for the victor.[23] Strabo already knew the competing claims for the two Heracleses, and says that it was in fact the Heracleidae under the leadership of Oxylus who founded the first Games.[24] Pausanias further mentions eight more times when the Olympic Games were put on, namely, by Clymenus, Endymion, Pelops, Amythaon, Pelias and Neleus together, Augeas, the Theban Heracles, and Oxylus (different such lists are provided by Phlegon of Tralles and Eusebius[25]), and these also further included chariot racing, horse racing, wrestling, and the *pankration*.[26] Pausanias makes it clear that all these instances were not consecutive, nor were they put on every four years, making one wonder why he stated that the tradition of a four-year Olympiad was already established by the Cretan Heracles at the very first Games. The answer might simply be that Pausanias has conflated two different traditions. In fact, Pausanias rather says that, some time after Oxylus (the length of time, says Pausanias, is uncertain), it was King Iphitus who began the first Olympic Games of the unbroken tradition which lasted until Pausanias' own day (and, as we know, beyond).[27] Pausanias further claims that the Pythia was involved, a tradition also found in Phlegon of Tralles, Eusebius, and a Platonic scholiast.[28]

It is usually assumed that Iphitus' Games were the starting point for the *Register* of Hippias and others after him;[29] however, if there were indeed already a tradition in the time of Pindar (a tradition which has also slipped into Pausanias' account) that Heracles had established the first Olympic Games and also the four-year cycle of the Games, it would make more sense that this was normally considered the starting point. On the other hand, if indeed it were widely believed that the Games were not regularly held until later, how are we to know that Hippias, or whoever the earliest scholars on this question were, started from Iphitus and not, let us say, from Oxylus (as, we have seen, Strabo later did)? Indeed, it has not been emphasized enough that in the fourth century BC, Ephorus said simply that Iphitus celebrated the Olympic Games, and, as far as we can tell from the text handed down by Strabo, did not make Iphitus (or Oxylus for that matter) first in the continuous tradition of Olympiads.[30]

It is Aristotle who is first known to have considered Iphitus the founder of the first of the continuous Olympic Games. Aristotle knew the tradition that Heracles was the founder of the Olympic Games,[31] but Plutarch relates that Aristotle credits Iphitus together with the Spartan Lycurgus with establishing the Olympic truce, on the evidence of a discus at Olympia which preserved an inscription to that effect (no doubt a forgery).[32] Pausanias later specified that the discus was in the Temple of Hera at Olympia.[33] The peripatetic Hieronymus of Rhodes also said that Iphitus and Lycurgus established the first Olympic Games, presumably on the authority of Aristotle;[34] much later, Phlegon of Tralles (a contemporary of Pausanias) also mentioned the discus of Iphitus, and added Cleosthenes of Pisa to make a trio of founders.[35] It seems fair to argue, as Mahaffy has in his 1881 article, that there was no complete list of victors going all the way back to Iphitus to provide proof that his Games were the starting point of the continuous tradition;[36] rather, the chroniclers worked down from Iphitus because of the evidence of the discus.

It is normally assumed that Aristotle compiled a list of Olympic victors. Indeed, as we have seen, it is often said that he in fact revised Hippias' *Register*. According to Diogenes Laertius, however, Aristotle did not write an ἀναγραφὴ τῶν Ὀλυμπιονικῶν, or *Register of Olympic Victors*, as Hippias supposedly had according to Plutarch, but rather simply an Ὀλυμπιονῖκαι, or *Olympic Victors*, in one book.[37] The fragments attributed to the work include no more than anecdotes about individual victors,[38] and so for all we know Aristotle simply set out the evidence concerning what was known of victors in various (but not necessarily all) Olympic Games, as well as the foundation of the Games by Heracles and their renewal by Iphitus and Lycurgus, and no complete list of victors need have been provided.

The same could be argued with regard to Eratosthenes' *Olympic Victors*;[39] none of the fragments points to a complete list, and the fact that some victors' Olympiads are mentioned does not mean that all were. That

Eratosthenes followed Aristotle, however, is certain. Diogenes Laertius notes at the beginning of his biography of the philosopher Empedocles that Eratosthenes' authority in his work *Olympic Victors* for Empedocles, grandfather of the philosopher, as a victor at the seventy-first Olympiad was Aristotle,[40] we may well assume from his own work *Olympic Victors*.[41] According to Clement of Alexandria, Eratosthenes placed the first Olympic Games 297 years before Xerxes' invasion of Greece (which occurred in 480 BC), yielding a date of 776 BC when counting inclusively.[42] Since Eratosthenes, on Aristotle's authority, accepted a victor for the seventy-first Olympiad (that is, 496 BC), a time not too distant, it would seem that he would have taken the date for the first Olympiad from Aristotle as well, and thus that Aristotle had already fixed Iphitus' and Lycurgus' renewal of the Games to 776 BC.[43] Eratosthenes, however, did at least deviate from Aristotle in that he did not date Lycurgus to the time of the first Games, but to 108 years before them.[44]

We cannot simply assume that, after Aristotle and Eratosthenes, all ancient scholars accepted the date of 776 BC for the first Olympic Games, and in fact there is some evidence to the contrary. A number of ancient authors calculate quite differently the number of years between the fall of Troy and the first Olympic Games. According to Censorinus, Eratosthenes placed the first Olympic Games 407 years after the fall of Troy (therefore dating the latter to 1072 BC) whereas Timaeus had given the length of time as 417 years, and Eretes and Sosibius, perhaps both contemporaries of Eratosthenes, had given 514 and 395, respectively.[45] Other intervals are found as well: for instance, in the fourth century BC, Dicaearchus gave 436 years, in the second century AD Clement of Alexandria had 338 years, and in the third century AD Solinus said 408 years.[46] Though it is quite possible that for many the date of the fall of Troy is different and not that of the first Olympiad,[47] and that all accepted 776 BC as the date of the first Olympic Games, this is uncertain. It seems quite certain, however, from Photius' testimony, that in the second century AD Phlegon accepted 776 BC as the date for the first Games,[48] as did Pausanias. Julius Africanus and Eusebius certainly gave it further currency, and it is the date found in all extant sequential chronologies.[49]

Two sources provide us with definite alternatives to the 776 BC date. In the first century AD, Velleius Paterculus said that the very first Games were put on by Atreus about 1,250 years before his own day, and that Heracles won every contest;[50] further, that Iphitus renewed the games 823 years before the consulship of Marcus Vinicius (which occurred, as is generally agreed, in AD 30)[51]—therefore giving us a date of 793 BC (though this could not have been a year in the continuous quadrennial Games).[52] Furthermore, on a bronze discus dedicated at Olympia by the pentathlete Publius Asclepiades of Corinth, who can be dated to the third century AD because of a reference to Flavius Scribonianus on the discus, he is named winner in the 456th Olympiad, thus placing the first Olympiad in the sixteenth century BC.[53]

Aristotle could set the beginning of the continuous Olympic Games at the time of Iphitus because of the discus in Olympia, but we are left without evidence as to how exactly he came up with the date 776 BC (or, for that matter, how anyone else's dates were set).[54] We certainly cannot simply presume that Aristotle provided a complete list of victors (in the *stadion,* as became the tradition, or some other event) from Iphitus' Games down to his own time, as is usually assumed. He may well have had access to information to compile a complete or fairly complete list, especially from perhaps ca. 500 BC on, but in all probability there was little reliable information on early winners.

One important piece of evidence was no doubt the tombstone of Coroebus, which Pausanias says was on the boundary between Heraea and Elis, and named him as the first winner of the *stadion.*[55] The correspondence between Coroebus' first victory and the foundation of the Olympic Games was variously interpreted by ancient authors. According to Eusebius, the mysterious Aristodemus of Elis, perhaps from the third or second century BC, as well as Tiberius Claudius Polybius, claimed that the first recorded victor, Coroebus, competed in what was really the twenty-eighth Olympiad, but that this was considered the first Olympiad since no winners were known before it.[56] This is a tradition also found in Phlegon of Tralles, who further places an Iphitus at this Olympiad, although he also places an Iphitus, though surely not the same one, at the first Olympiad, and an Iphitus at the sixth Olympiad.[57] Callimachus, in the third century BC, mentions instead that the first recorded victor of the renewed Olympic Games, Coroebus, won only during the fourteenth Olympiad;[58] however, in neither case can we presume that 776 BC was considered the usually reckoned first Olympiad.[59] It is only first in Pausanias that Coroebus is made the winner of the foot race in Iphitus' first Olympiad Games, which can be dated to 776 BC.[60]

In the end, we may presume that just as the discus of Iphitus gave Aristotle the evidence for the name of the first founder of the continuous Games, so the tombstone of Coroebus gave Callimachus (or someone else before him) the evidence for Coroebus' victory. Since so little was known of either Iphitus or Coroebus,[61] it was anyone's guess when exactly their respective contributions to the Games were made, and whether they were made at the same time. Once this matter of Iphitus and Coroebus was somehow settled, it was simply a matter for the scholars from the fifth or fourth centuries BC on to find or invent names to fill in the gaps in the list of Olympiads until the time when the victors were certainly known.[62] Plutarch, as noted above, was very skeptical of the accuracy of the one *Register* which he referred to as that of Hippias, saying that there were those who claimed that it was based on no sure evidence.[63] We too should certainly be skeptical of all the early dates for the Olympic Games transmitted by ancient authorities, even Aristotle's venerable 776 BC.

In conclusion, we can say nothing certain about the ancient research into the origins of the Olympic Games or the Olympic victors until we come to Aristotle, who obviously conducted a careful study of the question, and who seems to have accepted 776 BC (in our terms) as the beginning of the continuously recorded quadrennial Games. This was further accepted by Eratosthenes and others after him (notably from the second century AD on), but certainly not by all ancient researchers on the question. Although the *communis opinio* discussed at the beginning of the paper concerning the *Register of Olympic Victors* remains one possible interpretation, it is in fact far from being the only one.

Notes

1 Gardiner 1973 [1925], 86.

2 See, for instance, Mouratidis 1985, 12 n. 18, and Miller 2004a, 226–27.

3 Christesen, forthcoming (I thank the author for allowing me to look at the manuscript before publication). This important work provides for the first time a full collection and systematic discussion of all Olympic victor lists, and the works (chronographies and chronicles) which used them for the purpose of historical reckoning (many of which I leave out of my discussion, including Timaeus). I am highly indebted to his work, though I differ from him on a number of issues.

4 This has been argued by Heidrich (1987, 29–31), who is followed by Shaw (2003, 35–36, 76–77, and 241–42).

5 Mahaffy (1881, 175–76), Mouratidis (1985, 2), Golden (1998, 63, and 2004, 114) and Tyrrell (2004, 44), among many others (see Shaw, 2003, 62–63), assume that Hippias set the date of the first Games at 776 BC. Pfeiffer (1968, 163) claimed that Eratosthenes was the first to fix 776 BC as the date of the first Olympic Games, based on the first known winner, Coroebus of Elis. Lämmer (1967, 108) attributes the date rather to Timaeus.

6 Plutarch *Vit. Num.* 1.4 Perrin = 1.6 Flacelière, Chambry, and Juneaux = Hippias, 86B3 D.-K. = *FGrH* 6F2 and 416T3 (τοὺς μὲν οὖν χρόνους ἐξακριβῶσαι χαλεπόν ἐστι καὶ μάλιστα τοὺς ἐκ τῶν Ὀλυμπιονικῶν ἀναγομένους, ὧν τὴν ἀναγραφὴν ὀψέ φασιν Ἱππίαν ἐκδοῦναι τὸν Ἠλεῖον, ἀπ᾽ οὐδενὸς ὁρμώμενον ἀναγκαίου πρὸς πίστιν). Though this is listed by Jacoby as a fragment, no actual words of Hippias are preserved in this passage. All translations in this paper are the author's.

7 See Plato *Ap.* 19e (= Hippias, 86A4 D.-K.) and *Hp. mai.* 281a (= A6 D.-K.) and 282d-e (= A7 D.-K.) and Xen. *Symp.* 4.62 (= A5 D.-K.) and *Mem.* 4.4.5–7 (= A14 D.-K.).

8 Plato *Hp. mai.* 285d = Hippias, 86A11 D.-K.

9 Plato *Hp. mi.* 363c and 364a = Hippias, 86A8 D.-K.

10 Plato *Hp. mi.* 368b = Hippias, 86A12 D.-K.

11 Philostratus *V S* 1.11 = Hippias, 86A2 D.-K.

12 Philostratus *V S* 1.11.7 = Hippias, 86A2 D.-K. (ἔθελγε τὴν Ἑλλάδα ἐν Ὀλυμπίᾳ λόγοις ποικίλοις καὶ πεφροντισμένοις εὖ).

13 Pausanias 5.25.5 = Hippias 86B1 D.-K.

14 See, for instance, den Boer 1954, 51, and Mosshammer 1979, 93–95. Christesen, forth-coming, argues convincingly that the earliest list would be based on disparate and incomplete information.

15 See Paus. 3.2.1 (= *FGrH* 416F4), 5.4.5–6 (= F1), 5.7.6–8.1 (= T9), 5.21.8–9 (= F5), 6.2.2–3 (= F3), 6.4.2 (= T7b), 6.6.3 (= T1), 6.8.1 (= T2), 6.9.2 (= T4), 6.13.9–10 (= F2), 6.22.2–4 (= T7a), and 10.36.9 (= T8a). These writings were also used by Philostratus (*De arte gymn.* 2).

16 Eusebius *Chron.* 1.190 Schoene (αἱ παρ᾽ Ἕλλησιν ἀναγραφομέναι Ὀλυμπιάδαι), and see 1.192 Schoene.

17 See den Boer 1954, 42–44; Mosshammer 1979, 86–87; and Shaw 2003, 51. Herodotus (1.59, 5.71, 6.35–6, and 6.125) and Thucydides (3.8.1 and 5.49.1) mentioned Olympic victors but did not use their victories as chronological markers (see Shaw 2003, 49–50, 61).

18 Stephanus of Byzantium *Ethn.* s.v. Δύμη = Philist., *FGrH* 556F2 (...καὶ Φίλιστος Σικελικῶν α΄· ἐπὶ τῆς ὀλυμπιάδος καθ᾽ ἣν ὁ Οἰβώτας <ὁ Δυμαῖος> ἐνίκα στάδιον).

19 Pausanias 6.3.8 and Julius Africanus *Ol.* 6. For Oebotas, see Moretti 1957, 60 no. 6.

20 For skepticism concerning this date, see, for instance, Mahaffy 1881, 164; Gardiner 1973 [1925], 85–86; Bickerman 1980, 75; Mouratidis 1985, 1, 10; Morgan 1990, 47–49; Peiser 1990; Golden 1998, 43–45, and 2004, 64; and Wacker 1998, with the recent comments of Lee 2001, 76. Many general accounts still present 776 BC as the date of the first Olympics without comment, such as Swaddling 1999, 7, while Finley and Pleket (1976, 6) even speak of the first Olympic Games as "traditionally and credibly dated in [*sic*] 776 BC."

21 Pindar *Ol.* 10.22–75 (every four years at 57, and the events at 60–75), and see *Ol.* 2.3–4 and *Ol.* 3.11–13 (on the wreath).

22 Lysias *Olymp.* 33.1–2. For this point, see Robinson 1981, 34.

23 Pausanias 5.7.6–10, and see also 5.13.8 and 14.6–9.

24 Strabo 8.3.30. See also Diodorus Siculus 5.64.6 and Dinon *FGrH* 690F2.

25 Phlegon (*FGrH* 257F1.1) speaks of Peison, Pelops, Heracles, and then Iphitus putting on Games. Eusebius (*Chron.* 1.192 Schoene) speaks of one of the Idaean dactyls, then Aethlios, Epeius, Endymion, Alexinos, Oinomaos, Pelops, the Theban Heracles, and then Iphitus; he further says (1.194 Schoene) that many say that 419 years passed between Heracles' Games and the first ones in the continuous tradition.

26 Pausanias 5.8.1–5.

27 Pausanias 5.4.5, 5.4.6, 5.8.5, and 8.26.4: Ἴφιτος...τὸν ἀγῶνα διέθηκεν ἐν Ὀλυμπίᾳ...καί οἱ προσταχθῆναι φασιν ὑπὸ τῆς Πυθίας ὡς αὐτόν τε Ἴφιτον δέοι καὶ Ἠλείους τὸν Ὀλυμπικὸν ἀγῶνα ἀνανεώσασθαι.... Ἰφίτου δὲ τὸν ὀγῶνα ἀνανεωσαμένου κατὰ τὰ ἤδη μοι λελεγμένα, τοῖς ἀνθρώποις ἔτι ὑπῆρχε τῶν ἀρχαίων λήθη...ἡνίκα δὲ τὸν ἀγῶνα τὸν Ὀλυμπικὸν ἐκλιπόντα ἐπὶ χρόνον πολὺν ἀνενεώσατο Ἴφιτος καὶ αὖθις ἐξ ἀρχῆς Ὀλύμπια ἤγαγον [Iphitus... arranged Games in Olympia....And they say that it was decreed by the Pythia that it was necessary for Iphitus himself and the Eleans to renew the Olympic Games....When Iphitus renewed the Games, as has been already related by me, there was among men a forgetfulness of the old traditions....When Iphitus renewed the Olympic Games after

having not been held for a long time and again from the start they held the Olympic festival].

28 Pausanias 5.4.6 (who mentions one oracle), Phlegon *FGrH* 257F1.3, 6, 7, 9, and 10 (who mentions five different oracles), *Pl. Schol. Rep.* 465d (who mentions one oracle, a conflation of two in Phlegon), and Euseb. *Chron.* 1.192, Schoene (who mentions two oracles); for these oracles, see Fontenrose 1978, 268–70.

29 See, most recently, Tyrrell 2004, 44.

30 Strabo, 8.3.33 = Ephor., *FGrH* 70F115: Ἔφορος δέ φησιν... Ἰφιτόν τε θεῖναι τὸν Ὀλυμπικὸν ἀγῶνα [Ephorus says that... Iphitus put on Olympic Games]. Ephorus goes on to say that Pheidon of Argos later celebrated the Olympic Games, but that the event was not recorded by the Eleans. One may wonder how Ephorus came across this information.

31 *Schol. Aristid. Panath.* 323 Dindorf = Ar., fr. 637 Rose³ (attributed to his *Peplos*).

32 Plutarch *Vit. Lyc.* 1.1 = Ar., fr. 533 Rose³: οἱ μὲν γὰρ Ἰφίτῳ συνακμάσαι καὶ συνδιαθεῖναι τὴν Ὀλυμπιακὴν ἐκεχειρίαν λέγουσιν αὐτόν, ὧν ἐστι καὶ Ἀριστοτέλης ὁ φιλόσοφος, τεκμήριον προσφέρων τὸν Ὀλυμπίασι δίσκον ἐν ᾧ τοὔνομα τοῦ Λυκούργου διασώζεται καταγεγραμμένον [And some say that he (i.e., Lycurgus) flourished together with Iphitus and established the Olympic truce (with him), of whom Aristotle the philosopher is one, alleging as proof the discus at Olympia on which survives the inscribed name of Lycurgus]. This fragment has usually been attributed to the *Lacedaemonian Constitution*, but it may well belong to Aristotle's *Olympic Victors*. Bollansée (1999) rightly argues that this provides no evidence as to Aristotle's view on the date of the foundation of the Games, only on the beginnings of the truce. On the forgery, see Mouratidis 1985, 8–9, and Christesen, forthcoming, who argues convincingly for a sixth century date for the discus.

33 Pausanias 5.20.1.

34 Athenaeus *Deipnosophistae* 14.635f = Hieron., fr. 33 Wehrli. Eusebius (*Chron.* 1.194 Schoene) also speaks of these two founders, noting that both were descendants of Heracles. See also Heraclides Lembus, fr. 10 Dilts on the truce (presumably also following Aristotle).

35 Phlegon *FGrH* 257F1.2–9. This trio is also found in *Schol. Pl. Rep.* 465d.

36 Mahaffy 1881, 174.

37 Diogenes Laertius 5.26, and see *Vit. Menag.* 122.

38 Aristotle *FHG* 261–264 and possibly fr. 561 Rose³ (assigned to this work by Christesen, forthcoming). Elsewhere, Aristotle mentions the Olympic victors Diocles (at *Pol.* 2.12 [=1274a33]) and Dorieus (at *Rh.* 1.2 [= 1357a19–22]), but without providing the number of the Olympiad in which each won. Aristotle also mentions (*Pol.* 8.4 [= 1339a1–4]) that only two or three of the Olympic victors won both as boys and as men. Christesen posits that *IG* II 2.2326, a fragmentary victor list from the early third century BC, is a copy of Aristotle's work on Olympic victors. This is far from certain, though it is true that a number of inscriptions from Delphi (*SIG*³ 275 et al.) preserve a list of Pythian victors compiled by Aristotle (see the full discussion in Christesen), whereas the other known fragments of Aristotle's work on Pythian victors (615–617 Rose³) give no indication that it includes a victor list. Aristotle may have felt confident about compiling a Pythian victor list, whereas the difficulties in compiling an accurate Olympic victor list may have proved too daunting for him.

39 Eratosthenes *FGrH* 241F4–8, 11, 14, 15, and 44, and see *Etym. Magn.*, s.v. Elis (these are all the fragments attributed to the work by Christesen, forthcoming).

40 Diogenes Laertius 8.51 = Eratosth. *FGrH* 241F7 = Ar., fr. 71 Rose³: λέγει δὲ καὶ Ἐρατοσθένης ἐν τοῖς Ὀλυμπιονίκαις τὴν πρώτην καὶ ἑβδομηκοστὴν Ὀλυμπιάδα νενικηκέναι τὸν τοῦ Μέτωνος πατέρα, μάρτυρι χρώμενος Ἀριστοτέλει [Also Eratosthenes says in his *Olympic Victors,* using Aristotle as a source, that at the sev-

enty-first Olympiad the father of Meton (Empedocles, the philosopher's father) was a victor]. Julius Africanus (*Ol.* 71) also places Empedocles in the same Olympiad. See further Diog. Laert. 8.51–53 for various authorities on this victory. Others claimed that it was Empedocles the philosopher who was the Olympic victor (Athen., *Deipnosophistae* 1.3e and *Suda*, s.v. Ἀθήναιος). For Empedocles the victor, see Moretti 1957, 81 no. 170.

41 See Pfeiffer 1968, 80 n. 2.

42 Clement of Alexandria *Strom.* 1.138.1–3 = Eratosth. *FGrH* 241F1a.

43 Möller 2005, 254, assumes that Eratosthenes came up with the date of 776, but Christesen, forthcoming, shows that Aristotle already must have had it.

44 Clement of Alexandria *Strom.* 1.138.1–3 = Eratosth. *FGrH* 241F1a.

45 Censorinus *De die nat.* 21.3 = Eratosth. *FGrH* 241F1c (and see 1a) = Tim. *FGrH* 566F125 = Eret. *FGrH* 242F1 = Sosib. *FGrH* 595F1 (and see 2). Eratosthenes' calculations were clearly followed by Apollodorus (*FGrH* 244F61a, in Diod. Sic. 1.5.1), and later authors also keep to his 407-year length of time, such as Tatian (*Ad Graec.* 41.3) and Porphyry (in Euseb. *Chron.* 1.190 Schoene and *Suda*, s.v. Homer).

46 Dicaearchus fr. 58 Wehrli, Clement of Alexandria *Strom.* 2.85.15 and Solin., 1.28.

47 For the variety of ancient dates for the fall of Troy, see Shaw 2003, 52–53 and 242–43, and Möller 2005, 249–50. Jerome (*Chron.* s.a. 776 BC), who accepts 776 BC as the first Olympiad, places this 405 years after the fall of Troy, while Eusebius, who also accepts the 776 BC date, has 408 years (*Praep. Evang.* 1.10).

48 Photius *Bibl.* 97 = Phleg., *FGrH* 257F12.

49 On this point, see Christesen, forthcoming.

50 Velleius Paterculus 1.8.2.

51 Velleius Paterculus 1.8.1.

52 This date is calculated by subtracting 30 from 823 and then adding one year because of inclusive counting (which was typical in antiquity) and subtracting one year because there was no year 0. Inclusive counting, however, was not universally used, and therefore precise reckoning is often impossible for the modern scholar.

53 *IvO*, 240/241. See Moretti 1957, 173 no. 930, and Lämmer 1967, for the strong possibility that this is not a lapsus.

54 For an account of the possibilities as to how the 776 BC date was devised, including calculations made by counting back from 576 or 476 BC, see Christesen, forthcoming.

55 Pausanias 8.26.3–4. This shows clearly that our Coroebus is not the same mentioned in 1.43.7–1.44.1, whose grave was in Megara.

56 Eusebius *Chron.* 1.194 Schoene = Aristod. *FGrH* 414F1 = Tib. Claud. Polyb. *FGrH* 254F2.

57 Phlegon *FGrH* 257F1.1 (twenty-eighth Olympiad), 1.2–9 (first Olympiad), and 1.10–11 (sixth Olympiad). Pausanias (5.4.6) mentions a tradition that Iphitus' father was also named Iphitus. See further Robinson 1981, 242.

58 Eusebius *Chron.* 1.194 Schoene = Callim., fr. 541 Pfeiffer. For Coroebus, see Moretti 1957, 59 no. 1.

59 Golden (1998, 63–64) assumes this and thus places Aristodemus' date for the real beginnings of the Games at 884 BC (he also mistakenly refers to this date as Eratosthenes'). It is of interest, however, that Eratosthenes (*FGrH* 241F1 in Clem. Al., *Strom.* 1.138.1–3) dated Lycurgus' floruit to this year.

60 Pausanias 5.4.5–6, 5.8.5–6, and 8.26.4. Strabo (8.3.30 = *FGrH* 416T5) had made Coroebus the winner of the first Olympiad celebrated by Oxylus. Eusebius (*Chron.* 1.194, Schoene), Julius Africanus (*Ol.* 1), and Syncellus (197c) simply place Coroebus in the first Olympiad (dated to 776 BC) without saying who celebrated it.

61 Interestingly, Athenaeus (*Deipnosophistae* 9.382b), citing no sources, has a character say in passing that Coroebus, victor at the first Olympic Games, was a cook.

62 See Mahaffy 1881, 165, with the conclusion (at 178) that the names of the victors of
    the first fifty Olympiads are not genuine. Shaw (2003, 15) argues for reliability only from
    the fifth century BC on; for the earliest sources, see 60–61. See also Christesen, forth-
    coming, on this issue. The fact that all the early victors are Eleans or close neighbours
    in the late lists can be used to support either the position that these are genuine or that
    they are fabrications, since on the one hand this could be explained by the local nature
    and small size of the early Games, and on the other hand it could point to patriotic inven-
    tion.

63 For the difficulty of this passage and what Plutarch might have meant here, see Mossham-
    mer 1979, 93–94. See also Plut. *Quaest. conv.* 5.2 (= *Mor.*675c), which den Boer (1954,
    46–47) cites to show that Plutarch could at least take seriously the traditional order of
    the introduction of events at the Olympic Games.

The Transformation of Athletics in Sixth-Century Greece

Paul Christesen

At the close of the sixth century the Greeks were literally a nation of athletes.
— Gardiner 1930, 42

While much has been written about how the ancient Greeks were, as Gardiner observed, a nation of athletes, the temporal component of this phenomenon has been largely ignored.[1] It was not until the first half of the sixth century BC that athletics came to play a dominant role in Greek life and identity. Consider the situation as it stood in the seventh century. The Olympic Games were the only regularly scheduled athletic contests in Greece, and were just beginning to develop a Panhellenic rather than a regional profile.[2] Informal local competitions were common but were largely restricted to elites.[3] Athletic motifs appeared in art but with nowhere near the frequency that would later become the norm.[4] Architectural forms specifically dedicated to athletics could be found in neither sanctuaries nor cities.[5] In short, seventh-century Greece was not a nation of athletes.[6]

All this changed in the first half of the sixth century, when both the amount and the social significance of athletic activity increased sharply. The Pythian, Isthmian, and Nemean Games were founded (in 586, 580 and 573, respectively), and athletic competition was added to numerous local festivals, including the Panathenaea (in 566).[7] The first athletic victor statues were erected.[8] Stesichorus wrote the first purely athletic epic,[9] and Ibycus wrote the first *epinicium*.[10] Both the absolute number and percentage of surviving Athenian black-figure vases with athletic scenes from the first half of the sixth century are dramatically higher than those in the preceding half century.[11] The first formal stadia were built at this time,[12] and the earliest gymnasia were founded.[13]

The sixth-century transformation of Greek athletics should come as no surprise, since one of the axioms of sport history is that sport is shaped by, and can itself shape, larger cultural and historical patterns.[14] The Archaic period was a time of incessant, wrenching change, and athletics evolved in conjunction with the rest of Greek society. The diachronic development of Greek athletics can, as a result, only be appreciated and understood when Greek sport is situated in its social and historical context. A complete account of the complex, dynamic relationship between sport and society in ancient Greece would need to give due consideration to a wide range of factors, such as the cultic elements of athletics and a cultural orientation towards competition. When the focus is narrowed to the transformation of athletics in the sixth century, however, one factor stands out as being of overriding importance: the political overtones of athletic activity.

There are two dominant schools of thought in the relatively limited amount of scholarship that examines the causes of the sixth-century transformation of Greek athletics. One school sees the creation of the hoplite phalanx as the key factor. Some members of this school argue that the need for physical fitness among hoplites was met through the use of athletics, which in turn brought about fundamental changes in the scale of athletic activity in Greece. Other members of this school argue that the phalanx sharply circumscribed opportunities for individuals to distinguish themselves on the battlefield, so that strong agonistic instincts were channelled into athletics, which in turn produced a massive surge in athletic activity.

Unfortunately, the chronological evidence does not support either of this first school's viewpoints. The hoplite phalanx was probably introduced in the early part of the seventh century, long before the transformation of athletics in the sixth century. If the introduction of the hoplite phalanx did directly affect athletics, one would expect a significantly earlier change in the scale and nature of athletic activity in Greece. It is unlikely that the sudden, sharp increase in athletic activity in the first half of the sixth century was directly caused by the introduction of the hoplite phalanx a century earlier.

According to the other school of thought, *poleis* (Greek city states) during the Archaic period imposed limits on the opportunities for individuals to gain distinction by political and military means, as a result of which athletics became the primary arena for competition in *philotimia* or "distinction." There are a number of problems with this perspective. To begin with, everything that is known about the socio-political history of Archaic Greece indicates that competition was alive and well in a variety of spheres in most, if not all, Greek *poleis* through the end of the sixth century and beyond. It is not clear, therefore, that athletics was the competitive arena of last resort. Further, there was no distinct change in overall socio-political trends in Greece in the first half of the sixth century that could, in and of itself, account for a sudden change in the structure of athletic activity.[15]

Economics no doubt played an enabling role in the transformation of Greek athletics in the sixth century, with increasing wealth creating more leisure time for more people. This, however, cannot explain what happened in the field of Greek athletics in the sixth century, since the existence of a greater pool of resources is not inherently determinative of how those resources were allocated. The Greeks chose to expend significant resources on athletic activity, specifically nude athletic activity, in the sixth century. The challenge is thus to explain why they chose to do so.[16] During the Archaic period, participation in athletics became a means by which non-elites could make a regular, public claim to socio-political privilege, and this in turn brought about fundamental changes in the place of athletics in Greek life and consciousness.

The politicization of athletics is a familiar element of modern-day sport, most obviously in the context of the Olympic Games, which are infused with competitive nationalism. While this sort of politicization was not entirely foreign to ancient Greece, athletic activity in Greece was political primarily because athletics was a collective activity. This is a pivotal concept in the analysis that follows, so a clear definition is a necessity. A collective activity can be defined as an iterated form of group interaction that establishes membership in and the boundaries of communities, that expresses the realities of the prevailing socio-political system, and that has the potential to express and reify competing visions of what that system ought to be.[17]

Collective activities were inherently political in the seventh and sixth centuries because, as Christian Meier has remarked in discussing the Archaic period, "Politics and relationships between citizens as citizens did not represent an independent fact that could be abstracted from the totality of social events."[18] What Meier calls the "discovery of politics"—the construction of a distinct political realm in fifth-century Athens, and the privileging of participation in that realm as the most important marker of full membership in the community—resulted in a marked decrease in the socio-political importance of other forms of communal practice. Before that time, however, many activities, which would become more social than political by the end of the Classical period, were simultaneously social and political.[19] A particularly clear example of a collective activity can be found in commensality. The elite symposium and the demotic *eranos* (a meal contributed to by each diner, like a potluck) embodied sharply variant notions of the normative socio-political order. In choosing a particular form of commensality, therefore, individuals were making overtly political statements.[20]

It is apparent from the Homeric poems that athletics was a collective activity as early as the eighth century.[21] Homer describes a society in which a social contract of sorts bound *basileis* ("chiefs") and *demos* (people) together. *Basileis* provided physical protection on and off the battlefield, and material support in times of hardship, in exchange for labour, gifts, obedience, and respect. The power and prestige of any given leader were largely dependent upon the resources, particularly the resources of manpower, at his disposal. Since the relationship between leader and follower was personal and subject to dissolution at any time, ambitious leaders competed to display their physical prowess and generosity to actual or potential followers. The result was constantly shifting intra-community status hierarchies.[22]

Athletics played a vital role in elite competition because athletic activity provided a relatively peaceful, rule-governed form of competition closely linked to military prowess. This helped build and stabilize socio-political structures by enabling leaders to communicate important information about their ambitions and capabilities in a regular, non-destructive fashion. The mere fact of participation in such competition was a public statement of some importance. To be invited or perhaps allowed to participate in athletics meant that one was seen as a suitable competitor by other *basileis*, and was therefore in and of itself a sign of status. This explains Euryalus' anger at Odysseus for declining an invitation to participate in the athletic contests held in his honour in Phaeacia. The invitation to compete with the male members of leading families in the community was a mark of honour, which was not to be refused lightly. When Odysseus does refuse, Euryalus immediately attacks his social status:

> Then Euryalus answered him and abused him to his face, "No, stranger, you do not seem like a man experienced in contests, of which there are

many among men. Rather you seem like a captain of sailors going to and fro in a many-benched ship, a man who is both concerned about his cargo and watchful of his goods and his rapacious profits. You do not seem like a man who competes for prizes." (*Od.* 8.145–64)

Athletics was thus a collective activity that reflected and underpinned the socio-political structure of the eighth century. Both political leadership and participation in athletics were limited to elites. *Basileis* and athletes were one and the same group. Further, the relationship between *basileis* was marked by constant competition that created shifting intra-community status hierarchies, and athletics both reflected and enabled this endless struggle for pre-eminence.

The sixth-century transformation of Greek athletics was brought about by the confluence of two changes, one in the structure of socio-political institutions and one in the structure of athletic activity. The political history of most Greek *poleis* during the Archaic period was marked by a progressive formalization of institutions of governance and a prolonged struggle between mass and elite over who would have access to and control over those institutions. Ian Morris has termed the non-elite group the "middling" citizens because this group consisted of those men who were neither very rich nor poor.[23] In the parlance of fifth-century Athens, these men were *penêtes* (workers), rather than *plousioi* (rich) or *ptôchoi* (poor).[24] The "middling" view of the *polis* was a community in which both *penêtes* and *plousioi* (though not *ptôchoi*) formed a citizen body with minimal internal rank distinction. Elites, on the other hand, sought to impose a much more restrictive notion of community.

The structure of athletic activity in Archaic Greece was fundamentally altered by changes in the nature and significance of athletic nudity. When one discusses athletic nudity, it is necessary to be specific about precisely what type of athletic nudity one has in mind. This is because there were at least two different categories of athletic nudity in ancient Greece, each with its own distinct history. One of those categories might be called initiatory athletic nudity, that is, athletic nudity occurring in the context of initiation rites.[25] This type of nudity was doubtless of great antiquity in Greece, almost certainly going back at least to the late Bronze Age.[26] Its significance was, however, limited because it was by definition extraordinary. Nudity of this type marked its context as being beyond the realm of everyday life.[27] The relevant literary and artistic sources make it clear that the incorporation of athletic nudity into everyday life did not begin until the middle of the seventh century and proceeded gradually thereafter as initial resistance to public nudity, even amongst a limited group of males, was overcome.[28] This was a very different kind of nudity than initiatory nudity, and carried with it a very different meaning. Larissa Bonfante has given the label "civic nudity" to this type of undress because it was very closely associated with being a male citizen and with service in the hoplite phalanx. Bonfante defines civic nudity as non-formal, nude athletic activity that took place on a regular basis, typically in gymnasia.[29]

The advent of civic nudity fundamentally altered the socio-political significance of athletic activity. Civic nudity was inherently political because active participation in the defence of the community was, at least from the time of Homer, one of the basic claims to socio-political privilege.[30] When civic nudity was adopted by the majority of the hoplites in any given community, it emphasized the military significance of non-elites and their concomitant claim to political rights. The participation of elites and non-elites in the same activity, on the same terms, simultaneously minimized the difference between these two groups, while the absence of clothing, one of the most commonly employed status markers, limited socio-economic stratification.[31] Civic nudity was, therefore, potentially a collective activity that reified the "middling" socio-political vision.

The advantages that accrued to non-elites from civic nudity were dependent upon their being included in the group of males who exercised in the nude on a regular basis. Everyday athletics in the eighth century had been the preserve of the elite, and there was no reason why the addition of nudity necessarily brought with it the extension of such activity to non-elites.[32] Civic nudity also had the potential to become a means by which elite monopolization of socio-political privilege was represented and consolidated, provided that non-elites were excluded from participation. This did not escape the keen eye of Aristotle. A little-noticed feature of his much-quoted comments on the historical development of *politeiai* (state constitutions) is the inclusion of nude exercise in the list of means by which the elite separated themselves from the non-elite:

> The pretexts used in the various kinds of *politeia* are five in number and concern the assembly, the magistracies, the courts, the bearing of arms, and nude exercises [*gymnasia*] (*Pol.* 1297a14–7).

> They legislate in the same manner about both the possession of arms and gymnastics [*toû gymnazesthai*]. For it is possible for the poor [*aporois*] not to possess arms, but the rich [*euporois*] not possessing arms are fined. And if the poor do not exercise in the nude [*mê gymnazôntai*], there is no fine, but there is a fine for the rich, so that the rich will, on account of the fine, take part while the poor do not because they do not fear a fine (*Pol.* 1297a29–35).[33]

A more stringent regime seems to have been implemented in the sixth century at Rhegium. Phytius, Theocles, Helicaon, and Aristocrates, all disciples of Pythagoras, established a *gymnasiarchê politeia* (roughly a constitution based on control or regulation of the gymnasium) in which socio-political privilege and access to the gymnasium were both sharply restricted.[34]

The struggles between elite and non-elite throughout the Archaic period did not come to an absolutely clear conclusion, but the "middling" vision of an inclusive socio-political community prevailed in much of Greece by the end of the sixth century. Broad participation in civic nudity was both a cause and effect of this outcome, and civic nudity became a primary means of distinguishing male citizens from all other members of their communities, particularly slaves.[35] Aristotle (*Pol.* 1264a17–22) observes that Cretans of his time granted their slaves most of the privileges enjoyed by citizens, except the rights to exercise in the nude and to possess arms. Both Aeschines (*In Tim.* 138) and Plutarch (*Vit. Sol.* 1) mention a law ascribed to Solon that forbade slaves to exercise or oil themselves in gymnasia. Here are Aeschines' comments on this law:

> The laws states that, "a slave will not exercise in the nude [*gymnazesthai*] or rub himself with oil in the palaistrai." There is no addition stating that, "the free man will anoint himself with oil and exercise in the nude [*gymnazesthai*]." For the lawgivers, observing the good that comes from nude exercise [*gymnasiôn*], forbade slaves to take part, and in so doing they thought that they were issuing an invitation to do so to the free.[36]

The enduring socio-political importance of civic nudity is reflected in a third-century inscription recording an alliance between Hierapytna and Praisos in Crete that gave citizens of both *poleis* the right to use the gymnasia in each city (*IC* III iv 1B 68–78).

The sixth-century transformation of Greek athletics, then, was driven by the emergence of civic nudity as a collective activity that embodied an inclusive socio-political vision. As civic nudity was gradually adopted by Greek communities in the second half of the seventh century and early sixth centuries, it became imperative for non-elites not only to participate in athletics but to make their participation evident to everyone in their community. The result was a sharp increase in the amount of athletic activity in Greece and in the resources devoted to commemorating athletic activity.[37] Being an athlete was a strong claim to socio-political privilege, and it was this that made Greece into a nation of athletes.

Notes

1 All dates are BC unless otherwise indicated. All translations of ancient Greek sources are my own.

2 On the geographic extent of participation in the early Olympic Games, see Morgan 1990, 57–105. The Homeric Hymn to Apollo (11. 146–50) mentions boxing matches at the festival of Apollo on Delos, but the date of this hymn remains uncertain. The section of the Hymn that mentions boxing is typically dated to the early sixth century. See Kirk 1985.

3 Irregularly scheduled funeral games were the predominant form of organized athletic contests before the sixth century; see Roller 1981. On the structure of Greek athletics prior to the sixth century, see Laser 1987, 6–25 and 88–184.

4 The key evidence comes from pottery. See Legakis 1977, 370–88.

5 See nn. 12–13, below, for bibliography.

6 The application of the term "nation" to ancient Greece is problematic, and it is used here solely as an echo of Gardiner's phrasing. For recent thinking on Greece as a "nation," see Cohen 2000, 3–10, 79–103.

7 Brodersen 1990; Gardiner 1930, 28–42; Gebhard 2002; Miller 1978; Osborne 1990. This upswing in athletic activity also had an impact on the venerable Sanctuary of Zeus at Olympia. Sometime in the very early sixth century, the Sanctuary received its first permanent stone architecture in the form of a temple dedicated to Zeus and Hera. This edifice was the start of a major building program that in the succeeding decades brought the construction of numerous treasuries and the stadium. See Drees 1968, 111–29; Mallwitz 1988; Schilbach 1992.

There has been considerable discussion as to whether the (re-)foundation dates for the Pythian, Nemean, Isthmian, and Panathenaic festivals given in the ancient sources are precisely accurate. Gardiner, for instance, dates the reorganized Pythia to 582, but Miller 1978 (see also now Brodersen 1990) argues persuasively for a date of 586. For present purposes, it is sufficient that these dates are approximately correct, which is beyond question.

8 On victor statues, see in particular Pausanias 7.60.1–2. The following modern sources are also relevant: Gardiner 1915, 216; Hyde 1921, 26–37; Lattimore 1988; Kurke 1993, 141–49; Steiner 1998.

9 On Stesichorus, see Segal 1985, 186–201.

10 See Golden 1998, 74–88 for a good brief history of *epinicia*. On Ibycus, see Barron 1984 and Jenner 1986.

11 Legakis 1977, 370–88. See also Goossens and Thielemans 1996; Hollein 1988, 71–103.

12 On stadia, see Romano 1993, 1–42. Ongoing excavations at Isthmia, Nemea, and Olympia continue to augment what is known about early stadia. See Brulotte 1994; Gebhard 2002; Miller 2002; Schilbach 1992.

13 For brief overviews of the history of the gymnasium, see Glass 1988 and Mussche 1992. For full-length treatments, see Delorme 1960 and Glass 1967. For early Athenian gymnasia, see Kyle 1993, 64–84.

14 See Müller 1995, 11–13 for a summary of the relevant argumentation and pertinent bibliography. The terms "sport" and "athletics" are used interchangeably throughout, though there is a considerable literature that suggests variant definitions. See Blanchard 1995, 27–60.

15 For these points of view, see Delorme 1960, 9–32; Stein-Hölkeskamp 1989, 104–22; Müller 1995, 115–25, respectively. The date of the introduction of the hoplite phalanx remains a subject of some dispute. Both Singor 1995 and Storch 1998 contain good overviews of the relevant scholarship.

16 On the growth of the Greek economy during the Archaic period, see Starr 1982.

17 On collective activities in general, see Murray 1983b and Schmitt-Pantel 1990a. For a brief historiographical review of the study of collective activities, see Bremmer 1990.

18 Meier 1984, 30. Dougherty and Kurke (1993, 2) have aptly characterized Archaic Greece as "predisciplinary"; the boundaries between what later became separate spheres such as politics, economics, and religion were incipient, if extant at all.

19 See Meier 1990, 29–81 and passim; Meier 1984, 1–62.

20 On commensality as collective activity, see Murray 1983a; Murray 1983b; Murray 1990; and Schmitt-Pantel 1990a and 1990b.

21 On athletics as a collective activity, see Scanlon 2002, 3–24, 323–34; Schmitt-Pantel (1990a, 199) gives athletics the barest mention. Scanlon is interested in demonstrating that athletics served as a form of *paideia* (education) for youths on the verge of adulthood: "The primary concern of this study is to characterize Greek athletics and body culture in its connection with religion, sexuality, and rituals for bringing youths to adulthood" (3). His lengthy study does an excellent job of exploring the connection between athletics, initiation, and pederasty, but Scanlon examines the importance of athletics for adults in very general terms and does not consider why (and how) athletics played such an important role in Greek society. The best work on athletics as a collective activity is that of Mark Golden (1998), who argues that athletics was a means of creating a "discourse of difference" between Greeks and barbarians, boys and men, males and females. Although Golden does not use the term, the boundary-creating functions of athletics are precisely the function fulfilled by collective activities.

22 This view of Homeric society is based on Donlan 1998, as well as Donlan 1999, 1–34. See also Donlan 1982a; Donlan 1982b; Finley 1965, 74–107; and Snodgrass 1980, 15–159. Other scholars see Homeric Greece as a much more stratified society than that described here, with a correspondingly strong emphasis on the importance of hereditary position. For an eloquent defense of this view, see van Wees 1992, 63–167 and passim.

23 The view of Archaic Greek social history sketched here is derived from Morris 2000, 109–94. Other relevant work includes (but is not limited to) Donlan 1999, 35–75, 95–111; Morris 1996; and Morris 1997.

24 On the definition of the rich and poor in ancient Greece, see Davies 1984, 1–14; den Boer 1979, 151–78; Markle 1985; and Morris 1996. The Greeks seem to have divided the socio-economic spectrum into three more or less distinct segments. The very wealthy were called *plousioi* or *euporoi*, the very poor *ptôchoi*, and the large group located in between *penêtes* or *aporoi*. The difference between the *plousioi* and the *penêtes* seems to have been defined by whether or not the household in question had at its disposal enough dependents to free the adult male members of the nuclear family from the necessity of daily productive activity. The difference between *penêtes* and *ptôchoi* lay in the ability of the former to support themselves from their own resources. Dependence thus created a hierarchy. *Plousioi* were in a position to live a life of relative leisure (though they did not necessarily do so) because they controlled dependent labour; *penêtes* were independent but needed to work on a daily basis to provide for themselves; *ptôchoi* regularly depended on the largesse of others.

25 On categories of nudity in ancient Greece, Bonfante 1989 is essential. A fairly consistent picture of Greek initiatory athletics emerges from what is known about Cretan rites and the *Heraea*. On the Cretan rites, see Aristotle Fr. 611.15; Dosiadis *FrGH* 458 F1 (*ap.* Athen. 143a-d); Ephorus *FrGH* 70 F149 (*ap.* Strabo 10.483); Nikolaos *FrGH* 90 F103 (*ap.* Stob. 4.2); Plato *Laws* 636d; *IC* I ix 1 99–100 (Dreros); *IC* I xix 1 17–8 (Mallia and Lyttos); *IC* I xvi 5 21 (Lato and Olous); *IC* II v 24 7–9 (Axos). For modern accounts, see Burkert 1985, 260–62; Dover 1989, 185–96; Leitao 1995; Scanlon 1999; Scanlon 2002, 74–77; Vidal-Naquet 1986, 113–17; Willetts 1955, 120–23; Willetts 1962, 43–53, 60–67, 116–17, 201–14; and Willetts 1965, 110–18.

26 See Koehl 1986; Koehl 1997; and Koehl 2000.

27 Nudity is just one type of special costume associated with initiatory rites. Other forms
    of costume included various kinds of transvestism. The most relevant example is the use
    of male garments by the female competitors in the *Heraea* at Olympia. See Serwint
    1993.

28 The best treatment of the relevant evidence is McDonnell 1991. See also McDonnell 1993
    and Shapiro 2000.

29 Bonfante (1989) establishes the connection between participation in civic nudity and mem-
    bership in the hoplite phalanx. She does not, however, explore how this connection
    came into being. It is unlikely that civic nudity came into being solely to help keep
    hoplite soldiers physically fit, both because the chronology is problematic (see n. 15) and
    because there is no obvious reason why hoplites needed to take their exercise in the nude.
    Civic nudity was a significant departure from an entrenched custom of clothed athletic
    activity with clear military dimensions, a custom that could easily have been adapted to
    the requirements of hoplites. There is, therefore, need for further investigation of the
    link between hoplites and civic nudity. I hope to address this subject in detail in the
    near future.

30 See, for instance, *Il.* 9.574–80 and 12.310–21. See also Hanson 1996 and Vidal-Naquet
    1968. For a contrary view, see van Wees 1995.

31 The levelling aspects of nudity in the specific context of democratic Athens are well
    treated in Miller 2000.

32 The importance of numbers in the clash of hoplite phalanxes and the link between the
    training of hoplite numbers and civic nudity did, however, tend to create a certain pres-
    sure towards greater inclusion.

33 On these passages, see Aristotle (trans. Robinson) 1995, 109–11.

34 See Iamblichus, *Life of Pythagoras*, 27.130.5, and Mann 2001, 184.

35 The link between political inclusion and civic nudity is reflected in a fragment of Erx-
    ias' *History of Colophon* (*FHG* IV 406), which records the dedication of a gymnasium
    to Eros in Samos and the simultaneous creation of a festival of Eleutheria, probably on
    the occasion of the overthrow of Polycrates in the second half of the sixth century.

36 The attribution of legislation to Solon is always problematic. Regarding the Solonic leg-
    islation on athletics, see Kyle 1984. A Hellenistic inscription from Beroea in Macedo-
    nia (*SEG* XXVII.261) similarly bars slaves from gymnasia, though this law may have
    sprung from concerns about pederastic relationships. An English translation of the
    Beroea inscription can be found in Miller 2004b, 133–38. For a discussion of the con-
    tent of the inscription, see Cantarella 1992, 28–33.

37 It is possible to arrive at some idea of the increase in the general level of athletic activ-
    ity that occurred in the sixth century, based on what is known about the relative num-
    bers of elite and non-elite members of hoplite phalanxes in ancient Greece. In Classical
    Athens, there seems to have been a general notion that the *plousioi* and those perform-
    ing liturgies were identical. Given prevailing estimates as to the population of Athens and
    the number of liturgists, this would indicate that something like the wealthiest 5 per cent
    of households fell into this group. Perhaps 33 to 50 per cent of the adult males of any
    given community possessed sufficient wealth to serve in the hoplite phalanx. The emer-
    gence of civic nudity, and the extension of everyday athletic activity from elites to all mem-
    bers of the phalanx, would thus have produced a six to tenfold increase in the number
    of athletes. It need hardly be said that this is a very rough calculation and cannot be
    pressed too far, but it does give a sense of scale. On the number of liturgists, see Davies
    1967; Davies 1971; Rhodes 1982. On service in the hoplite phalanx, see Cartledge
    2001, 166, and van Wees 2001.

The Ancient Olympics
and Their Ideals

Nigel B. Crowther

"To construct a better and more peaceful world" is one of the aims expressed in the modern Olympic Charter.[1] "International understanding," "brotherhood," and "peace" are catchwords often associated with the Olympic movement of today. But are these simply recent concepts, or do they have a basis in the ancient world? This paper will discuss the ancient Olympic Games in terms of nationalism and internationalism, understanding between nations, war and peace, and especially brotherhood and unity. Bearing in mind the enormous timespan of the Games, it is the intention here to concentrate particularly, although not exclusively, on the fifth and fourth centuries BC, which provide much relevant material for this purpose.

Nationalism and Internationalism

The Greek concept of nationalism was different from the one with which we are familiar in the modern world.[2] Greece was not a specific entity until the modern state came into existence in 1825. Ancient Greece consisted of numerous city states, the *poleis,* which were fiercely independent and not united until the time of Philip II of Macedon.[3] Yet there was a sense of Greek ethnicity that separated Greeks from non-Greeks, who were referred to as barbarians.[4]

No founding charter of the ancient Olympic Games has survived, nor has any evidence yet been found that one existed, so that little is known for certain about the earliest times. Indeed, if the Games preceded the introduction of the alphabetic script into Greece, knowledge about them would have depended on oral tradition.[5] It is only in the middle of the sixth century BC that written regulations dealing with the Olympic festival, the *leges sacrae* as they are called, first appear. Consequently, much about the ideals and regulations at Olympia has to be deduced from a time many years later than the first recorded festival of 776 BC.[6] To be Greek, however, always seems to have been an ideal of the Games. This was true in the earliest times, when the Games were probably local, being only for the city state that controlled the festival, whether Pisa or Elis, or at the most for the inhabitants of the Alpheus valley.[7] We find the same ethnic ideal also in the sixth century BC, when the Eleans explained the rules of the festival to the Egyptian Psammis that anyone from Elis or the rest of Greece could compete at Olympia (Hdt. 2.160).[8] Even several hundred years later, in the second to third century AD, when Greece was ruled by the Romans, we know from Philostratus (*De Gymnastica* 25) that the ideal was still to be Greek, since to qualify for competition at Olympia an athlete (at least a boy athlete, and presumably an adult) had to have a legitimate father and family, be free-born, belong to a tribe, and have a native city. It was understood that he was to be of Greek birth.[9] In this respect, the ancient Games are comparable not with the Olympics of 1896, or of course with those of today, but with the Zappas Olympic Games held in nineteenth-century Athens, where contestants, like their ancient counterparts, came from the Greek-speaking world.[10]

Over time, as athletes came to the Games not only from the old, established centres but also from the fringes of the Greek world, the concept of being Greek became less clearly defined.[11] Macedonians, Egyptians, Lycians, Lydians, Phoenicians, Romans, and others, including even a member of the royal family of Armenia, eventually gained admittance to Olympia.[12] Aspiring competitors from these regions were allowed to compete for various reasons. Some were declared eligible if they could prove Greek ancestry. In the fifth century, Alexander I, king of Macedon, was initially rebuffed, for instance, when he tried to enter the Games, since the other competitors protested that the contest was not for foreigners, but for Greeks. Nevertheless, Alexander proved that he was an Argive, and was judged to be Greek (Hdt. 5.22).[13] Non-royal Macedonians, however, do not appear in the victory list until the late fourth century.[14] Some athletes became qualified because of cultural assimilation, when their cities, notably in Egypt and Asia Minor, became part of the Greek world after the conquests of Alexander the Great.[15] On occasion, a foreign member of royalty or a noted dignitary probably participated by invitation, but these were few in number, to judge from the victory lists.

As for the Romans, who had no Greek heritage, it was no lofty ideal of internationalism and brotherhood that led to their admittance to the Games, but harsh reality.[16] After 146 BC, as Greece lost its independence and eventually became a Roman province, Rome became politically involved in the affairs of Olympia.[17] This is the time when the Elean organizers of the festival had to suffer "the indignities of Roman affronts to Hellenic ideals."[18] The Eleans probably accepted the participation of the Romans in the Games, notably members of the aristocracy, for external, political, and especially economic reasons. It was at the end of the first century BC that noble Romans began to appear in the records as victors in equestrian events: the first of these was the future emperor Tiberius, victor in the *quadriga* in 4 BC.[19] It is significant for understanding the relationship of Elis and Rome that inscriptions from Olympia honour him, not only as a victor, but also as a patron and benefactor of the city of Elis.[20] Clearly the Eleans were interested more in the financial considerations of such a distinguished competitor to enhance the festival than in any sense of internationalism. It is unlikely, therefore, that the Romans were made eligible en masse for the Olympic Games after their conquest of Greece, as seems to be confirmed by the victory lists.[21] Roman competitors were accepted at the Games as a prudent and political compromise by the Eleans to add to the prestige of the Games, and especially to retain control of the festival in the Roman period.[22]

National elements, and even shades of being Greek, can be seen during the course of the events themselves at Olympia: in the boxing match of 212 BC, the crowd supported the underdog, Aristonicus, against Cleitomachus of Thebes. Because his rival seemed to be a match for him, Cleitomachus called upon the spectators to support him against his opponent, since he was fighting for the glory of Greece against an Egyptian; the crowd changed sides during the contest and cheered to victory their champion from the Greek Mainland (Polyb. 27.9.7–13).[23] Even though both boxers (presumably) were technically qualified for the Games, for the name Aristonicus is Greek, the crowd was asked to make an ethnic distinction between them. By 212 BC the Greek Mainland had been unified, and Egypt was thought of as a different part of the Greek world. Moreover, as late as the fourth century AD, under Roman rule, a would-be athlete at Olympia is advised to make Greece appear as strong as possible, since foreigners were present at the Games ([Julian], *Ep. ad Themistium* 9 [263a]).[24] Even after a thousand years, therefore, being Greek was still a significant factor at the Games, which continued to display elements of nationalism.

Understanding between Nations

Olympia did not champion understanding between nations, nor between city states. This is evident from the fact that the Olympic festival was controlled not by a cross-section of Mediterranean states, or even by a union of Greek states, but solely by and for one city.[25] There was no equivalent, therefore, of an International Olympic Committee, or even a national Olympic committee. This domination by a single city and the consequences thereof are significant for understanding Olympia, since it was the city of Elis that had almost complete authority over the festival for most of its thousand-year history and treated it as its own, almost as if it were part of the city. This control over Olympia increased the status and power of Elis throughout Greece. The political manoeuvres of the Eleans in regard to Olympia can be illustrated from an incident in 420 BC, when they accused the Spartans of breaking the Olympic truce (*ekecheiria*).[26] At this time the Eleans were apparently interested not simply in maintaining Olympic regulations, but in preserving their territorial claim to the neighbouring city of Lepreon, which had been championed by Sparta.[27] At Olympia, both athletes and visitors were at the mercy of the Eleans, who had the ultimate authority over those who were allowed to visit the Games or to compete;[28] however, although they had the right to exclude other cities from taking part in the festival, as far as we know they never did so, except when cities were in breach of the regulations. In general, the Eleans acted fairly in regard to Olympia, but on occasion they are known to have misused their power, as in the incident with the Spartans just mentioned.[29]

War and Peace

Unlike those of the modern era, the ancient Olympics were not cancelled because of war; those of 480 BC are an early example of the doctrine that the "Games must continue," whatever may be happening in the outside world. These Games were held at a time when the Greeks were fighting against the Persians only a few hundred kilometres (or a few days' march) away from Olympia, and when the famous battle of Thermopylae was being fought in central Greece (Hdt. 7.206). Moreover, the victors in these Games came from different parts of Greece—and not only from the area around Olympia, as one might have expected, for the distinguished boxer Theagenes travelled from the northern island of Thasos, which Xerxes closely bypassed in his campaign.[30] In addition, [Dai]tondas and Arsilochus entered a four-horse chariot from Thebes, a city no more than a hundred kilometres from the battlefront.[31]

Archaeologists have shown that many, if not most, of the surviving dedications at Olympia are associated with war rather than with peace, at least before the fifth century BC and to a certain extent beyond. It was common to offer arms to Zeus in thanksgiving for the oracle's advice in military matters.[32] Hardly any of the memorable battles of Greek history were fought (directly or indirectly) without the aid of an Olympic seer,[33] and one tenth of the spoils in war was traditionally dedicated to the god of Olympia. Many of these consecrations of armour, it should be emphasized, did not commemorate battles of Greeks against foreigners, but those of Greeks against Greeks.[34]

This practice of offering weapons at Olympia, however, is more scantily documented in the fifth century and later.[35] It was in part replaced there by other kinds of victory memorials—for instance, an image of Zeus was dedicated by the Greeks who fought against the Persians at Plataea in 479 BC. A bronze slab records the terms of the thirty-year peace between the Athenians and the Spartans in 445 BC. The offering of the Eleans in thanks for regaining control of the Sanctuary from the Arcadians in 364 BC bears the inscription "from the Eleans for concord."[36] Moreover, some Greek philosophers and historians opposed the dedication of weapons and criticized the association between armour and Greek festivals: in the fourth century BC, for example, Plato (*Resp.* 5, especially 469E–470A) attacked the custom of offering arms taken from Greeks; in Plutarch (*Mor.* 401C–D), one finds a similar denunciation. Yet we can deduce that in the fourth century BC and afterwards, Greeks still dedicated armour in sanctuaries.[37]

It has been proposed that Olympia became particularly famous as a festival not because of any idealism about peace, but because the professional seers of Olympia were so often consulted before battle, and because the help of Zeus was requested in war.[38] A case may be made, therefore, that the Olympics grew from war, not from peace. Yet we should not, of course, think of war as an ideal of Olympia.[39]

Brotherhood and Unity

Did the Olympic Games in the ancient world promote a feeling of brotherhood and unity, and if so, to what extent? Generally, Panhellenism was not a major goal of the Greek people, but was used rather as a "tool of political propaganda,"[40] for as we have seen the Greek ideal was not a united nation but the *polis*, the independent city state. Even so, two etiological myths are sometimes cited to support the view that Panhellenism was found in the early Olympic Games.[41] According to one legend, strife broke out among the people of the Peloponnese, since the worship of Zeus had been neglected. Therefore, Lycurgus of Sparta, Iphitus of Elis, and Cleosthenes of Pisa decided to revive the Olympic Games, to proclaim a truce between competing cities and to add athletic events.[42] According to Lysias in the early fourth century (in a speech quoted by Dionysius of Halicarnassus, *Lys.* 30), Heracles, one of the legendary founders of the Games, believed that the Olympic festival would be the beginning of friendship among the Greeks, and would unite the estranged Greek cities. Yet it is probable that later Greek writers invented these myths about the early Games, since they wished to see Panhellenism in the Games of their time.[43]

Some scholars suppose that as early as the sixth century BC, when the athletic circuit began, Olympia and the other major festivals reflected the development of national unity in Greece through common shrines, gods, and athletics.[44] Moreover, they believe that the Olympic festival itself had Panhellenic features, such as the treasure houses in the Sanctuary and the sacred envoys, who were sent there by a city to act on behalf of that city. Yet these are Panhellenic in the sense that they represented different cities in the Greek world, but did not promote brotherhood. Cities used the treasure houses for propaganda, which should be considered as examples of competition among the Greeks rather than as support for Greek unity. At all events, these features seem to be largely a by-product of the festival, and not a founding ideal. One should also bear in mind the offering of weapons at Olympia, which as we have seen were sometimes dedicated by Greeks against Greeks.

In the fifth and fourth centuries BC, however, elements of brotherhood and unity did begin to appear at Olympia, as we have already hinted.[45] The impetus came in part from forces outside Olympia, from various intellectuals who used the crowds at the Games as a sounding board for their own purposes, but it also came from the Olympic festival itself in several ways: first, it promoted the famous truce; secondly, it appears that

Olympic officials were used as ambassadors of peace; finally, it set up a court to mediate disputes among the Greek people using the sanctity of Olympia.

Before examining these three elements at Olympia, we should first comment on the "outside forces," the rich and famous, the politicians and intellectuals, who certainly had an effect on the Games.[46] The Athenian general Themistocles, during his visit to the festival in 476 BC was constantly singled out by the crowd as one who had saved Greece from Persia four years earlier. He was applauded and admired for his achievement, even to the neglect of the athletes (Plut. *Them.* 17.2).[47] As well, some intellectuals actively used Olympia to further their own political ideals. We should observe, however, that this does not reflect any Panhellenism in the Games, but that Olympia with its crowds provided the opportunity for such activities. In the late fifth century BC, Gorgias there delivered his Olympic oration (of which only fragments survive); this was a rare plea for the unification of the Greeks.[48] In 388 BC, the orator Lysias gave his famous Olympic speech, a call to free the Greeks from the Sicilian tyrants, especially from Dionysius of Syracuse (Dion. Hal. *Lys.* 29, Diod. Sic. 14.109.2–3). In 380 BC, Isocrates distributed his *Panegyricus* (187–8) at Olympia, an appeal for a Greek alliance against the barbarians.[49] We should not necessarily assume from these examples, however, that the festival itself became a hotbed of Panhellenism; nevertheless it did provide perhaps the largest assembly of Greeks at one time.[50] All these individuals seem to have been passionate about their ideals, although significantly Isocrates (*Paneg.* 5.13) was aware that his orations in general, and those of others, would have little effect in reality.[51] Indeed, no united front emerged from these speeches at Olympia against either the Persians or other foreigners.[52]

Yet what of the elements from within Olympia? It was the Eleans themselves who were largely responsible for the Olympic truce, as we have seen, for messengers, *spondophoroi*, were dispatched to all Greek cities to announce the sacred truce, which among other things guaranteed safe conduct to travellers to and from Olympia.[53] It may be argued, however, that unity was the effect rather than the purpose of the truce, which simply guaranteed the sanctity of Olympia. Certainly the truce had limitations in an international sense, for it had no meaning to the Persians, who were said to be unaware that the Games of 480 BC were being held and had to be informed of them by Greek deserters. Moreover, one of the Persian leaders, Tigranes, was surprised that the prize at Olympia was simply an olive wreath and not money (Hdt. 8.26).[54] Even if this last statement is a cliché, it does demonstrate yet again the marked differences between Greeks and foreigners.

In addition to the Olympic truce, which was controlled by Elis, but often with the assistance of Sparta, it seems that Olympia was also associated with the Panhellenic truce, which the Spartans had organized in 481 BC throughout Greece to counteract the Persian invasion. This produced a confederation of Greeks, the Greek League, which agreed not only to guarantee safety to travellers but also, unlike the Olympic truce, to end all wars among its members. It appears that it was the Olympic judges, the *Hellanodikai*, who were appointed as official supervisors of this truce. Their important political role outside Olympia, however, was short-lived, for this truce does not seem to have continued for long after the Persian Wars.

The third feature to be considered in terms of brotherhood and unity at Olympia is the Olympic court,[55] which dealt with matters not of a sporting nature, nor of immediate concern to the festival itself, but with political and civic affairs among the Greek states. The epigraphical sources are meagre, so that it is difficult to determine its exact nature, but one surviving verdict of the court involves litigation between Athens and Boeotia on civic matters confirming the decision of the lower court at Olympia. A second decision concerns a dispute between the Thessalians and the Thespians over the paying of damages.[56] It may not be coincidental that these judgments are dated between 476 and 472 BC, the two Olympiads that immediately followed the Persian Wars. This court seems to have become for a short time a "symbol of harmony among all Greek states."[57] Yet it was an ideal that for whatever reason never really took hold in the Greek world. We can conjecture that, since the court consisted entirely of Eleans, it may not have been viable or acceptable to the other Greeks because of its political overtones. There is no evidence for the continuation of this court, or of the Greek League, which appears to have been accepted by the Greeks in a time of crisis for only a brief period, and disappeared when the threat of the Persians eased.

Conclusion

In summary, we may state that despite the romantic notions and idealism of Victorian scholars, still promulgated by some today in an attempt to link the ideals of the modern Games with those of the ancient, it is clear that there was no real attempt by the Eleans to foster "international understanding," "brotherhood," or "peace" at the ancient Olympics. Some have rightly spoken of the inter-city nature and expansion of the later Olympics throughout the Mediterranean, but this is not true internationalism, where all people are eligible to compete, and are willingly accepted by the organizers of the festival. Foreigners did attend the Games, but the festival generally did not encourage their participation as competitors, even though on occasion a few who were not Greek by birth, heritage, or cultural assimilation were victorious. This is different from the modern Olympics, which stress the importance of nations taking part en masse. Since the ancient festival honoured Zeus, the criterion in the Games was excellence, *arete*. The emphasis there was on allowing only the best to compete, not on mass participation. Directly or indirectly, Olympia furthered nationalistic tendencies, and even by tradition commemorated victories in war over both foreigners and Greeks. Attempts to promote "understanding," "brotherhood," and "peace" were always within the context of the Greek world, as in the fifth century, when Olympia seems to have tried genuinely to mediate among the city states, but for less than a decade in the case of "brotherhood." It was in a cultural rather than in a political sense that the Games united the Greeks.[58] For most of its history, the Olympic Games did not advance the ideals of even a Greek *ethnos*, but the political agenda of the *polis* to which they belonged.

Notes

1 Olympic Charter 1984, Lausanne 1984 (Rule 1, p. 6); see Lämmer 1982–83, 72 n. 2. This paper is in part a response to an earlier presentation at the conference, which followed the traditional (or more utopian) view that the ancient Olympics promoted international understanding, peace, and unity. It has been much improved by comments from my colleague, Antony Littlewood. This article first appeared in Crowther 2004, 11–22, with update, p. 51.

2 The concept of nationalism in the ancient world is complex, but see Hornblower and Spawforth 1998, 488–89.

3 There were literally hundreds of these city states, small in population (many would have 5,000 people or fewer), with their own laws, calendars, and measurements. For the relatively few federal "states" within Greece, see Larsen 1968.

4 See Herodotus (8.144) on Greeks and Persians. Renfrew (1988, 23) believes that the Panhellenic Games played a fundamental role in the development of Greek ethnicity. This is true to a certain extent, but this was hardly the purpose of the Elean organizers of the Olympic Games, as we shall see. For more on ethnicity, see n. 11, below.

5 See Siewert (1992, 114), who argues against the view that 776 BC is a significant date because it coincides approximately with that of the introduction of writing to the Greek world. He points out that from the eighth and seventh centuries, many offerings have been discovered at Olympia, but no inscriptions.

6 On this date see Golden (1998, 63–65), who points out that Elis was too tiny a community to have victors in the early and mid-eighth century. One should also consult Mallwitz (1988), who dates the first Games to about 700 BC, and Peiser (1990), who dates them to the early sixth century. For the problems of reckoning by specific Olympiads, however, and of the victory list probably compiled by Hippias in the fifth century, see

now Shaw (2003), who believes that 776 BC "is…a fixed point that may be, and probably is, spurious" (p. 242). This work reached me too late to be incorporated into the article. See also now the article by Astrid Möller (2005), and the paper by Max Nelson in this volume.

7 Hence, for a few Olympiads, the Games probably had little significance beyond the immediate area of Olympia. The surviving victory list shows that the earliest victors were local and that there was no victor from the eastern Peloponnese until 732 BC (one from Cleonae); see Moretti 1957, no. 12. Morgan (1990, 47) rightly remarks that the first festival hardly suggests a Panhellenic institution; see also Lee 1988b.

8 For more on this visit to Egypt and its implications, see Decker 1974.

9 At least this is the way the passage is usually interpreted, although Philostratus does not mention the word "Greek." Like others, I consider the word πατρίς (native country, fatherland) here to be the equivalent of πόλις (city state). This regulation was not unique to Olympia, but Philostratus states that both an Olympic judge and a Pythian President of the Games ensure that boy athletes meet these regulations. It is unknown whether this is Philostratus' own wording, or whether he is following an earlier source; at all events the regulation seems to apply to his own day. See also the passages in Polybius (27.9.7–13) and [Julian] (*Ep. ad Themistium* 9 [263a]) discussed below.

10 The Zappas Games began in 1859; see Young 1984, 28–43, and the corrected version, Young 1996a, 13–23. Young (1996a, 191, n. 35) believes that the first truly international Olympic competition was held at the Liverpool Olympic Festival of 1867. Conceived by Charles Melly and John Hulley, who co-founded the Liverpool Athletic Club, the Liverpool Olympic Festivals were held from 1862 to 1867.

11 On ethnicity in the ancient world, see, for example, Morgan 1991, and bibliography. See also Nielsen (1999, 19, with references), who comments on such features as a collective name, common ancestry, shared language, shared history, shared culture, association with a specific territory, sense of solidarity, and political and economic associations. This is a complex problem, and further discussion is outside the scope of this paper. I argue here that although the Eleans had specific rules regarding eligibility at the Games, as we have seen, they also seem to have admitted whomever they pleased for their own considerations, sometimes without regard to ethnicity.

12 This was Varazdat(es), victorious in boxing in AD 369; see Moretti 1957, no. 944, for references. We still do not have a detailed study of Olympic victors from the less established parts of the Greek world.

13 Is it significant that Herodotus states that it was his fellow competitors, not the Elean officials, who protested against his eligibility? If so, Alexander may have been one of the first royal competitors to be invited by Elis. See below for other possible invited contestants. It may be that Elis did not challenge his qualifications, so that a royal competitor might add to the prestige of the Games. Another royal Macedonian, Archelaus, son of Perdiccas, won in the *quadriga* in 408 BC (Moretti 1957, no. 349).

14 Van Nijf 1999, 177. The first non-noble Macedonian known to have been victorious at Olympia is Kliton in the *stade* of 328 BC (Moretti 1957, no. 463).

15 See Moretti 1957, Indice II, for a list of these cities.

16 Polybius (2.12.8) says without elaboration that the Corinthians admitted the Romans to the Isthmian Games for the first time [in 228 BC]. We can deduce that the Romans were probably invited there for political reasons, since they had conquered the Illyrians, the enemies of the Greeks (Corinthians).

17 The site periodically suffered financial declines from the late Republic onwards, which were redressed to some extent by Augustus and Hadrian. The cult of the emperor appeared in the *Altis*; see Scanlon 2002, 47, for details.

18 Scanlon (2002, 40) offers a good discussion of the status of Olympia in Roman times, and comments on the increasing number of successful athletes from outside mainland

Greece. He remarks that the success of the cities in Asia Minor was due to economic and political reasons. He notes rightly that the Eleans still supplied the officials and controlled the content of the festival; yet it is recorded that on occasion the Eleans sent to Rome for a final decision. See Crowther 2000, 136–37. There is no detailed treatment, to my knowledge, of the relationship between the Eleans and Romans in running the Games.

19 See Moretti 1957, no. 738.

20 Dittenberger and Purgold 1966, nos. 369 and 371.

21 From the general population (non-nobles) of Rome, there are no definite Roman victors; see Moretti 1957, no. 684, for the only possible, but doubtful, example.

22 See below for political abuses of Olympia by the Eleans.

23 See Moretti 1957, no. 584, and Pausanias 6.15.3. Walbank (1979, 308) remarks that Aristonicus was probably a Greek and that the term "Egyptian" carried contemptuous overtones.

24 Foreigners at Olympia were not unusual in the role of spectators, as in 476 BC (below). These may have included invited dignitaries, who were travelling officially in Greece. According to Pausanias (5.12.5), Arimnestus, the king of Etruria, was the first foreigner to present an offering to Zeus at Olympia. For the indifferent reaction of a foreigner to the Olympics, see Lucian (*Anach.*), where Greek athletics and the Olympic Games are said to be alien to Scythian customs. Similarly, in 480 BC, according to Herodotus (8.26), the Persian Tigranes was said to be ignorant of the proceedings at Olympia (below).

25 See Sinn 2000, 1.

26 On the meaning of the term *ekecheiria*, see Lämmer 1982–83, and below, n. 53.

27 Roy 1998, 368.

28 Sourvinou-Inwood 1990, 296–97.

29 For more on the control of Olympia by Elis and its consequences, see Crowther 2003.

30 Moretti 1957, no. 201.

31 Moretti 1957, no. 206.

32 Sinn 2000, 15–22.

33 Sinn 2000, 19.

34 Recent excavations at Olympia (mostly in wells and in the older stadium) have unearthed more armour than at any other site in Greece, even though it was customary to make such dedications at other athletic festivals. See Jacquemin 2001. These consisted especially of helmets used in battle against other Greeks, according to Rausch (1998, 126–28, with references). Some of these helmets can be found today in the Archaeological Museum of Olympia.

35 See Jackson 1992, who states that no armour has been discovered in the enlarged stadium at Olympia, dating to the period after the Persian Wars.

36 According to Drees (1968, 130–31). Similarly, instead of offering weapons at Olympia, we may note that the Messenians dedicated the enormous statue of Nike to commemorate success in the Peloponnesian War. According to Thucydides (5.47.11), Athens, Argos, Mantinea, and Elis erected a bronze column to honour their military alliance against Sparta. Some of these memorials dedicated by the Greek states at Olympia are described by Pausanias (5.23–4).

37 Neither Plato nor Plutarch mentions Olympia by name, but it was no different from other festivals in this regard. Siewert (1996, 144–45) suggests that the end of dedicating arms coincided with the rise of Panhellenism (below), and believes that it was actually forbidden after 440 BC.

38 See Siewert 1992, 116.

39 It is understandable that dedications would be made to Zeus, as the god who bestows victory, and that this practice became customary at Olympia, the important centre of the cult of Zeus, where as many people as possible could view the offerings honouring the

god. This was for propaganda reasons and had nothing to do with the Games, except that they drew extremely large crowds (see below, n. 50).

40 Perlman 1976, 30; see also Flower 2000 for a useful bibliography on Panhellenism.

41 Raubitschek 1988, 36.

42 Raubitschek (1988, 35–36) traces this legend back from Phlegon of Tralles (*FGrH* 257 fr. 1) and Pausanias (5.4.5, 5.8.5) in the second century AD to Isocrates, and perhaps even to Hippias in the fifth century BC. See Pausanias (5.20.1) and Strabo (8.357–8). Raubitschek (1992, 185) also suggests that the truce was originally for the people of the Peloponnese.

43 According to Bollansée (1999, 563), these intellectuals presented the Olympic truce as the "gist of the Panhellenic movement," and propagated the view that the truce was closely associated with the foundation of the Games to suit their own ideals of Panhellenism.

44 McGregor 1941, 286, and Raubitschek 1992.

45 See Sinn 2000, 54–57.

46 On this aspect of the festival, see Weiler 1997.

47 If this story is true, it is another instance of nationalism at Olympia, although one of the few occasions we know of when the crowd was more interested in a politician and the success of the Greeks in war than in the athletes themselves.

48 See Aristotle (*Rh.* 1414b), Clement of Alexandria (1.51 [2.33.18 Str]). Flower (2000, 92–93) suggests that this speech was delivered in 408 BC, rather than later in the fourth century.

49 Kokolakis 1992, 158. A certain Peregrinus (Lucian *Peregrinus*) may have instigated the Greeks there to revolt against the Romans, perhaps in AD 157. The historian Herodotus is said to have sought the quickest route for fame as a writer for himself by reciting his *Histories* to the assembled Greeks (Lucian, *Herodotus*, 1). Even if this account is apocryphal, it may still represent the opinions of some people of the day about Olympia.

50 This increased interest in Greek unity at Olympia may have coincided with the building of the new stadium, which in the middle of the fourth century BC could accommodate over forty thousand people; see Romano 1993, 22. This was almost double the capacity of the previous stadium.

51 See Perlman 1976, 3 n. 7. Perlman (1969) points out that Isocrates recommended Athens and Sparta as joint leaders against Persia in the *Panegyricus,* but in the *Philippus* he began to look outside the traditional Greek *poleis* for a leader; see also Perlman 1976, 25–29. Sinn (2000, 56) believes that it is no coincidence that Alexander the Great had a proclamation read at Olympia concerning the plight of refugees in the civil wars.

52 Mann 2001, 25.

53 For the truce, its duration, and breaches by the Greeks, see Lämmer 1982–83, who dispelled the notion that the truce guaranteed a complete amnesty; see also Kyle 1998, 114, for a bibliography. The ancient sources on the truce and the dating of the Olympics are hard to reconcile. Bollansée (1999, 564) argues that the truce could not have been a founding ideal if the Games began as a celebration only for local inhabitants, but it could have been a founding ideal, if one follows Lämmer, who suggests that the term *ekecheiria* at Olympia originally referred not to a truce, but to the Sanctuary as a holy place. Bollansée also seems to propose the view that Iphitus founded the Games alone, and that Lycurgus came later and instituted the truce.

54 See Kyle 1996, 123 n. 1, for prizes like this as a mark of Greek ethnicity.

55 Little is known about the courts at Olympia. See Siewert 1992, 115; Crowther 2003.

56 Sinn 2000, 55, and Siewert 1981.

57 Sinn 2000, 56.

58 Mann 2001, 25.

Olympic Losers: Why Athletes Who Did Not Win at Olympia Are Remembered

Victor Matthews

In Moretti's index of Olympic victors we find listed more than seven hundred names.[1] To these men, of course, went the fame and glory associated with Olympic success. In the opening to *Olympian* 8, Pindar invokes Olympia as the mother of golden-crowned games and as the "mistress of truth" (1–2). For some, however, their moment of truth at Olympia meant not happiness at success, but shame at defeat. Little attention was and has been paid to those who lost at Olympia, the vast majority of whom now languish forgotten in anonymity. Some indeed may have preferred it this way; note how Pindar (*Pyth.* 8. 86–87) describes the defeated opponents of the boy wrestler Aristomenes slinking home via the back streets to avoid the taunts of their enemies. There are, however, some instances where the names of men who lost at Olympia have been recorded. This paper will examine what these circumstances were, and will discuss some of the factors which have caused the names of some Olympic losers to be passed down to posterity.

In the large body of agonistic literature (epinician odes and epigrams) honouring Olympic victors, it is very rare to find the name of a defeated opponent. Pindar, while commenting derisively on the unhappy homecomings of the opponents of two wrestlers (*Ol.* 8. 67–69 and *Pyth.* 8.

83–87), refrains from identifying any of them (coincidentally four in each case). Simonides, however, in one poem, displayed no such scruple about naming a defeated athlete:

ἐπέξαθ᾽ ὁ Κριὸς οὐκ ἀεικέως
ἐλθὼν ἐς εὔδενδρον ἀγλαὸν Διὸς
τέμενος. (F 507 *PMG* / Campbell)

[Crius not surprisingly got himself shorn (Campbell; "was fleeced," Bowra) when he came to the well-treed glorious precinct of Zeus.]²

This fragment is preserved by the scholiasts on the *Clouds* of Aristophanes, who himself shows that it was a song well known at Athens (1355 ff.). The scholiasts tell us that Crius (whose name means "ram") was an Aeginetan who appears to have been famous and distinguished (Sch. RVE), and that he was a wrestler (Sch. EΘMRs). At first glance, the Sanctuary of Zeus could be either Olympia or Nemea.³ Some scholars have assumed the latter,⁴ but when we see that Simonides' epithet εὔδενδρον is used by Pindar in a specific reference to Olympia, ὦ Πίσας εὔδενδρον ἐπ᾽ Ἀλφεῷ ἄλσος (*Ol.* 8.9), we may think it more likely that Simonides too was referring to Olympia.

Crius would thus appear to have been an Aeginetan wrestler who lost at Olympia, but does he owe his mention in the literary record solely to having a name suitable for an effective pun? As noted above, a scholiast states that Crius was well known and distinguished, and in fact he is almost certainly the same man who was an Aeginetan leader in the early fifth century,⁵ mentioned by Herodotus (6.50, 73) as the target of yet another play on his name. When the Aeginetans chose to medize ca. 491 BC, an Athenian delegation denounced them at Sparta, whereupon King Cleomenes crossed to Aegina to arrest their leaders. He was opposed especially by Crius, son of Polycritus, and when forced to leave, asked Crius his name. Upon being told that it was "Ram," he said, "Now tip your horns with bronze, Mr. Ram, for great trouble is coming your way"—in other words, Crius should get ready to be sacrificed. Not long afterwards, Cleomenes returned with his new colleague Leotychidas, arrested Crius and nine others, and sent them into Athenian custody (Hdt. 6.73). Thus Mr. Ram was well and truly "fleeced," and Simonides' poem should be viewed in the light of this ongoing Athenian–Aeginetan hostility.⁶ Simonides exploited Crius' name and earlier athletic defeat in a poem that obviously pleased his Athenian friends. Since Crius's son, Polycritus, commanded an Aeginetan ship at Salamis in 480 BC (Hdt. 8.92), it is clear that his father's athletic defeat must have been well before his political role in the late 490s. Crius was likely born closer to 540 than to 530 BC, so that his adult wrestling career probably lay within the period 520 to 500 BC. If he was a contestant in the Olympics of 520, 516, or 512 BC, he may have been well and truly "fleeced" by the great Milo of Croton (victor, 532–516 BC) or his fellow-townsman and successor Timasitheus (winner in 512 BC).

On a few rare occasions, we do find the sort of situation that we are more familiar with in the modern world, when both victor and vanquished are identified because of the memorable nature of their contest. In the ancient Olympics, this is almost always a combat sport. One such example is a double reference in Aristophanes' *Wasps* (1190–94; 1382–86) to how the pankratiast Ephoudion or Ephotion (Moretti, no. 253), though old and grey, fought a fine battle against his younger opponent Ascondas.[7] The scholiast to Aristophanes dates Ephoudion's victory to the 79th Olympiad (464 BC)—a date which appears to be confirmed by P. Oxy. 222, which rules out all dates from 480 to 448 BC except 464 and 460. The loser, Ascondas, is only named because of the exceptional circumstances of the victor's age and ability, which were still memorable over a generation later.

Another Olympic combat final where both victor and vanquished are remembered from an account written many years later is the boxing final of 212 BC. Polybius (27.9) describes aspects of this fight in order to illustrate the sudden enthusiasm of the Greeks for Perseus of Macedon in 171 BC. Polybius says that, when a humble and inferior fighter is up against a famous and invincible opponent, the sympathy of the crowd goes at once to the underdog. They cheer him on, especially when he manages to get in a telling blow. They may even try to ridicule the stronger opponent simply out of sympathy for the weaker man. On the other hand, if someone calls attention to their error, they will very quickly change their minds. He tells us that this is what the boxer Clitomachus (Moretti, nos. 584, 589) did. He was the famous fighter with the invincible reputation whose challenger, Aristonicus of Alexandria, had been trained and sent to Olympia by Ptolemy IV. The onlookers immediately took the side of Aristonicus, happy to see that someone, at least for a while, dared to oppose Clitomachus. The challenger landed a few good blows, and the enthusiasm and applause of the crowd grew. Clitomachus paused, and asked them what they were thinking of in cheering on Aristonicus. Was it that he himself was not fighting fairly, or did they not know that he was fighting for the glory of Greece, while Aristonicus was fighting for King Ptolemy? Did they want to see an Egyptian defeat the Greeks and carry off the Olympic crown or see a Theban and Boeotian proclaimed winner of the men's boxing? These words, says Polybius, changed the attitude of the crowd, and Aristonicus was beaten by it rather than by Clitomachus.

Despite winning this boxing title, Clitomachus himself was also an Olympic loser in 212 BC. Not every champion, of course, can win every time, and we have several examples of a former champion meeting his match in another great athlete, especially in the combat events, where a number of practitioners excelled in more than one discipline. Clitomachus was one of these. Pausanias (6.15.3–5), who, with reference to the boxing final, records only that Clitomachus fought "with vigorous spirit and unwearied body" after his previous exertions, provides interesting details about Clitomachus' defeat in his earlier contest, the *pankration,* in which he was the defending Olympic champion. Clitomachus apparently had sufficient confidence to enter both events in 212 BC because he had previously won an unprecedented treble in boxing, *pankration,* and wrestling at the Isthmian Games (most likely in the spring of that same year).[8] This triple success was probably also responsible for his great fame, mentioned by Polybius; however, it was his misfortune at Olympia in 212 BC to come up against another great champion, the local man Caprus of Elis (Moretti, nos. 587, 588), who had entered both *pankration* and wrestling. After Caprus had won the latter event, Clitomachus asked the *Hellanodikai* to hold the *pankration* before he sustained damage in the boxing (presumably he had suffered this experience during his treble at the Isthmian Games).[9] The authorities granted his request, but despite this concession, Clitomachus lost the *pankration* to Caprus. Pausanias also supplies the name of the man whom Caprus had vanquished in the wrestling, his fellow Elean, Paeanius, the defending champion from 216 BC (6.15.10; Moretti, no. 583).

A clash of two great champions rather similar to that of Clitomachus and Caprus occurred at Olympia in 480 BC when Euthymus, the boxing victor in 484 BC (Moretti, nos. 191, 214, 227), was pitted against the famous Theagenes of Thasos (Moretti, nos. 201, 215), who wished to win both the boxing and the *pankration* (Paus. 6.6.5). Euthymus was defeated, but then Theagenes himself lost the *pankration* because he was too exhausted after the boxing final to contest it. Pausanias (6.11.4) adds the detail that because Theagenes was unable to fight, Dromeus of Mantinea (Moretti, no. 202) became the first man to win the *pankration akoniti* (without dust, meaning "without having to fight"). In a curious judgment, the *Hellanodikai* bade Theagenes pay a talent to Zeus and another to Euthymus on the grounds that he had entered the boxing to spite Euthymus! At the next Games (476 BC), Theagenes paid his fine to the god, but compensated Euthymus by not entering the boxing, which Euthymus duly won (as he did again in 472 BC). Theagenes, meanwhile, won the *pankration* of 476 BC.

There are several examples in which a previous Olympic champion returned for what turned out to be one Games too many. These included the famous Milo of Croton, winner of six Olympic wrestling crowns (including one boy's title) between 540 and 516 BC (Moretti, nos. 115, 122, 126, 129, 133, 139). In 512 BC, however, he was defeated by his younger townsman Timasitheus (Moretti, no. 145) when he must have been at least forty years old (Paus. 6.14.5). Another champion who returned only to suffer defeat was the giant Poulydamas of Scotousa (Moretti, no. 348), "tallest of men since the heroes" (Paus. 6.5.1), who won the *pankration* in 408 BC but came back from the Persian court for the Games of 404 BC only to be defeated by Promachus of Pellene (Paus. 7.27.6; Moretti, no. 355).

There are also instances of the opposite situation, where a man who had been a loser returned to win an Olympic crown. Pausanias (6.9.3) notes that Taurosthenes of Aegina (Moretti, no. 308) was outwrestled by Cheimon of Argos (Moretti, no. 298), but came back at the next festival and overthrew all his opponents.[10] The reason that Pausanias mentions Taurosthenes, however, is surely the fantastic story that an apparition of the wrestler turned up the very same day in Aegina to announce his victory.

An interesting case of a loser who became a victor is that of Artemidorus of Tralles (Moretti, no. 799) who failed in the boy's *pankration* at Olympia because, Pausanias (6.14.2) says, he was too young (τὸ ἄγαν νέον). Although we know that boys as young as twelve could and did compete at Olympia,[11] it is surely unlikely that Artemidorus was actually younger than twelve. More probably he failed because of physical weakness, since Pausanias goes on to tell that, when the time came for the Ionian festival at Smyrna, he had improved so much in strength (ἐς τοσοῦτο ἄρα αὐτῷ τὰ τῆς ῥώμης ἐπηύξητο) that he prevailed in the *pankration* on the same day not only over his opponents from Olympia, but also over the *ageneioi* (beardless youths) and the adult men. He went on to win an Olympic victory as an adult in AD 69 (212th Olympiad) and to become a *periodonikes* (circuit winner), if he is the Ti. Claudius Artemidorus honoured in an inscription at Ephesus.[12] Clearly Pausanias only mentions Artemidorus' early defeat because of his dramatic transformation into a winner.

A variation on the theme of the Olympic loser who later became a winner is the case of Tisamenus of Elis, who went on to fame in a very different field. His story is told by Herodotus (9.33–5) and Pausanias (3.11.6–8; 6.14.13). A member of the Elean prophetic family, the Iamidae, Tisamenus consulted the Delphic oracle about having children, but received the response that he would win "the five greatest contests." He mistakenly interpreted this oracle as referring to athletics, trained for the pentathlon, and came within one fall (or within one contest, i.e., wrestling, out of the three victories needed to win) of winning at Olympia against Hieronymus of Andros (Moretti, no. 173). According to Herodotus, it was the Spartans who realized that the response given to Tisamenus referred not to athletics but to war, and they set about persuading him to become their leader alongside their kings. In Pausanias' version, it was Tisamenus himself who saw the true implication of the prophecy, and the Spartans, when they heard of it, persuaded him to migrate from Elis and become the Spartan state diviner. According to Herodotus, this happened only after hard bargaining, which included the granting of Spartan citizenship to both Tisamenus and his brother Hegias. The outcome was a series of Spartan victories in five battles in the period 479–457 BC, at Plataea, Tegea, Dipaea, Ithome, and Tanagra.

While one would expect that many of Pindar's Pythian, Isthmian, and Nemean victors failed to win at Olympia, it is nonetheless surprising to find the poet admitting as much, even with a qualification. In *Nemean* 6.61–3, for the boy's wrestling victor, Alcimidas of Aegina, Pindar states that "a random lot robbed you, my boy and Polytimidas [a relative] of two wreaths at the Olympic festival." Apparently Alcimidas and Polytimidas were unlucky in the draw for their wrestling bouts; that is, one or more of their opponents, most likely the one they met in the final, had benefited from a bye, while they had not.

Bacchylides (*Ode* 11. 24–36) presents a rather similar case when celebrating the Pythian victory of another boy wrestler, Alexidamus of Metapontium, declaring that "if someone had not turned aside the path of upright justice, he would have garlanded his hair with the grey olive." The poet goes on to say that Alexidamus had brought many a boy to the ground with his cunning skills, but "either a god was responsible or else the judgments of mortals, which often go astray, snatched the highest prize from his hands." In other words, Alexidamus "was robbed," presumably at the previous Olympics two years prior to his Pythian victory.

Another Pindaric example of an accomplished athlete who had not won at Olympia is the wrestler Theaeus of Argos, who had recently won twice in his native city (*Nem.* 10). Pindar mentions earlier victories at the Pythians and three each at the Isthmian and Nemean Games (25–28). The time span needed to compete in at least three Isthmian and Nemean Games (six years) would encompass two celebrations of the Olympics, and it is hard to imagine that Theaeus had not competed in at least one. Yet Pindar (*Nem.* 6.29–36) still expresses hope that Theaeus will win at Olympia, "the peak of the ultimate games," and he prays to Zeus for the victory for which the wrestler himself is too modest to ask, despite his two recent victories at the Panathenaea. Then Pindar takes another approach, pointing out to Theaeus that honour for athletic success often attends his maternal family, with the help of the Charites and the Tyndaridae. These maternal relatives had won equestrian victories at the Isthmus and Nemea, as well as elsewhere in the Peloponnese, and it is tempting to think that Pindar (37–48) is here suggesting to Theaeus that *he* should now switch to the equestrian events in his quest for an Olympic victory.

The supreme reputation of Olympia in athletics is also evident when Pausanias states (10.9.1–2) that he does not think it worth mentioning any dedications by athletes or musicians at Delphi, since he has already included in his description of Elis those who had left any kind of glory behind. He does, however, make one exception, a statue of Phayllus of Croton, who, he says, had no victory at Olympia, yet won twice in pentathlon and once in the *stade* at the Pythian Games. Pausanias' words imply what we would naturally suspect, that Phayllus *did* compete at Olympia, but did not win. Pausanias goes on to tell that Phayllus fought at Salamis in his own ship, equipped by himself and manned by Crotoniates domiciled in Greece. It is clear that Pausanias made an exception of Phayllus for his exemplary patriotism, not for his athletic prowess.[13] Herodotus (8.47) states that of the Western Greeks, only the Crotoniates helped the Greeks at Salamis, with the single ship of Phayllus, thrice a Pythian victor. His patriotism was also remembered by Alexander the Great nearly one hundred and fifty years later when he sent a share of the spoils of Gaugamela to Croton to honour the zeal and courage of Phayllus (Plut. *Alex.* 34.2). The athlete himself made a dedication on the Athenian Acropolis in which he combined reference to his Pythian victories with his success in the naval battle against the Asiatic enemy.[14]

Phayllus' exploits seem to have ensured his continuing popularity at Athens. Over half a century later, Aristophanes can cite him as a famously fast runner. At *Acharnians* 214, the chorus boasts of being able, in youth, to follow close behind Phayllus, even carrying a load, and at *Wasps* 1206, Philocleon tells how he beat "the runner Phayllus"—in a lawsuit, by two votes.[15] Despite his lack of an Olympic victory, Phayllus was also remembered, though only in late sources, as the greatest Greek jumper.[16]

An interesting case where an apparent loser may have been the real winner is that of Leon of Ambracia in the *stade* race of 396 BC (96th Olympiad). In mentioning the statue of the victor Eupolemus of Elis (Moretti, no. 367), Pausanias (6.3.7) tells us that two of the three *Hellanodikai* judging the event declared Eupolemus the winner, while the third voted for Leon. When the Ambracian lodged a protest, the Olympic Council levied a fine on the two judges who had voted for Eupolemus, yet the result was allowed to stand. This unwillingness to reverse an official decision is similar to practice in modern major league baseball, where an umpire's call, even if shown to be wrong by videotape replay, is not overturned.

An important category of Olympic losers consists of athletes who were disqualified for infringements of the Olympic rules. It is indeed something of a paradox to realize that the first historical Olympic athletes mentioned by Pausanias in his description of Elis come not in his list of victory statues in Book 6, but in his description of votive offerings in Book 5. These athletes are named in Pausanias' discussion of the bronze statues of Zeus, known as *Zans*, which were dedicated from the fines paid by contestants who had dishonoured the Games (ἀθληταῖς … ὑβρίσασιν ἐς τὸν ἀγῶνα, 5. 21.2).

The six earliest images were set up in the 98th Olympiad (388 BC), said to have been the first occasion of criminal conduct at the Games (Paus. 5.21.3), when Eupolus of Thessaly bribed those who had entered the men's boxing: Agetor of Arcadia, Prytanis of Cyzicus, and Phormio of Halicarnassus, the defending champion from 392 BC (Moretti, no. 387). All four boxers were fined, and four of the six statues were furnished with elegiac inscriptions intended to deter future contestants from cheating. The first inscription read that one won at Olympia through speed of foot or strength of body, not with money; the second, that this statue was erected to honour the divinity through the piety of the Eleans and to be a source of fear to lawbreaking athletes. The inscription on the fifth statue praised the Eleans for fining the boxers, and that on the sixth stated that the statues were a lesson to all the Greeks not to give bribes for an Olympic victory.

The next disqualified athlete to be identified by Pausanias (5.21.5–7) is Callipus of Athens, who bribed his opponents in the pentathlon in the 112th Olympiad (332 BC). Unfortunately, Pausanias does not name those who accepted the bribes, though they too were fined. Pausanias says that the Athenians sent their famous orator, Hyperides, to persuade the Eleans to cancel the fine. When their request was denied, the Athenians refused to pay the fine and to attend the Olympic Games. Finally, the Delphic oracle declared that no responses would be given to the Athenians until they paid the fine. When they did so, six more *Zans* were set up, all with inscriptions. The sending of Hyperides may indicate that it was ultimately incumbent upon the state of which the offender was a citizen to pay the fine, as suggested by Donald Kyle,[17] but it also shows that, just as today, a state might support an offending athlete against an athletic governing body, viewing an Olympic victory as a matter of national prestige.[18] Also striking is the effective co-operation between the religious athletic authorities at Olympia and Delphi to ensure that the penalty was in fact paid.

Pausanias' next tale of bribery at Olympia (5.21.8–9) identifies two wrestlers as offenders, for one of whom his state paid the fine. In the 168th Olympiad (68 BC), a wrestler called Eudelus accepted a bribe from a Rhodian, Philostratus. From their fines, two *Zans* were erected, and the inscription on one recorded that the Rhodians paid up for the wrongdoing of their athlete.

Yet another example of athletes identified for bribery at Olympia by Pausanias (5.21.15) comes from the 226th festival in AD 125. The authorities detected that two boxers, both from the Arsinoite nome of Egypt, had colluded for a sum of money. Pausanias names the one who gave the bribe as Sarapammon, and the other as Didas.

Pausanias (5.21.16) expresses amazement that athletes should show so little respect for the god at Olympia as to offer or accept a bribe in the contests, and even more so that an Elean should have the effrontery to do so. Yet, he tells, at the 192nd Olympiad (12 BC), the Elean Damonicus, father of the boy wrestler Polyctor, bribed the father of his son's opponent, Sosander of Smyrna (the name of both father and son). Pausanias states that the *Hellanodikai* imposed fines not on the boys, but on their fathers, since they were the ones who had done wrong. Of the two resultant *Zans*, one was set up in the gymnasium at Elis,[19] presumably as a pointed warning to Elean citizens, the other in the *Altis* at Olympia.

I have included these athletes who were involved in bribery as Olympic losers, because I cannot believe that they were allowed to retain their crowns, any more than Ben Johnson could keep his gold medal from the 100 metres at the 1988 Seoul Olympics. Yet some scholars allege that bribery proved after the event did not deprive a winner of his title and wreath.[20] Indeed, Moretti lists Eupolus (no. 384), Callipus (no. 460), and Polyctor (no. 733) as Olympic victors. In the case of Sarapammon, through a misreading of Pausanias, he assigns the victory instead to Didas (no. 841). Similarly, Rutgers, in his edition of Sextus Julius Africanus, has included these athletes as victors solely on the evidence of Pausanias.[21]

Pausanias, however, never calls any of them an Olympic victor, and in only two of the cases do the offenders seem even to have been contending in a final. Sarapammon and Didas were fighting ὑπὲρ ἦ αὐτῆς... τῆς νίκης (5.21.15), which must surely refer to the final bout, while the boy competitors, Polyctor and Sosander, were wrestling ἐπὶ τῷ στεφάνῳ (5.21.16), which again would seem to mean the final. In the other instances, it is not clear how far the competitions had proceeded. Eupolus bribed those who had entered the boxing competition (τοὺς ἐλθόντας τῶν πυκτῶν, 5.21.3), and all were fined. Similarly, Callipus, having entered the pentathlon, bought off those who were going to compete against him (τοὺς ἀνταγωνιουμένους).[22] Nor is it obvious whether the men who accepted the bribes intended to "throw" their event or withdraw, allowing Eupolus and Callipus an *akoniti* victory. Since all the athletes in these two contests seem to have been involved in the corruption, it is easy to suppose that no Olympic champion was declared. In the case of Philostratus and Eudelus, they were the only wrestlers to engage in bribery (presumably at an early stage in the competition), and the event was won by Strato of Alexandria (Moretti, nos. 700, 701).[23]

In a striking passage, Pausanias (5.24.9–10) draws his readers' attention to the statue of Zeus Horkios in the Council Chamber at Olympia, before which the athletes, their fathers, brothers, and even their trainers had to swear an oath, over a dismembered boar, to do no wrong to the Olympic Games (μηδὲν ἐς τὸν Ὀλυμπίων ᾿αγῶνα ἔσεσθαι παρ᾿ αὐτῶν κακούργημα). Moreover, the adult athletes had to pledge that they had been in full training for ten consecutive months, and the officials who examined the boys and colts (that is, for admittance to their age-group events) had to swear to decide justly and without bribes and to keep secret all information as to whether or not an entrant was accepted. Surely no one who failed to keep these solemn oaths would be permitted to retain an Olympic wreath.

One athlete who clearly did lose his wreath for breaking the rules is Cleomedes of Astypalaea (Paus. 6.9.6). In the boxing event of 492 BC,[24] he killed his opponent, Iccus of Epidaurus, and was convicted by the *Hellanodikai* of foul play and deprived of his victory (καταγνωσθεὶς δὲ ὑπὸ τῶν Ἑλλανοδικῶν ἄδικα εἰργάσθαι καὶ ἀφῃρημένος τὴν νίκην). Going mad with grief at the decision, he returned to his native island, where he pulled down a school on top of sixty children. When the angry citizens began to stone him, he took refuge in the temple of Athena, where he climbed into a chest and closed the lid. By the time the box was finally broken open, Cleomedes had disappeared. An Astypalaean embassy, sent to Delphi to ask what had happened to Cleomedes, received the response, "most recent of heroes is Cleomedes, honor him with sacrifices since he is no longer mortal."[25] Clearly, Cleomedes was remembered because of his mysterious disappearance and subsequent heroization as much as for the death of his opponent and his disqualification; however, since Cleomedes was deprived of his victory, he should not appear as he does (no. 174) in Moretti's list of Olympic victors.

In addition to those athletes disgraced for bribery at Olympia, Pausanias names two others fined for discreditable conduct whom we can list as Olympic losers. At the 218th Olympiad (AD 93), the boxer Apollonius from Alexandria failed to arrive at the required time, and offered the excuse that he had been delayed by unfavourable winds (Paus. 5.21.12–14). A rival, Heraclides, also of Alexandria, proved this pretext to be a lie, stating that Apollonius had arrived late because he had been collecting money prizes at games in Ionia. The Eleans then excluded Apollonius, and any other boxer who had not come in time, from the contest, which led to Heraclides being crowned *akoniti*. Apollonius then wrapped his hands in the *himantes* (ox-hide straps) as if for a fight and attacked Heraclides, who already had the wreath on his head. No doubt it was because of Apollonius' lie and violent conduct that the authorities imposed the fine. Some years earlier, in the 201st Olympiad (AD 25), another Alexandrian, the pankratiast Sarapion, was so overawed by his opponents that he ran away the day before the competition. Pausanias (5.21.18) reports that he was the only man ever fined at Olympia for cowardice.

To sum up, we do in fact know the identities of a goodly number of Olympic losers, almost exclusively contestants in fighting events. There is a wide range of reasons (sometimes overlapping) for their mention by ancient writers. Only rarely do we have a direct statement that an athlete was a loser without any reference to the victor. More often a loser is named (1) as part of the story of a more famous victor; (2) as failing in defence of a previous Olympic title; (3) as failing at one Olympiad but achieving victory at a later one; (4) as a victor in the other great Games who has not won at Olympia; (5) rarely, as a victim of the luck of the draw or a wrong decision by the judges; or (6) as being disqualified for bribery or other discreditable conduct.

It is noteworthy that many of these losers who are identified by name are also either former or future Olympic victors, while those who met defeat at the hands of a particularly notable champion also merit respect, as do those who were the victims of cheating. Those who were guilty of cheating, of course, can be seen as deserving the infamy of having their names passed down to posterity.

The general reluctance of ancient sources to name opponents may be reflected in the imaginary chariot race at the Pythian Games described by the messenger in Sophocles' *Electra* 698–763. Orestes had won all the previous contests prior to the chariot race which resulted in his supposed death. Naturally, in the circumstances, all attention is upon him, and he is fully proclaimed as an Argive, named Orestes, son of Agamemnon (693–4). In the chariot race, although nine opponents are mentioned,[26] they are referred to only in terms of ethnicity (an Achaean, a Spartan, two Libyans, an Aetolian, a Magnesian, an Aenian, an Athenian, and a Boeotian), and not by name. This is true even of the Athenian, who was the apparent winner following Orestes' accident.

Notes

1 Moretti 1957.
2 Campbell 1991, 371; Bowra 1961, 313.
3 See Campbell 1991, 371; Bowra 1961, 313; Molyneux 1992, 61, n. 90.
4 For example, Henderson 1998, 193, in his note on *Clouds* 1356; Page 1951, 140–41.
5 See Bowra 1961, 314; Molyneux 1992, 51; Huxley 1978, 240.
6 Note Huxley 1978, 240.
7 This story is suggested by Bdelycleon to his father in the play as an example of sophisticated conversation.
8 In addition to Pausanias (6.15.3), this treble is recorded in an epigram, *AP* 9. 588 = no. 67' in Ebert (1972, 198–200). Ebert dates Clitomachus' exploit at Isthmia to 218 BC, suggesting that the epigram would have mentioned his Pythian victories (all in *pankration*, probably 218, 214, and 210 BC) if they were before the Isthmians. This assumption is unwarranted, since the epigram is celebrating Clitomachus' unique triple victory and makes no reference to *any* previous victories elsewhere. Moretti (1957, on no. 584) dates the triple to 216 BC, but Clitomachus' known victories in the great Games up to and including 214 BC were all in *pankration* (Pythian in 218 and 214 BC, Olympian in 216 BC). While it is possible that Clitomachus tried but failed to win the boxing at Delphi in 218 and/or 214 BC, Pausanias (6.15.4) implies that the festival of 212 BC was the first occasion on which he had attempted such a double at Olympia. I would thus suggest that Clitomachus' Isthmian triple took place in 212 BC and that his success there led him to attempt the Olympic double later that year.
9 The language of the Isthmian epigram (ll. 3–6) suggests that the order of the three events there was boxing, *pankration*, wrestling.
10 If Cheimon is to be identified with the Cimon of Argos recorded under 448 BC in *P. Oxy.* 222, Taurosthenes' victory would be in 444 BC; see Moretti (1957, 100–103).
11 Damiscus of Messene, winner of the boys' *stade* in 368 BC (Paus. 6.2.10–11; Moretti 1957, no. 417). See Crowther 1988a, 305–306.
12 See Moretti 1957, 158.
13 Note Habicht 1985, 115–16.
14 The inscription is *IG* I². 655 = *SIG*³ 30; see Moretti 1953, nos. 11, 25–29; Raubitschek 1949, no. 76; Kyle 1993, 153, n. 174.

15 See Kyle 1993, 132.

16 For example, Zenobius 6.23; Schol. Ar. *Ach.* 214; *Suda.*

17 Kyle 1993, 120 n. 39.

18 Note Kyle 1993, 160.

19 Pausanias (6.23.4) also mentions this statue when describing the city of Elis, but there he refers to the fines imposed on Sosander of Smyrna and Polyctor of Elis, that is, on the boys, not the fathers.

20 For example, Finley and Pleket 1976, 66.

21 Africanus (ed. Rutgers) 1980, 59, 66, 84, 93.

22 The future tense of this participle is not apparent in the translations of either Levi (Pausanias 1971, 260) or Jones (1977, 505).

23 Pausanias himself is needlessly puzzled by the fact that the Elean records listed Strato as the winner; see Africanus (ed. Rutgers) 1980, 82 n. 1.

24 This date reflects the best understanding of what Pausanias (6.9.4) says in reference to the chariot victory of Gelon in the 73rd Olympiad (488 BC) and the incident with Cleomedes at the Olympiad prior to this one (6.9.6); note Moretti 1957, 82.

25 For the translation "most recent" rather than "last" for ὕστατος, see Fontenrose 1968, 74; cf. Poliakoff 1987, 123–24, with n. 13.

26 Lloyd-Jones (1994, 228) fails to realize that the fifth contestant, with Thessalian mares (703–4), is Orestes himself. For the correct interpretation, see Sophocles (ed. Kells) 1973, 141.

Judges and Judging at the Ancient Olympic Games

David Gilman Romano

Introduction

A reporter from the Canada News Wire called me in February 2002, during the Salt Lake City Olympic Games, to talk about the ancient Olympic Games. He was specifically interested to know what happened in antiquity to judges who were caught cheating. "Did they string them up?" he asked. The reporter was calling in reference to the figure-skating controversy involving Canadian pairs skaters Jamie Salé and David Pelletier, who at the time had been denied a gold medal after a questionable judges' decision. A Russian pair, Elena Berezhnaya and Anton Sikharulidze, were awarded the gold, but it was reported that the French judge, Marie-Reine Le Gougne, had been pressured to vote for the Russian pair instead of the Canadian. Salé and Pelletier were eventually also awarded gold medals in an emotional ceremony, making four gold medal winners in all.[1]

I replied to the Canadian reporter that an answer to his question was not easy. While there were difficulties and in fact serious controversies in antiquity involving judges and judging, as far as I knew there were no recorded instances where the judges were "strung up." The reporter was clearly disappointed. When I told him about some judging difficulties in antiquity, he listened patiently for a while, but was clearly interested in a different kind of story.

When invited at about this same time to participate in the conference *Onward to the Olympics*, it seemed only appropriate to address the topic that the Canadian reporter didn't really want to hear. What do we know about judges and judging from the ancient Olympic Games? What were their duties? What was their training? Where did they work? What kinds of problems did they have? Fortunately, we have information from a number of ancient authors on the subject, together with some epigraphical and historical documents. A little archaeological evidence also relates to the *Hellanodikai* at Olympia.[2]

Historical Accounts of the *Hellanodikai*

Herodotus (2.160) tells the story about the Egyptian King Psammis (594–587 BC), who received a delegation from Elis. The Eleans boasted about the excellent way in which they organized the Olympic Games, and asked if the Egyptians could suggest any way to do it more fairly. King Psammis collected his most learned subjects, and, after listening to the Eleans' explanation of their organization of the Olympic contests, asked if the Eleans allowed representatives of all Greek states to compete in the Games, including their own from Elis. When told that all Greeks were welcomed, the Egyptian reply was that such a principle was not fair at all, since surely Elean athletes would be favoured over visiting ones. The Egyptians recommended that if they really wanted fair play at the Olympics, they should not allow anyone from Elis to compete.[3]

Centuries later, Pausanias (5.9.4–6), one of the best sources on the subject, gives much good information about judges at Olympia, including a brief history of *agonothetes*, *athlothetes*, and *Hellanodikai*, explaining how the number of judges evolved.

> The rules for the *agonothetes* of the games are not the same now as they were at the first institution of the festival. Iphitus held the games as likewise did the descendants of Oxylus after Iphitus. But at the 50th festival (580 BC) two men appointed by lot from all the Eleans were entrusted with the management of the Olympic Games, and for a long time after this the number of *agonothetes* continued to be two. But at the 95th festival (400 BC) nine *Hellanodikai* were appointed. To three of them were entrusted the chariot races, another three supervised the pentathlon, the rest superintended the remaining contests. At the second festival after this (392 BC) the tenth *athlothete* was added. At the 103rd festival (368 BC), the Eleans having twelve tribes, one *Hellanodikas* was chosen from each. But they were

hard pressed in a war with the Arcadians and lost a portion of their territory, along with all the demes included in the surrendered district, and so the number of tribes was reduced to eight in the 104th Olympiad (364 BC) At this time the number of tribes equaled the number of *Hellanodikai*. At the 108th festival (348 BC) they returned again to ten which has continued unchanged down to this day.[4]

Table 1. Evolution of the Number of Judges at Olympia According to Pausanias

?	Iphitos
?	Descendants of Oxylos
50th Olympiad [580 BC]	Two Elean men are appointed by lot as *agonothetes*
95th Olympiad [400 BC]	9 *Hellanodikai*
97th Olympiad [392 BC]	10 *Hellanodikai*
103rd Olympiad [368 BC]	12 *Hellanodikai*
104th Olympiad [364 BC]	8 *Hellanodikai*
108th Olympiad [348 BC]	10 *Hellanodikai*

Pausanias uses the words *agonothetes*, *athlothetes*, and *Hellanodikai*. An *agonothete* was literally one who "made the contest," an *athlothete* was one who "offered the prize," and the *Hellanodikai* were literally the "Greek judges." All of these words can be translated as "judge" and sometimes "umpire," although we should be careful about which term is actually used and when. There was an earlier word for "judge," διαιτητής (or διαιτατής) *diaitetes*, meaning "arbitrator" or "umpire," which occurs on two sixth-century inscriptions from Olympia.[5]

It appears that the first use of the word *Hellanodikas* occurs in Pindar (*Ol.* 3.12), where an Aetolian *Hellanodikas* is mentioned in connection with Theron's victory at Olympia in the *tethrippon* (476 BC).[6] There is also an early bronze inscription from Olympia which mentions a *Hellanodikas* in the context of an Elean *rhetra* or treaty (fig. 1).[7] It is dated by Jeffery to the second quarter of the fifth century, and would therefore seem slightly later than the reference in Pindar.[8]

There are several interesting aspects to the passage by Pausanias (5.9.4–6), who first mentions the term *Hellanodikai* in connection with the 95th Olympiad in 400 BC. Since Pindar refers to a *Hellanodikas* in 476 BC, and the bronze inscription mentions a *Hellanodikas* ca. 475–450 BC, it would seem that *Hellanodikai* were clearly in existence before 400 BC.[9]

Figure 1. Bronze inscription from Olympia. The shaded word is *Hellanodikas*. From Wilhelm Dittenberger and Karl Purgold, *Die Inschriften von Olympia* (Berlin, 1896), no. 2. Courtesy of DAI, Athens.

Pausanias is probably saying that the number changed in 400, not the name, which may well have occurred seventy-five or more years earlier. Why were the number of officials increased from two *agonothetes* to nine *Hellanodikai* (or *athlothetes*)? This is likely to be symptomatic of a change in organization, or perhaps the size or makeup of the festival. More officials were likely needed to carry out the duties required by more athletes and more events. It is known, for instance, that the *hoplitodromos* was added to the Olympic program in 520 BC and three equestrian events were added during the fifth century: the *apene*, a mule cart race, in 500 BC; the *kalpe*, a race for mares, in 496 BC (both of which were discontinued in 444 BC); and the *synoris*, the two-horse chariot race, in 408 BC. Furthermore, the Sanctuary went through an important building phase in the fifth century, with the construction of the Temple of Zeus, 472–457 BC, and the construction of Stadium III, 465–455 BC (fig. 2).[10] Pausanias states that three judges were assigned to the chariot races, three to the pentathlon, and three to the other contests. This need to increase the number of judges may also be reflected in the lengthening of the festival from two days to five days, which occurred about the same time.[11]

Following the early inheritance of the position of *agonothete* by Iphitus and Oxylus, according to Pausanias, the first *agonothetes* at Olympia, appointed in 580 BC, were chosen by lot, and it may have been that the judges were appointed by lot from the body of Elean citizens throughout the history of the festival.[12] If Herodotus' story of Psammis is true and chronologically accurate, it would have been only a few years after the visit of the Elean delegation that the Eleans selected the first *agonothetes* by lottery. This might be explained as a partial concession to the criticism of Psammis that the Eleans could not be objective if they allowed fellow citizens to participate in the Olympic Games. At least with a lottery, any Eleans acting as judges for the Olympic Games would be selected as a result of chance.[13]

Pausanias (6.22.2–3) also tells us that in two instances the neighbouring Pisatans controlled the Games instead of the Eleans. In the first instance, the tyrant Pheidon of Argos held the Games (Pausanias says it was the eighth Olympiad in 748 BC) with the Pisatans.[14] In this case, Pheidon could have been the *agonothete*. In the 34th festival, in 644 BC, the king of Pisa, Pantaleon, together with an army held the Olympic Games and in this case Pantaleon could also have been termed an *agonothete*. There was a third known instance, mentioned by Pausanias in the same passage, when the Arcadians held the Games in 364 BC. So in these cases, "holding the Games" and controlling the Sanctuary were likely to have been understood as the same. In all these cases, according to Pausanias (6.22.2–3), the festivals were termed "non-Olympiads" by the Eleans and were not included in their written Olympic lists.[15]

The Duties of the *Hellanodikai* at Elis and at the Olympic Games

From Pausanias we know some details about the gymnasia of Elis, as well as the responsibilities of the judges before and during the Olympic festival:

> One of the noteworthy things in Elis is an old gymnasium. In this gymnasium the athletes go through the training through which they must pass before going to Olympia. High plane trees grow between the tracks inside a wall. The whole of this enclosure is called xystus (ξυστός).... The track for the competing runners called by the natives the Sacred Track (ἱερός δρόμος) is separate from that on which the runners and pentathletes practice. In the gymnasium is the place called plethrium (πλέθριον). In it the *Hellanodikai* match the wrestling competitors according to age and skill.... There is another enclosed gymnasium, but smaller, adjoining the larger one and called Square because of its shape. Here the athletes practice wrestling, and here when they have no more wrestling to do, they are matched in contests with the softer gloves.... There is also a third enclosed gymnasium called Maltho from the softness of its floor and reserved for the ephebes for the whole time of the festival.... In this gymnasium is also the Elean *Bouleuterion,* where take place exhibitions of extemporary speeches and recitations of written works of all kinds. (6.23.1–7)

> One of the two ways from the gymnasium leads to the agora and to what is called the *Hellanodikaion*. It is above the grave of Achilles and by it the *Hellanodikai* are able to go to the gymnasium. They enter before sunrise to match the runners, and at midday for the pentathlon and for such contests that are called heavy. (6.24.1)

In the *Hellanodikaion*, the *Hellanodikai*-elect live for 10 consecutive months, those who are instructed by the guardians of the law (νομοφύλακες) as to their duties at the festival. Near to the stoa where the *Hellanodikai* pass the day is another stoa, a street being between the two. The Eleans call it the Corcyrean.... The stoa is in the Doric order and double, having its columns both on the side towards the agora and away from it. Down the center of it the roof is supported not by columns but by a wall... (6.24.3–5)

Speaking about the statue of Zeus in the *Bouleuterion* at Olympia, Pausanias says:

Zeus Horkios holds in each hand a thunderbolt. Besides this image it is the custom for athletes, their fathers, their brothers as well as their trainers (*gymnastai*) to swear an oath upon slices of boar's flesh that in nothing will they transgress against the Olympic games. The athletes take this further oath, that for ten successive months they have strictly followed the regulations for training. An oath is also taken by those who judge the boys, and the foals entering for races, that they will decide fairly and without taking bribes, and that they will keep secret what they learn about a candidate, whether accepted or not. (5.24.9)

According to Pausanias, the *Hellanodikai* were instructed by the Guardians of the Law (νομοφύλακες) as to their duties at the festival. These Guardians may have been members of the Elean Council, or former *Hellanodikai*.[16] The ten-month period for the judges to be in residence in the *Hellanodikaion* was an extended length of time. What were the duties of the *Hellanodikai* during this period, and specifically what did they do before the arrival of the athletes one month before the Olympic festival? Since the *Hellanodikaion* was near the agora in the center of Elis and adjacent to the various athletic gymnasia, *dromoi*, and the hippodrome, the *Hellanodikai* would certainly have been able to watch the Elean athletes who were likely practising in some of these facilities during the ten months of their residence.[17]

The *Hellanodikai* may also have been involved in the organization and administration of the truce, the *ekecheiria*, as well as the dispatching of the envoys, the *spondophoroi* who announced the truce, and the *theoroi*, who were sent out all over the Greek world to announce the approaching Olympic Games.[18] Records were kept of where these heralds went, the schedule of their visits to distant cities, and the hosts for these envoys.[19] The same heralds who left Elis months before the festival at Olympia might also have brought back to Elis and to the *Hellanodikai* news of the athletes from these Greek cities, near and far.[20] The *Hellanodikai* might have received letters of intent of athletes to come to Elis the next year, or possibly letters might have been carried back by the *theoroi*. Perhaps the athletes needed to pledge in advance that they planned to train for ten months before the festival, since it would be very unlikely that athletes show up without warning in Elis a month before the Olympic Games were to begin and then pledge that they had been training for ten months. The athletes must have known of this regulation before arriving at Olympia, and might have made a prior commitment to satisfy it. The *Hellanodikai* might also have handled the paperwork that necessarily accompanied the planning for the athletic events, the physical arrangements for the events, the equipment, as well as the entries of the individual athletes.[21]

The principal reason for the period of thirty days' training in Elis before the Olympic Games would have been to give the *Hellanodikai* an opportunity to watch the athletes practise and compete in order to see which of them were worthy of advancing to the contests at Olympia.[22] There was no way to screen athletes in advance of their arrival at Elis, since there were no stopwatches in antiquity and the foot measure varied from city to city. There were therefore no means to compare the fitness and achievements of the athletes before their arrival, since athletes could not have submitted qualifying times or distances from local contests. The athletes would come to Elis based only on their reputations, which undoubtedly would include lists of victories over local and regional opponents, and on the recommendations of their coaches and patrons. Certainly some athletes would be known far and wide. The *Hellanodikai* would need to compare the athletes according to event and age, and weed out those who were not competitive, since even the most famous athletes would not necessarily be fit to compete in the Olympic Games.

They would also determine whether or not the athlete was qualified with respect to his birth and family.[23] We know from Herodotus (5.22), for instance, that Alexander I of Macedon had to prove his Greek lineage to the *Hellanodikai* before being allowed to race at Olympia, probably in 500 BC. He was judged to be a Greek, an Argive, and was allowed to run in the *stadion* race. According to Herodotus, Alexander finished in a dead heat for first in the race.[24]

Archaeological Evidence for the *Hellanodikai*

The ancient city of Elis has been investigated by Austrian and Greek archaeologists since 1910.[25] Their research has focused on the public centre of the city, including the area of the agora and the theatre. The remains of a large Doric stoa, ca. 98 m in length, with a double colonnade separated by a wall, correspond well with the description in Pausanias (6.24.4, above).[26] Other buildings mentioned by Pausanias, including the *Hellanodikaion* and the gymnasia, have not yet been identified but should be close by (fig. 2).

German archaeologists have been excavating at Olympia since 1875.[27] As a result, much is now known about the layout of the Sanctuary.[28] Some of their discoveries relate to the *Hellanodikai*—for example, the *Bouleuterion*, or Council House, which was built in several phases (fig. 3). The southern and northern apsidal wings were constructed in the sixth century BC. Joining the two apsidal wings was a central square hall built in the fifth century where the statue of Zeus Horkios, the Oath God, was located, in front of which, or perhaps around which, the athletes, trainers, and relatives took the Olympic oath of fair play.[29] A colonnade was added on the east side of the building, also in the fifth century. It is worth noting that the central hall may have been an open-air room, ca. 14 m x 14 m,

Figure 2. Reconstruction drawing of the agora area of Elis. From N.D. Papahatzis, Παυσανίου Ἑλλάδος Περιήγησις (Athens, 1979), vol. 3, fig. 360.

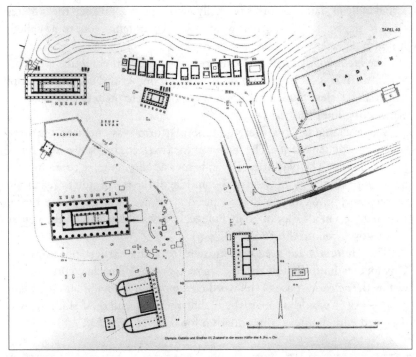

Figure 3. Sanctuary of Zeus at Olympia, ca. 450 BC. The shaded area is the central hall of the *Bouleuterion*. From Alfred Mallwitz (ed.), *X. Bericht über die Ausgrabungen in Olympia* (Berlin, 1981), tafel 40. Courtesy of DAI, Athens.

which would have included room for the statue. The space was large enough for about 344 men to stand at close quarters.[30] The *Bouleuterion* was located to the west of the stadium and southeast of the Temple of Zeus.

Pausanias (6.20.8–9) tells us that the *Hellanodikai*, as well as the athletes, entered the stadium at Olympia through the κρυπτὴν ἔσοδον or "hidden entrance." This entrance is sometimes identified as the vaulted tunnel at the northwest corner of the stadium.[31] By the second century BC, the athletes probably warmed up before their competitions in the gymnasium and the palestra complex on the west side of the Sanctuary,[32] but before the construction of these training facilities, the athletes may have used more convenient areas closer to the stadium, perhaps an area near the *Bouleuterion* where the judges carried out some of their functions (fig. 3).[33] It has been suggested that the athletes assembled for their individual events along the corridor on the east side of the Echo Stoa after its construction in the middle of the fourth century (fig. 4).[34] Today, such an area is called a "clerking" area, where the athletes check in before their race and are assigned heats, lanes, etc. It is typically a holding area to keep the athletes close to the track and in order, waiting for the athletic event to be called. It is also a place where rules can be reviewed.[35]

The *Hellanodikai* had a special area reserved for them in the Olympia Stadium III. It is located south of the track about a third of the way from the west end, close to the 200-foot marker, (i.e., 54 to 66 m east of the western starting line) (figs. 4–5).

This rectangular, two-tiered, stone platform was enclosed on three sides by a wooden barrier. The higher of the two steps had space for a number of chairs.[36] The platform originally measured 5.25 m. x 10.24 m, and had an opening 0.95 m. wide in the middle of the north side to reach the racecourse (fig. 6). In the Roman period, the area was expanded twice, totalling 9.60 m x 14.45 m, to include eight rows of benches on the higher south slope, behind the podium (fig. 7).[37]

The *Hellanodikai* area was known from the earliest phase of the Olympia Stadium III, now dated ca. 470–455 BC.[38] This date corresponds well with the earliest use of the word *Hellanodikas* from Pindar *Olympian* 3, 476 BC. It would appear, then, that the new enlarged stadium was designed with ample accommodation for the *Hellanodikai*.[39]

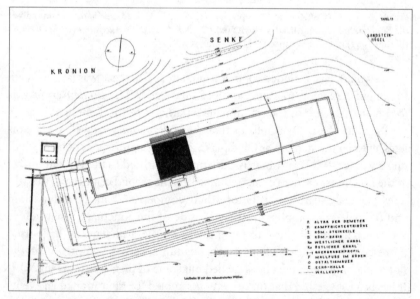

Figure 4. Stadium III at Olympia. The shaded area is the proposed *plethrion*, 100 feet square. From Emil Kunze (ed.), *VIII. Bericht über die Ausgrabungen in Olympia* (Berlin, 1967), tafel 11. Courtesy of DAI, Athens.

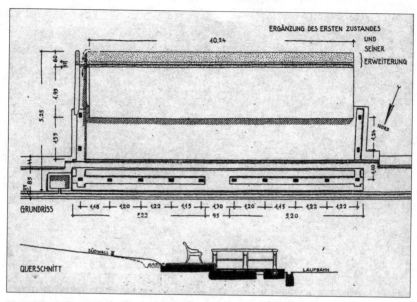

Figure 5. *Hellanodikai* area in Stadium III, phase 1. From Emil Kunze and Hans Schleif, *III. Bericht über die Ausgrabungen in Olympia* (Berlin, 1941), tafel 3. Courtesy of DAI, Athens.

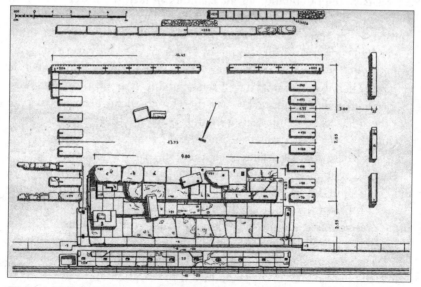

Figure 6. *Hellanodikai* area in Stadium III, phase 2. From Emil Kunze and Hans Schleif, *III. Bericht über die Ausgrabungen in Olympia* (Berlin, 1941), tafel 4.

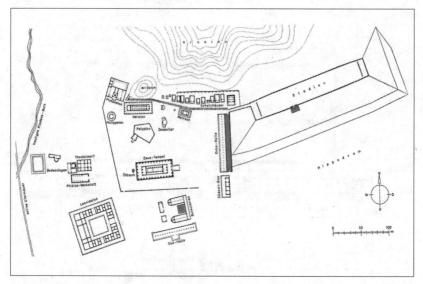

Figure 7. Sanctuary of Zeus at Olympia, ca. 300 BC. The shaded areas include the central hall of the *Bouleuterion*, the east corridor of the Echo Stoa, and the *Hellanodikai* area in the stadium. From Hans-Volkmar Herrmann, *Olympia: Heiligtum und Wettkampfstätte* (Munich, 1972), 162. Courtesy of DAI, Athens.

Seats were not common in the stadium. In fact, there were very few, limited to the *Hellanodikai*, the Priestess of Demeter Chamyne (whose throne was opposite the *Hellanodikai* on the north side of the track),[40] and individual stone seats for *proxenoi* of Greek cities.[41] Why were the seats for the *Hellanodikai* located where they were? Some reasons may be offered. First, the sun would have been behind the spectators on the southern embankment for most of the day, therefore reducing problems of glare for the judges. Second, the seats were in good view of the vaulted entrance, so judges could watch athletes coming and going. Third, this location is perhaps where combat events, such as boxing, *pankration*, and wrestling were held, and possibly some events of the pentathlon: the javelin, discus, and long jump (fig. 4).[42] It is unlikely that the *Hellanodikai* could judge the start or finish of the foot races from these seats, so the judges of the running events must have moved closer to the starting and finishing lines. Pausanias, in his discussion of Leon of Ambracia (6.3.7), mentions that the three judges were standing on the track (see below). It is also possible that the *Hellanodikai* area in the stadium was the location of the awarding of the prizes following certain events, since it is likely that the *Hellanodikai* awarded the victorious athletes the wreath of olive leaves.[43] The lower area of the enclosure in front of the chairs may have been the location of the award tables. The judges' area was in a good location to be seen fairly easily by most of those on the embankments of the stadium.[44]

The Sixteen Women

Pausanias (6.24.10) mentions that a committee of Sixteen Women organized the games for Hera at Olympia. He says that there is, in the agora of Elis, a building for the women called the Sixteen, where they weave the *peplos*, or robe, for Hera. These are the married women who hold the games for Hera at Olympia; we learn later in Pausanias (5.16.2–4) that the Sixteen Women are the *agonothetes* of the Hera festival. The Sixteen Women were originally chosen, says Pausanias (5.16.5), as the oldest, the most noble, and the most esteemed woman from each of the sixteen cities of Elis for the purpose of making peace between Elis and Pisa. Pausanias (5.16.7) mentions that later on they were entrusted with the Heraea games, and were chosen by selecting two from each of the eight tribes of Elis. They were responsible for weaving the *peplos* for Hera, for organizing the foot races for the unmarried girls, and for organizing the choral dances to Hippodameia and Physcoa.[45]

It has been noted that the *Hellanodikai*, as well as their predecessors the *diaitetes,* seem not to have had any religious affiliation.[46] The Sixteen Women, as *agonothetes*, clearly did have an association with the religious festival of Hera.[47]

Judging Controversies

There were several notable occasions when the judges at Olympia were involved in controversy. I mention only a few of the most well-known examples here. One such story involved Eupolemus of Elis. Pausanias (6.3.7) describes the statue of Eupolemus, who won the men's *stade* race at Olympia in 396 BC, as well as two pentathlon victories at the Pythian Games and another at the Nemean Games. With regard to his victory at Olympia, Pausanias tells us that there were three *Hellanodikai* standing at the finish of the race, and that two declared Eupolemus the winner while the third voted for Leon of Ambracia; however, through the Olympic Council, clearly protesting the original decision, Leon had the two judges who voted for Eupolemus fined. This story suggests that Leon was the real winner of the race and that the decision by the other two judges in favour of Eupolemus was flawed because of local bias towards the Elean athlete.[48]

Another story involved Troilus, an Elean, who in 372 BC, at the 102nd Olympiad, won victories in the two-horse chariot race and in the four-colt chariot race. At the same time, Troilus was a *Hellanodikas*. A bronze inscription from a statue of Troilus reads:

> I was *Hellanodikas* at Olympia when Zeus granted my first Olympic Victory with prize-winning horses and then my second in succession, Again with horses. Troilus was the son of Alkinous.

From Pausanias (6.1.4) we know that Troilus' statue was made by Lysippus, and that Troilus won two chariot races in 372 BC. Pausanias goes on to say that from this date on, Elis proclaimed that no horse belonging to a *Hellanodikas* could compete.[49]

A story in Pausanias (6.6.4–6) illustrates the kind of moral dilemma facing the *Hellanodikai* on occasion. It concerns Euthymus of Locris, who won the boxing match in 484 BC at the 74th Olympic festival. At the next festival, in 480 BC, Euthymus wished to defend his title, but the great Theagenes wanted to win both the *pankration* and boxing at the same festival. Theagenes defeated Euthymus in boxing; however, Euthymus so exhausted his challenger that Theagenes could not win the *pankration* later. As a result, the *Hellanodikai* fined Theagenes a talent for the god and a talent for the harm done to Euthymus, for they ruled that it was out of spite that Theagenes entered the boxing contest. The *Hellanodikai* also fined Theagenes to pay a sum privately to Euthymus. At the 76th festival in 476 BC, Theagenes paid in full the money owed to the god, and as compensation to Euthymus did not enter the boxing contest. Euthymus won the boxing in both 476 and 472 BC.[50]

What was the greatest scandal for the *Hellanodikai*? It was probably the incident involving the Roman emperor, Nero, who had long been interested in Greek athletics. He had founded the Juvenalia games at Rome in AD 59, and the Neronia in AD 61, and had built a gymnasium in the city as well. One of his greatest desires was to tour Greece and compete in the Olympic Games and the other Panhellenic festivals. Nero arranged for all four of the great Games festivals to be held in a single year, AD 66–67, so that he could compete and win in each and thereby become a *periodonikes*, a circuit victor. The Olympic Games scheduled to have been held in AD 65 were postponed to 67. According to the Roman author Dio Cassius (62.14), Nero bribed the *Hellanodikai* with one million *sesterces* in order to compete in this extraordinary Olympic Games. Not only did he win in the regularly scheduled events of the heralds, four-colt and four-horse chariot races, but he had three new events added to the Olympia program: singing to the lyre, tragedy, and the ten-horse chariot race. Suetonius (*Nero* 24) tells us that

> after he had been thrown from the car and put back in it, he was unable to hold out and gave up before the end of the course; but he received the crown just the same.

When Nero departed Olympia, he left as a six-time Olympic victor, all victories from the same Olympic Games. This put Nero at the head of the list of most victories at a single Olympic festival. He had also accomplished the best single one-day/festival Olympic equestrian achievement in the history of the Olympic Games. He had won three equestrian events. Only three of his predecessors at Olympia had managed to win two equestrian events on the same day, one of them being Troilus of Elis in 372 BC.[51] Pausanias (10.36.9) mentions that the Olympic festival of AD 67 was omitted from the Elean records, meaning that it lacked credibility. Nero's successor, Galba, was eager to have Nero's bribe paid back to Rome.

Conclusions

What can we learn from the evidence about ancient judges and judging at Olympia? To begin with, we should note that at least for a part of the historical period, according to Pausanias, the *Hellanodikai* were chosen by lot from the body of Elean citizenship. Secondly, the *Hellanodikai* were in residence at Elis in preparation for the Olympic Games for ten months, a substantial period of time, and although not all of their duties are known, it is likely that they were busy with preparations for the athletes' participation at Olympia. Thirdly, the Eleans did have trouble with respect to conflicts of interest. Perhaps Psammis was right in the early sixth century BC, and there should have been totally impartial judging at the Olympic Games. Certainly the Eleans would have been hard pressed to disallow their own citizens from the competitions, and why would they want to promote a festival with athletic contests in which their own citizens could not participate? Could there have been instituted a committee of judges from a cross-section of Greek city states?[52] Can we in the modern day learn something from their experiences, since we seem to have some difficulties of our own?

Did they string them up? No, the judges who were caught cheating in antiquity were fined, as were the athletes who were guilty of the same charges. It would appear that monetary fines were the ultimate solution to infractions at ancient Olympia. Following the Salt Lake City scandal in

2002, the International Skating Union (ISU) adopted a new set of judging rules with a broader pool of judges, half of them selected at random to judge anonymously. Marie-Reine Le Gougne—the French judge who admitted to pressure to vote, but *for* the Canadians—was suspended by the ISU.

Notes

1   Schmemann 2002.

2   For recent articles on the subject of the *Hellanodikai* at Olympia, see Crowther 1997 (Crowther 2004, 71–81), and Crowther 2003 (Crowther 2004, 53–64). Note also the article by Slowikowski 1989.

3   Diodorus 1.95 also describes this meeting. Lloyd (1988, 164–67) believes that this event "is almost certainly unhistorical."

4   The translations of Pausanias in this paper are based largely on those of the Loeb Classical Library editions by W.H.S. Jones (1977). Anglicizing the Greek terms for the organizers of the Games is problematic, but here I have used "athlothete" and "athlothetes" for all "cases" of "ἀθλοθέτης" and "ἀθλοθέτες" (singular and plural, respectively), "agonothete" and "agonothetes" for all "cases" of "ἀγωνοθέτης" and "ἀγωνοθέτες," and *"Hellanodikas"* and *"Hellanodikai"* for all "cases" of " Ἑλλανοδίκης" and " Ἑλλανοδίκαι" (singular and plural, respectively).

5   Siewert 1992, 114–15; Golden 1998, 15; Crowther 2003, 64–66 n. 18. Siewert has proposed a plausible explanation for how the earlier term of διαιτατήρ or διαιτατής was changed to Ἑλλανοδίκαι between 500 and 480 BC. He suggests that Sparta, which had created an anti-Persian coalition of Greek states in 481 BC, gave support to the Elean judges in Olympia to watch over the Panhellenic truce against the Persians. Since the anti-Persian forces called themselves oἱ Ἕλληνες, Siewert suggests that the Olympic διαιτατής were renamed Ἑλλανοδίκαι.

6   Pausanias (5.4.1–4) tells us that King Oxylus came from Aetolia and brought with him Aetolian colonists. This Aetolian tradition was likely very long remembered, and so a given *Hellanodikas* from Elis might still be remembered as having come from these Aetolian colonists in Elis. Pausanias (5.15.12) does mention the fact that the Eleans offer sacrifice in the *Altis* at Olympia to the divine heroes worshipped in Elean territory and in Aetolia. He also mentions (5.4.4) that Aetolus, son of King Oxylus, was buried right at the gate leading to Olympia and was honoured with sacrifices like a hero every year by the gymnasiarch.

7   Dittenberger and Purgold 1896, no. 2.

8   Jeffery 1961, 220, no. 15.

9   See the argument by Siewert 1992, 114–15. See also Golden 1998, 42.

10   For the date of the construction of Stadium III, see Schilbach 1992, 37. For the date of the construction of the Temple of Zeus, see Mallwitz, 1972, 211–34.

11   Lee 2001, 100–103, has suggested such a change in the Olympic program in 468 BC from two days to five days.

12   Philostratos (*V A* 3.30) suggests that the lottery system for selection of judges at Elis may not be the best method, since there may not be enough just men in Elis to serve. Since Pausanias (5.9.4–6) mentions that one judge was selected from each tribe of the Eleans, there may have been a series of lotteries.

13   Crowther 1997, 77–81.

14   Herodotus (6, 127) also refers to this event. For a recent study of Pheidon, see Foley 1997.

15   See Moretti 1957, 121, who mentions that the festival of 364 BC was organized by the Pisatans and that the Eleans considered the festival as ἀνολυμπιάς (a non-Olympiad).

16 The fact that the Elean Council House was found within the Maltho gymnasium (Paus. 6.23.7) is interesting in itself, since it suggests a close association of the civic and religious elements of the Council and the *Hellanodikai*.

17 It is known that Eleans who were former Olympic victors could become *Hellanodikai*. According to Pausanias (6.8.1), Euanoridas of Elis, who earlier had been a boy's wrestling victor at both Olympia and Nemea, was *Hellanodikas* and, as such, recorded the names of Olympic victors at Olympia.

18 This may be especially true based on the theory of Siewert (above, n. 5), who suggests that the *Hellanodikai* were formed to protect the Panhellenic truce against the Persians.

19 See Perlman 2000, 63–66, for a discussion of the *theorodokoi* for Olympia.

20 Perlman (2000, 72) notes that the *theoroi* could set out on their journeys almost one year in advance of the festival they were announcing.

21 Dio Chrysostom, 31.111, mentions that letters of reference sometimes sent to the Eleans were left unopened until after the contest.

22 Crowther (1991, 66) suggests that the thirty-day training period before the Olympic Games in Elis could have been introduced in 471 BC as a result of the growth of the festival in importance and size. Philostratus (*VA* 5.43) implies that the festivals at Delphi and Isthmia also had similar periods of training. Philostratus (*De Gymnastica* 54) mentions that the *Hellanodikai* are strict with their orders for the training of the athletes, even threatening to whip their coaches if they should disobey.

23 Philostratus, *De Gymnastica* 25.

24 Is it possible that the race was rerun and Alexander lost? Roos, 1985, has called into question the validity of this story, since the name of Alexander I does not appear in the victor lists. See also Romano 1990.

25 See Mitsopoulos-Leon 1998, 182–85.

26 The stoa can no longer be identified with the fifth-century Corcyrean Stoa but may have been a replacement building for it dating from the fourth to second century BC. See the report by Hector W. Catling, 1980, 34.

27 See Kyrieleis 2002.

28 See Mallwitz 1972.

29 Mallwitz 1972, 235–40.

30 This calculation is based on an estimated 0.5 square metres of space for each standing person. Multiplying 14 x 14 m = 196 m^2, then subtracting 24 m^2 for the space in the middle of the hall for the statue, altar, and room to manoeuvre would leave an area of 172 m^2, and dividing this by 0.5 would equal 344. The space would have been large enough for approximately this number of individuals to take the oath at the same time, although it would have been very crowded. In fact, it is likely that there were fewer than this number to give each individual more space. If athletes were joined by coaches and family members, the total number of athletes would have been less than this number. It is also possible, of course, that there were several different groups of athletes who came at different times to the *Bouleuterion* to take the oath. See Crowther 1993, 48–52, for estimates of numbers of athletes at Olympia. Miller (2004a, 118) estimates that two hundred athletes took part in the Olympic Games, then adds an unknown number of trainers, family, etc.

31 For instance, Swaddling 2004, 31. The vault was built after Stadium III was constructed. See Mallwitz 1972, 186–92, and Heilmeyer 1984, 251–63. Another interpretation for the κρυπτὴν ἔσοδον has been made by this author, suggesting that at the western entrance to the vault on the south side was an entrance to the corridor, 96 m long and 8 m wide and running along the east side of the Echo Stoa, that could have been used by athletes and judges. Considering this interpretation, the κρυπτὴν ἔσοδον would not have been the vault itself but rather the entrance to the small vestibule in front of and to the south of the western vault entrance. See Romano 1981, 128 n. 20.

32 The palestra was built in the third century, the gymnasium in the second century BC. See Mallwitz, 1972, 278–89.

33 Since Pausanias (6.23.7) tells us that the *Bouleuterion* in Elis was located inside the Maltho gymnasium, perhaps a similar relationship of athletes' facilities and place for judges existed at Olympia. Could the space around the *Bouleuterion* therefore have been an early (informal) area for a gymnasium?

34 Koenigs (1984, 84) suggests that the space was used by athletes for washing, undressing, and waiting. Miller (2001, 190–210) is in general agreement with Koenigs.

35 This would seem to be a more likely interpretation for both the east corridor of the Echo Stoa at Olympia as well as for the so-called *"apodyterion"* ("undressing room") at Nemea. See Miller 2001, 139–78.

36 Depending on the size of the chairs, there would be room for eight to twelve, close to the number needed for ten *Hellanodikai*.

37 Kunze and Schleif 1941, pls. 2–4.

38 Schilbach 1992, 33–37.

39 The spectator capacity of the Olympia III stadium was ca. 43,000, whereas its predecessor held ca. 24,000. See Romano 1993, 22.

40 Directly below the altar of Demeter have been found stone posts that originally supported five wooden benches, each approximately 32 m in length and parallel to the side of the racecourse.

41 For the seats of *Gorgos* and *Euwanios*, see Mallwitz 1972, 184–85; also Romano 1993, 19–22.

42 It is admittedly speculative; however, Pausanias (6.23.3, above), in his discussion of the *Hellanodikai* at Elis, mentions the *plethrion,* a place for matching wrestling competitors according to age and skill. A *plethron* was 100 linear feet or 100 square feet, and was of some significance. The distance between the *Hellanodikai* area on the south side of the stadium and the location of the throne of the Priestess of Demeter and the benches on the north side of the stadium, the width of the *dromos,* is approximately 100 Olympic feet or 32 m. Is it possible that 100 feet of the length of the stadium (perhaps between the 150- and 250-foot markers of the stadium from the west end) was a similar *plethrion* with special importance for some field events? The *dromos* is approximately 32 m wide at this point, so that there might be a 100-foot square (a *plethrion*) in front of both the *Hellanodikai* seats and the seats below the Priestess of Demeter. See above, note 39 and fig. 5. The use of the western *balbis* as a *bater* for pentathlon events is discussed in Hugh Lee's essay in this volume.

43 This is the implication from Pindar *Ol.* III. 12. From Lucian, *Herm.* 39–45, it is known that the lots for competitors in the wrestling and the *pankration* at Olympia were drawn at the area of the *Hellanodikai* in the stadium, and that the procedure was supervised by the judges. I thank Aileen Ajootian for this reference. Pausanias (5.12.5) mentions seeing a bronze tripod in the Temple of Zeus, once used to display the victor's crowns, and later (5.20.2) describes a gold and ivory table made by Kolotes in the Temple of Hera used to display the crowns. Pausanias does not say that the award ceremony takes place in either temple. Lee (2001, 69–75) has gathered the ancient testimonia concerning the awarding of prizes at Olympia and the possibility of a separate award ceremony at the end of the competitions, and concludes that there is no evidence to suggest a ceremony on the last day of the festival, including the awarding of olive crowns. It is more likely, he suggests, that the athletes received their awards immediately following the contest, in connection with a public proclamation by a herald.

44 Note that the *Hellanodikai* also had an area in the hippodrome, though as yet not located. Pausanias (6.13.9) mentions this when he describes the victory of the mare of the Corinthian, Pheidolas.

45 See Scanlon 2002, 98–99.

46 Siewert 1992, 116; Crowther 2004, 3. Pausanias (5.16.8) does mention that before any ceremony performed by the *Hellanodikai* or the Sixteen Women (organizers of the girls' contests in honour of Hera at Olympia), they first sacrifice a pig and purify themselves with water at the Piera Spring on the road from Olympia to Elis.

47 Plutarch, *Mor.*, [*Mulierum virtutes* 15] (Loeb Classical Library, 1931, vol. 3, 251e–f) mentions that there existed Sixteen Women of Elis who were sacred to Dionysus, suggesting the possibility that the same sixteen women may have had several religious roles in the city. I thank Gerald Schaus for this reference. See also Frazer's *Pausanias*, 1913, vol. 3, 592–93.

48 See the full discussion of this incident in Crowther 1997, 149–60. The parallel to the pairs figure-skating controversy at Salt Lake City in 2002 is obvious, but instead of two declared winners, we hear only of the victory statue of Eupolemus.

49 It is not clear if the *Hellanodikai* were still being selected by lot at this time.

50 See Crowther 2001a, 39.

51 Romano 2004, 121.

52 This was previously suggested by Crowther 1997, 158–59.

Heroic and Athletic Sortition
at Ancient Olympia

Aileen Ajootian

The heroic charioteers in Book 23 of the *Iliad*, before their race at Patroclus' funeral games, were assigned lanes by lot. Each driver put a token,
a *kleros*, into a container of unspecified type. Achilles shook it, allowing
one marker to fly out at a time, establishing lane order, and incidentally
giving the best driver the worst position. What Homeric *kleroi* looked
like, what marks they bore, is unknown. Elsewhere in the *Iliad*, the
Achaeans employed this simple method of allotment both for athletics
and for war, shaking a container until one *kleros* popped out, uninflu-
enced by human intervention. A brief survey of sortition scenes in Homer
reveals that in military episodes a helmet served as the receptacle for lots.
In athletic encounters, the form of the vessel is not always specified.[1]

Other ancient sources record the use of lots in athletic competition. In
Sophocles' *Electra* (709–10), for example, Orestes and the other charioteers in the race at the Pythian Games received lane assignment through
random allotment.[2] The use of lots in mythological horse races was par-
alleled by actual practice. Pausanias (6.20.11), in his detailed, albeit late,
account of the hippodrome at Olympia, located somewhere south of the
stadium, stated that competitors in equestrian events were apportioned
lanes by lot. Archaeological evidence corroborates the literary record.

Letters painted in red on the plastered surface of the unusual curved starting line, or *balbis*, of the early fifth-century stadium at Corinth, for example, marked at least sixteen lanes (fig. 1).[3] *Alpha* was the first character, at
the south end of the starting line, and the letters continued north, labelling
lanes along the *balbis*, up to *pi*.[4] Circa 5 cm high,[5] the letters were painted
between the front and back grooves cut in the starting blocks for athletes'
feet, and were meant to be viewed from the runners' perspective, behind
(east of) the starting line.[6]

    The ordering system for stadium lanes used at Corinth differs from the
"alphabetic numbers" employed in Classical Attica and other regions,
where the twenty-four Ionian characters, plus three added ones, were split
into three groups of nine.[7] Thus, *alpha* through *theta* represented numbers
1 through 9; *iota* through *koppa*, an added character, stood for 10 through
90; *rho* to *omega* for 100 to 900. At Corinth, the letters painted on the
starting line of the fifth-century racetrack functioned instead as labels.[8] In
Classical Attic inventory inscriptions, letters served to highlight successive headings in lists.[9] A similar labelling system ordered the ranks of
jurors in the Athenian court. The entire group of *dikasts* (jurors) was
divided into ten sections, each assigned a letter, *alpha* through *kappa*.
Some eighty-nine bronze fourth-century jurors' tokens, or *symbola*,
inscribed with these letters, determined the section to which their owners
were assigned.[10] Jurors also received seat assignments in court by means
of bronze *symbola* bearing one of twenty-five letters (a character was
added to make the division of quantities like 200, 400, and 500 easier).[11]
At the theatre in Boeotian Mantineia, a similar labelling system is documented in the third century BC to assign seating in various sections of the
cavea. Clay tokens were each inscribed with the owner's name and
patronymic on one side, and one of twenty-five letters on the other.[12]
Similarly, painted letters labelled the sixteen lanes of Corinth's early Classical racecourse, and would probably have corresponded to *kleroi* inscribed
alpha through *pi*. The labelled starting line of Corinth's stadium provides
rare evidence for a system of organizing runners in their lanes through allotment.[13] Presumably there would have been other equipment on hand, clay
or bronze tokens and a container from which athletes took the lots.

    In the first half of the second century AD, Lucian, who witnessed
Olympic festivals, provided the fullest description of allotment employed
for sacred athletics (*Hermotimus* 40).[14] The namesake of his dialogue
described allotment, not for chariot races, but for the assignment of partners and byes in the heavy events, wrestling and *pankration*. Lucian's
account of athletic sortition at Olympia is embedded in a long dialogue con-

Figure 1. Early Classical starting line of the racetrack at ancient Corinth. American School of Classical Studies, Corinth Excavations 1980-50-2. Photo by I. Ioannidou and L. Bartzioti.

cerning the pros and cons of philosophical schools. Hermotimus, the philosophy enthusiast, reported that at Olympia he watched the process close up, sitting near the *Hellanodikai*. These officials, according to Pausanias (6.20.8–9), had special stone seats along the south side of the racetrack. Their stadium furniture survives, on the opposite side of the track from the marble altar for Demeter Chamyne.[15]

The sortition procedure observed by Lucian's Hermotimus apparently took place near the judges' seating. Small lots (*mikroi kleroi*), inscribed with letters, were thrown into a silver vessel that Lucian called a *kalpis*, dedicated to the god. The competitors prayed to Zeus, then each one picked a lot from the vessel. A whip-wielding *mastigophoros* was standing by to make sure no one looked at his letter. The athletes stood in a circle, and the *alytarch*, another Sanctuary official, or maybe one of the *Hellanodikai*, went around to inspect each lot. It is apparent from Hermotimus' description that for allotment in the heavy events, alphabetic numbers α through ε were employed, rather than the labelling system of lane assignments. Hermotimus described the way in which, depending on how many contestants there were, partners and byes were arranged by means of odd and even letters (symbolizing numbers).

A few archaeological notes can be added to this ancient literary vignette. The term *kalpis* was used for several vase shapes, from a *hydria* to a *pyxis*, but modern critics generally consider a *kalpis* to be a type of *hydria* with neck and body formed with a curving, uninterrupted profile, rather than the neck set off distinctly from the body.[16] In Athens, *hydriae* are named as the containers for Classical dikastic procedures.[17] While lot casting was not a popular subject in Classical vase painting, *hydriae* are employed for some kind of voting or lot casting on a mid-fifth-century red-figure *kylix* in Dijon (fig. 2).[18]

Schmidt proposed allotment as the motif in this scene.[19] Beardless youths stand near the *hydriae* punctuating the outside of the *kylix*, while bearded men sit next to the vessels. In addition, a late fifth or early fourth-century red-figure bell krater by the Nikias Painter, said to be on the Paris art market, depicts two helmeted men, otherwise nude, apparently taking lots from a *hydria*.[20] One reaches into the vessel; the other may be waiting his turn. Behind them, a column supports a statue of Athena bearing an *aphlaston* (curved stern of a ship). To the right of the central group stands a draped man holding what has been identified as a torch, but this attribute may actually be the long branch wielded by a judge.

The use of *hydriae* for athletic lot casting is documented in the Roman period on the reverse of a bronze imperial coin from Prostanna (Pisidia), minted under Gordianus III (AD 238–244).[21] The obverse bears this emperor's portrait. On the reverse are three athletes, one reaching into a *hydria* for his lot; the other two have already received their tokens and are looking at them. In Hermotimus' account, then, the silver *kalpis* containing *kleroi* could have been a *hydria* bearing an inscribed dedication to Zeus. This text may also identify the vessel as official Olympic equipment.

In fact, some official paraphernalia have been recovered at Olympia, including terracotta *karpometra*, standard units of measure for food.[22] These late Classical vessels bore painted labels identifying their function and ownership (*DEMOSION* and *OLYMPIA*).[23] In addition, some 114

Figure 2. Red-figure *kylix*, Stieglitz Painter. Musée archéologique, Dijon, 1301. After *Agora* XXVIII, pl. 5. Photographs © Musée des Beaux-Arts Dijon.

Hellenistic bronze tokens have turned up, chiefly in the southeastern quadrant of the site, just outside the *Altis*, east of the *Bouleuterion* and south of the Classical stadium.[24] The inscribed monogram on many of these disks identifies them as property of the city of Elis, in control of Olympia on and off through the Classical period. Similar tokens found at Elis itself suggest that they were used for administrative purposes at both places. A few bronze tokens found at Olympia are uninscribed, suggesting that perhaps they were marked at the site as needed, but so far none has been recognized as a *kleros* employed in athletic allotment.[25]

Bronze *hydriae*, whole vases and fragments, including the form called a *kalpis*, have also been recovered at Olympia.[26] They range in date from the early sixth century BC through the Classical period, and various regional types have been identified, including Laconian and South Italian. None of them preserves an inscribed dedication such as the one Lucian describes, and it is not possible to identify any of them securely as allotment containers.[27] Find-spots are not very helpful; *hydriae* have been found across the site in wells, in the so-called Southeast Building, near the Prytaneum, even in the Alpheus River.

Despite the absence of securely identifiable equipment, it is evident that allotment was a routine and important process at Olympia. Not only were athletic matters settled there by means of sortition, but the *Hellanodikai* themselves were selected this way, using the simplest form of an administrative procedure common to civic life in ancient Greece.[28] Well documented archaeologically and in ancient testimonia, the Classical democratic allotment system for choosing public officials and members of the *Boule* (Council) in Athens was admittedly more complex than shaking a container full of *kleroi*. Some of the civic paraphernalia survives in Athens and elsewhere, including bronze *pinakia* bearing jurors' names, and marble *kleroteria* employed to assign male citizens their governmental duties.[29]

It is considerably more difficult to reconstruct the archaeological evidence of sortition equipment for sacred athletics—the vessels and the metal or clay *kleroi* probably in use at Panhellenic sanctuaries.[30] Yet such items must have been commonplace, used many times over at the festivals, a standard part of the competition process. Furthermore, the sortition ceremony itself would have been a familiar phase of the proceedings, both for contestants and for viewers, judging from Lucian. It is always risky to speculate on what ancient Greeks saw, or how they interpreted their experience, but the Panhellenic setting of Olympia encouraged a thematic relationship among the buildings and dedications as they filled the *Altis*, and the programmatic possibilities of these specialized victory monuments may have elicited specific responses from viewers in antiquity.[31] In the first half of the fifth century BC, a deliberate, visual equation was made between Homeric, heroic sortition and the preliminary events conducted routinely at the site during the sacred Games.

The so-called Achaean Dedication at Olympia, made by the early Classical Aeginetan artist Onatas, was a Homeric tableau set up just east of the Temple of Zeus.[32] Pausanias (5.25.8–10), a critical source of information on monuments in the *Altis*, was the only ancient authority who mentioned the over life-size statue group. The monument was labelled with inscriptions which he recorded, providing a full record of the dedicants, divine recipient, theme, and artist.

> There are also offerings dedicated by the whole Achaean race in common; they represent those who, when Hector challenged any Greek to meet him in single combat, dared to cast lots to choose the champion. They stand, armed with spears and shields, near the great temple. Right opposite, on a second pedestal, is a figure of Nestor, who has thrown the lot of each into the helmet. The number of those casting lots to meet Hector is now only eight, for the ninth, the statue of Odysseus, they say that Nero carried to Rome, but Agamemnon's statue is the only one of the eight to have his name inscribed upon it; the writing is from right to left. The figure with the cock emblazoned on the shield is Idomeneus the descendant of Minos. The story goes that Idomeneus was descended from the Sun, the father of Pasiphaë, and that the cock is sacred to the Sun and proclaims when he is about to rise. An inscription too is written on the pedestal:
>
>> To Zeus these images were dedicated by the Achaeans,
>> Descendants of Pelops the godlike scion of Tantalus.
>
> Such is the inscription on the pedestal, but the name of the artist is written on the shield of Idomeneus:
>
>> This is one of the many works of clever Onatas,
>> The Aeginetan, whose sire was Micon.
>>   (translation W.H.S. Jones—Loeb ed.)

Pausanias identified the dedicants, the whole Achaean race (*ethnos*), and described the theme, which clearly reflects an episode in the *Iliad* (7.67–200) (n. 1 above, no. 2). The Homeric Greeks, called Achaeans, like the fifth-century dedicants at Olympia, placed lots into a helmet held out by King Nestor to determine which warrior would accept the Trojan Hector's invitation to fight in single combat. According to Homer, when Hector issued his challenge, only Menelaus volunteered. After the remonstrances of Agamemnon and Nestor, nine Greek warriors, all named, then stepped forward. Now one man had to be chosen. Each warrior put a *kleros*, perhaps imagined by Homer's audience as a potsherd, marked with his own *sema*, or sign, into Agamemnon's helmet. Nestor, averting his gaze, shook the helmet, so that one lot would pop out. Then heralds showed the *kleros* to each warrior until Ajax claimed his own *sema*. The action then turned to the warriors' contest; they fought to a draw.

Pausanias located Onatas' Homeric statue group near the Temple of Zeus. Nineteenth-century German discoveries at Olympia supported his statement: the limestone foundation levels of a large curved base (ca. 1.20 m wide) was located some seventeen metres southeast of the temple, and a separate round base was found about seven metres further east (fig. 3). The arc of the curved base, roughly 12 m long, inscribes a circle on the ground about 81.68 m in diameter. The round base, with a diameter of 1.5 m, sits inside the imaginary circumference of the curved socle (figs. 3–6). The bases' stratigraphic relationship to the Temple of Zeus confirms that the two installations were erected at about the same time.[33] The Zeus Temple, traditionally considered one of the few early Classical buildings with a secure date, was probably constructed sometime between 470 and 456 BC, so Onatas' Achaean Dedication may have been erected at about the same time.[34]

A Homeric scene was recreated by nine large, probably bronze, statues of the "Achaean" soldiers, holding shields and spears. They stood on the semicircular socle, facing east towards Nestor, poised opposite on the round support. Only the bases survive, but various early Classical statues or Roman sculptural types have been suggested as belonging to the monument, including the so-called Riace bronzes.[35] These warrior statues found off the coast of Riace Marina in Calabria probably do not pertain to the bases, but they give an idea of the material, the large scale (ca. 1.97 m tall), and the early Classical style of Onatas' lost works.

Pausanias documented Onatas' monument fully, but he did not report that an ancient processional way circa seven metres wide separated the curved base supporting the warriors awaiting the cast of the lot from the round base upon which Nestor stood. The two separate elements apparently were recognizable as a single thematic unit, as Pausanias himself gives witness. Visitors walking north along the path between the bases may have recognized the story from inscriptions or other identifying signs, such as shield blazons (Idomeneus' shield had a cock). Once the arrested poses of the Achaean heroes on one side and Nestor with inverted helmet on the other side had been identified, visitors might quickly recognize the unity of the two elements and imagine the outcome of the scene.

Figure 3. Olympia, model of the *Altis*. DAI neg. 68/802.

Figure 4. Olympia, foundations of Onatas' early Classical Achaean Dedication. Photo by the author.

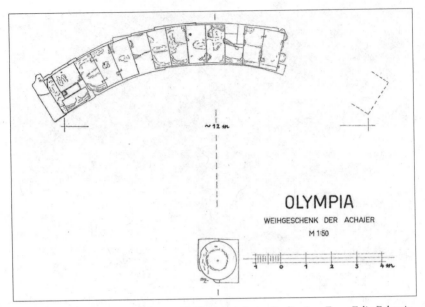

Figure 5. Olympia, plan of Onatas' early Classical Achaean Dedication. From Felix Eckstein, *Anathemata* (Berlin, 1969). Courtesy Dietrich Reimer Verlag.

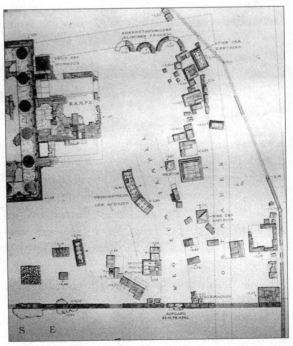

Figure 6. Olympia, plan of the east side of the *Altis*. From *Olympia, Karte und Pläne*, map 6e.

Freezing the action as it commenced, with the warriors looking across the space separating them from Nestor, Onatas exploited viewers' experience of the Homeric story, forcing them to imagine the interaction of the statues and to finish the narrative that he had begun. The three-dimensional recreation of a well-known Homeric episode through the interplay of spectator and statue, however, is only one way in which Onatas' monument at Olympia may have fused the heroic world and the contemporary Panhellenic setting, thus bringing the two realms closer together by superimposing one on the other via the ancient viewer's experience.

The choice of Hector's opponent by random lot portrayed by the Achaean Dedication at Olympia illuminated and heroized an administrative procedure that must have been a convention of Olympic athletics. Considering the widespread and traditional use of lots to assign positions, heats, partners, as well as administrative posts in Panhellenic competitions, the Achaean Dedication east of the Temple of Zeus at Olympia could have expressed several kinds of meaning for ancient viewers. It combined the moment before the Homeric military *agon* (contest or struggle), when the Greeks waited for Nestor to cast the *kleros*, with the assignment of lots for Olympic athletics, an act performed and witnessed over and over for centuries at the Sanctuary.

The visual and symbolic equation of Onatas' bronze Homeric soldiers with generations of mortal athletes at Olympia may have conveyed its meaning through the physical arrangement of the installation. As we have seen, Lucian—in the long description of sortition for heavy events at Olympia—reported that the athletes all received randomly assigned lots marked with letters and then stood in a circle while the judges came around to inspect these tokens. Admittedly he provides a late glimpse of Olympic procedures, but perhaps his report reflected long-established tradition. Onatas may have set the bronze Achaeans on a semicircular base, modelling this heroic composition on the Olympic athletic conventions of his own time. The bronze Achaeans on their curved base inscribe a circle on the ground, perpetually witnessing Nestor about to shake the helmet full of lots.[36] The monument thus becomes an enduring paradigm for a critical phase of Panhellenic athletics, and generations of athletes at Olympia, in turn, waiting for lane, partner, and bye assignments by lot, reflected the timeless pose of the bronze heroes.

One challenge we face in reading Olympia's sacred topography is that it changed over time, transformed by successive phases of building and dedications. In the late Archaic period, the racetrack, Stilbach's Stadium II, was roughly aligned with the middle of the so-called "Treasury Row" to the north in the *Altis*.[37] By 465–455 BC, when the Temple of Zeus and the Achaean Dedication were under construction, the next phase of the Stadium, IIIA, was relocated further east, out of the *Altis* altogether, to accommodate the ever-increasing crowds of spectators attending the sacred events.[38] Thus when the Zeus temple and Onatas' sculpture group were being installed, the location of athletic allotment was probably not near the judges' seats bordering the Classical stadium, as Lucian reported seven centuries later. In the Archaic and early Classical periods, allotment must have taken place somewhere within the *Altis* itself.

Even before the Zeus temple dominated it, the southeastern quadrant of the *Altis* had been appropriated for victory monuments, both military and athletic. About 17 m north of the Achaean Dedication along the north-south path was the Eretrian bull dedication set up early in the fifth century BC.[39] Another monument predating Onatas' statue group was a bronze *quadriga* dedication set up ca. 488 BC by Gelon, tyrant of Sicilian Gela. The inscribed base of this work celebrated Gelon's victory in an Olympic chariot race.[40] In addition, an enormous bronze statue of Zeus stood ca. 13 m south of the Achaean group. This work celebrated the Greek victory over the Persians at Plataea in 479 BC. These earlier monuments flanked a processional way that ran north, past the *Bouleuterion* just south of the *Altis*, then through the sacred zone east of where the Zeus temple would be built, leading towards the older stadium.

Onatas' Achaean Dedication undoubtedly drew some of its meaning from such earlier installations that lined the path going north. In fact, the sculptor set Nestor's base so close to the Geloan chariot monument (fig. 4)—less than a metre to the west—that one wonders if he intended the earlier work's victorious symbolism to provide a backdrop for his own. Perhaps Onatas' design was also influenced by the custom of athletic sortition for all events that would have occurred somewhere close to the earlier stadium (II), still within the *Altis*. Just possibly, this preliminary phase of Olympic competition had traditionally been performed in the area later bracketed by the Achaean Dedication's two bases.

Onatas' design relied on his knowledge of Olympic procedures, and drew some of its meaning from its position within the *Altis*. Athletes swore their oath not to cheat before the Altar of Zeus Horkios located east of the *Bouleuterion*, at that time not separated from the *Altis* by the late-fourth-century wall.[41] They then would have processed north on the path leading from the *Bouleuterion* and Zeus altar, following the path north towards the stadium aligned with the treasury terrace. Onatas set the Achaean dedication inside the *Altis*, but still close to the Zeus Horkios altar. Although we cannot be sure, Onatas may have forged a visual and ideological connection between the critical moment in the athletes' procession when they swore not to cheat and their passage north, flanked by the large bronze statues of the Achaean Dedication, east of the Temple of Zeus. Pausanias identified the theme of the temple's eastern pedimental sculptures as the moment before the fateful chariot race between the young hero Pelops and the local King Oinomaus, a story that provided a quasi-historical backdrop for the Panhellenic site.[42] Over life-sized marble statues stand motionless just before this race; the bearded king and his challenger flank the central figure of Zeus. Oinomaus opens his mouth slightly; he is speaking, a very unusual detail in sculpture of this period. According to Säflund, the king is setting out the rules of encounter for the chariot context.[43] But Hirschfeld had earlier proposed that Oinomaus in the east pediment, like a mortal athlete, might be in the middle of swearing his oath before Zeus not to cheat in the chariot race about to begin.[44] This suggestive interpretation of the east pediment's central group binds the temple closely to the topography of the *Altis*. Having just sworn their oath to support fair play, athletes processed below a similar scene re-enacted in marble above in the east gable of the Zeus temple, and walked between the two parts of the Achaean Dedication where bronze statues performed allotment.

Olympic traditions made their mark upon the sacred landscape. The function of specific areas at the Sanctuary was reinforced by the shared experience of athletes and viewers, and was perhaps formalized, as the Sanctuary developed, by monuments that recognized the traditional meaning and ceremonial use of specific spaces. Onatas' Homeric sculptural program, linking the athletes with their ancestor Pelops, also provided them with a broader ideological connection to the heroic past of Greece.

*I thank Gerald Schaus and Stephen Wenn for inviting me to participate in the conference *Onward to the Olympics*, and for their careful editing of this essay. I am grateful to David Romano for useful references and discussions concerning the stadium at Olympia.

Notes

1 1. *Iliad* 3.325: Paris and Menelaus determine by lot which of them will throw his spear first. Hector is in charge of the procedure, putting their two *kleroi* into a helmet. Like Nestor in no. 2 (below), he averts his gaze, ensuring an objective outcome. 2. *Iliad* 7.175–83: Hector challenges the Achaeans to single combat. His opponent is selected by means of allotment. Agamemnon's helmet serves as a receptacle for lots. Nestor shakes it until one lot pops out. 3. *Iliad* 23.352: Competitors in the chariot race honouring Patroclus at his funeral games place lots in a container of unspecified type. 4. *Iliad* 23.862: Teucer and Meriones employ lots and a bronze helmet to determine the order of their archery competition. 5. *Iliad* 24.400: The Myrmidon messenger and squire of Achilles, Argeïphontes (Hermes in disguise), tells Priam that lots were cast to determine

which of seven brothers would accompany the expedition to Troy. 6. *Odyssey* 9.331: Odysseus asks his men to choose by lot the four who will help him hold the stake to blind Polyphemus. 7. *Odyssey* 10.206: Eurylochus is selected by lots cast in a helmet to lead his group of men on an exploration of Circe's island. 8. *Odyssey* 14.209: Odysseus, in disguise, tells Eumaeus a story about his upbringing; after his father died, his brothers born in wedlock cast lots as a means of dividing their father's possessions.

2 Lloyd-Jones and Wilson 1990, 55; Davidson 1988, 65; Kamerbeek 1974, 99; Sophocles (ed. Kells) 1973, 142–43.

3 Morgan 1937, 549–50; Williams and Russell 1981, 7–8; Jeffery 1990, 440 D; Romano 1993, 43–79, esp. 46, and figs. 29–30; Pfaff 2003, 137. This phase of the stadium is late Archaic, according to Pfaff (2003, 137), who notes that the earliest stratified levels of the track date to the late sixth century BC, based on pottery finds (and see Williams and Russell 1981, 2).

4 Williams and Russell 1981, 7.

5 Williams and Russell 1981, 7.

6 Romano 1993, 51. The issue of whether or not runners remained in the same lane for the whole race remains a topic of debate: Crowther 1992, 68; Crowther 1997, 154–55. Strips of coloured earth embedded in the early Hellenistic stadium surface at Nemea may have indicated lanes (Valavanis 1999, 30 n. 8; Miller 2001, 38, 44 n. 96).

7 Tod 1950, 126–39; Woodhead 1959, 107–11; Richardson 1985, 13–15; McLean 2002, 61–63, no. 2.09.

8 Tod 1954, 1–8.

9 Tod 1954, 1.

10 *IG* V2323, nos. 22–107: Tod 1954, 1.

11 Boegehold et al. 1995 (*Agora* XXVIII), 34, 70.

12 Tod 1954, 1.

13 Stella Miller (1983, 93–95) reported an inscribed "Λ" (*lambda*) on a block from a possible Hellenistic phase of the starting line. Three blocks from the Archaic starting line at Nemea (on display at the Nemea Museum) bear inscribed letters: inv. nos. A 215 (*gamma*; see Miller 2001, 241, fig. 375), also A 380 (*rho*), A 401 (*chi*).

14 Citations to Lucian are from Kilburn's edition: Kilburn 1990.

15 Romano 1993, 22.

16 Richter and Milne 1935, 11–12; Kanowski 1983, 39–42.

17 Aristotle, *Ath. Pol.* 63–69; Boegehold et al. 1995 (*Agora* XXVIII), 37; also Xenophon, *Hellenika* I.7.9 for a special vote to determine whether Athenian generals were guilty of neglect in recovering sailors after the Athenian victory at Arginusae. Each *phyle* (tribe) was to vote, using two *hydriae*. See Isokrates, *Trapeziticus* 33, where the banker Pasion is accused of various infractions that included opening official sealed *hydriae* (kept on the Acropolis) containing votes.

18 Attributed to the Stieglitz Painter: *ARV* 2 829.37; Dijon, Musée Archéologique 1301; Boegehold *et al.* 1995 (*Agora* XXVIII), 210; von Bothmer 1975, 15. Other terms for vessels containing ballots and *kleroi* include: *dadoi, kadiskoi, amphoreis* (Boegehold et al. 1995 [*Agora* XXVIII], 210; Aloni 1983, 43–49).

19 Schmidt 1967, 80.

20 *ARV*2 1334.18: unpublished (the Beazley Archive illustrates this vessel; see "term word" *hydria*, item no. 153). The vessel preserves much of its added white paint, perhaps meant to represent silver.

21 Robert Weir mentions this coin in his paper for this collection. I thank him for alerting me to the coin and for kindly providing information and references (*Sylloge Nummorum Graecorum Sammlung von Aulock* 1957, 514; Franke 1968, 54, no. 257). There are similar reverses from other sites in Pisidia: Baris (Severus Alexander 222–235 AD): *SNG Sammlung von Aulock* 1965, 5011; also from Roman Caria, at Aphrodisias (Gal-

lienus 253–268 AD, obverse of Salonina): *SNG Sammlung von Aulock* 1968, 2476. On this reverse athletes stand around a vessel, no one reaches inside it: no. 514; Franke 1968, 54, no. 257.

22 Schilbach 2000, 323–37; Hamdorf 1981, 192–208.

23 Schilbach 2000, 323; Hamdorf 1981, 204–208.

24 Baitinger and Eder 2002, 163–87.

25 Baitinger and Eder 2002, 241–43.

26 Gauer 1991, 93–110; for a catalogue of *hydriae* at Olympia: 257–266, including six *kalpides*: 265, Hy 74–79.

27 A fifth-century bronze *hydria* found in a well at Nemea bears an inscribed dedication to Zeus on its rim; it is on display at the Nemea Museum.

28 On the Hellanodikai: Crowther 1997, 149–51.

29 Boegehold et al. 1995 (*Agora* XXVIII), 37–38, 58; Camp 1990, 247–48; Dow 1939, 1–34; see also Moretti 2001, 133–43; on *pinakia*: Kroll 1972, 92–94.

30 Clay disks (mostly 4th to 3rd century BC) bearing impressions of designs carved on metal rings or engraved on gems have been found near civic buildings in Athens (Lang and Crosby 1964 [*Agora* X], 125). Their function is not known, but they were probably not sealings (Lang and Crosby 1964 [*Agora* X], 124–26). They may have been used as a form of identification.

31 On this issue see Elsner 2001, 3–20.

32 Ajootian 2003, 137–63; Harrison 1985, 47–53; Dörig 1977, 3, 20–21; Ridgway 1970, 89, A. 6; Eckstein 1969, 27–62.

33 Mallwitz 1972, 211–34; on the date of the building, 211; Harrison 1985, 52.

34 Sinn 2000, 58–67.

35 Hoffman and Konstam 2002, 153–65; Moreno 1998; Mattusch 1996b, 29–30; Cohen 1991, 465–502; Harrison 1985, 47–51; Ridgway 1984, 313–26.

36 The early Classical racetrack at Corinth, with letters marking the lanes, was slightly curved. Romano (1993, 49–53) has worked out the mathematical system that may have been used to project the course of the track. While the starting lines of Stadium II and III at Olympia apparently were straight, Onatas, plotting the space for his sculpture group, must have relied on existing survey and computational techniques, like those used to plot the starting line at Corinth.

37 Schilbach 1992, 204–206; Mallwitz 1988, 94.

38 Schilbach 1992, 206.

39 Eckstein 1969, 50–53.

40 Eckstein 1969, 54–60.

41 Pausanias 5.24.9–10; 7.19.1; Lorimer 1936, 176–77.

42 On the sculpture of the Zeus temple, see now Barringer 2005.

43 Säflund 1970, 99, 124.

44 Hirschfeld 1877, 309.

Fabulous Females and Ancient Olympia

Donald G. Kyle

One of the most dramatic changes in the modern Olympics since 1896 is the presence of female athletes.[1] Pierre de Coubertin and the early Olympic establishment opposed the very idea, but we have come a long way since 1896.[2] One might say that we have never looked back, but we do look backwards, to Greece and ancient Olympia, sometimes seeking validation and heroines. This paper on females (girls and women, by age and biological nature) and Olympia in the Archaic and Classical ages uses "fabulous" in the classical sense—of fictitious or improbable tales, wondrous and not real things. It discusses girls' races for Hera at Olympia, the ban on women at the Olympics and the story of a mother who snuck in, the issue of virgin girls attending the Olympics, and the chariot victor Cynisca of Sparta.

Enthusiasm and Evidence

The earnest pursuit of evidence for ancient women's athletics in recent years has produced modest returns.[3] Admittedly, there is an embedded male bias; we have found more than we might have expected, and much more may once have existed and may yet be found.[4] Works keep turning to literature on Spartan females, to later ages, and to myths of Atalanta, itself a myth of inversion (and ultimate taming) that undermines the argument for female sport.[5] Of course, we keep turning to Pausanias, who gives the most detailed and sometimes the only information about aspects of female sport and Olympia. Writing around AD 170, he had a keen eye for topography, monuments, and inscriptions, but he also used oral sources.[6] He was not credulous or uncritical, but he was not an eyewitness to any athletic contests at Olympia. Even with Pausanias, even when supplemented by archaeology, the evidence for Greek female athletics remains meagre compared to the abundant and ubiquitous evidence for males. Few female contests in Classical Greece were arguably "athletic" by ancient Greek terms—that is, high-level competition for prizes in public contests. Certainly many females visited Olympia as pilgrims; they sacrificed, made dedications, and served as priestesses.[7] Some, however, now suggest that there was widespread female athletic competition in ancient Greece, and that there were female spectators at the ancient Olympics.

The Heraea

The best case for female athletics at Olympia is the Heraea, the festival of Hera.[8] Discussing her temple, Pausanias says (5.16.2–8) the Sixteen Women from Elis organized races for *parthenoi* or virgin girls, who wore a distinctive costume (5.16.2–3). Nancy Serwint has identified the costume as the *exomis* of male soldiers and workers, which suggests a liminal inversion and further points to the origins of the Heraea as an initiation rite.[9] The girls used the Olympic stadium, but their sprints, the sole event, were shorter (by one-sixth) than the males'. Their prizes included an olive wreath, a portion of meat, and permission to dedicate "icons" (εἰκόνας)—perhaps inscribed statues or painted images of themselves.[10] With three age classes, the Heraea, at least originally, was not a puberty rite but a "social initiation" rite sanctioning the girls' status in the local community.[11] Yet how athletic was the Classical Heraea, and was it Panhellenic (open to non-Elean girls)?

Spartan Female Physical Education

Sparta certainly had institutionalized female physical education, patterned to a degree on the training of boys and including public nudity and (probably for girls only) contests of "strength and speed" (Xen. *Lac.* 1.3–4; Plut. *Lyc.* 14.2–15.1).[12] Statuettes of Laconian workmanship (e.g., Athens National Museum, Collection Carapanos no. 24; Scanlon 2002, fig. 4-3) depict Spartan female runners in short chitons, sometimes lifting their hems. Outside sources (e.g., Eur. *Andr.* 590–601, Ibycus frag. 339) called them "thigh-flashers," and the Spartan character Lampito in Aristophanes' *Lysistrata* is proud of her fitness.[13] Pausanias (3.13.7) mentions a race for the "eleven Daughters of Dionysus" at Sparta, but such races were local initiation rites.[14] Other Spartan statuettes (mostly mirror or patera handles) of girls, some topless and some nude, perhaps look athletic, but Andrew Stewart identifies them as mementos of maturation rituals (especially choral dances)—women's luxury goods for personal use in Sparta.[15] Overall, Sparta's female program included exercises, parades, choral dances,[16] and initiatory runs, all tied to cults and to the conditioning and maturation of girls within Sparta.[17] As Xenophon (*Lac.* 1.4) and Plutarch (*Lyc.* 14.2, 15.1) explained, the aim of Sparta's female physical education was erotic and eugenic—nudity to inspire breeding and fitness to assist healthy childbirth.[18] Plato, however (*Resp.* 5.452–57), shows that the idea of nude female sport was seen as ridiculous outside of Sparta. None of the salacious testimonia places Spartan girls at Olympia.

The Arcteia *in Attica*

Many turn to the *Arcteia* of Artemis in Attica to argue that maidens' races were widespread. A group of ritual vases depicts lightly clad or nude young girls seemingly running near an altar. Some see an athletic race here, but Thomas Scanlon sees a ritual chase, analogous to a hunt, part of an initiation rite in which the girls fled from society, and were pursued and tamed to return to society.[19] Gloria Ferrari sees the girls as "figurative nudes" that refer not to contemporary practice but to the mythical past, perhaps to Artemis and Callisto (and Callisto's transitions from maiden to bear to constellation). She suggests that the girls performed a circular dance (in imitation of the movement of stars) in a rite that marked them as legitimate citizen females of Athens who could marry and bear citizen sons.[20] Scanlon, therefore, sees a liminal ritual chase, while Ferrari sees a local circular dance. Neither sees an athletic contest. Athens thus offers evidence of maturation rites, which were of great importance in the lives of girls throughout Greece, but there is insufficient evidence for early, widespread female athletics.

Later Girls' Races

Girls did compete at major athletic contests later, but the evidence comes from long after Classical Greece. A first-century AD inscription records victories of the daughters of Hermesianax in running at Delphi, Isthmia, and Nemea, but it makes no mention of Olympia or the Heraea.[21] By the first century AD female athletic competition was widespread under the Roman Empire but not in the Olympics.

Date and Extent of the Heraea

We should reconsider the antiquity and authenticity of the Heraea as an athletic contest. Some feel that the races in some form had a long, early history, possibly as old as the Olympics or older. Pausanias (5.16.4) says that the races are credited to "ancient times," but the myth that Hippodameia established the race out of gratitude to Hera for her marriage is a fabricated *aition* ("cause" or reason) pointing to a local initiation rite.[22] The story that the Sixteen Women made peace between Elis and Pisa may suggest that the Heraea began (or was reorganized) in the 580s,[23] but how Panhellenic was it?

Spartan Girls at the Heraea?

Assuming an early and Panhellenic Heraea and early Spartan girls' sport, some suggest that, because of proximity and economy of travel, most runners and winners in the Heraea were Spartan girls.[24] Cultic or initiatory parallels can be cited, but the hard evidence is limited and questionable. One statuette is often taken as a dedication by a Spartan Heraean victor.[25] Only this statuette has the exact short Heraean costume as described by Pausanias (with the right breast bare).[26] This small piece is of Laconian craftsmanship, but it is not inscribed, and it was found not at Olympia or Sparta but in the area of ancient Epirus. Did it belong to a Spartan victor, or was it designed for sale at the Heraea, or neither? Moreover, some interpret this figure, with her head turned backwards, as a dancer, not a runner, with an open stance for its attachment to a larger vessel.[27] She may be a dancer and a decoration, not a runner and a dedication.

Prizes and Evidence

If numerous Spartan and other Greek girls won the Heraea over several centuries, why do we not read about the Heraea until Pausanias? Why do we not have the name of one historical virgin victor? The only victor known by name is the mythical Chloris, granddaughter of Zeus and niece of Pelops (Paus. 5.16.4). The Vatican "Atalanta," a sculpture of a running girl, may be a copy of an original Greek victor statue of ca. 460 BC, but the dating is much debated. By its costume and palm, it refers to victory in the Heraea.[28] If the Vatican runner is Chloris, however, we still lack even a copy of a mortal's victor statue.

Despite speculations about Panhellenic participation, the sprint at the Heraea began as, and remained, a race of passage, a transitional rite for local Elean girls. It developed over time into a limited reflection of the male games, but the runners were not nude, and there were no trainers, other events, or known victors. There is simply too little evidence for major Heraean games with girls coming from afar.[29]

Women at the Male Olympics?

Were the Ancient Olympics completely a "men's club"? Females, young and mature, apparently could watch athletics at Delos, Athens, and possibly Cyrene,[30] but Olympia retained its old and sacral ban on women (*gynaikes*).[31] Pausanias (5.6.7) writes:

> As you go from Scillus along the road to Olympia, before you cross the Alpheus, there is a mountain with high, precipitous cliffs. It is called Mount Typaeum. It is a law of Elis to cast down it any women who are caught present at the Olympic games, or even on the other side of the Alpheus, on the days prohibited to women. (Loeb ed.)
>
> [κατὰ τούτου τὰς γυναῖκας Ἡλείοις ἐστιν ὠθεῖν νόμος, ἢν σωραθῶσιν ἐς τὸν ἀγῶνα ἐλθοῦσαι τὸν Ὀλυμπικὸν ἢ καὶ ὅλως ἐν ταῖς ἀπειρημέναις σφίσιν ἡμέραις διαβᾶσαι τὸν Ἀλφειόν.]

Topographically, the reference to crossing the Alpheus in Book Five was the appropriate place to clarify any exceptions to the ban on women (the Priestess of Demeter and the virgins discussed below), but Pausanias mentions only a certain mother who supposedly defied the ban.

A Mother Invades the Games?

Pausanias goes on to say (5.6.7–8) that the only woman who watched the Olympics was Callipateira (or Pherenice), from the famous athletic family of Diagoras of Rhodes.[32]

> However, they say that no woman has been caught, except Callipateira only; some, however, give the lady the name Pherenice and not Callipateira. She, being a widow, disguised herself exactly like a gymnastic trainer (ἄνδρι γυμναστῇ), and brought her son to compete at Olympia. Peisirodos, for so her son was called, was victorious, and Callipateira, as she was jumping over the enclosure in which they keep the trainers shut up, bared her person (ἐγυμνώθη). So her sex was discovered, but they let her go unpunished out of respect for her father, her brothers and her son, all of whom had been victorious at Olympia. But a law was passed that for the future trainers should strip before entering the arena. (Loeb ed.)

Some dismiss this story as an apocryphal etiology, but still retell it. Some accept it, perhaps due to the firm historicity of the family;[33] however, the motifs of forbidden access, transvestite disguise, titillating disclosure, and miraculous reprieve sound like some *logos* from Herodotus. Perhaps Pausanias just passed on a local explanation for the nudity of trainers, but it is likely more a matter of confusion than credulity. For example, Pausanias first calls the woman Callipateira ("well fathered"), but he admits that "some" call her Pherenice ("bearer of victory"). In another passage (6.7.2), Pausanias retells the basic points: a mother, disguising herself as a male trainer, took her son to the Olympic Games; however, he then presents Callipateira as the mother of Eucles rather than Peisirodos, whose invasive mother he leaves nameless.[34] Like most later sources, let's call the invasive mother Pherenice.

A scholiast on Pindar (*Ol.* 7) simply says that a daughter of Diagoras, whom he calls Callipateira, "was prevented from spectating at the Olympic Games because she was a woman."[35] If this is correct, she perhaps tried but she was turned away from Olympia. In his version, like that of Pausanias, Aelian (*VH* 10.1) has the mother bring the boy to compete, and, like the scholiast, he suggests that she showed up and was denied access. Then, however, he becomes creative:

> Pherenice brought her son to the Olympic festival to compete. The presiding officials refused to admit her as a spectator (κωλυόντων δὲ αὐτὴν τῶν ἑλλανοδικῶν τὸν ἀγῶνα θεάσασθαι), but she spoke in public (παρελοῦσα) and justified her request by pointing out that her father and three brothers were Olympic victors, and she was bringing a son who was a competitor. She won over the assembly (τὸν δῆμον), the law excluding women was abolished [lifted temporarily], and she attended the Olympic festival (τὸν εἴργοντα νόμον τῆς θέας τὰς γυναῖκας, καὶ ἐθεάσατο Ὀλύμπια). (Loeb ed.)

Aelian's idea that she appealed and won a dispensation is likely taken from a nearby passage in Pausanias (5.6.6, just before noting the ban at 5.6.7), saying that Xenophon had requested and won a dispensation from the Olympic council to be allowed to keep his estate at Scillus.[36] Aelian grafts that reprieve onto the mother, and he has her excused from the ban instead of from punishment.

The latest source, Philostratus (ca. AD 230, *Gym.* 17, trans. Sweet) expands even further on Pausanias:

> The Eleans say ... that there was a woman from the island of Rhodes named Pherenike, daughter of the boxer Diagoras; her physical appearance was

such that the Eleans at first thought she was a man. At Olympia she wrapped herself in her cloak and trained her son Peisidoros [ὥς δὲ Ἠλεῖοί φασι, Φερενίκη ἡ Ῥοδία ἐγένετο Διαγόρου θυγάτηρ τοῦ πύκτου, καὶ τὸ εἶδος ἡ Φερενίκη οὕτω τοι ἔρρωτο, ὡς Ἠλείοις τὰ πρῶτα ἀνὴρ δόξαι. εἴλητο γοῦν ὑπὸ τρίβωνι ἐν Ὀλυμπίᾳ καὶ Πεισίδωρον τὸν ἑαυτῆς υἱὸν ἐγύμνασε], who was a skilled boxer, the equal of his grandfather. When the Eleans learned about the trick, they hesitated to execute Pherenike because of their admiration for Diagoras and his children, since the members of Pherenike's family were all Olympic victors, but they passed a law that the gymnastes must take off his clothes and submit to a physical examination [ἐπεὶ δὲ ξυνῆκαν τῆς ἀπάτης, ἀποκτεῖναι μὲν τὴν Φερενίκην ὤκνησαν ἐνθυμηθέντες τὸν Διαγόραν καὶ τοὺς Διαγόρου παῖδας – ὁ γὰρ Φερενίκης οἶκος ὀλυμπιονῖκαι πάντες –, νόμος δὲ ἐγράφη τὸν γυμναστὴν ἀποδύεσθαι καὶ μηδὲ τοῦτον ἀνέλεγκτον αὐτοῖς εἶναι].

Speculating, to add credibility to the story, that the mother looked somewhat masculine, Philostratus says that Pherenice wore a trainer's cloak and trained her son herself at Olympia. In gender-segregated Greece, being from a family of athletes did not mean that Pherenice could train her son. Pindar (*Ol.* 8.54–8) says that the trainer Melesias taught from personal experience, and (8.59–64) that someone without experience does not give good advice. Also, athletes had to spend a month before the Games at Elis, and Pherenice could not have remained disguised that long.[37]

Philostratus may have borrowed from his own story of the young *pankratiast* Mandrogenes of Magnesia, who said he owed his *pankration* win to his trainer (*Gym.* 23, trans. Sweet): "after his father's death the household had come under the control of his mother, who was not only wellborn but had virtues of a man as well." That well-born widow with manly virtues, however, hired a trainer and stayed at home while her son competed. Even if widowed, would Pherenice have brought her son herself? Why not send one of her Olympic victor brothers? Her brother Dorieus was still alive and was probably at the games of 404, when Diagoras' two grandsons competed. Dorieus could have trained and registered both boys.[38] It seems likely, then, that Pherenice's supposed training of her son is Philostratus' embellishment of Pausanias' idea that she disguised herself as a trainer.

No Punishment?

Apprehended, Pherenice justifiably deserved punishment. The judges could have used the death penalty, or at least a fine, exclusion, or flogging. In 420 they had flogged Lichas, a mature man from a family of victors, when he was caught defying a ban on Sparta by sneaking into Olympia,[39] yet they apparently did not punish this guilty woman at all. It seems that the key to Pausanias' story of the mother's narrow escape lies in his account (6.7.4–5, two sections after 6.7.2 on Pherenice) of how Dorieus was captured fighting against Athens at sea and brought to Athens in 407. The Athenians were furious and threatening, but in the assembly they were so impressed with his physique and so respectful of his fame that they released him without the slightest punishment, even though severe punishment was justified.[40] Pausanias confuses these two stories of siblings.

Simply put, the mother was not exposed or killed because she was not at the Games. Etiological ingenuity syncretized a change of Olympic regulations with a storied athletic clan. The tale of Pherenice grew taller over the centuries. Her disguise and exposure stem from her gender, and her release at Olympia is borrowed from her brother's release at Athens. Dorieus' experience at Athens is well substantiated; Pherenice's visit to the Olympics just seems fabulous.

Virgin Olympic Spectators?

Were there immature female spectators at the Olympics? Pausanias, discussing the stadium at Olympia in Book Six (6.20.8–9), mentions the Priestess of Demeter Chamyne: "Opposite the umpires is an altar of white marble; seated on this altar a woman looks on (θεᾶται γυνὴ) at the Olympic games, the Priestess of Demeter Chamyne ['of the earth'], which office the Eleans bestow from time to time on different women (τιμὴν ταύτην ἄλλοτε ἄλλην)" (Loeb ed.). Scholars feel that Demeter's cult area preceded the stadium of Zeus, and so her priestess could attend.[41] Pausanias then adds (6.20.9) that "they do not prevent maidens from watching" (παρθένους δὲ οὐκ εἴργουσι θεᾶσθαι). Earlier (5.6.7), he noted the ban on women but made no reference to girls, and here he does not mention the ban on women but notes that a mature priestess watches and maidens are not excluded. This apparent inconsistency may be due to a problem with the text, or a slip by Pausanias, but most now defend the text and Pausanias.[42] Two questions arise: why would virgins not be excluded, and, if not excluded, did virgins actually attend the male Games?

Virgins and Cults of Zeus at Olympia

According to the initiation model and its element of seclusion, rites for one sex should include a ban on the other sex at Olympia; perhaps, however, maidens were seen as "asexual" or "pre-sexual."[43] Yet Pausanias calls them *parthenoi,* which indicates their sex, rather than the generic *paides.* Also, if maidens were sexless, why were they excluded, along with women, from other places at Olympia? Pausanias (5.13.10) says that maidens and "likewise (ὡσαύτως)" women, "when they are not shut out from Olympia (ἐπειδὰν τῆς Ὀλυμπίας μὴ ἐξείργωνται)," are permitted to climb the lower level (*prothysis*) of the ash altar of Zeus, but "men only" are allowed at the higher level.[44] Just a few sections before discussing the stadium and maidens (6.20.8–9), Pausanias (6.20.2–6) also mentions the sanctuary (between the Treasuries and the Hill of Cronus) of Eileithyia, a goddess of childbirth, within which Sosipolis, a local Elean god, was worshipped. Except for one old, devout priestess, neither women nor girls were allowed into the shrine of Sosipolis, a form of Zeus as an infant.[45] In both these situations, virgins were thought to be sexual enough to be banned along with women. Only men—not women or virgins—could go to the top of the Altar of Zeus. In the cult of Sosipolis or the infant Zeus, only one priestess could enter the inner sanctum, not women or virgins. At the Olympic Games of Zeus, only a priestess of Demeter might watch; women could not enter, but could virgins watch? Consistency based on these situations would suggest that virgins could not watch. Yet we resist the notion of the ancient Olympics (with one exception) as an all-male gathering.

Could Pausanias have been confused? In his day, female sport and spectatorship were far more public. Under Rome, maidens raced in the Capitoline Games (Suet. *Dom.* 4.4; Dio 67.8.1), women and Vestal Virgins attended the circus and amphitheatre (Suet. *Aug.* 44.3), and Vestals attended athletic contests (Suet. *Ner.* 12.4).[46] Did Pausanias accept stories about females from the perspective of his own Second Sophistic age, as we want to accept them from our own age of increased familiarity with female athletics at all levels?

Virgin Viewers?

The assumption that virgins watched the Olympic Games in order to meet possible husbands has been canonized by no less than the *Oxford Classical Dictionary.*[47] Following Stephen Instone's 1990 article on the erotic overtones of athletics in Pindar,[48] works now suggest that fathers brought eligible maidens to the male Olympics seeking marriage arrangements, that girls were allowed to watch the Games to meet possible future husbands, prepare for marriage, and learn about the male world, and that the Panhellenic Heraea and Olympics were held close together in time, making it convenient for fathers and daughters (or whole families) to attend the Heraea, and then the Olympics (mothers supposedly camped out nearby and waited during the male Games).[49] We simply do not know, however, when the Heraea was held,[50] and the one-cow sacrifice does not suggest a Panhellenic feast.[51] Women's rites were usually held in seclusion, not on a Panhellenic stage. Rather, like other female-only local festivals, the Heraea was probably separate and segregated in time and attendance.

Nevertheless, did virgins attend the male Olympics as spectators? If virgin spectators were at Olympia, why did Pindar not mention them at a crown game? Did someone check the age and condition of young girls entering the site? Placing virgins with their fathers at the Olympics seems culturally incongruous. Fathers arranged marriages for their daughters, but bringing the girls to the men at Olympia reverses the pattern in Greek suitor contests. If fathers wanted girls to see athletes, the gymnasium at home was more convenient; athletic fields (beyond Sparta) were male turf.[52] Male nudity at Olympia was erotic but not eugenic. As the myth of Zeus and Ganymede suggests, athletic eros at Olympia was male and pederastic.[53] If moved by Eros, mature males, not young girls, went to watch nude young men.

For a father to take his girl with him to Olympia would make him a laughingstock and inhibit his social life. Greek fathers, moreover, worried about sexual abuse of children—male or female—and the "Olympic Village" was a tent town with only limited security. Any father with a young girl in the midst of tens of thousands of males would have been anxious about the safety of her purity, something essential to beneficial marriage prospects. So even if virgins, in general, were not banned from the male games, realistically, they were not there. Their spectatorship is a modern "invented tradition." Sources on crown games mention slaves, sophists, magicians, horses, and dogs, but only Pausanias mentions the possibility of virgins. Why?

A Possible Solution

A simpler solution, returning to and preserving Pausanias' text (6.20.9), is suggested by his verb θεάομαι, used of both the priestess and the virgins. We have been looking for virgins and overlooking "the looking." At the Olympian Games at Ephesus, in imitation of the original Olympics, a Priestess of Demeter was selected, not for life, but "from time to time" to sit on the altar and "watch" the rites.[54] She was not there as a fan to "see" the Games but, as an honorific privilege, to assist in the ritual by watching and witnessing "the Olympia." Note that Pausanias' comment on virgins comes in a passage about officials and special seats, the *Hellanodikai* and one priestess on one altar, and it follows clarifications of when women and virgins are allowed at Olympia. Pausanias adds that virgins are not excluded from "watching." If this means that a virgin daughter, or a virgin unmarried woman, could sit in as (or with, like Persephone) the Priestess of Demeter for the festival, the numerous virgin viewers vanish.

Cynisca and Olympic Victory

Cynisca of Sparta was the first woman to win an Olympic victory, the four-horse chariot race in both 396 and 392 BC.[55] Her victory epigram on an inscribed base at Olympia is also in the *Palatine Anthology*, 13.16:[56]

> Kings of Sparta were my fathers and brothers, and I, Cynisca, winning the race with my chariot of swift-footed horses, erected this statue. I assert that I am the only woman in all Greece who won this crown. (Loeb ed.)
>
> [Σπάρτας μὲν βασιλῆες ἐμοὶ πατέρες καὶ ἀδελφοί·
> ἅρμασι δ'ὠκυπόδων ἵππων νικῶσα Κυνίσκα
> εἰκόνα τάνδ' ἔστησα· μόναν δέ με φαμι γυναικῶν
> Ἑλλάδος ἐκ πάσας τόνδε λαβεῖν στέφανον]

This sounds assertive, and Pausanias says that Cynisca was ambitious to win at Olympia, but Xenophon and Plutarch say that her brother Agesilaus pressured her to compete. Was the victory engendered by the princess or engineered by the king? Was she a proud pioneer or a political pawn? Sarah Pomeroy calls Cynisca "the first female star in Greek athletics," "an expert in equestrian matters" with a "single-minded devotion to racing," "champing at the bit" to compete at Olympia.[57]

Was Cynisca truly a wealthy, competitive woman acting on her own? We know little about her beyond her wins and dedications at Olympia. She was the daughter of King Archidamus, and probably half-sister to Agis and full sister to Agesilaus.[58] Her name, "puppy" or "little hound," came from her grandfather, and probably referred to hunting as a pastime of elite Spartans.[59] She perhaps went through Sparta's female physical education system, perhaps hunted, and perhaps drove a (two-horse) chariot in the *Hyacinthia* as a girl, but these are all speculations.[60] A dedication to Helen at Sparta (*IG* V 1.235) bore her name, and Pausanias (3.15.1) saw a hero shrine for her by the Platanistas, but we should not extrapolate too much from the limited details. We are not certain when she was born or died, but she was at least 40 to 50 years old in 396—no longer a young princess.[61] We do not know if she was a wife or mother.[62] Since she probably inherited part of the estate of Archidamus in 427, and owners did not have to be present at Olympia to be declared victors, she certainly could have owned and entered a chariot team.[63] But did she act outside Sparta without consulting male relatives? Let's review the evidence.

The Sources

Cynisca's epigram sounds proud,[64] but that seemingly rock-solid evidence was probably composed by a male. Pausanias (3.8.2) suggests that it was written "by some man or other" (ὅστις δή). At best, the epigram was commissioned with instructions by Cynisca, or by her brother.[65] As well, the poem's features are formulaic. Similar claims to be the "first," the "one," or "only" person to do something are found in inscriptions claiming record-setting victories by many athletes. Cynisca set what David Young calls a "gender record," but her motives are not stated.[66]

The earliest prose source on Cynisca is Xenophon (*Ages.* 9.6). He perhaps knew her, but he says that Agesilaus initiated his sister's pursuit of Olympic victory: Agesilaus "persuaded his sister Cynisca to breed chariot horses, and showed by her victory that such a stud marks the owner as a person of wealth, but not necessarily of merit" (Loeb ed.). [Κυνίσκαν δὲ ἀδελφὴν οὖσαν πεῖσαι ἁρματοτροφεῖν καὶ ἐπιδεῖξαι νικώσης αὐτῆς, ὅτι τὸ θρέμμα τοῦτο οὐκ ἀνδραγαθίας, ἀλλὰ πλούτου ἐπίδειγμά ἐστι.]

Centuries later, Plutarch (*Ages.* 20.1, repeated in the *Spartan Sayings, Agesilaus* 49 (*Apoph. Lac.* 212B)) wrote:

> However, on seeing that some of the citizens (ἐνίους τῶν πολιτῶν) esteemed themselves highly and were greatly lifted up because they bred racing horses, Agesilaus persuaded (ἔπεισε) his sister Cynisca to enter a chariot in the contests at Olympia, wishing to shew the Greeks (Ἕλλησιν) that the victory there was not a mark of any great excellence, but simply of wealth and lavish outlay (ἀλλὰ πλούτου καὶ δαπάνης). (Loeb ed.)

Note Plutarch's suggestion that, while inspired by arrogant Spartan horse breeders, Agesilaus wanted to send a message "to the Greeks"—not just to the Spartans.

The latest source on Cynisca is Pausanias (3.8.1), who omits Agesilaus' role:[67] "[Cynisca]...was exceedingly ambitious to succeed at the Olympic games, and was the first woman to breed horses and the first to win an Olympic victory" (Loeb ed.). [φιλοτιμότατα δὲ ἐς τὸν ἀγῶνα ἔσχε τὸν Ὀλυμπικὸν καὶ πρώτη τε ἱπποτρόφησε γυναικῶν καὶ νίκην ἀνείλετο Ὀλυμπικὴν πρώτη.] Pausanias saw Cynisca's monuments and inscriptions,[68] but, again, he wrote from the perspective of an age familiar with greater opportunities for females in sport, and with wealthy, assertive Hellenistic queens and Roman empresses. The sources for Cynisca grew with time, and male authors credited motives to her. Plutarch followed Xenophon's near contemporary comments, but Pausanias elaborated upon the epigram's few words. A woman pressured by her brother to win at Olympia became more and more independent, ambitious, and admirable.

Politics and Chariots

Let's turn to the historical context. Cynisca's competition in 396 came at the end of decades of mounting tension between Sparta and Elis and Athens. Pausanias remarks (6.2.1) that Spartans became the most enthusiastic breeders of horses among the Greeks after the Persian invasion. Spartans won the chariot race in seven out of eight Olympiads from 448 to 420. Famous for horse breeding, and growing politically closer to Athens, Elis may have resented Sparta's success.[69] In 420, Cynisca's older brother, Agis, was king when Elis joined Athens in an anti-Spartan alliance (Thuc. 5.47; Xen. *Hell.* 3.2.21), terms of which were to be inscribed on a pillar at Olympia; Elis then fined and banned Sparta from the Olympics of 420 (Thuc. 5.49–50). As mentioned, despite the ban, the Spartan Lichas entered his chariot in 420, misrepresenting it as from Thebes. When the team won, Lichas revealed his improper presence and was flogged.[70] Sparta's anger about the ban and the insult to Lichas was deep and lasting.

Alcibiades and Sparta

Enter Alcibiades, a war hawk eager to undermine the Peace of Nicias. In the 420s he married Hipparete of the rich, horsey family of Callias II (Plut. *vit. Alc.* 8.1–3). At the Olympics of 416, Alcibiades entered more chariots and won more placements than ever before. His victory ode applauded his record, "which no other Greek has had," a triumph won "without labor" (ἀπονητὶ).[71] Advocating the Sicilian Expedition in 415, Alcibiades made a self-serving appeal to his Olympic fame, won through conspicuous expenditure.[72] Soon he deserted and headed to Sparta.

Already jealous of Alcibiades' popularity, Agis was personally offended by Alcibiades' rumoured seduction and impregnation of his wife, Timaea, who supposedly referred to her baby son Leotychidas in private as "Alcibiades."[73] Forced to leave, Alcibiades went to Persia, but he returned to Athens after 411 to bedevil Sparta's naval efforts. Hating him and fearing that Athens' hopes would persist as long as he lived, Agis probably arranged his murder in 404. He was not to come back again to rally Athens, but Sparta still had to purge the memory, the record, of the man. Then, in the Elean War of ca. 402–400, Agis led campaigns ravaging the Elean countryside, even fighting at Olympia, and forcing Elis to surrender.[74] In 400 Agis died, and Agesilaus' succession was controversial.[75]

Agesilaus and Cynisca

Short, and lame from birth, Agesilaus countered an ominous oracle, that a lame king would bring troubles, by charging that his rival Leotychidas was Alcibiades' bastard son.[76] As king, Agesilaus inherited Sparta's enmity against Elis and Athens, and the family's resentful memories of Alcibiades, who was gone but not forgotten. At Athens in 399, the trial of Socrates raised the issue of state rewards for wealthy equestrian victors (Pl. *Ap.* 36d-e). In 397, Isocrates' court speech (*Biga* 16.33) repeated Alcibiades' bragging about his victories. Alcibiades was still making headlines. How could Agesilaus' royal family get even with a dead man and exorcise his glorious ghost? Olympia, the site of Alcibiades' display, offered a Panhellenic stage for upstaging Alcibiades.

Agesilaus never considered competing at Olympia himself. He would not publicly condone chariot racing; just winning would not be enough, and losing would be too embarrassing. Why not have Cynisca compete? If she lost, it was just a woman losing. If she won, declaring Cynisca the "only" woman winner in all Greece would make a mockery of Alcibiades' claim to excellence. But where did Agesilaus get the idea of using a female competitor in a male sporting domain?

Agesilaus knew his Homer. Before sailing to Asia Minor in 396, he imitated Agamemnon by attempting to sacrifice at Aulis.[77] At Ephesus, when Agesilaus allowed rich men to provide cavalry horses to get out of military service, he said that he was following Agamemnon's example.[78] As he knew, in the chariot race in *Iliad* 23.295, Menelaus' team included the mare Aithe, a mare "eager to race." She had been given by a rich draft dodger (Echepolus) to Agamemnon, who in turn lent her to Menelaus. During the race, Antilochus threatened his male team lest they lose to a team of mares (*Il.* 23.407–9). What shame that would bring! Chariots and gender insults—a great idea. Centuries later, the mare Aithe, eager to compete and driven by the cuckolded Spartan king Menelaus, was revivified as the princess "Puppy," eager to race and driven to compete by Agesilaus, the brother of a cuckolded Spartan king.

Yes, Cynisca was an Olympic victor, but Agesilaus used his sister to show that Olympic chariot victories were won by wealth and not by manly excellence. Cynisca's victory was a vehicle for vengeance—an insult to the family via a female was avenged via a female, but it was male shame and honour at stake. To discredit Alcibiades, Agesilaus emasculated the Olympic chariot race. Cynisca, pushed by her brother, skirted the rules of the Olympic men's club and won, but she still could not attend the Olympics.

Conclusion

If the evidence and cases are problematic,[79] why are we still eager to find strong, competitive females at Olympia? If the ancient Olympics and the Heraea can be moved together in time, if virgins both ran and watched, then Olympia becomes more gender inclusive. Virgin runners and spectators would authenticate the Heraea as truly athletic, and modernize and liberalize the ancient Olympics. As well, we want to believe in Pherenice and Cynisca as resourceful heroines who would not be excluded or denied. Unfortunately, it is all too good to be true.

It is anachronistic to denounce or obscure the sexism of the ancient Games, but we can applaud the modern Games for accepting female sport, albeit slowly, and for surpassing the gender bias in the ancient paradigm. We should rejoice that female athletics have become, and will remain, a crucial and progressive component in the modern Olympics and in modern women's history. In the modern sense, that's fabulous.

Notes

1 Unless otherwise indicated, all dates are BC. Abbreviations follow the *Oxford Classical Dictionary*[3], and translations are from the Loeb Classical Library: Aelian, by A.F. Scholfield; *The Greek Anthology*, by W.R. Paton; Pausanias, by W.H.S. Jones and H.A. Ormerod; Pindar, by W. H. Race; Plutarch, by B. Perrin; Suetonius, by J.C. Rolfe; and Xenophon, by E.C. Marchant.

2 Daniels and Tedder 2000; Simri 1980.

3 Scanlon 2002 (including modified versions of earlier articles) and Dillon 2000 (an expanded version of his 1997 *Pilgrims and Pilgrimage in Ancient Greece* (London: Routledge), 194–96, and summarized in his 2002 *Girls and Women in Classical Religion* (London: Routledge), 130–31) offer recent and thorough discussions of female sport in Greece. See also Miller 2004a, 150–59, Golden 1998, 123–40; Frass 1997; Mantas 1995; Guttmann 1991; Arrigoni 1985; Lee 1984, 1988; Spears 1984; and Harris 1966.

4 Lämmer (1981) challenged attempts by proponents of modern women's sport to discover ancient Greek precursors and justifications for modern trends. He concludes that modern interest has led us to make too much of the sporting activities of Greek females, and that classical models have had very little to do with the progress of modern women's sport.

5 See Scanlon 2002, chap. 7, "Atalanta and Athletic Myths of Gender," 175–98. Myths of Atalanta, by contrast and outcome, ultimately reinforced social norms of athletic and erotic behaviour. See, similarly, Golden 1998, 134–37.

6 On Pausanias as a source in general, see Habicht 1985, especially 117–40.

7 Sinn 2000, 76–82. See Dillon 2002 on the important roles of females in Greek religion.

8 Scanlon (2002, chap. 4, "Racing for Hera—A Girls' Contest at Olympia," 98–120) argues that the original significance of the event, with its distinctive costume, clearly had more to do with initiation rites and prenuptial transitions than with mainstream athletics.

9 Serwint 1993. Wearing a costume of the opposite sex, the girls entered a sexually neutral state, experiencing "the other," before advancing towards readiness for marriage and female adulthood. Des Bouvrie (1995) presents Olympia as a liminal place where Greeks reinvigorated their social order and sacred truths through "gender elaborations" and "symbolic structuring."

10 Pausanias 5.16.3; Frazer 1965, 3:593. Scanlon (2002, 110) points to niches in temple columns "which probably held the paintings of victors," but he admits that there are no parallels for males or for females elsewhere.

11 Pausanias does not give the ages of the classes, so we cannot confirm any analogy to age classes of Spartan boys, female choruses, or athletic festivals (e.g., Isthmia, Athens). The Sixteen Women also organized choral performances for Hippodameia and for Physkoa, who was raped by Dionysus; see Calame 1997, 242–44, and Ingalls 2000, 15–16. These choruses were probably performed in the city of Elis as marriageable girls were presented to the community, in contrast with the secluded phase of initiation at Olympia.

12 On Spartan athletic competition overall, now see Hodkinson 1999. On women (150–51) he comments (151): "Participation may have involved only unmarried girls and not married women....It was therefore only a circumscribed version of agonistic activity...Spartan practice...appears unique in the incorporation of girls' athletic competition...as a regular part of their upbringing, in its extension to all girls of citizen households, and in the public character of the activity, practiced not in rural sanctuaries like Olympia and Brauron but in the very centre of the Spartan polis."

13 See Millender 1999.

14 On the Dionysiades and Spartan girls' races and choruses, see Dillon 2000, 466; 2002, 211–15. On this type of event as probably a prenuptial rite, see Serwint 1993, 418, and Scanlon 2002, 104–105, 134–35, 287–90. Constantinidou (1998, 22) notes the Dionysiades but concludes that the cult of Dionysus was a minor one at Sparta.

15 For an art historical perspective, see Stewart (1997, 108–18 and Appendix A), who disagrees with Scanlon's treatment (2002, 127–38, based on an earlier article) of the Spartan bronzes.

16 See Calame (1997, 191–202) on races and choruses in Sparta. Ingalls (2000, 3–12) discusses the effectiveness of choral training for educating girls about the power of their sexuality, the need for marriage, and their role in Spartan society.

17 Pomeroy (2002, 12–27) discusses exercises and contests, possible age classes or herds, and possible military aspects and value. Pomeroy, 12: "There is more evidence, both textual and archaeological, for athletics than for any other aspect of Spartan women's lives....Spartan women's intense involvement in such activities was probably unique in the Greek world." However, Ferrari (2002, 164–66) points out that nude female exercise at Sparta was a temporary privilege and only for young citizen females, who were not segregated or taken from their homes, who were not organized in age groups like the boys, and whose form of *pederastia* ended with marriage.

18 On Spartan girls' physical training, nudity, contests, and processions, see Scanlon 2002, chap. 5, "'Only We Produce Men'—Spartan Female Athletics and Eugenics," 121–38. He discusses female exercises and homoerotic pederasty with parallels to male experiences, but concludes that the purposes of most of the activities were eugenic, initiatory, prenuptial, and erotic. He admits (121) that the Spartan system was "strikingly anomalous," but he later suggests (135) that Sparta perhaps influenced the Heraea at Olympia and other states.

19 Scanlon 2002, chap. 6, "Race or Chase of 'the Bears' at Brauron," 139–74; Sourvinou-
    Inwood 1988, 15–105; Lonsdale 1993, 171–93; Dillon 2002, 19–23, 93–95, 220–21.
20 Ferrari (2002), especially chap. 7, "Fugitive Nudes," 162–78, argues that vases show how
    females were imagined, not how they actually were. She rejects the popular notion of
    women's initiations: unlike males, women did not go through procedures that brought
    about womanhood.
21 See Lee 1984, 1988c; Mantas 1995; Frass 1997; and examples collected in Moretti
    1953, 168–69. Inscription at Delphi of ca. AD 47: SEG^3 802; Moretti 1953, 165–69,
    no. 63, by a father for three daughters, all of whom won *stadion* races "first of the vir-
    gins" (as well as other events, such as the chariot race in armor and cithara singing). Dil-
    lon (2000, 462) notes the lack of reference to the Heraea or Olympia. Scanlon (2002,
    23–24) concludes: "Only later under the Roman Empire, in the first century AD, is there
    any evidence of young women personally competing in traditionally men's athletic fes-
    tivals in such contests as chariot racing or footraces. But even here girls probably com-
    peted only against other girls."
22 Harris (1966, 179–80) is suspicious of the antiquity and the *aition* of the Heraea. Läm-
    mer (1981, 19) feels that races at the Heraea were "not genuine contests with foreign
    or even Panhellenic participation, they were merely a traditional cultic ceremony for local
    girls." He suggests that it was not until Roman times that the ceremony took on a
    "superficial" parallelism (e.g., wreaths, judges) to the men's contests.
23 Scanlon (2002, 113–16, 120), favouring an early ritual under Spartan influence with ear-
    lier influences back to Crete, feels that an early initiatory cult with races for local girls
    was reorganized on a Panhellenic basis around 580, if not earlier.
24 Pomeroy (2002, 24–27), on female Spartan competitions, suggests (26) that "at least when
    the political relationship between Sparta and Elis was favorable, the girls who raced at
    the Heraea were mostly Spartans."
25 British Museum Bronzes no. 208; Scanlon 2002, fig. 4-1.
26 Scanlon (2002, 101–106, figs. 4.1–4) offers four statuettes (Brit. Mus. 208, Ath. Nat.
    Mus. Carpanos Coll. 24, Sparta Mus. 3305, and Palermo Nat. Mus. no. 8265 (42), all
    probably attachments to bronze vessels)—as well as the Vatican "Atalanta" statue—as con-
    necting Sparta and the Heraea. Hodkinson (1999, 150, n. 6 on 178), rejecting the
    Palermo example and adding Louvre 171, sees the figures as evidence of running within
    Sparta.
27 Constantinidou 1998, 24. Pomeroy (2002, 12–13, n. 97 on 25) admits that she may be
    a dancer.
28 Galleria dei Candelabri, Museo Pio-Clementino, Vatican, Inv. 2784. Some prefer a first
    century BC date, and some see a dancer and not a runner; Serwint (1993, 407–11, fig. 2)
    identifies the iconography as that of the Heraea. Stewart (1997, 33, 241) accepts her argu-
    ment and notes a parallel early Hellenistic sculpture in the Louvre, which wears the
    exomis but has both breasts bare.
29 Bernardini (1986–87, 17–26) finds examples of girls' runs significant for ritual or recre-
    ation, but she suggests that the Heraea retained the features of a local initiation rite
    and not a serious athletic contest. Cf. Pomeroy (2002, 24): "The women's race at the
    Heraea in Elis was the most prestigious, the equivalent of the Olympic competitions held
    for men."
30 Thucydides (3.104.3–4, citing the *Homeric Hymn to Apollo* 146–50), says the Ionians
    used to bring their wives and children to the festival of Apollo at Delos, which included
    athletic contests, just as they did in his day to the festival at Ephesus. Pindar (*Pyth.*
    9.97–103) says that girls and women, apparently as spectators, are enamoured of vic-
    tors in games at Cyrene: "When they saw you so often victorious as well in the seasonal
    festivals for Pallas, each of the maidens wished in silence that you, O Telesikrates, were
    her dearest husband or her son—also in the Olympic games and in those for deep-

bosomed Earth, and in all the local ones (καὶ πᾶσιν ἐπιχωρίοις)" (Loeb ed.). Instone (1990, 39) reads the text as favouring his argument for the pursuit of marriage ties at the games: "In the seasonal festivals of Pallas women saw you many times victorious... and in all the local ones." He prefers to suggest (39–42) that women and girls saw the victories of Telesicrates; but he admits (n. 28 on 41) that lines 97–103 "present complex problems." Scanlon (2002, 222–23) would interpret the references to Pallas and Olympian games as applying to the Panathenaic games at Athens and the great Olympic Games. Further on female spectators, see Scanlon 2002, 219–26; Dillon 2000, 457–59.

31   Originally the ban was perhaps tied to the seclusion of a male initiation rite or hero cult rite. Despite Aelian NA 5.17, it is unlikely that athletic sexual abstinence and the fear of lost ability through intercourse with women lay behind the ban. On the ban, gender-exclusive festivals, and associations of women with pollution, see Cole 1995.

32   Moretti 1957, 111–12, no. 356, "Peisi(r)rodos." On the family, see Paus. 6.7.1–7; Pind. Ol. 7; and references in Moretti (1957) by names (Diagoras, Acousilaos, Damagetus, Dorieus); see also Frazer (1965, 4:20, 25–29); Harris (1966, 123–24). Dorieus, the youngest son, won the Olympic pankration three times (432, 428, 424); see Moretti (1953, no. 23); Paus. 6.7.4. Two older brothers won at Olympia earlier and lifted Diagoras in celebration: Paus. 6.7.2–3; Pind. Pyth. 10.22; Plut. Vit. Pel. 34.4; Cic. Tusc. 1.46.111.

33   Dillon 2000, 459–60, at 460: "This is probably an aetiological myth explaining why the trainers were naked, but it was a credible story to Pausanias, Aelian and presumably others, underlining the prohibition on women attending the Olympic festival." Golden (1998, 108–9) says that Pherenice or Callipateira accompanied her son to Olympia. Later, at 132, he retells Pausanias' story, saying "she lived to have the tale told about her."

34   See Pausanias 6.7.2: "The sons too of the daughters of Diagoras practiced boxing and won Olympic victories: in the men's class Eucles [men's boxing 404], son of Callianax and Callipateira, daughter of Diagoras; in the boys' class Peisirodus [boys' boxing 404], whose mother dressed herself as a man and a trainer, and took her son herself to the Olympic games (ὃν ἡ μήτηρ ἀνδρὸς ἐπιθεμένη γυμναστοῦ σχῆμα ἐπὶ τῶν Ὀλυμπίων αὐτὴ τὸν ἀγῶνα ἤγαγεν)." On the confusion of the names, with Pherenice and Peisirodus as the main tradition, see Jüthner (1969, 228–30) and Frazer (1965, 3:482).

35   Hypoth. c. Pind. Ol. 7c (Drachmann 1.197); noted by Instone 1990, 32; Dillon 1997, 194; Frazer 1965, 3:482.

36   See Pausanias 5.6.6: "The guides (ἐξηγηταὶ) of Elis said the Eleans recovered Scillus again, and that Xenophon was tried by the Olympic Council (Ὀλυμπικῇ βουλῇ) for accepting the land from the Lacedaemonians, and, obtaining pardon (συγγνώμης) from the Eleans, dwelt securely in Scillus" (Loeb ed.).

37   Crowther 1991.

38   Pausanias (6.7.4) says that his name was proclaimed, with Peisirodus, as Thurian.

39   Thucydides 5.50; Xen. Hell. 3.2.2 (see below). Note the motifs of sneaking into Olympia despite prohibition, a family of victors, and exposure in excitement over victory. Still, Lichas was flogged. As Crowther and Frass (1998, 60) note: "No competitor or individual, whatever his rank or age, apparently was exempt from being whipped at Olympia."

40   Pausanias 6.7.4–6: "Before he was brought to them the Athenians were wroth with Dorieus and used threats against him; but when they met in the assembly and beheld a man so great and famous in the guise of a prisoner, their feelings towards him changed, and they let him go away without doing him any hurt, and that though they might with justice have punished him severely" (Loeb ed.). Similarly, Xenophon (Hell. 1.5.19) says the Athenians released him even without a ransom. He was later executed at Sparta (Paus. 6.7.6–7, with Androtion FGrH 342 F46).

41   Dillon 2000, 461–62. Sinn (2000, 74) logically suggests that the priestess had a special place in the stadium because this old vegetation cult had an earlier claim to the location.

Her cult area was disrupted by the development of the stadium, and the special altar-seat marked her earlier ownership. He further suggests that Demeter's tie to the earth may explain why the surface of the spectator area remained earth and never received stone seating. He adds that "it would not be unusual if the cult of Demeter/Chamyne had been reserved for unmarried girls, who had to undergo a sequence of initiation rites as preparation for their future role as wives and mothers." Pausanias (6.21.1–2) also mentions a sanctuary of Demeter Chamyne on the other side of the Hippodrome with a statue of her and Persephone, "the Maid."

42 Frazer (1965, 3:482) says that "maidens were free to view them [the games]." Stewart (1997, 34) notes that *parthenoi* were freely admitted." Harris (1966, 183), taking *parthenoi* as "unmarried women," sees the passage as corrupt, probably because "a scholiast's note referring to the girls' races has made its way into the text." On Nero's reference to the priestess as a precedent (Suet. *Ner.* 12.4), Harris points out that this "would have been meaningless if all virgins had been admitted at Olympia." Golden (1998, 132–33) does not see Pausanias as inconsistent because Paus. 5.6.7 refers to "women" and does not include girls. Dillon (2000, 457, 466–68) sees no need for emendation: there are no variant readings of the text, Pausanias is careful in his use of terms for females, and Nero's actions primarily concern females of status, who happen to be virgins.

43 As Stewart (1997, 11–12) notes, girls were *parthenoi* until the loss of their virginity as wives. *Parthenoi* were seen as asexual or presexual: "her sexuality—or lack of it—is socially constructed, in that she is officially a presexual being, defined by public knowledge of her virginity…she represents femininity in its unripe, unfinished form."

44 Pausanias 5.13.10. With "likewise" setting off "women" somewhat, the next clause is usually read as applying only to women. See, e.g., Golden 1998, 132–33: "This passage establishes that *gunaikes* make up a set separate from girls and suggests that it is their presence which is remarkable." One might, however, see some ambiguity about whether "when not excluded" applies to women only, or to women and virgins.

45 See Pausanias 6.20.2: "The old woman who tends Sosipolis herself too by an Elean custom lives in chastity (ἁγιστεύει "lives piously" or "performs sacred rites"), bringing water for the god's bath and setting before him barley cakes kneaded with honey"(Loeb ed.). See Dillon (2002, 75–78) on the marital status and sexual abstinence of various priestesses, and (230–31) on the cult of Eileithyia. On Sosipolis, see Robert 1893; Frazer 1965, 4:75–76.

46 Suetonius *Ner.* 12.4: "He invited the Vestal virgins also to witness the contests of the athletes, because at Olympia the priestesses of Ceres were allowed the same privilege" (Loeb ed.). The invitation of the Vestal Virgins, not just the priestess of Vesta, may be Nero's misunderstanding, or he knew what specific virgins might watch at Olympia. See below.

47 See Instone 1996, 207: virgin girls were allowed to watch, "a custom perhaps derived from a conception of the games as an occasion for girls to meet future husbands."

48 Instone (1990) argues persuasively that Pindar emphasized the beauty of athletes, their desirability in both homosexual and heterosexual terms, to enhance their status with women and increase their chances for advantageous marriages. However, he conjectures too much (32) from one Pindaric reference to an athlete's homecoming and a non-crown game situation (i.e., Cyrene) in *Pyth.* 9: "in the context of sexual and marital references in Pindar's odes it is necessary to bear in mind that a large festival would have provided an excellent opportunity for marriages to be arranged by fathers, and was one of the better opportunities women had for meeting men. Unfortunately no specific details known to me survive about this fringe-part of the Olympic Games…, but it is not improbable that fathers with eligible daughters would have attended the athletics festivals in the hope of arranging a marriage with a young man of good background and

outstanding physical ability." He admits (33): "Pindar mentions the unmarried female spectators in *Pythian Nine* (98–10), though it is not clear at which games he says they were spectating, who wished that the victor could be their husband or son." Instone (33) feels that Achilles Tatius 1.18 suggests that males at Olympia sent love gifts to girls via the Alpheus, but the passage refers to a supposed direct connection (Plin. *HN* 31.55) between the Alpheus and the fountain of Arethusa in Syracuse. The Alpheus is said to carry the gifts from males at Olympia directly to their beloveds, but the girls are not at Elis.

49 Scanlon (2002, 117–18, 287) speculates that the Heraea, for practical reasons, took place just prior to the men's games, that the Heraea may have been open to male and female spectators, that non-local maidens traveled to the Sanctuary with their whole families to attend the Olympics, and that the women left when the Olympic Games were held. The video *Blood and Honor at the First Olympics* (Ancient Mysteries Series, A&E, 1996, Act 4, "The Nude Olympics") claims that virgins were allowed to attend the Games to learn about men and to view excellent males.

50 Dillon (2000, 461–62) admits uncertainties but presses on:

> While it is not known whether these contests took place at about the same time as the Olympics, it is possible that they were held either immediately before or directly after them, as this would have been the best arrangement for encouraging attendance. How well frequented the Heraia were is unknown, but it would have been convenient for spectators of the Olympics, and possibly the fathers of male competitors, to bring daughters with them in order to take part in these games at the same time. It is possible to go further and suggest that in some cases they could have been the sisters of male competitors. Fathers accompanied boy competitors to Olympia…and athletic daughters could well have come to Olympia with them. The fact that parthenoi were allowed to attend the Olympic festival naturally points to their presence in Olympia at that time, and it is surely unreasonable to suppose that Pausanias is referring to local parthenoi only in his statement that parthenoi attended the games. It would make sense if at least some of the parthenoi who attended the male competitions had come to Olympia to compete in the Heraia, and that the Heraia were held either directly before or after the Olympic festival…; if this were the case, permitting parthenoi to watch the Olympic contests would have allowed their fathers to chaperone them while they themselves watched the contests. However, it is also completely possible that the Heraia were not held in conjunction with the Olympic festival, and that they attracted only local parthenoi competitors.

Later, he simply says (468, 469) that *parthenoi* competed in the Heraea and attended the men's games.

51 Crowther (2001b, 38), notes both Dillon's ideas and the lack of evidence: "It has been suggested that for logistical reasons the Heraia may have been held directly before or after the regular Olympics for males, although there is no evidence of this."

52 Apparent depictions on vases of nude women exercising or bathing probably refer to women getting ready for bed, or to Spartan women. See Scanlon 2002, 190–93; Bérard 1986.

53 Pindar (*Ol.* 10.40–5) says that an enamoured Poseidon abducted Pelops, as Zeus abducted Ganymede. Pausanias (5.24.5) notes images of Zeus and Ganymede in the *Altis* at Olympia. Scanlon (2002, chap. 8, "Eros and Greek Athletics," especially 211–19, and n. 40 on 399) thoroughly discusses the well-attested connections between pederasty and sport.

54 Robert (1974) discusses four inscriptions of the imperial period from Ephesus. Perhaps Pherenice asked for this honour, to "watch" in the role of the priestess, and perhaps Nero knew Olympic customs better than we thought.

55 For a full discussion, see Kyle 2003. On the dates of her wins, see Moretti 1957, nos. 373, 381, pp. 114–15; 1953, no. 17, pp. 40–44. On the context and chronology of Spartan events, see Cartledge 1987.

56 On the inscription, see *IvO* no. 5.160 (= *IG* V 1.1564a = Moretti 1953, no. 17. *Anth. Pal.* 13.16; see Ebert 1972, no. 33, pp. 110–12.

57 Pomeroy 2002, 19–24. In a new video (*The Spartans*, PBS, 2003), Bettany Hughes echoes this opinion: Cynisca was "obviously a tomboy," an "equestrian expert," who "made no secret of her ambition." Like others, Pomeroy relies heavily on Pausanias' characterization of Cynisca as very ambitious (see below). Scanlon (2002, 21–23) feels that Agesilaus used a female victory to challenge the significance of male chariot victories, and he adds that Cynisca and other female equestrian victors "won some political capital for the fatherland, but also the prospect of some visibility as women attracted them to the competition." Golden (1998, 133–34) sees "traces of the play of gender" in the victories of Cynisca and her female chariot victor successors.

58 See Cartledge (1987) for genealogies of Spartan kings (fig. 7) and the ancestry and family of Agesilaus (figs. 3, 9.1).

59 Herodotus (6.71.1) mentions her grandfather Zeuxidamus (father of Archidamus), whom some Spartans called Cyniscus. Cf. Cyniscus, son of Cyniscus, of Mantinea, Olympic boy boxing victor ca. 460 (Paus. 6.4.11). Pomeroy (2002, 21) finds Cynisca's name "unusual" and speculates that it may have been "a nickname for an especially tomboyish woman." She also notes (18), from Xen. *Cyn.* 13.18, that some Spartan women hunted.

60 Pomeroy (2002, 19–21) collects evidence to make a case for extensive Spartan female equestrianism, both in knowledge and practice. She feels (20) that girls raced chariots but admits that Athenaeus' text (*Deip.* 4.139f, citing Polycrates) is unclear. See Scanlon 2002, n. 69 on 346.

61 Moretti 1953, 41, 43; Pomeroy 2002, 21.

62 Pomeroy (2002, n. 79 on 22) comments: "Perhaps she had been widowed at a young age. In any case, no husband nor children are recorded for her, and her brother's attempts to manipulate her...suggest that she did not have a husband. Her single-minded devotion to racing may not have left any time for wifely duties."

63 Hodkinson (1988, 96–103) relates Cynisca's chariot racing to internal factors in Sparta. Discussing the influence of inheritance and marriage patterns, he argues that a system of "universal female inheritance" contributed to increasing inequalities in land ownership and the pursuit of status through wealth, as in hippotrophy, from the mid-fifth century on. Further on the resources and influence of Spartan women, see Pomeroy 2002, especially chap. 4, "Elite Women," 73–94.

64 Cynisca's monuments (Paus. 6.1.6) included a group: a chariot, charioteer, and horses in bronze, and a victor statue of Cynisca, located near the Temple of Hera. Her second monument (Paus. 5.12.5), located in or near the porch of the Temple of Zeus, included smaller than life-size bronze horses.

65 See Pomeroy (2002, 141–42): "Another text where a woman's voice may be heard is the epigram composed in honor of Cynisca's chariot victories...Cynisca is depicted as speaking in the first person. If she did not write the epigram herself, she may well have commissioned the poet and given orders about the content."

66 Young (1996b, especially 180–81 on Cynisca) shows that victors kept and cherished records of their achievements.

67 Pomeroy (2002, 21, 23) cites Pausanias twice as evidence of Cynisca's equestrian ambition. See, similarly, Pomeroy 2002, 23: "With the increase in private wealth, much of it in the hands of women, and with their keen interest in athletics and knowledge of horses, it was natural that Spartan women would own racehorses." She suggests (76) that

Cynisca "defied her brother," and she seems to take Agesilaus' attitude to his sister as disdainful (93).

68 Pausanias (3.8.1) comments that "after Cynisca other women, especially women of Lacedaemon, have won Olympic victories, but none of them was more distinguished for their victories than she." He (3.17.6) notes a statue near the Bronze House at Sparta of a Spartan woman named Euryleonis (Moretti 1957, no. 418), who won the *synoris* at Olympia, perhaps in 368 BC. Further on later female equestrian victors, see Moretti 1953, 41–43; Mantas 1995, 128–29; Dillon 2000, 464–65.

69 Hodkinson (1988, 96–98) relates the hippotrophic increase to other signs of internal shifts in demography, concentrations of land ownership, and the pursuit of status. Crowther (1988b, 301–10) notes that, while Elis had the most recorded equestrian victories in general (including six in the *tethrippon*), the greatest chariot racing rivals were Athens (with twelve) and Sparta (with sixteen).

70 Thucydides 5.50; Xen. *Hell.* 3.2.21; Paus. 6.2.3, 3.8.3; Diod. Sic. 14.17.1. Hornblower (2000, 212) calls this "one of the most tense and dramatic moments in the history of the Olympic Games."

71 Euripides apud Plut. *Vit. Alc.* 11, frag. 755 Page *PMG*.

72 Thucydides 6.16.1–2. See Kyle 1987, A4, 115–16, 130–31, 136–37, 163–68.

73 Plutarch, *Vit. Alc.* 23.7–9; *Vit. Ages.* 3.1–2. According to Plutarch, Alcibiades claimed that he seduced Timaea because he wanted his descendants to rule Sparta. Cartledge (1987, 113) notes (from Thuc. 8.6.3) that "Alcibiades" was originally a Spartan name, and that Alcibiades' family had ritualized guest-friendship ties at Sparta. Cartledge agrees that Agis was probably not the natural father of Leotychidas, and he calls this "perhaps the greatest domestic scandal in all of Spartan history." Further, see Hamilton 1991, 26 and n. 85.

74 Xenophon, *Hell.* 3.2.21–31; Paus. 3.8.3–5, 5.20.4–5; Diod. Sic. 14.17.4–12. For a recent discussion, see Unz 1986. Cartledge (1987, 249–52) relates Agis' campaign against Elis to personal revenge, and also to political considerations and economic needs. Falkner (1996, 17) suggests that "in addition to satisfying a need for vengeance, the conquest of Elis gave Sparta control of the coastline of the north-west Peloponnese and access to the Adriatic and the routes to the west."

75 Hamilton (1991, 7–39) psychologically relates Agesilaus' character to his deformity, his experience in the *agoge*, his awkward accession, and various personal insults. He views Agesilaus as a man of "deep-seated emotions—especially hatred, resentment, and unbridled ambition," someone capable of "nursing a political grudge" (7–8).

76 Pausanias 3.8.9–10. On the accession, see Cartledge 1987, 20, 111–15; Hamilton 1991, 26–29.

77 Xenophon, *Hell.* 3.4.3–4; Plut. *Vit. Ages.* 6.4–6; Paus. 3.9.2–3. See Hamilton 1991, 30–32, 95–96; Cartledge 1987, 212, 290–91, 357.

78 Xenophon, *Hell.* 3.4.15–16; *Ages.* 1.23–4; Plut. *Vit. Ages.* 9 and *Sayings of the Spartans, Agesilaus* 12 (209b-c).

79 Scanlon 2002, 23: "Participation in those few games for women were [was] restricted to unmarried girls, and the contests themselves were in all known instances footraces. That is, the games for women were not meant as demonstrations of the excellence of adult females, who were kept in the house, but as celebrations by maidens of their transitional prenuptial status between the 'wildness' of adolescence of the past and the 'tameness' to come with marriage."

The *Halma*: A Running or Standing Jump?

Hugh M. Lee

No consensus has existed as to whether the ancient Greek long jump, the *halma*, was a running or a standing jump; indeed, eminent scholars are arrayed on each side of the issue.[1] The matter has remained in doubt because there was no known literary passage to settle the question definitively. Much of the argument has therefore centred on Greek art, with advocates on each side claiming to find support in vase paintings of jumpers. A passage in the work of the first-century AD rhetorician Quintilian (*Inst.* 10.3.6), however, neglected until recently, makes it clear that the jump was preceded by a run at least in Quintilian's time. That a running jump was also the practice in Greece centuries earlier is made clear by an Attic red-figure *kylix* in Boston. Before presenting the evidence, however, it is useful to review the two sides of the question.

According to E.N. Gardiner, "The jump in the pentathlon was, it seems, a running long jump with weights," a conclusion with which Jüthner, Hyde, Harris, Patrucco, Yalouris, Sweet, Young, and Miller concur.[2] Support for the running jump is based principally on vase paintings (see, e.g., fig. 1) showing athletes running with the *halteres*, the Greek jumping weights.[3]

Figure 1. Interior of a red-figure *kylix* by Oltos from Vulci. From des Vergers, *L'Étrurie et Les Étrusques*, III, Plate XXXVIII.

Gardiner describes the jump as follows:

> The modern long-jumper depends for his impetus on his pace, and tries to reach his maximum speed at the take-off. The jumper with weights depends for his impetus partly on the swing of the weights, partly on the run. The run is shorter and not so fast. He begins with a few short springy steps, holding the weights by his side or swinging them slightly.... As he nears the take-off he checks his run and takes two or more long slow strides, swinging the weights once or twice vigorously forwards and backwards, taking off with his last forward swing.[4]

Gardiner adds that the runner took off on one foot.[5] He also believes that the Greeks did the standing jump in practice, but not in the pentathlon competition, stating: "We know that the Greeks practised a standing jump with and without weights."[6]

    To the contrary, Ebert asserts that the jump was a standing one, an opinion he shares with Gardner, Schröder, Drees, Finley and Pleket, Decker, and Sinn.[7] According to Ebert, the athlete stands with his feet

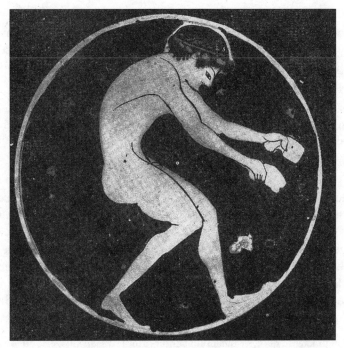

Figure 2. Interior of a red-figure *kylix* in Graz dated to about 500 BC.

close together and parallel to each other, bends his knees as he swings the weights backward, then launches both feet in the air as the weights come forward. Advocates of the standing jump also claim that the visual evidence supports their position.[8] Vase paintings showing athletes standing or crouching with a weight in each hand are interpreted as jumpers standing with feet parallel, swinging the weights before leaping. Even depictions of athletes drawn with one foot in advance of the other are interpreted as the standing jump (see fig. 2). Ebert argues that the artist employs an artistic convention, wishing to show both legs in profile but intending them to be understood as being side by side.[9]

Ebert also rejects the running jump on empirical grounds. Modern jumpers employing weights in a running jump actually find that the use of weights weighing 2.5 kg not only diminishes the athlete's speed in his approach but also hinders the pumping action of the arms, yielding results inferior to those of someone jumping without weights. Moreover, adds Ebert, modern athletes using *halteres* have attempted the run and jump as described by Gardiner, but could not co-ordinate the movement of the arms and legs in the manner prescribed.[10]

Reflecting the unsettled nature of the question, Swaddling borrows from both camps. Employing a drawing illustrating a standing jump, she comments: "Though we are used to seeing a running start, it is not certain that this method was used in antiquity." She then adds, however, paraphrasing Gardiner:

> It seems quite possible, to judge from surviving illustrations, that a short run was used, that the jumper started with the weights held close up to his body, ran a short way still holding them to the front, then as he neared the take-off point he swung them back at arm's length and then forward on the moment of take-off.[11]

Such has been the scholarly impasse. Recently, however, Olaf Grodde, in his monograph *Sport bei Quintilian* (1997), discusses the passage (*Inst.* 10.3.6) which clearly indicates that a run-up was employed.[12] This crucial passage, being buried in the middle of Quintilian's lengthy treatise, had escaped the attention of scholars of Greek athletics, nor indeed has Grodde's discovery received the recognition it deserves. Quintilian, when discussing the value of revision, compares it to the jump, the javelin throw, and shooting an arrow:

> Nam praeter id quod sic melius iunguntur prioribus sequentia, calor quoque ille cogitationis, qui scribendi mora refrixit, recipit ex integro vires et velut repetito spatio sumit impetum; *quod in certamine saliendi fieri videmus, ut conatum longius petant et ad illud, quo contenditur, spatium cursu ferantur*; utque in iaculando brachia reducimus et expulsuri tela nervos retro tendimus.[13]

> For beside the fact that thus we secure a better connection between what follows and what precedes, the warmth of thought which has cooled down while we were writing is revived anew, and gathers fresh impetus from going over the ground again. *This we see to happen in the jumping contest. The competitors seek a longer attempt and bring themselves in a run to the jumping pit.*[14] Similarly, in throwing the javelin, we draw back our arms, and in archery pull back the bow-string to propel the shaft.[15]

What do all three sports have in common? The *akontist* grasps the javelin, the archer puts arrow to bowstring, the jumper leaps from the takeoff line. In each case, however, there is a withdrawal or recession of some kind. The *akontist* draws back his arm before throwing. Were he to keep his hand in the plane of his body when first grasping the spear, he would not be able to throw it very far. Similarly, the archer does not release the arrow at the point from which he fixes the arrow to the bow-string, for the arrow would simply fall to the ground. Rather, he first pulls back bowstring and arrow. Like the flight of the javelin and the arrow, the jump is enhanced if the athlete draws himself back in some way. He draws back his body in the sense that he takes several steps back from the take-off line. While it could be argued that the backward swing of the weights could be seen as the equivalent of the akontist drawing back his arm or the archer pulling back the bowstring, what is significant is that Quintilian unambiguously singles out the run-up. Indeed, a late Archaic vase from Poggio Sommavilla by the Harrow Painter may depict an athlete pacing off the distance to the starting point of his run, just as modern high and long jumpers do.[16] He then retraces that distance with a run before leaping. Quintilian's use of the word *cursu*, and his analogies to the javelin throw and archery, make it clear that some kind of run preceded the jump.

For each athletic event, there is considerable benefit in withdrawing from the original starting point and then retracing the ground to that point. Similarly, says Quintilian, going over what one has written, namely revising, will lead to a better result. The passage cannot be explained without a run-up to the jump. In support of a running long jump during the Roman period is the black and white mosaic from Tusculum, on which a jumper holding weights is clearly depicted as running.[17]

A controversy still remains, however, for, as Grodde indicates, there are now two possibilities: (1) either the jump was always preceded by a run-up, or (2) an original standing jump became a running one in Roman times.[18] Grodde himself supports the former. He uses the example of a vase painting showing an athlete with a backward lean who holds the weights straight out in front at chest level. His straight right leg is flat on the ground and forward, and his left leg is bent, while the weight of his body is placed on the balls and toes of his left foot. Grodde argues that such a position is not possible with the standing jump and should rather be interpreted as the phase of the running jump in which the athlete is transferring his horizontal thrust into a vertical one. Gardiner thus interprets jumpers in a similar stance.[19] On the other hand, Miller, an advocate of the running jump, believes that an athlete in such a position is shown at the moment preceding the run-up:

> The athlete would lean back, bracing himself on his right leg, which was bent at the knee and extending his left leg forward. Holding a halma (sic) in each hand and extending his arms in front of him, he would stand poised, listening to a flute player....We should picture the athlete, then, rocking back and forth as he listens to the music and then breaking forward into his run.[20]

While the vase painting adduced by Grodde may not be clear-cut evidence of a running jump, there are indeed others which appear to show athletes running while carrying weights. Gardiner gives the example of the vase painting by the early red-figure artist, Oltos (see fig. 1).[21] As noted above, however, Ebert has argued that the alleged running position of the legs is artistic convention, the legs really being parallel to one another.[22] Furthermore, opponents of the running jump could even concede that there are vase paintings of athletes running with weights, while denying that they are doing so as part of the long jump.

There is, however, a red-figure *kylix* in Boston (01.8033) by the late Archaic artist known as the Telephos Painter which clearly depicts a running phase of the long jump (see figs. 3–4). The position of the body and limbs of two jumpers, one on each side of the vase, suggest a run, and the context indicates competition.

On side A (fig. 3), the jumper is depicted with a forward lean while pushing off on the ball and toe of his right foot. His left leg is raised high off the ground and bent at the knee at an angle greater than ninety degrees. His hands holding the *halteres* are extended straight ahead and parallel to the ground. Either he is still running and will in the next instant plant his left foot and take off into the air, or he has planted the right foot and swung the weights forward as he pushes off into his ascent. In either case, the jump, whether off the left or the right foot, is, as it were, the last long stride of the run-up. With the standing jump, on the other hand, both feet would leave the ground together.

The context informs us that he is jumping rather than merely running with weights. The jumper is flanked by an *akontist* on the left and an official on the right facing both athletes. Between the jumper and the official is a pillar. The pillar is the *kampter*, the post which was inserted into the stone sill or *balbis* which marked the limit at each end of the track. The *balbis* also seems to have been the *bater*, the takeoff point, for the jump, as well as the foot marker used by javelin and discus throwers.

Philological evidence indicates that the takeoff board was called the *bater*. The second-century AD grammarian Julius Pollux comments (iii, 151): "The place from which the jump is made is the *bater*, whence the expression, 'He has hit the *bater* with a bang.'" A few lines earlier (iii, 147), he associates the *bater* with the stone blocks embedded in the ground at each end of the course, and which define the boundaries of the track: "Where they start from is called the *aphesis*, *hysplex*, *gramme*, and *balbis*, that round which they turn, the *nyssa* and *kampter*; where they stop, the *telos*, *terma*, and *bater*, but to some, the *balbis*." Such stone blocks can be seen

Figure 3. *Akontist*, jumper, and official on a red-figure *kylix* by the Telephos Painter, Boston 01.8033, *ARV*² 817.4. Courtesy Museum of Fine Arts, Boston.

Figure 4. *Discobolus, akontist*, and jumper. Reverse of Boston 01.8033. Courtesy Museum of Fine Arts, Boston.

today in numerous ancient Greek stadia—for example, at Olympia, Delphi, and Nemea. The connection between the *bater* and the javelin throw is made especially clear on a red-figure *kylix* in Berlin, which shows both the *kampter* and an *akontist* in the act of throwing. The association of the *bater* with the *balbis* locates the jump and throws together at one end of the stadium.[23]

On the Boston vase, the *akontist* is clearly in the act of throwing. His arm is drawn back just as Quintilian had described, with the weight on his back (right) foot. It is extremely unlikely, of course, that a jumper and an *akontist* would compete at the same moment, so the artist must be representing two different moments at the same place in the stadium. But the moments are analogous, namely in competition and immediately before the launching of the javelin and the takeoff into the air.

The similar athletic scene on side B (fig. 4) lends further support to this interpretation. There we observe, from left to right, a *discobolus*, an *akontist*, the *kampter*, and a jumper, who in terms of composition has replaced the official and like him faces to the viewer's left; however, whereas the trainer/official can be interpreted as observing the *akontist* and the jumper while each performs, it is highly unlikely that the jumper on the reverse is leaping towards the *discobolus* and the *akontist*. Rather, we would seem to have three analogous athletic moments in competition.[24] The *akontist* is shown at a slightly later stage than on side A, for he has now transferred his weight to the left foot while his trailing right foot is off the ground.

There are two possible ways to interpret this jumper. Either he is leaping off his left foot, or he will take one more step and jump off his right foot. If he and his counterpart on side A are both jumping off the left foot, jumper B is shown at a slightly later moment, having already planted his left foot on the *bater* and begun to swing the *halteres* forward. If both athletes are taking off from the right foot, then jumper B is depicted at an earlier moment. He has planted the left foot and, in the next instant, will transfer his weight onto the balls and toes of his left foot and raise his right leg into the bent position like the jumper on side A.

The *discobolus* is in the act of throwing. In the next moment he will swing the discus behind his back while pivoting on his right foot and rotating his body clockwise into the position familiar to us from Myron's famous statue.

In brief, the presence of the pillar and the official, the fact that the two *akontists* and a *discobolus* are in the midst of throwing, and the stances of the two jumpers indicate a running long jump.

A running long jump also yields the clearest interpretation of Pollux's remark, quoted above, that the jumper hits the *bater* with a bang. He must be referring to the noise made by the planting of the foot immediately prior to the leap. The standing jump, on the other hand, cannot so easily explain this passage.

The passage from Pollux concerning the *bater* provides one more important clue concerning the performance of the *halma*, and suggests a reply to the empirical objections against a running jump. According to Aristotle (*De Anima* 3.705a; also *Problems* 5.8.881b), "A pentathlete using *halteres* jumps farther than one without them."[25] Proponents of the standing jump claim that Aristotle's statement is true only of a standing jump. With a running jump, the use of weights decreases the length of the jump.

Ebert cites the results of practical experiments, conducted under his supervision, in which athletes jumped with and without weights. For *halteres*, they used dumbbells weighing 2.5 kg. Working with Ebert were East German athletes, including Walter Meier, that country's record holder in the decathlon.[26] To quote Drees, who summarizes Ebert's results, "In the running jump the weights proved a hindrance, *reducing* normal performance more than a meter. In the standing jump, however, performances were *improved* by fifteen to twenty centimeters," or about 6 to 8 inches.[27] As Ebert's athletes discovered, the carrying of weights weighing 2.5 kg would not only diminish one's speed but also inhibit the pumping of the arms, a technique which contributes to speed. Furthermore, Greek *halteres* could weigh more than 2.5 kg and so presumably be an even greater hindrance.[28]

Modern jumpers employ an approach of about 40 metres, good enough to get close to top speed, which is obviously a factor in achieving distance. Everything else being equal, the greater the velocity, the longer the jump. It is no accident that Jesse Owens and Carl Lewis were both great sprinters and great jumpers. Given the length of the modern approach, Ebert's conclusion that the running jump without the weights yields superior results is valid.

Sweet, an advocate of the running jump, disagrees with Ebert, and comments that "Ebert's athletes did not use the same techniques as the Greeks."[29] It may not, however, simply be a matter of technique. A relevant issue may well be the length of the run-up used.

We have seen that the *balbis*, the starting line for the foot races, also served as the *bater* for jumping. At Olympia, the distance between the *balbis* and the border of the track where the stands begin was only 10.5 m, and similar distances are to be found in other Greek stadia (fig. 5).[30]

Gardiner had in fact already proposed a shorter run, as had Yalouris, although neither made explicit reference to the dimensions of the area behind the *balbis*.[31] Gardiner seems to have based the distance of the run-up on the experiences of a jumper named G. Rowdon, who used an approach of 14 yards in the high jump with weights. Although he was

Figure 5. West end of the stadium at Olympia. Photo by Gerald Schaus.

aware of the layout of the stadia at Olympia, Delphi, Pergamon, Epidaurus, and Athens, he does not connect it to the short run-up.[32] Perhaps, from practical experience, the Greeks learned that a short running approach of approximately 10 metres would exceed the same jump without weights, since speed would be much less of a factor and the *halteres*, instead of being an impediment, might be employed to advantage. The distance between the *balbis* and the edge of the stadium floor seems to reflect that knowledge. If the technique described by Gardiner, namely the movements of arms and legs, is unworkable, as Ebert contends, it remains for us to discover the proper technique.[33]

Conclusion

The literary testimony of Quintilian, joined to the evidence from vase painting, now makes it clear that the *halma* was a running long jump with weights. The run-up, however, was most likely a short one of about 10 m, not the modern sprint of 40 m, and was limited by the distance between the end of the stadium and the *balbis*, which served as the *bater*.

Addendum

German colleagues have brought to my attention the dissertation by Harald Schmid, *Der Weitsprung in der griechsichen Antike. Eine Neubewertung unterschiedlicher Theorien unter Berücksichtigung eigener biomechanischer Versuche* (Mainz, 1997). Thanks to Wolfgang Decker, I have seen a photocopy of pages 66–83, which deal with the question of the run-up and the use of weights. Schmid (1997, 67–68) is aware of Gardiner's advocacy of a short run-up and also the short distance between the *balbis* and the end of the stadium; however, he confines his biomechanical researches to a jump using a 30-m run-up. Six athletes do the running jump employing no *halteres,* and then *halteres* of increasing weight. The result (Schmid 1997, 76–78) is that, as the weight of the *halteres* increases, speed declines and thus the length of the jump. I have not seen the second volume of his dissertation, which is a catalogue of vase paintings illustrating the jump, and so do not know whether he includes the Boston *kylix* (figs. 3–4), nor how he would interpret those paintings. Thus, to the best of my knowledge, Schmid's researches do not exclude the possibility that, with a shorter run-up, one can jump farther with weights than without.

Notes

I wish to thank Gerry Schaus for his helpful suggestions and corrections. Any errors that remain are of course my responsibility. My gratitude also to Ingomar Weiler and Peter Mauritsch in Graz for their help in obtaining the photo of the Graz *kylix.*

1 An invaluable resource for the ancient texts and bibliography on the Greek long jump is Doblhofer and Mauritsch 1992.
2 Gardiner (1930, 144), reiterating the position that he enunciated earlier (1904, 187–90, and 1910, 301–307); Jüthner 1912, 2275 (a change from his earlier view, 1896, 14); Hyde 1938, 417; Harris 1966, 8; Yalouris 1976, 181; Patrucco 1972, 80–81; Sweet 1987, 46; Young 2004, 35; Miller 2004a, 67. See also Legrand 1875, 1055, and Schmid (1997, 67–83), who is a kinesiologist.
3 Gardiner 1930, 149: "The positions represented on the vases prove that the Greek long jump with weights was generally a running jump."
4 Gardiner 1930, 147.
5 Gardiner 1930, 147.
6 Gardiner 1930, 144. As an example of the standing jump, he (1930, 149, fig. 22) gives the bronze statuette of an athlete holding the *halteres* above his head; however, the two vase paintings (figs. 99 and 110), which he cites as examples of the standing jump without weights, are more likely runners in the starting position.
7 Ebert 1963, 49–62; see also p. 66, the "Text zur Bildreihe," and the sequential photographs of an athlete performing the standing jump while using five-pound dumbbells. He repeats his opinion later (1980, 62). See also P. Gardner 1880, 212; Drees 1968, 74–75; Finley and Pleket 1976, 34; Decker 1995, 99; Sinn 2000, 41–42. Mahaffy (1901, 30) curiously states: "We may infer from the use of weights (*halteres*) that the jump was a standing one."

8 Ebert (1963, 51) asserts, "Auch die Darstellungen des Halterensprunges auf Vasenbildern passen weitaus in der Mehrzahl eher zu der Vorstellung eines Sprunges *aus dem Stande*…Frühere Erklärer haben hier jedoch nicht immer richtig interpretiert."

9 Ebert 1963, 52–53 and Plate 5 figure 9. For the *kylix* in Graz, see Diez 1954, 13–14; also Lehner, Lorenz, and Schwarz 1993, 35–37, with reiteration of Ebert's interpretation of a standing jump on p. 37.

10 Ebert 1963, 50.

11 Swaddling 1980, 55; 1999, 77. Mezö (1930, 114) also believes that the Greeks practised both the standing and running jump. Doblhofer and Mauritsch (1992, 92) do not mention Mezö's book, but list his later contribution (1958, 165–72), which I have not seen, among the works supporting the running jump.

12 Grodde 1997, 43–44, 92.

13 Grodde uses the edition of Rahn (1995).

14 The jumping pit, *ad illud, quo contenditur, spatium,* is literally "the area being contested" or perhaps the area "to which one hastens." The Greek word for the jumping pit is *skamma,* which comes from the word "to dig," and indeed, there are vase paintings showing athletes using picks to dig up the hard ground of the stadium for wrestling and the long jump. We should note, however, that the modern jumping pit, which is filled with sand, was softer than the ancient. For the Greek long jump, it seems more likely that the ground, after being dug up, was then smoothed down, thus providing a softened but firm surface.

15 The translation is that of Butler—Quintilian (trans. Butler) 1958, 95—except for the sentence *Quod…ferantur,* where I have provided my own. Butler instead writes, "The competitors take a longer run and go at full speed to clear the distance which they aim at covering." I believe that his translation of *conatum longius* to refer to the approach and not the attempt is erroneous, and his translation of *cursus* as "at full speed" goes beyond the literal meaning of the Latin. Quintilian tells us that the athletes run. They could be doing so at a slow or moderate pace. Indeed, as I indicate later, they are clearly not running at top speed. Butler's text of this passage from *Inst.* 10.3.6 is identical with Rahn's.

16 *ARV*[2] 274.42. Patrucco 1972, 89, fig. 22; Jüthner 1896, 9, fig. 10; Jüthner 1968, 170, fig. 42. The interpretation that the jumper is pacing off his approach is mine.

17 Gardiner 1930, 108, fig. 70, with the caption, "a jumper running at full speed."

18 Grodde 1997, 42–44, 92.

19 Grodde 1997, 42–44, and fig 4. He does not give the provenance for the painting; however, a similar position of the athlete can be seen in Gardiner 1930, 148, fig. 102, except that the left leg is straight and forward, and the right leg is bent and placed behind; also fig. 104, in which the athlete's stance is more upright. Gardiner is equivocal as to whether an actual jump, or a practice drill for the jump, is depicted: "In the running jump he (the athlete) takes off from one foot, and this is what we see constantly represented on vases. The position most commonly depicted is the top of the upward swing when the body is usually leaning slightly backwards and the front foot is slightly raised from the ground…But our illustrations probably represent not the actual jump so much as practice for the jump."

20 Miller 2004a, 66–67.

21 *ARV*[2] 6.84. Gardiner (1904, 188–89) states:

> The run so depicted is by no means incompatible with the use of the *halteres.* The modern long-jumper depends principally on pace, and, as has been pointed out, pace is inconsistent with the use of *halteres.* But the Greek jumper certainly does not sprint: like the modern high jumper he takes a few short, springy steps, intended to give elasticity to the limbs, and so to prepare for the final spring.

22 Ebert 1963, 49–62; 1980, 62.

23 Lee 1976. For further insight on the finish line in foot races, see Crowther 1999.

24 Professor Victor J. Matthews, commenting on the oral presentation of this paper, has suggested the interesting possibility of a literal interpretation of this scene, namely that if we assume the jump was a single one, there is in fact enough room, approximately 10 metres, between the *balbis* and the stands for the jumper to leap in a direction opposite to that in which the throws are being made. However, this seems the less likely possibility. First, the javelin and discus were thrown in the direction of the centre of the stadium, making it more probable that the jump was also in that direction. Furthermore, a jump towards the middle allowed more spectators to obtain a better view of the contest. In this connection we note too that the stone seats for the judges at Olympia were located about 60 metres up the track from the western *balbis*.

25 The translation of Aristotle is by Sweet (1987, 48).

26 Ebert 1963, 49–50.

27 Drees 1968, 75. More recently, Dr. Alberto Minetti, professor of Biomechanics and Exercise Physiology at the Manchester Metropolitan University (Minetti and Ardigo, 2002, 141–42), has found that, with the use of halteres weighing between 2 to 9 kg, a standing long jump will be increased by 6 per cent, or about 7 inches, for a jump of 10 feet.

28 Doblhofer and Mauritsch 1992, 71–72, 75; Gardiner 1930, 145–47.

29 Sweet 1987, 48.

30 Mallwitz 1972, 182.

31 Gardiner (1930, 147): "The run is shorter and not so fast." Ebert (1963, 50) questions the movement of the arms and body as proposed by Gardiner.

32 Gardiner (1930, 151–52) notes that in these displays, jumps were performed with weights and without, and with a run-up and without. For his discussion of the stadia, see 1930, 128–35. His description (1930, 152) of the high jump technique of Rowdon is as follows, with the difference from the long jump being that in the high jump the jumper throws away the weights: "The jumper starts about 14 yards from the posts taking two thirds of the distance with short quick steps hardly swinging the weights at all, after which he takes one or two comparatively long slow strides, swinging the bells together twice and at the second swing taking off the ground as the bells come to the front."

33 Ebert 1963, 50.

ᢙᢩ

Connections between Olympia and Stymphalus

Gerald P. Schaus

Introduction

When Greece surprisingly won the European soccer championship in 2004, the entire country exploded in a frenzy of celebration. Its national team overcame incredible odds to defeat the traditional soccer powers of Europe. Greece played the role of giant-killer, and as an overwhelming "underdog" against the representatives from much larger nations, the team stirred passions of fanatical patriotism. A hundred thousand overjoyed fans poured into the centre of Athens, Omonia Square, within a half hour of the victory, and the scene was repeated in virtually every corner of Greece, as I myself witnessed from tiny Lafka, near Stymphalus.

Most devoted sports followers have experienced this same emotional explosion at some point in their lives. Supporting a team or player from a small population centre with little expectation of winning, who goes all the way to a championship game and wins it, brings out this feeling of immense pride and overpowering joy almost every time. So, with regard to the great Olympic Games of antiquity, it is worth having a look at the success of one such small population centre to appreciate what many such centres must have experienced over the course of the Games' history.

The small city state of Stymphalus is located in a pleasant valley surrounded by mountains in northeastern Arcadia. At 600 metres above sea
level and a long day's walk from the coast, it was relatively isolated from
the more wealthy trading cities of Corinth, Sicyon, or Argos. The valley
is about 12 km long and 2 km wide, so that its adult population at the best
of times could hardly have surpassed five thousand.[1] The ancient city nes-
tles at the foot of Mount Cyllene, close to a small lake whose spring-fed
waters are trapped in the low spot of the valley till they reach the level of
a natural chasm, or *katavothros*, and so disappear below Mount Apelau-
ron. The area is little known in Greek history before the fourth century.
Homer (*Il.* 2.608), in his Catalogue of Ships, mentions a contingent from
Stymphalus accompanying the Achaean army of Agamemnon to fight
against Troy, while Pausanias indicates that the city had been relocated to
its present position, although no indication of date is provided for the
event. The earlier town is noted by Pausanias as still having three sanctuaries of Hera in his time.

The area is better known from Greek mythology. It was the scene of
Heracles' Sixth Labour, the ridding (killing or scaring away) of the Stymphalian birds, a serious local nuisance. The birthplace of the god, Hermes,
was nearby on the slopes of Mount Cyllene, and the goddess Hera returned
here after her divorce from Zeus.

Archaeological investigation of the ancient site of Stymphalus—under the
auspices of the Canadian Institute in Greece, the conference co-sponsor,
and directed by Hector Williams of the University of British Columbia—has
established the existence of an orthogonally planned city shortly before ca.
350 BC.[2] Evidence from coins and pottery confirms that the city began to
flourish at just about this time, suggesting a date for the city's relocation
alluded to by Pausanias. By the late fourth or early third century, the city suffered a setback at the hands of the Macedonians, and in the second century
it was dealt a major blow from Roman invaders as part of Mummius' destruction of Corinth and the Achaean League between 146 and 140 BC. Strabo
(8.388), by the late first century BC, says that Stymphalus was one of ten Arcadian cities that then lay in ruins, surely a result, at least in part, of the Roman
solution to Greek resistance. These preliminary remarks bring us to Olympia
and the Olympic Games. One might expect Stymphalus to leave any mark
it might make on Olympic history during the city's era of prosperity in the
Late Classical and Hellenistic periods. To be sure, our records of winners at
the Games are far from complete, and it is possible that some athletes from
this small Arcadian city were successful at Olympia after its relocation; however, not a single Stymphalian appears in the Victor Lists from this time.

The content of this paper would be remarkably brief and uninteresting if it relied on Stymphalus of the fourth century and later for its substance. There was, however, one short period in Olympia's history when Stymphalus stood out brilliantly. It may have been as brief as twelve years or as long as twenty-eight, but it has nevertheless left a legacy to us today: first, in a beautiful piece of ancient sculpture; second, in a poem ranked as one of Pindar's finest victory odes, and third, in a concern for proper diet in the training regimen of top athletes. A fourth item in our athletic inheritance from Stymphalus occurs a little later and has less impact: some archaeological evidence for Stymphalus' civic sports facilities.

Metope of the Stymphalian Birds

The great Temple of Zeus at Olympia was built under the direction of Libon, local architect of Elis, between 470 and 457 BC. As part of its sculptural decoration, a series of metopes was created for placement above the columns of both the east and west porches.[3] In all, there were twelve metopes, six in each porch. Not surprisingly, they depicted the Twelve Labours of Heracles—the ultimate *athloi* (heroic deeds or struggles), performed by the greatest of Greek heroes. With Athena's help, Heracles accomplished these impossible tasks to pay the penance imposed by the oracle at Delphi, eventually leading to his acceptance among the gods on Mount Olympus.[4]

Traditionally, the Sixth (sometimes counted as the Fifth) Labour was the killing of the monstrous Stymphalian birds. The Olympia metope representing this myth shows the young Athena sitting on a large rock, looking back at the approaching hero as he brings her a sample of his deadly handiwork (fig. 1).[5] The order of the Labours was not yet closely fixed in the fifth century, so at Olympia the killing of the Stymphalian birds is placed third from the left, above the central opening leading into the opisthodomus.[6] It therefore had a prominent position in the middle of the west porch. Bernard Ashmole has described it as "one of the most unexpected and most charming creations of ancient art."[7] Among the best preserved of the twelve metopes, it displays the serious expression and stark simplicity of the early Classical or Severe style.

The composition revolves around a central feature, the dead birds (now missing) in the hand of Heracles, for which Athena reaches. Directly below this focal point, one notices the very unusual landscape element in the scene, a large rough rock on which Athena sits and her bare feet rest. Ashmole was especially drawn to the rock. He says,

Figure 1. Metope from the Temple of Zeus, Olympia, depicting Heracles bringing the Stymphalian birds to Athena. DAI neg. 1984/928. Photo by G. Hellner. Courtesy Deutsches Archäologisches Institut Athen.

> Athena is pre-eminently the goddess of the citadel, especially of course of the Acropolis of Athens, but also of acropolis rocks everywhere. That is what the rock symbolizes, and that is why it is a lofty one.... She is in fact on guard, but she spares a moment from her guard-duties to turn round and look down graciously at the tribute her protégé has brought her.[8]

Its prominence is surely deliberate; its impact is consciously contrived. Although Ashmole regarded the rock as a symbol for acropolis rocks everywhere, the scene depicts a particular moment in time and space. The hero, Heracles, has killed the birds of Stymphalus and brought them to his patron, Athena. The artist may therefore also have a particular "rock" in mind, and if so, two possibilities stand out, either Mount Olympus or one of the mountains that overlooks the Stymphalian Lake where the birds had gathered in such numbers before Heracles carried out his slaughter. The former possibility, Mount Olympus, is far from the Labour's location, and it can be argued that it is premature for Heracles—in the midst of his Labours—to make a visit to Olympus to display the dead birds. The latter possibility, a site overlooking Stymphalus, is preferable, especially if Athena has some known association with this place. If one may be permitted to speculate, although the lake is surrounded by mountains and any rocky hilltop might be imagined in this metope, one candidate stands out: the acropolis ridge of the ancient city of Stymphalus itself, which rises sharply right beside the lake.

Interestingly, it was almost at the summit of this ridge, overlooking the lake, that a sanctuary probably dedicated to Athena Polias (that is, in her aspect as protectress of the city) was uncovered during Greek excavations in the 1920s and Canadian excavations in the 1990s.[9] The coincidence of the sanctuary and the representation of Athena seated on the rock is therefore hard to ignore. There are, however, at least two reservations that must be considered before accepting any real link. The first, of course, is the assumption that the rock in the metope is an identifiable location; the second is that evidence for cultic activity in the sanctuary as early as the time of the metope, about 466–462 BC, is very poor, to the point where we may seriously doubt its existence. One exciting discovery speaking in its favour is a beautiful, if now fragmentary, late Archaic *kore*, ca. 490 BC, found right inside the temple.[10] How it arrived at the site, while so little other fifth-century material exists, is puzzling. In the end, whether the rock represents Stymphalus' acropolis or not, the Olympia metope depicting Heracles' labour at Stymphalus stands out among early Classical sculpture.

Hagesias and Pindar's Sixth Olympian Ode

A second connection between Olympia and Stymphalus revolves around the victory of a man named Hagesias[11] at the 78th Olympiad in 468 BC (although others have suggested the 76th or 77th Olympiad). Hagesias, a citizen of both Syracuse and Stymphalus and a friend and ally of Hieron, the tyrant of Syracuse, won the mule chariot race (*apene*) at Olympia. Despite the diminished prestige of winning the mule race rather than the horse chariot race, Hagesias celebrated his victory with a monument as costly as any fine bronze statue raised by other Olympic champions. He invited Pindar, who was near the height of his career, to write an epinician ode in honour of his accomplishment.[12] The result was Pindar's lovely Sixth Olympian.[13] To judge from lines in the poem, Pindar employed Aineas, perhaps a relative of Hagesias from Stymphalus, to bring the ode to Stymphalus, to train and lead the chorus, and then to take the whole choral troop to Syracuse for a second victory performance.[14]

As a way to reinforce the importance of Stymphalus, and create a sympathetic connection between the poet and his honouree, Pindar declares himself to be a grandson of Stymphalus through a mythical connection between Thebes and the victor's city. He himself is a son of the city of Thebes, represented by the nymph Theba, and so the grandson of Theba's mother, Metopa, who is the nymph of the great spring that gushes out of the ground and provides water to Lake Stymphalus.

Nisetich makes special mention of the difficulty of this passage, noting: "A far more complex and difficult passage—perhaps the most vexing example in Pindar—occurs in the sixth Olympian ode."[15]

> The flute's whistling note
> puts me in mind of a shrill whetstone that hones my speech
> for what I'll say, pierced with enthusiasm:
> the mother of my mother was from Stymphalus, blossoming Metopa,
> mother of horse-riding Theba,
> from whose delightful spring I drink
> as I plait the intricate
> song for spearmen. (11. 81–87) (trans. F. Nisetich)

Both before this passage and immediately afterwards, Pindar focuses on Hagesias' own connection to Stymphalus and then hints that the chorus, after its performance at Stymphalus, will leave and sail to Syracuse:

> Pour out a word for Syracuse
> and Ortygia, where Hieron is king,...
> May time to come never disturb his bliss.
> And may he welcome
> to the feast
> Hagesias' reveling friends [i.e., the chorus for this victory ode] as they come
>
> from home to home, leaving behind the walls
> of Stymphalus, their mother Arkadia, nurse of flocks.
> On a winter's night, two anchors
> best secure the ship.
> May the god in his favor
> give glory to both these cities. (11. 92–93...97–102) (trans. F. Nisetich)

Dromeus, the Great Long-distance Runner

The third Olympian legacy from little Stymphalus was one of victory in the *dolichus*, or long distance race. Shortly after the Persian Wars, several great runners emerged in Greek athletic records. One was a sprinter, Astylus of Croton, who won both the *stade* and the *diaulus* (a two-*stade* race) in three consecutive Olympiads, but who shamed his accomplishment by changing his citizenship from Croton to Syracuse after his first double victory. Two others—Dandes of Argos in the *stade* and Ergoteles of Cnossus in the *dolichus*—were double *periodonikai*, but little else is known about them.[16] The last great runner of this era was Dromeus of Stymphalus, a champion in the *dolichus*. Pausanias is our source of information:

> A man from Stymphalus, by name Dromeus (*Runner*), proved true to it (his name) in the long race, [ἀνὴρ δὲ ἐκ Στυμφήλου Δρομεὺς ὄνομα, καὶ δὴ καὶ ἔργον τοῦτο ἐπὶ δολίχῳ παρεσχημένος], for he won two victories at Olympia, two at Pytho, three at the Isthmus and five at Nemea. He is said to have also conceived the idea of a flesh (meat) diet; up to this time athletes had fed on cheese from the basket. The statue of this athlete is by Pythagoras. Paus. 6.7.10 (Loeb trans.)

Dromeus won all four ancient Greek "grand slam" events in his athletic specialty, and he did it two times over and then some. In other words, he was crowned at least twice at each of the four Panhellenic Games festivals, including a presumed string of eleven Panhellenic contests without defeat (see below). If he had won just once more at Isthmia, he would have been undefeated for two full Panhellenic cycles, the Isthmian and Nemean Games being biennial. His accomplishment is stellar, matched by few others and surpassed only by the wrestler, Milo, up to this time.[17]

It is interesting that this *periodonikes* (i.e., winner of the circuit or "periodos") could afford to have a statue of himself raised in the Sanctuary at Olympia by one of the best sculptors of the day, despite being from a small city in the relatively poor region of Arcadia. His proud home area might possibly have contributed to the great expense, or his family if it had money, but being a champion runner, Dromeus might easily have afforded the cost himself from wealth to be made in competing in major prize games throughout Greece.[18] David Young, for example, has calculated that the winner of the *stade* race at the Panathenaic Games in Athens, one of hundreds of prize games in Greece, could make the equivalent of $67,800 (1980 U.S. dollars) for a single victory.[19] Pausanias tells us that Dromeus' statue was sculpted by Pythagoras, probably Pythagoras of Rhegion (originally from Samos?), a pupil of Clearchus, known also for

depicting other famous athletes, including Astylus, the sprinter, Leontiscus, the finger-breaking wrestler, and Euthymus, a great boxer.[20] Given the
dates for the career of Pythagoras, and already knowing the *dolichus* winners for 476 to 464 BC at Olympia, Dromeus must fall either before or after
this period, i.e., 484–80 or 460–456 BC.[21]

Pausanias (6.7.10, above) adds one further detail of interest to his
comments on Dromeus, noting that this great Panhellenic champion in
long distance running introduced the practice of a meat diet rather than
one depending on fresh cheese. Pythagoras, the philosopher from Samos
who moved to South Italy ca. 530 BC is said to have had a similar idea,
influencing Eurymenes of Samos and perhaps also Milo of Croton, both
wrestlers.[22] In the latter part of the sixth century, for example, Milo was
said to have carried a young bull into the *Altis*, killed it, and eaten it all in
a day. What may be new here is that it was a long distance runner, commonly the least bulky of all athletes, who pioneered a meat diet in his
sport rather than a heavy wrestler or boxer.

To summarize, within a very brief period, a beautiful depiction of
Stymphalus' mythic connection to Heracles' Labours was raised on the
Temple of Zeus at Olympia, ca. 466–462 BC, while Hagesias' mule team
victory was commemorated by the great poet Pindar with a choral performance at Stymphalus ca. 468 BC, and Dromeus' two long distance race wins
at Olympia were celebrated in a statue by Pythagoras erected close to the
Zeus temple in the *Altis*, perhaps dated 460–456 BC rather than 484–480.
Through Olympia, fame came swiftly and brilliantly to the small valley, and
then began to fade, well before the ancient city was even laid out in well-
planned blocks at its present location.

Did Stymphalus suddenly neglect its athletic endeavours? Almost certainly not. Four students of the site—starting with Ludwig Ross in 1840[23]
and including myself—have independently observed the long rows of seats
along the lower eastern face of the acropolis at Stymphalus, and thought
that they suited the needs of spectators in a stadium. Discounting walls
known only through field parch marks at the east end of the hypothetical
dromus, since their date is unknown, the boundaries of this *dromus* are
given by a short stretch of wall and the cut-back edge of the acropolis
bedrock along the north side near the east end of the hypothetical track,
and the north edge of the scene building discovered in AD 2000 quite far
in front of the *cavea* seating (see fig. 2).

Between these north and south limits, there is a clear distance of more
than 13 metres, which would allow for a running track with eight lanes.[24]
The fit is tight but possible, stretching from what has been identified as a

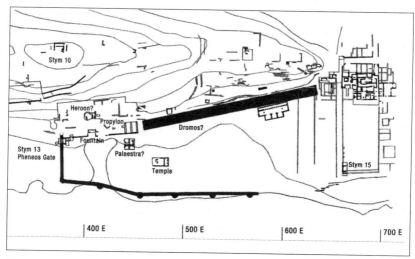

Figure 2. Plan of Stymphalus with proposed location of running track ("Dromos"). By Ben Gourley, Stymphalus Project.

monumental *propylaea* or gate building along the broad pedestrian road leading from the main westward or so-called Pheneus Gate, past the theatre *cavea*, to a rock-cut council (?) room at the end of the acropolis ridge, a distance of over 210 metres.[25] Close beside this tentative race track, near the monumental *propylaea* or putative entranceway to the stadium, Anastasios Orlandos identified a palestra conveniently located near the fountain house, where water for athletes to cleanse themselves after their exercises could easily be obtained.[26] It is possible, then, that Stymphalus provided for its athletes with a stadium, gymnasium or palestra, a nearby source of water, and a monumental entranceway to the stadium, just as many other Greek states had, and yet never again basked in Olympic glory.

Notes

1   *RE*, VII (4A) (1931) 436–53, "Stymphalos." Frazer's description of the valley (1965 [1898], 268–70) is good. The present adult population in the demos of Stymphaleia (which comprises ten villages) is about 3,000. The villages are scattered around the edges of the valley, with 150 to 700 residents each: Asprokampos, Drosopygi, Kaiseri, Kalliani, Kastania, Kefallari, Kyllene, Lafka, Psari, and Stymphaleia.

2   Preliminary publication of the work at Stymphalus in recent years is found in Hector Williams et al., 1996, 76–88; 1997, 44–57; 1998, 285–97; 2002, 135–87.

3   These are discussed most recently by Barringer (2005).

4   Heracles' service to his cousin Eurystheus is sometimes said to be blood-guilt payment for the murder of his own children, or alternatively the payment required by King Eurystheus to allow Heracles to return to Argos.

5 The metopes have often been discussed. See, for example, Hermann 1987, 151–200; Ashmole 1972, 60–89.

6 Pausanias (5.10.9) describes the themes of the six metopes over the west porch in reverse order, from right to left.

7 Ashmole and Yalouris 1967, 25.

8 Ashmole 1972, 70–71. Similar large rocks occasionally appear in contemporary Athenian vase painting, sometimes as landscape elements, such as on the Niobid krater (see Robertson 1992, 180, figs. 191–192), but sometimes also as specific topographic references. See, for example, an Athenian red-figure cup by the Penthesilea Painter with Theseus driving a bull to the Acropolis of Athens represented by an old man (his father?) sitting on a tall rock (Ferraro 44885, *LIMC* VII, 2 pl. 627, "Theseus 44"), or an Athenian red-figure amphora from Numana, near Ancona, with Zeus and Hera (?) sitting on tall rocks representing Mount Olympus and Iris standing between them holding an *oinochoe* (divine oath-taking, Iris with Styx water?), dated ca. 480–470 BC (Baldelli, Landolfi, and Lollini 1991, 24, colour plate opposite). For the rocks depicted on the Parthenon frieze and their meaning, see Fehl 1961, 1–44—esp. pp. 13–14, for the idea that the rocks on the east frieze represent a setting on Mount Olympus; p. 25 for the rocky setting of Mount Olympus for the east pediment, and pp. 30–33 for the rocky support below the shield of the Athena Parthenos representing the Acropolis of Athena. My thanks are owed to Alan Shapiro for these references. Ashmole 1972, 71, is also taken by the meaning of the goddess's bare feet on the Olympia metope, suggesting that the direct contact of her feet on the rock reinforces both her strength, through contact with the powers of earth, and her beauty. He goes on to suggest a possible influence of the Stymphalian metope on Pheidias' sculpture of the Athena Lemnia (pp. 72, 74).

9 For Orlandos's brief preliminary reports, see Orlandos 1924, 117–23; 1925, 51–5; 131–39; 1927, 53–56; 1928, 120–23; 1929, 92; 1930, 88–91; for an early photograph and plan of the Sanctuary, Πρακτικα (1924), 121, figs. 4 and 5. A summary of Orlandos's work is in *JHS* 45 (1925), 225. The identification of the Sanctuary is based primarily on a one-word inscription, POLIADOS, carefully carved in fourth-century BC letters on a rectangular pillar found by Orlandos in the Sanctuary, though now lost; see Orlandos 1926, 134.

10 For a reconstruction of the *kore* with most although not all of the fragments, see Hector Williams et al. 1998, 297, pl. 8. Mary Sturgeon is preparing a study of the *kore* and a second fragmentary piece of sculpture, a temple-boy, for publication. A very few pieces of pottery, several terracotta figurines, and one coin from the Sanctuary are fifth century.

11 "Agesias" in some editions of Pindar. The name was given the aspiration in Otto Schroeder's edition of Pindar (1900, 1923); see Slater 1969, s.v. "Ἀγησίας." A family connection to the great soldier Agasias of Stymphalus, mentioned often in Xenophon's *Anabasis*, is tempting to consider. Farnell (1932, 40) argues that Hieron, tyrant of Syracuse, won the four-horse chariot race at Olympia in 468, but Pindar showed his disappointment at not being asked to compose the paean for that by not mentioning the victory at all in the Sixth Olympian. Other commentators have suggested 472 or 476 BC. One might read into lines 100–102 a foreboding of troubles for Hagesias, probably more evident in 468 than in 472, since Hieron may have already been ill, leading to his death the following year. A scholiast on line 98 notes that Hagesias was put to death after Hieron's tyranny ended in 467. Farnell (1932, 40) suggests that Hagesias held his victory celebration in Stymphalus rather than Syracuse to gain favour with his Arcadian relatives, in case he had to move there for refuge, but the celebration was more likely held in both cities. He also notes (p. 48) that Pindar's victory ode may have been performed at a festival of Hera Parthenia (6th *Ol.*, 88), and that it should have been in the late summer, after the Olympic festival. This, however, prompts one to ask how long it would

take to engage Pindar's services, to have him complete an ode, and then to have it prepared for performance by someone sent from Thebes with the manuscript.

12 Pindar praises the choice of an ode over a statue in his Fifth Nemean Ode. Scholiasts of this ode might have invented the story of Pindar demanding a price for his ode that was equal to the cost of two statues; see Farnell 1932, 186.

13 Farnell (1932, 31) notes: "The mule-victories may have been comparatively unimpressive, but this one inspired Pindar to compose one of his most beautiful odes, pervaded throughout with a sunny brightness and warmth and with the flush of happy excitement." According to Pausanias, the mule chariot race was removed from the Olympics after 444 BC, so Hagesias' victory was a rare one.

14 For the opinion that Pindar's odes were performed as monodies, see Lefkowitz 1988, 1–11. The name "Aineias" or Aeneas is relatively uncommon in Greece (Farnell 1932, 48). Besides the chorus leader in Pindar's Ol. 6, however, there is a second Aeneas who was a captain in the Greek army of Xenophon's Anabasis (4.7.13). A third was Aeneas of Stymphalus, general of the Arcadian Confederacy in 367 BC, probably also the Aeneas Tacticus who wrote a fourth-century BC manual on siege warfare (OCD³, s.v. "Aeneas (Aineias) Tacticus"). Another is found in Paus. 6.4 in connection with a statue of Thrasyboulus, son of Aeneas, an Iamid, from Mantineia. That Aeneas was a relative of Hagesias is speculation based on the rarity of the name in places other than Stymphalus; see Farnell 1932, 48, or Gildersleeve 1885, 180, l. 88.

15 Nisetich 1980, 58.

16 See below, n. 17.

17 Other double periodonikai about the time of Dromeus included Theagenes of Thasos, ca. 480–476 BC, in pankration and boxing, Dandes of Argos in the stade (ca. 476 BC), and Ergoteles of Cnossus in the dolichus (ca. 472–468 BC). For the prestige that resulted from winning at all four Panhellenic festivals, i.e., as a periodonikes, see Kennell 1988, 239–51. A list of the periodonikai is given by H.C. Montgomery in RE XIX, I (1937), col. 813ff., and some names are added by Moretti 1954.

18 It has been suggested that Dromeus' descendants held the office of proxenos and thearodokos (similar to a "foreign representative") at Delphi between 315 and 280 BC. See Moretti 1957, 85, and Daux 1943, 27 FII.

19 Young 1984, 115–27.

20 See Pausanias (6.4.4) for the statue of Leontiscus: "The statue was made by Pythagoras of Rhegium, an excellent sculptor if ever there was one. They say that he studied under Clearchus, who was likewise a native of Rhegium, and a pupil of Eucheirus" (Loeb trans.). Other statues by Pythagoras include those of the boys' boxing winner, Protolaus of Mantineia (Paus. 6.6.1); the boxer Euthymus, of Epizephyrian Locris (6.6.6); Astylus, the double winner of the stade and diaulus in three successive Olympiads (6.13.1); Mnaseas of Cyrene, a hoplite race winner (6.13.7); and Mnaseas' son, Cratisthenes of Cyrene, in a chariot group with Victory (6.18.1).
   Moretti 1957, 85 and 87, no. 188, discusses Pythagoras' statue of Dromeus, and proposed identifications by other authors. See Pliny, HN 34.59; Lechat 1905, 13; Picard 1939, 114; Hyde 1921, 181. Pythagoras' career stretches from 480 BC (his statue of Astylus at Olympia) to 448 (Cratisthenes at Olympia); see Lechat 1905, 36, table IV, who discusses all his known works and his career. Pythagoras of Samos/Rhegium is one of the five best-known artists of the Severe style, see Ridgway 1970, 83–84, who notes that "he must have been one of the major personalities of the period."

21 The earlier date is favoured by Robert 1900, 141–95, and Moretti 1957, 85, while the later date is favoured by Hyde 1921, no. 69. In the latter case, the Pythian victories must be in 462 and 458, the Isthmian in 460, 458, and 456, and the Nemean in 463, 461, 459, 457, and 455. See Klee 1918, 81, no. 56, and pp. 94, 102–103. This seems preferable to the earlier dates, since it would put Dromeus' statue right in the middle of

Pythagoras' sculpting career rather than at its very beginning. It is thought that Dromeus' descendants continued to enjoy the privileges of proxeny and *thearodokia* at Delphi much later, between ca. 315 and 280; see Moretti 1957, 85, and Daux 1943, 27.

22 See Moretti 1957, 74, no. 123, and 85, no. 188; Finley and Pleket 1976, 94.

23 Ross 1841, 54. Others include Conrad Bursian, when he visited the site in 1854 (Bursian 1868–1872, 197), as well as both the present author and Stephen Miller, excavator of the stadium at nearby Nemea. One-sided stadiums were not uncommon; they existed at Priene (Wiegand and Schrader 1904, 262 pl. 19), Didyma (Wiegand 1941, 140–41 pls. 79, 80, 84), and Pergamon (possible stadium, Romano 1981, 586–89). The idea of using theatre seating to view athletic events on a track in front of the *cavea* is also not unusual. Oliver Picard (lecture in Waterloo, ON, 1988) proposed such an arrangement for the theatre at Argos, and David Romano (1982, 588 and n. 16 for references to ones at Aizanoi, Sardis, Tralles, Rhodes, and possibly Pessinus) has proposed this for the theatre in front of the temple of Dionysus (or Athena Nicephorus?) at Pergamon.

24 Clearly a major road extended from the area of the Pheneus Gate, past the so-called heroon and a fountain house, through the monumental *propylaea* and along the foot of the acropolis ridge to the theatre. Unless it took a sharp detour around the stage building, this road must have passed straight through the orchestra and on to the residential area to the east of the acropolis. The crucial question is how wide this major road was after encroachments such as the stage building and the monumental statue (?) base near the *klepsydra* are taken into account. Unless this stretch of road between the Propylaea and the east end of the acropolis is excavated, it will not be clear how narrow the narrowest segments may have been. With the currently known limitations, a *dromus* with eight lanes, each 1.5 metres wide, would fit. For a small city like Stymphalus, this would seem to be sufficient. At Priene, a well-preserved starting line has eight lanes and a central position for a starter. The length of this starting line is 14.9 m. The starting positions average 0.85 m wide, and columns were placed between each position, approximately 0.63 m wide. There is also a series of eight turning post blocks set in front of the starting line, and these are just under 13 m from one end to the other, again with provision for a wider central space, for the starter (?). The track at Priene is estimated to have been 178 m long. See Wiegand and Schrader 1904, 262, fig. 264, pl. 19. The *dromus* at Didyma is even narrower, having a clear width of only about 10 m for what appears to be eight starting positions. See Wiegand 1941, 140–41, pls. 79, 80, 84.

25 I am indebted to Ben Gourley for the plan with hypothetical *dromus*. A long sondage (3 x 11 m) was excavated between the *cavea*/orchestra and the scene building in the 2000 season, with no results in either proving or disproving whether a stadium track existed here. This sondage, and another cutting near the far eastern end of the proposed *dromus*, failed to find distinctive road mettling, but instead found rather softer sandy fill. This is in fact consistent with a *dromus* surface which was regularly softened for running races. It is also interesting that vehicular traffic coming from the west was directed up a terraced road and through a gate halfway up the south face of the acropolis ridge (wheel ruts are still visible), rather than through the Pheneus Gate, which—with its threshold block and steps to reach the terrace above the fountain house—must have been for pedestrian traffic.

26 *Orlandos* 1924, 120; 1925, 52; 1927, 55–56, fig. 4; Delorme 1960, 235–37, fig. 59; 374–94 passim.

Commemorative Cash: The Coins of the Ancient and Modern Olympics

Robert Weir

This chapter discusses a phenomenon that apparently links the modern Olympics to their ancient counterpart, that of commemorative coins issued on the occasion of the Games. Scholars of either the modern Olympics or of modern numismatics do occasionally note the connection to illustrate the modern Games' heritage.[1] Nevertheless, students of ancient sport, knowing how dissimilar the two festivals were in many other respects, might well be immediately skeptical of such generalizations by non-specialists and suspect that this paper will indulge in the straw man fallacy by attacking what nobody—at least no specialist—believes seriously anyway. To be sure, the coins minted at Olympia between the fifth and second centuries BC bore little resemblance to the phenomenon current since 1952. Lest I violate the *asuleia* (or sacrosanctity) of this Olympic gathering by provoking an analog of the pitched battle that marred the Games of 364 BC, let me hasten to add that the modernist assessment holds up surprisingly well for the ancient coinages associated with athletic festivals such as the Olympics in the Roman period, in particular from the mid-second to mid-third century AD.

This chapter examines some of the modern, Olympics-related coinages to determine what makes them "commemorative," a term that one often takes for granted. It will then discuss how well, or not, the ancient coins fit the modern definition. In an ideal world, one would also evaluate the ancient coins more fairly, that is, according to their own standard(s) for what made a commemorative; but arriving at such a definition would certainly exceed the scope of this paper and could in the end prove impossible anyway.[2]

In 1939, and acting apparently under the influence of sporting commemoratives recently issued in Sweden and Estonia, the Finnish Numismatic Society decided that the Helsinki Olympics slated for 1940 ought to be marked by a special coinage, and held a public contest to decide the design.[3] The noted sculptor Felix Nylund submitted an allegorical tableau of the goddess Freedom crowning Youth, which took second place, but the eventual winner for the rescheduled Helsinki Games in 1952 was a more sober design that featured simply the Olympic rings flanked by the inscription OLYMPIA / XV / 1952 / HELSINKI.[4] This design was stamped onto the obverse of only about 600,000 silver coins in a single denomination, 500 markkaa (worth $2.25 US at the time).[5]

From this simple beginning, the great phenomenon of collectable Olympic commemoratives grew, albeit slowly at first. No commemoratives were minted to celebrate the 1956 Games in Melbourne, while Japan struck two commemorative silver coins of 100 and 1,000 yen for the 1964 Olympics in Tokyo, and Mexico issued a silver coin of 25 pesos to mark the 1968 Games in Mexico City. Both the Japanese and Mexican issues were produced in much greater numbers than the Finnish coins, bore fancier figurative designs, and in the former case were intended to leave the country, since English was used in the legend for the first time.[6] These early series clearly refer to the Olympic Games, but have little in the way of visibly Olympic content, except for the five interlocked Olympic rings. Despite their ostensible celebration of the Olympics, recognizable national identifiers predominated (i.e., the rising sun and Mount Fuji in 1964, an Aztec ball player and an eagle fighting a serpent in 1968).

Commemorative coins of the modern Olympics began to hit their stride with the issues celebrating the 1972 Olympics in Munich, which have established a model for almost all Olympic commemoratives of the past thirty years. These coins now downplayed their nationalist ties and instead emphasized their Olympic connections: whereas the obverse remained devoted to the host nation and bore an image of its head of state, national emblem, etc., the reverse was exclusively Olympic, and bore one of a wide variety of types that had been created especially for that Olympiad. Furthermore, several different coins were produced, not just the one or two varieties of the earlier series, a strategy which created both greater inter-

Figure 1. Mexico City Olympics (1968), 25-peso commemorative. Coin diameter 31 mm; frame diameter 33 mm. Courtesy Keith Greenham.

Figure 2. Munich Olympics (1972), 10-mark commemorative of Series 4. Coin diameter 25 mm; frame diameter 27 mm. Courtesy Keith Greenham.

est for the collector and greater potential revenues for the state. In the case of the 1972 Games, the Bundestag authorized the production of six different series of silver 10-mark pieces. Since four different mints made up the otherwise identical issues for each series, a truly avid collector could assemble a total of twenty-four sub-varieties; as well, staggering the release dates of the six series at regular intervals between January 1970 and August 1972 was intended to keep consumer interest high during the two years leading up to the Olympics.[7] Whereas all previous Olympic commemoratives had been issued at a price no higher than their face value, the Munich Olympic coins marked a further departure from precedent by issuing limited numbers of proof-grade coins—in other words, higher-quality coins intended solely for collectors and not for circulation—at a 50 per cent markup over their face value (i.e., for 15 DM). The total number of coins being struck was also higher than ever before, 100 million pieces, of which about 3 per cent were proof coins aimed at the collector market.[8]

Figure 3. Montreal Olympics (1976), $100 gold commemorative (14 karats). Coin diameter 22 mm; frame diameter 24 mm. Courtesy Keith Greenham.

The year 1972 also saw the first Olympic commemoratives minted by countries other than the host nation. Although these coins are outside the scope of the present survey, one can describe them in general terms as virtuoso pieces executed in precious metals almost exclusively for collectors worldwide. The minting countries, interestingly enough, have tended not to be the usual Olympic superpowers but lesser-known states from the Arab world, the Pacific region, or Africa.[9]

At the next Olympiad, the 1976 Games in Montreal, one could say that the commemoratives had completed their evolution, and we will end our consideration of the modern phenomenon with them. They are a collector's paradise. The Royal Canadian Mint issued the first gold Olympic commemorative in two purities of metal, 14 karat and 22 karat. The face value in both cases was $100, approximately equal to the intrinsic value of the 14 karat coin, which sold initially for $105.[10] The 22 karat coin, however, not only had a higher intrinsic value (and thus a $150 initial issue price) but it was struck also in the higher proof quality.[11]

Most collectors, however, were more interested in the $5 and $10 silver coins, with no fewer than twenty-eight different reverse types, which the Royal Canadian Mint issued in seven staggered series between December 1973 and June 1976. Each of the series was the work of a different artist and was thematically distinct (geography; ancient Olympic motifs; early Canadian sports; track and field sports; Olympic water sports; Olympic team and body contact sports; and Montreal Olympic venues, respectively). Virtually none of the silver coins was intended for circulation, and each type could be purchased either as a single loose coin, as a single encapsulated coin, as part of the Mint's four-coin series in one of three grades of boxed sets, or as part of a deluxe boxed set of all twenty-eight

Figure 4. Montreal Olympics (1976), a selection of $5 and $10 silver commemoratives. Series 2, temple of Zeus; Series 3, lacrosse; Series 5, diver; Series 7, Olympic village. Series 2 and 3 coin diameter 37 mm; frame diameter 39 mm. Series 5 and 7 coin diameter 30.5 mm; frame diameter 32 mm. Courtesy Keith Greenham.

silver coins. In each case, there was always a significant markup ranging from 45 per cent (for a single unencapsulated $10 coin of Series 1) to 178 per cent over the face value (for the boxed set of all twenty-eight silver coins in proof condition).[12] The gold coins, perhaps because they were more expensive to begin with, were generally less overvalued, just 5 per cent for the more common 14 karat coin, and 50 per cent for the scarcer 22 karat coin in proof condition.

Semi-annual reports submitted by the Postmaster General to Parliament between 1973 and 1981 not only confirm the profit motive behind the commemoratives' overvaluations but also give a glimpse of unforeseen vicissitudes that threatened to derail the process. Although the total number of coins produced was only about a quarter of that minted in Germany in 1972 (i.e., 25, 352, 307), Ottawa realized net proceeds of $124.5 million (or an average margin of 39 per cent above face value).[13] This compared well with the approximately 17 million DM profit (or a margin of

1.7 per cent) that Germany had made by striking some proof coins for collectors. Germany had put the profits of its coin program towards defraying the cost of the Games, and Ottawa planned to do the same on a grander scale—even, according to early estimates, paying off 80 per cent of the projected $350 million bill through the coin program alone.[14] Not only did the coin program fail to realize most of the $280 million in projected profits, however, but the actual price for the Games themselves swelled to an eventual $730 million, more than twice the original estimate. The initial omens had been good: a strong public interest resulted in the sale of about 6.9 million coins from Series 1, on the basis of which the Postmaster General projected a healthy profit of $250 million for the whole program of seven series.[15] One year after the program began, however, an unforeseen rise in the traditionally stable price of silver from $2.70 US to $5 US a troy ounce seriously eroded the coins' profitability.[16] In addition, Canada already faced reduced profits from a pledge to give a rebate to the respective national Olympic committees of 3 per cent of the face value of all coins sold in Canada and forty-five foreign countries.[17] Ottawa's response was a cautious compromise: the price of Series 2 through 7 was raised modestly, though not commensurately with the increased price of silver, for fear of losing customers;[18] smaller runs for Series 2 through 7 lowered production costs.[19]

Criteria for Commemorative Olympic Coins

	Modern	Greek (470–190 BC)	Roman (150–250 AD)
Issue may be initiated, types chosen, etc., by interested citizens submitting a proposal to the government	x		x
Multiple possible issuing authorities for the same Games held in the same place at the same time	x	x[20]	
Although legal tender in their issuing countries, most coins are aimed at collectors and are not intended to circulate	x		?[21]
Face value of the precious metal issues may actually be lower than their intrinsic value	x		
Usually sold at a premium over both face value and intrinsic value in order to generate a profit for the issuer	x	?	?
Issued for a limited time or in predetermined quantities	x	x	x
May be struck in various denominations and metals	x	x[22]	x
Often in excellent condition owing to lack of circulation	x		x[23]
Types make specific reference to host cities, athletic events, Olympic logos, etc.	x		x

On the basis of the modern phenomenon, I propose the definition of a modern commemorative according to the criteria tabulated above. It is obvious from the table that the Classical and Hellenistic Greek coins minted at Olympia fulfill few of the same requirements, but that the coins of Roman Olympia meet enough of them to be considered "commemorative." Even some of the correspondences, however, require either qualification or acknowledgement that we lack the evidence to make a sure determination and must instead rely upon probability.

The definitive study of the pre-Roman coins from Olympia is still Charles Seltman's *The Temple Coins of Olympia* (1921). It has withstood the test of time well despite some minor modifications to his chronology and the occasional discovery of new dies, or even new varieties, not noted by him.[24] Most importantly, no one in the past eighty years has, to my knowledge, objected to his primary assertion, namely that all of the silver and bronze coins minted between ca. 470 and 190 BC with the inscription "of the Eleans" were actually struck at Olympia, not Elis: the ethnic designation really denotes the Sanctuary's political masters for virtually the whole existence of the ancient Olympic Games, not the place of production.[25] If Seltman had not shown to almost everyone's satisfaction that the Elean coins were in fact Olympian, one would simply not think to consider them as commemoratives in the first place.

Until isotope analysis of some Olympia coins is done to ascertain either the origin of their silver from a precise mine or (as most scholars suspect) that they are a blend of many mixed batches of coin from all over Greece, one cannot say much about the circumstances of their manufacture. What seems plausible, on the basis of a similar phenomenon attested at the sanctuary of Delphi in the fourth century, is that Olympic officials amassed the motley coins offered by pilgrims at the Sanctuary and struck a new coinage from it, probably on the occasion of the great quadrennial festival.[26] For what it is worth, we have no evidence to suggest that the Olympic coins were connected with fundraising efforts in the way that the Delphic coins were.[27] Because no ancient authors mention the coins of ancient Olympia, one has only countermarks and hoard distributions to study for further insights into why they were made and how they were used. As Seltman noted, many, maybe even most, of the staters minted in the first few decades of production came to bear one or several countermarks; thereafter, countermarks were applied ever more sporadically, until they ceased to appear on coins by the mid-fourth century.[28] Although twenty-two of the recorded countermark varieties were geometrical or floral patterns, another twenty-nine were figurative, many of which corresponded to the coin types of Peloponnesian or island mints (e.g., the sea turtle of Aegina).[29] What this suggests is that for several decades the staters from Olympia were not widely recognized as "good money," and had to be certified by foreign states or private bankers either as equivalent to a local stater (or two drachmae) or at least as pure bullion.[30] Such a slow, and perhaps reluctant, acceptance of Olympian silver as currency may have been due to two factors, both the relatively small size of Olympic issues and the constant variations of type, perhaps from one Olympiad to the next, that ran counter to the traditional conservatism of coin types in fifth-century Greece.[31]

If it were not for the hoard evidence, one might think that the coins were struck in limited quantities as souvenirs of the Games and were never really intended to circulate (and thus their need for validation if they passed from the original owner into circulation), but Olympic coins occur commonly in hoards, often well worn from decades in circulation, though their appearances are largely limited to Peloponnesian hoards. To take one example, a small hoard of silver and bronze coins excavated at Arcadian Stymphalus in 1999 was dated on the basis of Macedonian regal coins to 290/280 BC, but it also contained an Olympic hemidrachmon that dates to 350/325 BC.[32] Examination of the find-spots of several hoards containing silver coins minted at Olympia reveals that 45 per cent of them were unearthed within one day's travel of Olympia (30 km); within a 90 km radius equivalent to three days' travel, one can account for 90 per cent of the Olympic coins.[33] If the coins of Olympia were distributed or sold as commemorative souvenirs, one would expect to find them all over the Greek world and without any particular concentration in the Peloponnese. Visitors flocked to Olympia from all of Greece and beyond, and so one would naturally expect them to carry such keepsakes back home before possibly burying them with other prized possessions, or boring of them and trying to spend them. In other words, the Olympic silvers give every appearance of being a functional coinage rather than a souvenir.

The issues of pre-Roman Olympia do not really qualify as commemoratives on the basis of their choice of types, either. Although the variations are numerous, the types almost all allude either to the cult of Zeus or (in many fewer instances) to that of Hera. The obverse typically bears the head of a god, usually Zeus, while the reverse invariably exhibits either some aspect of the Zeus cult (e.g., thunderbolt, eagle) or occasionally a figure of Nike. Nothing pertaining to Hera appears on any reverse. The Zeus and Hera heads could be interpreted as allusions to the two most prominent temples in the *Altis* and their cults, but the coins were thus, if anything, reflective of the religious aspect of the ancient Olympics, and not

Figure 5. Silver hemidrachmon of Olympia, ca. 350/325 BC. From Stymphalus hoard of 1999. Coin diameter 15 mm; frame diameter 17 mm. Courtesy Hector Williams, Stymphalus Projects.

the athletic contests. The only apparent allusion to the competition is the recurring figure of Nike, either running with a wreath or seated pensively, on the reverse of some staters of the fifth century.[34] Allusions to sporting events (usually equestrian) and to victory in them is quite prevalent on Classical Greek coinage, particularly in Magna Graecia, where some types even allude to specific victories by specific tyrants at the Olympic Games.[35] Given that this option existed, the mint masters at Olympia made a deliberate choice to ignore it in favour of the gods.

The instance of Delphi's Amphictyonic coinage of 336 BC suggests a reason why cult types were so important on sanctuary coins. Although Delphi hosted a quadrennial set of games modelled on the Olympics and almost as prestigious, they had never received notice on the local coinage, which traditionally preoccupied itself with the cult of Apollo. Because we know from inscriptions that precisely these coins were minted from pilgrims' gifts to the god, the choice of religious types makes sense. Once a gift had been made to a Greek god, it essentially belonged to him forever and could not be deconsecrated, or wholly reintegrated into the secular world, even by being melted down and restruck.[36] The god's mark was thus testimony either to his continued ownership or to his tutelary interest in the money.[37] At either venue, Delphi or Olympia, the athletic festival was originally and ultimately in honour of the patron deity, and one could see the god's image as a symbol, albeit highly abbreviated, of all that was associated with his sanctuary, both sacred and agonistic. The essential difference of modern commemorative representations is that they honour the Games themselves.

Figure 6. Bronze of Olympia, minted under Caracalla, AD 198–217. Coin diameter
(max.) 27 mm; frame width 57 mm. Courtesy American Numismatic Society.

By contrast, the coins of Roman Olympia move a little closer to the
modern practice. For instance, the types can allude to the venue itself,
and not just to cult. The pieces in question are a few varieties of bronze
minted for Hadrian (AD 117–138), Caracalla (AD 198–217), and Geta
(AD 198–209). Although the Roman ruler's bust occupies the obverse, the
reverse designs feature a winner's olive wreath, Pheidias' chryselephantine
cult statue of Zeus, or Skopas' Aphrodite Pandemus riding sidesaddle on
a goat.[38] Two "repeats" from the pre-Roman coinage are a bearded head
of Zeus, presumed to be a detail of the Pheidian statue, and a striding figure of Zeus hurling a thunderbolt, which is believed to represent the pre-
Pheidian cult image of the fifth century BC.[39] All of these coins are rare
today, and it is unfortunate that fewer still are from known archaeological contexts, since this makes it hard to say much about their adventures
after minting, whether they were circulating money or souvenirs.[40] Their
very rarity today, however, suggests that they never existed in any great
number, and invites a comparison with the equally rare bronzes from contemporary Delphi and nineteen other athletic centres of the second and
third centuries AD, for whose commemorative athletic coinages I have
done die-studies.[41] At almost every site, the number of dies employed for
a particular issue was very small, usually no more than half a dozen obverse
dies. At Hadrianic Delphi, in fact, the same four obverse dies with the
emperor's portrait were coupled with fourteen different reverse types![42]
Given these limitations, no great number of coins was ever struck at Hadrianic Delphi, and the same likely holds true for Roman Olympia.

Although we cannot be certain of all the circumstances of issue, it can
be said that these coins were commemoratives in the sense that they are
souvenirs of specific items that one would have seen only at Olympia or

Delphi. Since they were bronzes of token value, not silver coins, and issued in apparently very small quantities, they cannot have had much of an economic impact. Perhaps this would qualify them as souvenir issues, not currency. Other athletic venues of the third century AD that issued commemorative coins went further by illustrating athletic events, prize crowns, and temples of the imperial cult frequently associated with the new Olympics and Pythian Games of the Roman East.[43] Here too the total number of dies used to strike individual varieties was never large, almost always in the single digits per variety, and many cities struck no more than a single variety of coin per Pythiad.[44] The coins of Roman Olympia and Delphi, however, already had much in common with the sorts of topical references that would appear on the commemoratives from the 1964 Olympics through the present. In conclusion, whereas it might be anachronistic to speak of commemorative coins minted for ancient collectors, the Games-related issues of the second and third centuries AD exhibit many of the characteristics of types deliberately chosen to evoke the Games, as well as a limited production run that would have had relatively little economic impact had it gone into circulation.

Notes

1   For two examples, see Hoge 1995 and Ménard 1991, 8.

2   Any definition would have to include the element of intentionality, namely, the reason behind striking a certain coin with a certain type, and this intangible and ephemeral notion is naturally all but impossible to verify for any aspect of Classical antiquity. Inasmuch as one function of a commemorative was to remind the viewer of a specific Olympics-related event, one could make a strong case that several high-denomination silver pieces from fifth-century BC Sicily qualify for the title, such as the mule-drawn cart on tetradrachms of Anaxilas' Rhegium and the four-horse chariot on tetradrachms and dekadrachms of Hieron's Syracuse (Kraay 1976, 214; cf. Schreier 1972, Driega 1974, Eberhardt 1988, and Gadoury and Romolo 1996). Even here, however, there are complications. For instance, the chariot coins were Syracuse's standard type for much of the earlier fifth century, and continued in production long after Hieron had disappeared from power. Thus one has to draw a line somehow between a potential commemorative and something that merely retains the same types without the same intention behind its production.

3   Talvio 1979 and 1984.

4   Talvio 1994.

5   Ménard 1991, 47; 18,500 examples were actually struck in 1951 and bear that date, which makes them rare and desirable today—about $240 US in extremely fine (EF) condition, as listed on eBay in the autumn of 2003. The great majority, however (586,500), were minted in the Olympic year 1952 (about $40 US in EF condition, from the same source). Each coin's reverse is non-commemorative and bears the number 500 within an oak wreath, around which runs the inscription SUOMI FINLAND and, at the bottom, MARKKAA. The coin's alloy was actually 50 per cent silver, 40 per cent copper, and 10 per cent nickel. It weighed 12 grams and had a diameter of 32 mm.

6   See Ménard 1991 for more information. As she notes, Japan issued 80 million pieces of 100 yen and 15 million coins of 1,000 yen (60–61), while Mexico issued 30 million coins of 25 pesos (65). On Japan's use of English for the first time, see Ménard 1991, 59. The English legend in each case includes the denomination, the date of issue (1964), and the venue. The Japanese legends both omit "Tokyo 1964," for which they substitute "year 39 of the reign of Showa (i.e., Emperor Hirohito)."

7   Ménard 1991, 70–75.

8   Ménard 1991, 70–75.

9   See for instance, Danaher 1978, 28–39 (1972 Olympics), and 41–52 (1976 Olympics). A quick look online (e.g., at eBay's current offerings) or at any major catalogue of world coins will confirm that Olympic commemoratives are legion.

10 Ménard 1991, 113.

11 Ménard 1991, 112.

12 Ménard 1991, 86–115.

13 Canada Post (fifteenth report of 31 March 1981), 5. The face value of all the gold and silver coins struck by the Royal Canadian Mint was $279.3 million, for which collectors paid $388.2 million by the end of government sales on 31 March 1981.

14 Danaher 1978, 53.

15 Canada Post (second report of 30 September 1974), 10.

16 Danaher 1978, 57. The increased cost of bullion left little room to cover the additional expenses of production, advertising, and distribution, not to mention any sort of profit.

17 Canada Post (fifteenth report of 31 March 1981), 11. Distribution and sale of the host country's commemoratives abroad was another novelty of the 1976 Olympic commemoratives. By the close of the coin program in March 1981, Ottawa had paid out $4.75 million to Canada's own Olympic committee, and $3.63 million to the Olympic committees of forty-five other nations. The greatest interest came from West Germany ($1.22 million in rebates) and the United States ($1.08 million in rebates), and least enthusiastic was Mexico, which received precisely $2 back!

18 Ménard 1991, 88–111. The price for Series 2 coins and coin sets was anywhere between 14 per cent and 21 per cent higher than for Series 1, depending on the numismatic product in question, but there were no further increases thereafter (*pace* Danaher 1978, 57). A single $5 coin rose from $8.50 to $10 (unencapsulated), or from $10 to $11.50 (encapsulated). A single $10 coin likewise climbed from $14.50 to $17.50 (unencapsulated), or from $16.50 to $19.50 (encapsulated). The three grades of four-coin sets for Series 1, namely the Custom Set, the Prestige Set, and the Proof Set, retailed for $47.50, $52.50, and $72.50, but the same sets in the later series sold for $57.50, $62.50, and $82.50, respectively.

19 By the end of March 1976, the projected profits of the program had fallen to $155 million (Canada Post [fifth report of 31 March 1976], 14), which is not far off the final figure of $124.5 million (Canada Post [fifteenth report of 31 March 1981], 5).

20 This was more the exception than the rule: as mentioned elsewhere, some autocrats, usually of fifth-century Magna Graecia, advertised Olympic victories on their own coins.

21 Die-totals indicate that only small numbers of coins were made, thus possibly for collectors.

22 Silver fractions of the stater were struck from earliest days, but bronze coins were only introduced in the third century BC.

23 All issues were in bronze, which corrodes readily; however, corrosion should not be confused with degree of wear, which is often surprisingly slight for bronze coins from antiquity.

24 Seltman's inception date for the Olympic series in the late sixth century (1921, 1) was dependent upon stylistic similarities with the snake-bearing eagles on the earliest coins of Chalcis, but because the latter have since been down-dated well into the fifth century,

it may well be that the first Olympic coins were not struck before the synoecism of Elis in 471 BC (Schrader 1937; Nicolet-Pierre 1975, Kraay 1976, 104). They are, at any rate, not attested in hoards buried before 450 BC (Thompson, Mørkholm, and Kraay 1973, no. 1482, and Kraay 1976, 104).

25 The reverse ethnic denotation is generally FA or FALEION, but one example minted ca. 360 BC goes so far as to read FALEION next to the Zeus head on the obverse and OLUMPIA next to a nymph's head on the obverse. This could be translated as "Olympia belongs to the Eleans," if one takes it as an allusion to the events mentioned below. The exception to the Elean ethnic denotation seems to prove the rule. For a brief period in 364 BC, the people of nearby Pisa seized control of the sanctuary with the help of the Arcadians. The episode manifests itself numismatically in the form of two gold coins— only two specimens are known to exist—that bear the same "Olympic" types but the reverse ethnic denotation "of the Pisatans" (PISATAN). Seltman's other evidence is similarly circumstantial but seems to reinforce his hypothesis beyond a reasonable doubt. Possibly the coins were even produced in the sanctuary's two principal temples, the Zeus-type coins in the Temple of Zeus (ca. 470–192 BC), and the Hera-type pieces in the Temple of Hera (ca. 421–365 BC).

26 Kraay 1976, 103. For records of the Amphictyony's collection and reminting of pilgrims' donations, see most conveniently the inscriptions gathered by Jones 1993, 129–59, especially inscription no. 212 on pp. 140–44.

27 The Amphictyony was raising money for about fifty years to rebuild the Temple of Apollo, which had been ruined by an earthquake in 373 BC.

28 Seltman 1921, 75.

29 Seltman 1921, 5.

30 Kraay 1976, 103, especially n. 5.

31 Seltman (1921) counted 158 obverse dies for 300+ years' worth of Olympic staters. Within this span, the staters of Olympia were minted in thirty different series, although there can be minor variations within a single series. This would average out to a different series, and thus a different set of types, being minted every ten years, or after two or three Olympiads.

32 Seltman did not know this particular variety of hemidrachmon, with an olive wreath in the lower right field of the reverse, though later cataloguers have almost invariably assigned it to his Series XXIII (ca. 323–271 BC) on the basis of a somewhat similar hemidrachmon that he assigned there (plate VIII.30: same types and style, but different adjunct symbol on the reverse). However, the hemidrachmon in the hoard from Stymphalus, which most likely dates to ca. 290/280 BC on the basis of its regal Macedonian coins, is already heavily worn, and this suggests that its date of issue was not later than the third quarter of the fourth century BC.

33 Thompson, Mørkholm, and Kraay 1973, nos. 19, 23–24, 35, 37, 44, 48, 67, 73–75, 78, 83, 122, 130, 176–77, 195, 209, 245, 266, 302, 1482, and 1652. Other hoards are lacking precise find spots and are excluded from consideration (eidem nos. 20, 50–51, 68–69, 129, 222, 224, and 243), as are finds of bronzes struck at Olympia (eidem nos. 197, 216, 242, 302, and 353), since different factors affected the circulation of token bronzes. Although the separations of the hoards from Olympia have been reckoned as straight-line distances, a figure of 30 km as the crow flies is not inconsistent with what would be a day's travel by a less direct route on the ground. According to Xenophon, it took "five or six" days to walk to Olympia from Athens (*Memorabilia* 3.13.5), and in this case, the straight-line distance is 192 km. For the discovery of Olympic coins at Olympia, see Warren 1962 and Schultz 1979; cf. Seltman 1951.

34 Seltman 1921, Series II, IV–XIII.

35 Above, n. 2. For instance, it was Anaxilas of Rhegium's victory in the mule-car race in either 484 or 480 BC that was featured on the local coinage (Aristotle, fragment 578R).

Hieron's advertisement on contemporary coins of Syracuse of his victory in the four-horse chariot was likely the motivating factor (Kraay 1976, 214).

36 Surviving inventories of sacred treasuries make it abundantly clear that these accumulations typically included coins, both domestic and foreign, as the records from Athens, Delphi, and Delos demonstrate most clearly (Jones 1993, nos. 131–286).

37 Perhaps the prevalence of deities on Greek coins has some connection to the supposed location of most Greek "mints," which were usually very minor set-ups involving only a handful of workers within the confines of temples.

38 Gardner 1963 [1887], xxxviii and 76; Pausanias 6.25.2.

39 Schwabacher 1962.

40 Three Hadrianic bronzes, however, were found in the course of the Agora excavations (Kroll 1993, 237, nos. 753–55). A quick survey of two major collections reveals four examples of such coins among the 550,000+ ancient coins held at the American Numismatic Society in New York (three Hadrianic, 1944.100.38742–43, 1948.4.87, and one Caracallan, 1944.100.38744); the British Museum's own catalogue volume, from the nineteenth century, lists five examples (Gardner 1963 [1887], 75–76, nos. 156–160).

41 Three bronzes of Hadrian and the deified Faustina I likewise surfaced in the Athenian Agora (Kroll 1993, 203–204, nos. 589–91).

42 For results of the die-study undertaken as part of the 1994 graduate summer seminar at the American Numismatic Society, see Weir 2004, 82–86. The coins in question were all small bronzes (17–20 mm) with reverse types such as the Delphic *omphalos*, Apollo's crow, a Pythian victor's wreath, a lyre, a tripod, a tetrastyle temple façade, a seated Pan, and a seated Apollo.

43 Even so, the lyre-strumming Apollo who adorns the reverse of a first-century AD series of Delphic coins has been convincingly equated with the emperor Nero, who came to compete in the musical contests of the Pythian Games of AD 67 (Levy 1989).

44 Weir 2004, 181–94.

WORKS CITED IN PART I

Adshead, K. 1986. *Politics of the Archaic Peloponnese*. Aldershot, England: Avebury.

Africanus, Sextus Julius. 1980. *Olympionicarum Fasti*. Greek text with critical commentary, notes, and appendix by Johannes Rutgers. 1862. Reprint, Chicago: Ares.

Ajootian, Aileen. 2003. "Homeric Time, Space, and the Viewer at Olympia." In *The Enduring Instant: Time and the Spectator in the Visual Arts*, ed. Antoinette Roesler-Friedenthal and Johannes Nathan, 137–63. Berlin: Mann.

Aloni, Antonio. 1983. "Osservazione su gr. ΚΑΔΟΣ." *Acme* 36:43–49.

Andrewes, Antony. 1952. "Sparta and Arcadia in the Early Fifth Century." *Phoenix* 6:1–5.

Ancient Mysteries: Blood and Honor at the First Olympics. 1996. New York: A & E Home Video.

Aristotle. 1995. *Politics: Books III and IV*. Translated with introduction and comments by Richard Robinson. Oxford: Clarendon.

Arrigoni, Giampiera. 1985. "Donne e sport nel mondo greco: Religione e società." In *Le donne in Grecia,* ed. Giampiera Arrigoni, 55–201. Rome: Laterza.

Ashmole, Bernard. 1972. *Architect and Sculptor in Classical Greece*. New York: New York University Press.

Ashmole, Bernard, and Nicholas Yalouris. 1967. *Olympia: The Sculptures of the Temple of Zeus*. London: Phaidon.

Baitinger, Holger, and Birgitta Eder. 2002. "Hellenistische Stimmarken aus Elis und Olympia: Neue Forschungen zu den Beziehungen zwischen Hauptstadt und Heiligtum." *JDAI* 116:163–243.

Baldelli, Gabriele, Maurizio Landolfi, and Delia Lollini, eds. 1991. *La ceramica attica figurata nelle Marche.* Ancona.

Barringer, Judith M. 2005. "The Temple of Zeus at Olympia, Heroes and Athletes." *Hesperia* 74:211–41.

Barron, J.P. 1984. "Ibycus: *Gorgias* and Other Poems." *BICS* 31:13–24.

Bennett, Emmett L., Jr. 1958. *The Olive Oil Tablets of Pylos. Minos Suppl.* 2. Salamanca: Seminario de Filología Clásica, Universidad de Salamanca.

Bérard, Claude. 1986. "L'impossible femme athlète." *AION* 8:195–202.

Bernardini, Paola Angeli. 1986–87. "Aspects ludiques, rituels et sportifs de la course féminine dans la Grèce antique." *Stadion* 12–13:17–26.

Betts, John H. 1967. "New Light on Minoan Bureaucracy: A Re-examination of Some Cretan Sealings." *Kadmos* 6:15–40.

Bickerman, E.J. 1980. *Chronology of the Ancient World.* 2nd ed. Ithaca, NY: Cornell University Press.

Bilik, Ronald. 2000. "Die Zuverlässigkeit der frühen Olympionikenliste. Die Geschichte eines Forschungsproblems im chronologischen Überblick." *Nikephoros* 13:47–62.

Blanchard, Kendall. 1995. *The Anthropology of Sport: An Introduction.* Rev. ed. Westport, CT: Bergin and Garvey.

Blech, Michael. 1982. *Studien zum Kranz bei den Griechen.* Berlin and New York: De Gruyter.

Blitzer, Harriet. 1993. "Olive Cultivation and Oil Production in Minoan Crete." In *La production du vin et de l'huile en Méditerranée,* ed. Marie-Claire Amouretti and Jean-Pierre Brun. *BCH Suppl.* 26:163–75.

Boeckh, August. 1821. *Pindari Opera quae supersunt.* Leipzig.

Boegehold, Alan L., et al. 1995. *The Lawcourts at Athens: Sites, Buildings, Equipment, Procedure, and Testimonia. Athenian Agora* 28. Princeton, NJ: American School of Classical Studies at Athens.

Boer, Willem den. 1954. *Laconian Studies.* Amsterdam: North-Holland Publishing.

———. 1979. *Private Morality in Greece and Rome: Some Historical Aspects.* Leiden: Brill.

Bollansée, Jan. 1999. "Aristotle and Hermippos of Smyrna on the Foundation of the Olympic Games and the Institution of the Sacred Truce." *Mnemosyne* 52:562–67.

Bonfante, Larissa. 1989. "Nudity as a Costume in Classical Art." *AJA* 93:543–70.

Bowra, C.M. 1961. *Greek Lyric Poetry from Alcman to Simonides.* 2nd ed. Oxford: Clarendon.

Bremmer, Jan. 1990. "Adolescents, *Symposion,* and Pederasty." In *Sympotica: A Symposium on the Symposion,* ed. Oswyn Murray, 135–48. Oxford: Clarendon.

Brinkmann, A. 1915. "Die olympische Chronik." *RhM* 70:622–37.

Brodersen, Kai. 1990. "Zur Datierung der ersten Pythien." *ZPE* 82:25–31.

Brommer, Frank. 1986. *Heracles: The Twelve Labors of the Hero in Ancient Art and Literature.* Translated and enlarged by Shirley J. Schwarz. New Rochelle, NY: A.D. Caratzas.

Brulotte, Eric L. 1994. "The 'Pillar of Oinomaos' and the Location of Stadium I at Olympia." *AJA* 98:53–64.

Bruwaene, Martin van den. 1981. *Cicéron: De Natura Deorum,* Livre III. Brussels: Collection Latomus.

Burkert, Walter. 1983. *Homo Necans. The Anthropology of Ancient Greek Sacrificial Ritual and Myth.* Translated by Peter Bing. Berkeley and Los Angeles: University of California Press.

———. 1985. *Greek Religion.* Translated by John Raffan. Cambridge, MA: Harvard University Press.

Bursian, Conrad. 1868–1872. *Geographie von Griechenland.* Vol. 2, *Peloponnesos und Inseln.* Leipzig: B.B. Teubner.

Cairns, Francis. 1991. "Some Reflections on the Ranking of the Major Games in Fifth Century B.C. Epinician Poetry." In *Archaia Achaïa kai Elis: anakoinoseis kata to proto diethnes symposio, Athena, 19–21 Maïou 1989,* Meletemata 13, ed. A.D. Rizakis, 95–98. Athens: Kentron Hellenikes kai Romaïkes.

Calame, Claude. 1997. *Choruses of Young Women in Ancient Greece: Their Morphology, Religious Role, and Social Functions.* Translated by Derek Collins and Janice Orion. Lanham, MD: Rowman and Littlefield.

Camp, John McK. 1990. *The Athenian Agora.* 4th ed. London: Thames and Hudson.

Campbell, David A., ed. 1991. *Greek Lyric* III. Cambridge, MA: Harvard University Press.

Canada Post. *Report to Parliament: Olympic (1976) Act—Olympic Coins.* Fifteen semi-annual reports issued from 15 October 1974 through 31 March 1981.

Cantarella, Eva. 1992. *Bisexuality in the Ancient World.* Translated by Cormac Ó. Cuilleanáin. New Haven, CT: Yale University Press.

Cartledge, Paul. 1987. *Agesilaos and the Crisis of Sparta.* London: Duckworth.

———. 2001. *Spartan Reflections.* Berkeley: University of California Press.

Catling, Hector W. 1980. "Elis." *AR 1979–1980,* 34.

Chadwick, John. 1973. *Documents in Mycenaean Greek.* 2nd ed. Cambridge: Cambridge University Press.

Christesen, Paul. Forthcoming. *Ancient Greek History and Olympic Victor Lists.* Cambridge: Cambridge University Press.

Cicero, Marcus Tullius. 1955–58. *De Natura Deorum.* Edited by Arthur Stanley Pease. Cambridge, MA: Harvard University Press.

Cohen, Beth. 1991. "Perikles' Portrait and the Riace Bronzes: New Evidence for 'Schinocephaly.'" *Hesperia* 60:465–502.

Cohen, Edward E. 2000. *The Athenian Nation.* Princeton, NJ: Princeton University Press.

Cole, Susan G. 1995. "Women, Dogs, and Flies." *Ancient World* 26:182–91.

Constantinidou, Soteroula. 1998. "Dionysiac Elements in Spartan Cult Dances." *Phoenix* 52:15–30.

Cornford, Francis Macdonald. 1963. "The Origin of the Olympic Games." In Jane Ellen Harrison, *Themis: A Study of the Social Origins of Greek Religion.* 2nd ed. 1927. Reprint, London: Merlin.

Coubertin, Pierre de. 2000. *Olympism: Selected Writings.* Edited by Nobert Müller. Lausanne: International Olympic Committee.

Crowther, Nigel B. 1988a. "The Age-Category of Boys at Olympia." *Phoenix* 42:304–308. [Crowther 2004, 87–92.]

———. 1988b. "Elis and the Games." *L'Antiquité classique* 57:301–10. [Crowther 2004, 99–108.]

———. 1991. "The Olympic Training Period." *Nikephoros* 4:161–66. [Crowther 2004, 65–70.]

———. 1992. "Rounds and Byes in Greek Athletics." *Stadion* 18:68–74. [Crowther 2004, 215–21.]

———. 1993. "Numbers of Contestants in Greek Athletic Contests." *Nikephoros* 6:39–52. [Crowther 2004, 171–82.]

———. 1997. "'Sed quis custodiet ipsos custodes?' The Impartiality of the Olympic Judges and the Case of Leon of Ambracia." *Nikephoros* 10:149–60. [Crowther 2004, 71–81.]

———. 1999. "The Finish in the Greek Foot-Race." *Nikephoros* 12:131–42. [Crowther 2004, 203–13.]

———. 2000. "Resolving an Impasse: Draws, Dead Heats and Similar Decisions in Greek Athletics." *Nikephoros* 13:125–40. [Crowther 2004, 297–311.]

———. 2001a. "Victories without Competition in the Greek Games." *Nikephoros* 14:29–44. [Crowther 2004, 281–96.]

———. 2001b. "Visiting the Olympic Games in Ancient Greece: Travel and Conditions for Athletes and Spectators." *International Journal of the History of Sport* 18:37–52. [Crowther 2004, 35–50.]

———. 2003. "Elis and Olympia: City, Sanctuary and Politics." In *Sport and Festival in the Ancient Greek World,* ed. David Phillips and David Pritchard, 61–73. Swansea: Classical Press of Wales. [Crowther 2004, 53–64.]

———. 2004. *Athletika: Studies on the Olympic Games and Greek Athletics.* Nikephoros, Beiheft 12. Hildesheim: Georg Olms.

Crowther, Nigel B., and Monika Frass. 1998. "Flogging as a Punishment in the Ancient Games." *Nikephoros* 11:51–82. [Crowther 2004, 141–60.]

Danaher, Mary A. 1978. *The Commemorative Coinage of Modern Sports.* South Brunswick, NJ, and New York: A.S. Barnes.

Daniels, Stephanie, and Anita Tedder. 2000. *"A Proper Spectacle": Women Olympians 1900–1936.* Sydney: Walla Walla.

Daux, Georges. 1943. *Chronologique delphique.* Paris: E. de Boccard.

Davidson, J.F. 1988. "Homer and Sophocles' Electra." *BICS* 35:45–78.

Davies, John Kenyon. 1967. "Demosthenes on Liturgies: A Note." *JHS* 87:33–40.

———. 1971. *Athenian Propertied Families, 600–300 B.C.* Oxford: Clarendon.

———. 1984. *Wealth and the Power of Wealth in Classical Athens.* 1981. Reprint, Salem, NH: Ayer Co.

Davies, Malcolm. 1988. *Epicorum Graecorum Fragmenta.* Göttingen: Vandenhoeck and Ruprecht.

Davis, Ellen N. 1987. "The Knossos Miniature Frescoes and the Function of the Central Courts." In *The Function of the Minoan Palaces*, ed. Robin Hägg and Nanno Marinatos, 157–61. Stockholm: Swedish Institute of Archaeology.

Decker, Wolfgang. 1974. "La délégation des Éléens en Égypte sous la 26e dynastie." *Chronique d'Égypte* 49:31–42.

———. 1995. *Sport in der griechischen Antike: vom minoischen Wettkampf bis zu den Olympischen Spielen*. München: C.H. Beck.

Deger-Jalkotzy, Sigrid. 1999. "Military Prowess and Social Status in Mycenaean Greece." In *POLEMOS : Le contexte guerrier en Égée á l'âge du Bronze. Actes de la 7e Rencontre égéenne internationale, Université de Liège, 14–17 avril 1998,* ed. Robert Laffineur. *Aegaeum* 19:121–31.

Delorme, Jean. 1960. *Gymnasion: étude sur les monuments consacrés à l'education en Grèce*. Paris: E. de Boccard.

Des Bouvrie, Synnøve. 1995. "Gender and the Games at Olympia." In *Greece and Gender,* ed. Brit Berggreen and Nanno Marinatos, 43–52. Papers from the Norwegian Institute at Athens, no. 2. Bergen: Norwegian Institute at Athens.

Des Vergers, A. Noël. 1862–64. *L'Etrurie et les Etrusques*, III. Paris: Didot.

Detienne, Marcel. 1970. "L'Olivier: un mythe politico-religieux." *RHR* 177:5–23.

Devereux, Georges. 1966. "The Exploitation of Ambiguity in Pindaros O.3.27." *RhM* 109:289–98.

Diez, E. 1954. "Junger Athlet. Bild einer griechischen Schale in der Sammlung des Archäologischen Institutes der Universität Graz." In *Festschrift Leibeserziehung in der Kultur*, B. Günther et al. Graz: Styria.

Dillon, Matthew. 1997. *Pilgrims and Pilgrimage in Ancient Greece*. London and New York: Routledge.

———. 2000. "Did Parthenoi Attend the Olympic Games? Girls and Women Competing, Spectating, and Carrying Out Cult Roles at Greek Religious Festivals." *Hermes* 128:457–80.

———. 2002. *Girls and Women in Classical Greek Religion*. London and New York: Routledge.

Dittenberger, Wilhelm, and Karl Purgold. 1896. *Die Inschriften von Olympia. Die Ergebnisse der von dem Deutschen Reichveranstalteten Ausgrabung 5*. Berlin: DAI.

———. 1966. *Die Inschriften von Olympia. Die Ergebnisse der von dem Deutschen Reichveranstalteten Ausgrabung 5*. Reprint. Berlin: Hakkert.

Doblhofer, G., P. Mauritsch, and M. Lavrencic. 1992. *Weitsprung: Texte, Übersetzungen, Kommentar*. In *Quellendokumentation zur Gymnastik und Agonistik im Altertum*, ed. I. Weiler. Wien, Köln, Weimer: Böhlau Verlag.

Donlan, Walter. 1982a. "The Politics of Generosity in Homer." *Helios* 9:1–15.

———. 1982b. "Reciprocities in Homer." *Classical World* 75:137–75.

———. 1998. "Political Reciprocity in Dark Age Greece: Odysseus and His Hetairoi." In *Reciprocity in Ancient Greece*, ed. Christopher Gill, Norman Postlethwaite and Richard Seaford, 51–71. Oxford: Oxford University Press.

———. 1999. *The Aristocratic Ideal and Selected Papers*. Wauconda, IL: Bolchazy-Carducci.

Dörig, José. 1977. *Onatas of Aegina*. Leiden: Brill.

Dornseiff, Franz. 1921. *Pindars Stil*. Berlin: Weidmann.

Dörpfeld, Wilhelm. 1935. *Alt-Olympia: Untersuchungen und Ausgrabungen zur Geschichte des ältesten Heiligtums von Olympia und der älteren griechischen Kunst*. Vol 1. Berlin: E.S. Mittler und Sohn.

Dougherty, Carol, and Leslie Kurke. 1993. "Introduction." *Cultural Poetics in Archaic Greece*, ed. Carol Dougherty and Leslie Kurke, 1–12. New York: Oxford University Press.

Dover, Kenneth James. 1989. *Greek Homosexuality*. 2nd ed. Cambridge, MA: Harvard University Press.

Dow, Sterling. 1939. "Aristotle, the Kleroteria and the Courts." *HSCP* 50:1–34.

Drees, Ludwig. 1968. *Olympia: Gods, Artists, and Athletes*. Translated by Gerald Onn. New York: Praeger.

Driega, Alexander W. 1974. "Ancient Greek Olympic Commemoratives." *Canadian Numismatic Journal* 19(6):185–86.

Eberhardt, Josef. 1988. *Olympia-Münzen und-Medaillen von der Antike bis zu Neuzeit: neu bearbeitet und erweitert mit Katalogteil, Münzteil, Medaillenteil*. München: Schwaneberger.

Ebert, Joachim. 1963. *Zum Pentathlon der Antike. Abhandlungen der sächsischen Akademie der Wissenschaften zu Leipzig, Philologisch-historische Klasse*, Band 56, Heft 1. Berlin: Akademie.

———. 1972. *Griechische Epigramme auf Sieger an gymnischen und hippischen Agonen*. Berlin: Akademie.

———. 1980. *Olympia von den Anfängen bis zu Coubertin*. Leipzig: Koehler und Amelang.

———. 1997. "Zur neuen Bronzeplatte mit Siegerinschriften aus Olympia (Inv. 1148)." *Nikephoros* 10:217–33.

Eckstein, Felix. 1969. *Anathemata*. Berlin: Mann.

Elsner, Jas. 2001. "Structuring 'Greece.' Pausanias's *Periegesis* as a Literary Construct." In *Pausanias: Travel and Memory in Roman Greece*, ed. Susan E. Alcock, John F. Cherry, and Jas Elsner, 3–20. Oxford: Oxford University Press.

Evans, Sir Arthur. 1901. "Mycenaean Tree and Pillar Cult and Its Mediterranean Relations," *JHS* 21:99–204.

———. 1930. *The Palace of Minos: A Comparative Account of the Successive Stages of the Early Cretan Civilization as Illustrated by the Discoveries at Knossos*. Vol. 3. London: Macmillan.

Evjen, Harold D. 1986. "Competitive Athletics in Ancient Greece: The Search for Origins and Influences." *Opuscula atheniensia* 16(5):51–56.

———. 1992. "The Origins and Functions of Formal Athletic Competition in the Ancient World." In *Proceedings of an International Symposium on the Olympic Games, 5–9 September 1988*. William Coulson and Helmut Kyrieleis, 95–104. Athens: DAI.

Falkner, C. 1996. "Sparta and the Elean War, ca. 401/400 B.C.: Revenge or Imperialism?" *Phoenix* 50:17–25.

Farnell, Lewis Richard. 1909. *Cults of the Greek States*. Oxford: Clarendon.

————. 1921. *Greek Hero Cults and Ideas of Immortality.* Oxford: Clarendon.

Farnell, Lewis Richard, trans. 1930. *The Works of Pindar.* Vol. I. London: Macmillan.

————. 1932. *The Works of Pindar.* Vol. II. London: Macmillan.

Farrington, Andrew. 1997. "Olympic Victors and the Popularity of the Olympic Games in the Imperial Period." *Tyche* 12:15–46.

Fehl, Phillip. 1961. "The Rocks on the Parthenon Frieze." *JWI* 24:1–44.

Fehr, Karl. 1936. *Die Mythen bei Pindar.* Ph.D. diss., Zürich: Leeman.

Ferrari, Gloria. 2002. *Figures of Speech: Men and Maidens in Ancient Greece.* Chicago: University of Chicago.

Finley, Moses I. 1965. *The World of Odysseus.* Rev. ed. New York: Viking.

Finley, Moses I., and H.W. Pleket. 1976. *The Olympic Games: The First Thousand Years.* London: Chatto and Windus.

Flower, Michael A. 2000. "From Simonides to Isocrates: The Fifth-Century Origins of Fourth-Century Panhellenism." *Classical Antiquity* 19:65–101.

Foley, Anne M. 1997. "Pheidon of Argos: A Reassessment." In *Argolo-Korinthiaka I*, ed. John M. Fossey, 15–28. Amsterdam: Gieben.

Fontenrose, Joseph. 1968. "The Hero as Athlete." *California Studies in Classical Antiquity* 1:73–104.

————. 1978. *The Delphic Oracle: Its Responses and Operations, with a Catalogue of Responses.* Berkeley: University of California Press.

Forrest, W. G. 1960. "Themistokles and Argos." *CQ* n.s., 10:221–41.

Franke, Peter Robert. 1968. *Kleinasien zur Römerzeit: griechisches Leben im Spiegel der Münzen.* München: C.H. Beck.

————. 1984a. "Olympia und seine Münzen." *Antike Welt* 15(2):14–26.

————. 1984b. "Eliaka-Olympiaka." *MDAI (A)* 99:319–33.

Fränkel, Hermann. 1961. "Schrullen in den Scholien zu Pindars *Nemeen* 7 und *Olympien* 3." *Hermes* 89:385–97.

Frass, Monika. 1997. "Gesellschaftliche Akzeptanze 'sportlicher' Frauen in der Antike." *Nikephoros* 10:119–33.

Frazer, J.G., translation and commentary. 1913. *Pausanias's Description of Greece.* 6 vols. 2nd ed. London: Macmillan.

————, translation and commentary. 1965. *Pausanias's Description of Greece.* 6 vols. 1898. Reprint, New York: Biblo and Tannen.

Fröhner, Wilhelm. 1865. "Damnameneus ein dämon, kein gemmenschneider." *Philologus* 22:544–46.

Fuchs, Franz P. 1976. "Olympiamünzen der Neuzeit." *Haller Münzblätter* 2(1–2): 33–41.

Gadoury, Victor, and Vescovi Romolo. 1996. *Olympic Medals and Coins, 510 BC–1994.* Monaco: Victor Gadoury Publications.

Galaty, Michael L. 1999. *Nestor's Wine Cups: Investigating Manufacture and Exchange in a Late Bronze Age "Mycenaean" State.* BAR International Series 766. Oxford: J. and E. Hedges.

Galaty, Michael L., and William A. Parkinson. 1999. "Putting Mycenaean Palaces in Their Place." In *Rethinking Mycenaean Palaces: New Interpretations of an*

Old Idea, ed. Michael L. Galaty and William A. Parkinson, 1–8. Los Angeles: Cotsen Institute of Archaeology, University of California.

Gardiner, E. Norman. 1904. "Further Notes on the Greek Jump." *JHS* 24:179–94.

————. 1910. *Greek Athletic Sports and Festivals.* London: Macmillan.

————. 1930. *Athletics of the Ancient World.* Oxford: Clarendon.

————. 1973. *Olympia: Its History and Remains.* 1925. Reprint, Washington, DC: McGrath.

Gardner, Ernest Arthur. 1915. *A Handbook of Greek Sculpture.* 2nd ed. London: Macmillan.

Gardner, Percy. 1880. "The Pentathlon of the Greeks." *JHS* 1:210–23.

————. 1963. *A Catalogue of the Greek Coins in the British Museum.* Vol. 10, *Peloponnesus (Excluding Corinth).* 1887. Reprint, Bologna: Arnaldo Forni Editore.

Gauer, Werner. 1991. *Die Bronzegefässe von Olympia.* Vol. 1 (*Olympische Forschungen* 20). Berlin: De Gruyter.

Gebhard, Elizabeth. 2002. "The Beginnings of Panhellenic Games at the Isthmus." In *Olympia 1875–2000: 125 Jahre Deutsche Ausgrabungen,* ed. Helmut Kyrieleis, 221–37. Mainz am Rhein: Philipp von Zabern.

German, Senta. 1999. "The Politics of Dancing: A Reconsideration of the Motif of Dancing in Bronze Age Greece." In *Meletemata: Studies in Aegean Archaeology Presented to Malcolm H. Wiener as He Enters His 65th Year. Vol. I.,* ed. Philip Betancourt, Vassos Karageorghis, Robert Laffineur, and Wolf-Dietrich Niemeier, 279–82. *Aegaeum* 20, Vol. 1, 279–82.

Gildersleeve, Basil L. 1885. *Pindar. The Olympian and Pythian Odes.* New York: Harper and Bros.

Glass, Stephen L. 1967. *Palaistra and Gymnasia in Greek Architecture.* Ph.D. diss., University of Pennsylvania.

————. 1988. "The Greek Gymnasium." In *The Archaeology of the Olympics,* ed. Wendy J. Raschke, 155–73. Madison, WI: University of Wisconsin Press.

Golden, Mark. 1998. *Sport and Society in Ancient Greece.* Cambridge and New York: Cambridge University Press.

————. 2004. *Sport in the Ancient World from A to Z.* London and New York: Routledge.

Goossens, E., and S. Thielemans. 1996. "The Popularity of Painting Sports Scenes on Attic Black and Red Figure Vases." *Bulletin Antieke Beschaving* 71:59–94.

Graf, Fritz. 1974. *Eleusis und die orphische Dichtung Athens in vorhellenistischer Zeit.* Berlin: De Gruyter.

Graham, J. Walter. 1957. "The Central Court as the Minoan Bull-Ring." *AJA* 61:255–62.

Grodde, Olaf. 1997. *Sport bei Quintilian. Nikephoros,* Beiheft 1 Band 3. Hildesheim: Weidmann.

Guttmann, Allen. 1991. "Spartan Girls and Other Runners." In Allen Gutmann, *Women's Sports: A History,* 17–32. New York: Columbia University Press.

————. 1992. "Old Sports." *Natural History* (July):50–57.

Habicht, Christian. 1985. *Pausanias' Guide to Ancient Greece.* Berkeley and Los Angeles: University of California Press.

Halbherr, Federico, Enrico Stefani, and Luisa Banti. 1977. *Haghia Triada nel periodo tardo palaziale. Annuario. Scuola Archeologica di Atene* 39:9–296.

Hallager, Birgitta, and Erik Hallager. 1995. "The Knossian Bull—Political Propaganda in Neo-Palatial Crete?" In *Politeia: Society and State in the Aegean Bronze Age. Proceedings of the 5th International Aegean Conference,* ed. Robert Laffineur and Wolf-Dietrich Niemeier. *Aegaeum,* 12, 547–56.

Hallager, Erik. 1996. *The Minoan Roundel and Other Sealed Documents in the Neopalatial Linear A Administration. Aegaeum* 14.

Hamdorf, F.W. 1981. "Karpometra." In X. *Bericht über die Ausgrabungen in Olympia. Frühjahr 1966 bis Dezember 1976,* ed. Alfred Mallwitz, 192–208. Berlin: De Gruyter.

Hamilakis, Yannis. 1996. "Wine, Oil and the Dialectics of Power in Bronze Age Crete: A Review of the Evidence," *OJA* 15:1–32.

Hamilton, Charles D. 1991. *Agesilaus and the Failure of Spartan Hegemony.* Ithaca, NY: Cornell University Press.

Hanson, Victor D. 1996. "Hoplites into Democrats: The Changing Ideology of Athenian Infantry." In *Demokratia,* ed. Josiah Ober and Charles Hedrick, 289–312. Princeton, NJ: Princeton University Press.

Harris, H.A. 1966. *Greek Athletes and Athletics.* Bloomington: Indiana University Press.

———. 1972. *Sport in Greece and Rome.* London: Thames and Hudson.

Harrison, Evelyn B. 1985. "Early Classical Sculpture: the Bold Style." In *Greek Art: Archaic into Classical,* ed. Cedric G. Boulter, 40–65. Leiden: Brill.

Harrison, Jane Ellen. 1963. *Themis: A Study of the Social Origins of Greek Religion.* 2nd ed. 1927. Reprint, London: Merlin.

Haskell, Halford W. 1984. "Pylos: Stirrup Jars and the International Oil Trade." In *Pylos Comes Alive: Industry + Administration in a Mycenaean Palace,* ed. Cynthia W. Shelmerdine and Thomas G. Palaima, 97–107. New York: Fordham University.

Heidrich, Specht K. 1987. *Olympias Uhren gingen falsch: Die revidierte Geschichte der griechisch-archaischen Zeit.* Berlin: Mann.

Heilmeyer, Wolf.-Dieter. 1972. *Frühe Olympische Tonfiguren. Olympische Forschungen,* Vol. 7. Berlin: De Gruyter.

———. 1984. "Durchgang, Krypte, Denkmal: Zur Geschichte des Stadioneingangs in Olympia." *MDAI(A)* 99:251–63.

Hemberg, Bengt. 1950. *Die Kabiren.* Uppsala: Almqvist & Wilksells.

Henderson, Jeffrey, ed. and trans. 1998. *Aristophanes.* Vol 2. LCL. Cambridge, MA: Harvard University Press.

Hermann, John, Jr., and Christine Kondoleon. 2004. *Games for the Gods: The Greek Athlete and the Olympic Spirit.* Boston: MFA Publications.

Herrmann, Hans-Volkmar. 1962. "Zur ältesten Geschichte von Olympia." *MDAI(A)* 77:3–34.

Herrmann, Hans-Volkmar, ed. 1987. "Prähistorisches Olympia." In *Ägäische Bronzezeit,* ed. Hans-Günter Buchholtz, 425–36. Darmstadt: Wissenschaftliche Buchgesellschaft.

Hirschfeld, Gustav. 1877. "Olympia," *Deutsche Rundschau* 13:286–324.

Hitchcock, Louise A. 2000. "Engendering Ambiguity in Minoan Crete: It's a Drag to Be a King." In *Representations of Gender from Prehistory to the Present,* ed. Moira Donald and Linda Hurcombe, 69–86. New York: St. Martin's.

Hodkinson, Stephen. 1988. "Inheritance, Marriage and Demography: Perspectives upon the Success and Decline of Classical Sparta." In *Classical Sparta: Techniques Behind Her Success,* ed. Anton Powell, 79–121. Norman: University of Oklahoma Press.

———. 1999. "An Agonistic Culture? Athletic Competition in Archaic and Classical Sparta." In *Sparta: New Perspectives,* ed. Stephen Hodkinson and Anton Powell, 147–87. London: Duckworth.

———. 2000. *Property and Wealth in Classical Sparta.* London: Duckworth.

Hoeck, Karl. 1823. *Kreta.* Göttingen: C.E. Rosenbusch.

Hoffman, Herbert, and Nigel Konstam. 2002. "Casting the Riace Bronzes: Modern Assumptions and Ancient Facts." *OJA* 21:153–65.

Hoge, Robert W. 1995. "The Ancient Olympic Games: A Celebration in Coinage." *Society for Ancient Numismatics* 19(2):39–43.

Hollein, Heinz-Günter. 1988. *Bürgerbild und Bildwelt der attischen Demokratie auf den rotfiguren Vasen des 6.-4. Jahrhunderts v. Chr.* Frankfurt am Main: Peter Lang.

Hönle, Augusta. 1972. *Olympia in der Politik der griechischen Staatenwelt: Von 776 bis zum Ende des 5. Jahrhunderts.* Bebenhausen: Lothar Rotsch.

Hoops, Johannes. 1944. *Geschichte des Ölbaums (=Sitzungsberichte der Heidelberger Akademie der Wissenschaften. Philosophisch-historische Klasse, Jahrg. 1942/43, 3. Abhandlung 1942/43, 3).* Heidelberg: C. Winter.

Hornblower, Simon. 2000. "Thucydides, Xenophon, and Lichas: Were the Spartans Excluded from the Olympic Games from 420 to 400 B.C.?" *Phoenix* 54: 212–25.

———. 2004. *Thucydides and Pindar: Historical Narrative and the World of Epinikian Poetry.* Oxford: Oxford University Press.

Hornblower, Simon, and Antony Spawforth, eds. 1998. *The Oxford Companion to Classical Civilization.* Oxford: Oxford University Press.

Hubbard, Thomas K. 1986. "Pegasus' Bridle and the Poetics of Pindar's *Thirteenth Olympian.*" *HSCP* 90:27–48.

———. 1987a. "The 'Cooking' of Pelops: Pindar and the Process of Mythological Revisionism." *Helios* 14:3–21.

———. 1987b. "Two Notes on the Myth of Aeacus in Pindar." *GRBS* 28:5–22.

———. 2001. "Pindar and Athens after the Persian Wars." In *Gab es das griechische Wunder? Griechenland zwischen dem Ende des 6. und der Mitte des 5. Jahrhunderts v. Chr.,* ed. Dietrich Papenfuss and Volker Michael Strocka, 387–400. Mainz: Philipp von Zabern.

Hughes, Bettany, host/narrator. 2004. *The Spartans.* Alexandria, VA: PBS/Paramount Home Video.

Huxley, George L. 1969. *Greek Epic Poetry from Eumelos to Panyassis.* Cambridge, MA: Harvard University Press.

————. 1978. "Simonides and His World." *Proceedings of the Royal Irish Academy* 78:231–47.

Hyde, Walter Woodburn. 1921. *Olympic Victor Monuments and Greek Athletic Art*. Carnegie Institution of Washington Publication 268. Washington, DC: Carnegie Institution of Washington.

————. 1938. "The Pentathlum Jump." *AJP* 59:405–17.

Immerwahr, Walter. 1891. *Die Kulte und Mythen Arkadiens: I, Die arkadischen Kulte*. Leipzig: B.G. Teubner.

Ingalls, Wayne B. 2000. "Ritual Performance as Training for Daughters in Archaic Greece." *Phoenix* 54:1–20.

Instone, S. 1990. "Love and Sex in Pindar: Some Practical Thrusts." *BICS* 37:30–42.

————. 1996. "Athletics." In *Oxford Classical Dictionary*, 3rd ed., 206–207.

Isaakidou, Valasia, Paul Halstead, Jack Davis, and Sharon Stocker. 2002. "Burnt Animal Sacrifice at the Mycenaean 'Palace of Nestor,' Pylos." *Antiquity* 76:86–92.

Jackson, Alastar. 1992. "Arms and Armour at the Panhellenic Sanctuary of Poseidon at Isthmia." In *Proceedings of an International Symposium on the Olympic Games, 5–9 September 1988*, ed. William Coulson and Helmut Kyrieleis, 141–44. Athens: DAI.

Jacoby, Felix. 1922. "ΙΩ ΚΑΛΛΙΘΥΕΣΣΑ" *Hermes* 57:366–74.

Jacquemin, Anne. 2001. "Delphes au Vᵉ siècle ou un panhellénisme difficile à concrétiser." *Pallas* 57:93–110.

Jeanmaire, Henri. 1939. *Couroi et Courètes*. Lille: Bibliothèque universitaire.

Jeffery, Lilian H. 1961. *The Local Scripts of Archaic Greece*. Oxford: Claredon.

————. 1990. *The Local Scripts of Archaic Greece*. Rev. ed. New York: Oxford University Press.

Jenner, E.A.B. 1986. "Further Speculations on Ibycus and the Epinician Ode." *BICS* 33:59–66.

Jones, Melville. 1993. *Testimonia Numaria: Greek and Latin Texts Concerning Ancient Greek Coinage*. Vol. 1, *Texts and Translations*. London: Spink.

Jones, W.H.S., trans. 1977. *Pausanias Description of Greece*. Vol. 2. LCL. 1926. Reprint, Cambridge, MA: Harvard University Press.

Jongkees, Jan Hendrick. 1968. "Notes on Coin Types of Olympia." *Revue Numismatique*, ser. 6, 10:51–61.

Jost, Madeleine. 1985. *Sanctuaires et cultes d'Arcadie*. Paris: J. Vrin.

Jüthner, Julius. 1896. *Über Antike Turngeräthe*. Edited by Otto Benndorf and Eugen Bormann. Abhandlungen des archäologisch-epigraphischen Seminares der Universität Wien. Heft 12. Wien: Alfred Hölder.

————. 1912. In *Paulys Realencyclopädie der classischen Altertumswissenschaft, neue Bearbeitung*, ed. August F. Pauly, Georg Wissowa et al., 7.2:2273–6, s.v. *halma*. Stuttgart: Metzler.

————. 1968. *Die athletischen Leibesübungen der Griechen II. Einzelne Sportarten*. Edited by Friedrich Brein. Abhandlungen der Österreichische Akademie der Wissenschaften, Philosophisch-Historische Klasse, Sitzungsberichte 249, Band 2. Graz, Wien, und Köln: Hermann Böhlau.

————. 1969. *Philostratos über Gymnastik*. 1909. Reprint, Amsterdam: B.R. Grüner.

Kaibel, Georg. 1901. "ΔΑΚΤΥΛΟΙ ΙΔΑΙΟΙ." *Nachrichten von der königliche Gesellschaft der Wissenschaften in Göttingen, Philologische-historische Klasse,* 501–14.

Kamerbeek, Jan Coenraad. 1974. *The Plays of Sophocles*. Vol. 5. Leiden: Brill.

Kanowski, Maxwell George. 1983. *Containers of Classical Greece*. St. Lucia: University of Queensland Press.

Karl, H. 1979. "Antique Greek Coins as a Source for the Historian." *Canadian Journal of History of Sport and Physical Education* 10(2):76–90.

Kennell, Nigel M. 1988. "ΝΕΡΩΝ ΠΕΡΙΟΔΟΝΙΚΗΣ," *AJP* 109:239–51.

Kilburn, K., trans. 1990. *Lucian*. Vol. 6. LCL. Cambridge, MA: Harvard University Press.

Killen, John T. 1994. "Thebes Sealings, Knossos Tablets and Mycenaean State Banquets." *BICS* 39:67–84.

Kirk, Geoffrey Stephen. 1985. "The Homeric Hymns." In *The Cambridge History of Classical Literature*, ed. P.E. Easterling and B.M.W. Knox. Vol. I, 110–16. Cambridge: Cambridge University Press.

Klee, Theophil. 1918. *Zur Geschichte der gymnischen Agone an griechischen Festen*. Reprint, Chicago: Ares, 1980. Leipzig und Berlin: Basel dissertation.

Kleingünther, Adolf. 1933. *ΠΡΩΤΟΣ ΕΥΡΕΤΗΣ*. Leipzig: Dieterich.

Koehl, Robert. 1986. "The Chieftain Cup and a Minoan Rite of Passage." *JHS* 106:99–110.

————. 1997. "The Villas at Ayia Triadha and Nirou Chani and the Origin of the Cretan *Andreion*." In *The Function of the Minoan Villa*, ed. Robin Hägg, 137–47. Stockholm: Paul Åströms.

————. 2000. "Ritual Context." In *The Palaikastro Kouros: A Minoan Chryselephantine Statuette and Its Aegean Bronze Age Context*, ed. J.A. MacGillivray, J.M. Driessen, and L.H. Sackett, 131–43. London: British School at Athens.

Koenigs, Wolf. 1984. *Die Echohalle. Olympische Forschungen* XIV. DAI. Berlin: De Gruyter.

Kokolakis, Minos. 1992. "Intellectual Activity on the Fringes of the Games." In *Proceedings of an International Symposium on the Olympic Games, 5–9 September 1988*, ed. William Coulson and Helmut Kyrieleis, 153–58. Athens: DAI.

Kolf, Maria Christina van der. 1923. *Quaeritur quomodo Pindarus fabulas tractaverit quidque in eis mutavit*. Rotterdam: Brusse.

Körte, Alfred. 1904. "Die Entstehung der Olympionikenliste." *Hermes* 39:224–34.

Köhnken, Adolf. 1974. "Pindar as Innovator: Poseidon Hippios and the Relevance of the Pelops Story in Olympian 1." *CQ*, n.s., 24:199–206.

————. 1983. "Mythical Chronology and Thematic Coherence in Pindar's Third Olympian Ode." *HSCP* 87:49–63.

Kraay, Colin M. 1976. *Archaic and Classical Greek Coins*. Berkeley: University of California Press.

Kroll, John H. 1972. *Athenian Bronze Allotment Plates*. LCM. Cambridge, MA: Harvard University Press.

————. 1993. *The Greek Coins. Athenian Agora* 26. Princeton, NJ: American School of Classical Studies at Athens.

Krummen, Eveline. 1990. *Pyrsos Hymnon: Festliche Gegenwart und mythisch-rituelle Tradition bei Pindar.* Berlin: De Gruyter.

Kunze, Emil. 1967. *VIII. Bericht über die Ausgrabungen in Olympia. Die Arbeiten vom Herbst 1958 bis zum Sommer 1962.* Berlin: De Gruyter.

Kunze, Emil, and Hans Schleif. 1941. *III. Bericht über die Ausgrabungen in Olympia. Winter 1938/39.* Berlin: De Gruyter.

Kurke, Leslie. 1993. "The Economy of *Kudos.*" In *Cultural Poetics in Archaic Greece,* ed. Carol Dougherty and Leslie Kurke, 131–64. New York: Oxford University Press.

Kyle, Donald G. 1984. "Solon and Athletics." *Ancient World* 9:91–105.

————. 1993. *Athletics in Ancient Athens.* 2nd ed. Leiden: Brill.

————. 1996. "Gifts and Glory: Panathenaic and Other Greek Athletic Prizes." In *Worshipping Athena: Panathenaia and Parthenon,* ed. Jennifer Neils, 106–36. Madison, WI: University of Wisconsin Press.

————. 1997. "The First Hundred Olympiads: A Process of Decline or Democratization?" *Nikephoros* 10:53–75.

————. 1998. "Games, Prizes, and Athletes in Greek Sport: Patterns and Perspectives (1975–1997)." *Classical Bulletin* 74(2):103–27.

————. 2003. "'The Only Woman in All Greece'": Kyniska, Agesilaus, Alcibiades and Olympia." *Journal of Sport History* 30:183–203.

Kyrieleis, Helmut. 2006. *Anfänge und Frühzeit des Heiligtums von Olympia. Die Ausgrabungen am Pelopion 1987–1996.* Olympische Forschungen XXXI. Berlin: De Gruyter.

————, ed. 2002. *Olympia 1875–2000: 125 Jahre Deutsche Ausgrabungen.* Mainz am Rhein: Philipp von Zabern.

Ladany, S.P. 1975. "Leisure of Numismatism: The Price and Demand for Commemorative Coins." In *Management Science Applications to Leisure-Time Operations,* ed. S.P. Ladany, 360–66. Amsterdam: North-Holland Publishing.

Lamb, Winifred. 1919–21. "Excavations at Mycenae III: Frescoes from the Ramp House." *ABSA* 24:189–99.

Lämmer, Manfred. 1967. "Der Diskos des Asklepiades aus Olympia und das Marmor Parium." *ZPE* 1:107–109.

————. 1981. "Women and Sport in Ancient Greece: A Plea for a Critical and Objective Approach." In *Women and Sport: An Historical, Biological, Physiological and Sportsmedical Approach,* ed. Jan Borms, Marcel Hebbelinck, and Antonio Venerando, 16–23. *Medicine and Sport* 14. Basel and New York: Karger.

————. 1982–83. "Der sogennante olympische Friede in der griechischen Antike." *Stadion* 8–9:47–83.

Lang, Mabel. 1968. *The Palace of Nestor at Pylos in Western Messenia.* Vol. 2. *The Frescoes.* Princeton, NJ: Princeton University Press.

Lang, Mabel, and Margaret Crosby. 1964. *Weights, Measures and Tokens. Athenian Agora* 10. Princeton, NJ: American School of Classical Studies.

Larsen, Jakob A.O. 1968. *Greek Federal States: Their Institutions and History.* Oxford: Clarendon.

Laser, Siegfried. 1987. *Sport und Spiel. Archaeologia Homerica*, Lieferung T. Göttingen: Vandenhoeck und Ruprecht.

Lattimore, Steven. 1988. "The Nature of Early Greek Victor Statues." In *Coroebus Triumphs*, ed. Susan Bandy, 245–56. San Diego: San Diego University Press.

Lechat, Henri. 1905. *Pythagoras de Rhégion.* Lyon: A. Rey.

Lee, Hugh M. 1976. "The *TEPMA* and the Javelin in Pindar, *Nemean* vii 70–3, and Greek Athletics." *JHS* 96:70–79.

———. 1984. "Athletics and the Bikini Girls from Piazza Armerina." *Stadion* 10:45–76.

———. 1988a. "The Ancient Olympic Games: Origin, Evolution, Revolution." *Classical Bulletin* 74(2):129–41.

———. 1988b. "The 'First' Olympic Games of 776 B.C." In *The Archaeology of the Olympics: The Olympics and Other Festivals in Antiquity*, ed. Wendy J. Raschke, 110–18. Madison, WI: University of Wisconsin Press.

———. 1988c. "*SIG*³ 802: Did Women Compete against Men in Greek Athletic Festivals?" *Nikephoros* 1:103–17.

———. 2001. *The Program and Schedule of the Ancient Olympic Games. Nikephoros*, Beiheft 6. Hildesheim: Weidmann.

Lefkowitz, Mary R. 1988. "Who Sang Pindar's Victory Odes?" *AJP* 109:1–11.

Lefkowitz, Mary R., and Maureen B. Fant. 1992. *Women's Life in Greece and Rome: A Source Book in Translation.* 2nd ed. Baltimore: Johns Hopkins University Press.

Legakis, Brian. 1977. *Athletic Contests in Archaic Greek Art.* Ph.D. diss., University of Chicago.

Lehner, M., T. Lorenz, and G. Schwarz. 1993. Griechische und italische Vasen aus der Sammlung des Instituts für Klassische Archäologie der Karl-Franzens-Universität Graz. Graz: Akademische Druck und Verlagsanstalt.

Legrand, Philippe.-E. 1875. In *Dictionnaire des antiquités grecques et romaines*, ed. C. Daremberg and E. Saglio, 4:1054–56, s.v. *saltus*. Paris: Librairie Hachette.

Leitao, David DeCosta. 1995. "The Perils of Leukippos." *Classical Antiquity* 14:130–63.

Levy, Brooks. 1989. "Nero's 'Apollonia' Series: The Achaean Context." *Numismatic Chronicle* 149:59–68.

Lewis, David M. 1992. "Mainland Greece, 479–451 B.C." In *The Cambridge Ancient History*, ed. David M. Lewis, 2nd ed., 96–120. Cambridge: Cambridge University Press.

Lindgren, Margareta. 1973. *The People of Pylos: Prosopographical and Methodological Studies in the Pylos Archives.* 2 vols. in 1. *Acta Universitatis Upsaliensis. Uppsala Studies in Ancient Mediterranean and Near Eastern Civilizations* 3.

Linforth, Ivan M. 1941. *The Arts of Orpheus.* Berkeley: University of California Press.

Lloyd, Alan B. 1988. *Herodotus, Book II: Commentary 99–182.* Leiden: Brill.

Lloyd-Jones, Hugh, ed. and trans. 1994. *Sophocles.* Vol. 1. LCL. Cambridge, MA: Harvard University Press.

Lloyd-Jones, Hugh, and Nigel Guy Wilson. 1990. *Sophoclea: Studies on the Text of Sophocles.* Oxford: Clarendon.

Lobeck, Christian August. 1829. *Aglaophamus sive de Theologiae Mysticae Graecorum Causis.* Königsberg: Regimontii Prussorum, Borntraeger.

Lonsdale, Steven H. 1993. *Dance and Ritual Play in Greek Religion.* Baltimore: Johns Hopkins University Press.

Lorimer, Hilda L. 1936. "Dipaltos."*ABSC* 37:172–86.

Mahaffy, Sir John Pentland. 1881. "On the Authenticity of the Olympian Register." *JHS* 2:164–78.

———. 1901. *Old Greek Education.* New York and London: Harper and Bros.

Malalas, John. 1986. *The Chronicle of John Malalas.* Trans. Elizabeth Jeffreys, Michael Jeffreys, and Robert Scott. Melbourne: Australian Asscociation for Byzantine Studies.

Mallwitz, Alfred. 1967. "Das Stadion." *VIII. Bericht über die Ausgrabungen in Olympia. Die Arbeiten vom Herbst 1958 bis zum Sommer 1962,* ed. Emil Kunze, 16–82. Berlin: De Gruyter.

———. 1972. *Olympia und seine Bauten.* Darmstadt: Wissenschaftliche Buchgesellschaft.

———. 1988. "Cult and Competition Locations at Olympia." In *The Archaeology of the Olympics: The Olympics and Other Festivals in Antiquity,* ed. Wendy J. Raschke, 79–109. Madison, WI: University of Wisconsin Press.

Mann, Christian. 2001. *Athlet und Polis im archaischen und frühklassischen Griechenland. Hypomnemata* 138. Göttingen: Vandenhoeck und Ruprecht.

Mantas, Konstantinos. 1995. "Women and Athletics in the Roman East." *Nikephoros* 8:125–44.

Marinatos, Nanno. 1994. "The 'Export' Significance of Minoan Bull Hunting and Bull Leaping Scenes." *Ägypten und Levante* 4:89–93.

Markle, M.M. 1985. "Jury Pay and Assembly Pay at Athens." In *Crux: Essays Presented to G.E.M. de Ste. Croix on his 75th Birthday,* ed. Paul A. Cartledge and F. D. Harvey, 265–97. London: Duckworth.

Mattusch, Carol C. 1996a. *The Fire of Hephaistos: Large Classical Bronzes from North American Collections.* Cambridge, MA: Harvard University Art Museums.

———. 1996b. *Classical Bronzes: The Art and Craft of Greek and Roman Statuary.* Ithaca, NY: Cornell University Press.

McDonnell, Myles. 1991. "The Introduction of Athletic Nudity: Thucydides, Plato, and the Vases." *JHS* 111:182–93.

———. 1993. "Athletic Nudity among the Greeks and Etruscans." In *Spectacles sportifs et scéniques dans le monde Étrusco-Italique: actes de la table ronde organisée par l'Équipe de recherches étrusco-italiques de l'UMR 126 (CNRS, Paris) et l'École française de Rome, Rome, 3–4 mai 1991,* 395–407. Rome: École française de Rome.

McGregor, Malcolm F. 1941. "Cleisthenes of Sicyon and the Panhellenic Festivals." *TAPA* 72:66–87.

McLean, Bradley H. 2002. *An Introduction to Greek Epigraphy of the Hellenistic and Roman Periods from Alexander the Great down to the Reign of Constantine (323 B.C.–A.D. 337)*. Ann Arbor, MI: University of Michigan Press.

Melucco Vaccaro, Alessandra. 2000. "The Riace Bronzes 20 Years Later: Recent Advances after the 1992–1995 Intervention." In *From the Parts to the Whole: Acta of the 13th International Bronze Congress, held at Cambridge, Massachusetts, May 28–June 1, 1996*, ed. Carol C. Mattusch, Amy Brauer, and Sandra E. Knudsen. Vol. 1, 124–31. Portsmouth, RI: Journal of Roman Archaeology.

Meier, Christian. 1984. *Introduction à l'anthropologie politique de l'antiquité classique*. Translated by Pierre Blanchaud. Vendôme: Presses universitaires de France.

———. 1990. *The Greek Discovery of Politics*. Translated by David McLintock. Cambridge, MA: Harvard University Press.

Ménard, Michèle. 1991. *Coins of the Modern Olympic Games*. Vol. 1, *Issued by Host Countries*. Vanier, ON: M. Ménard.

Mezö, Ferenc. 1930. *Geschichte der Olympischen Spiele*. München: Knorr und Hirth.

———. 1958. "Das Rätsel des altgriechischen Weitsprungs." *Das Altertum* 4:165–72.

Millender, Ellen. 1999. "Athenian Ideology and the Empowered Spartan Woman." In *Sparta: New Perspectives*, ed. Stephen Hodkinson and Anton Powell, 355–91. London: Duckworth.

Miller, Stella G. 1983. "Excavations at Nemea, 1982." *Hesperia* 52:70–95.

Miller, Stephen G. 1978. "The Date of the First Pythiad." *California Studies in Classical Antiquity* 11:127–58.

———. 2000. "Naked Democracy." In *Polis and Politics: Studies in Ancient Greek History Presented to Mogens Herman Hansen on His Sixtieth Birthday*, ed. Pernille Flensted-Jensen, Thomas Heine Nielsen and Lene Rubinstein, 277–96. Copenhagen: Museum Tusculanum Press.

———. 2001. *Excavations at Nemea II: The Early Hellenistic Stadium*. Berkeley: University of California Press.

———. 2002. "The Shrine of Opheltes and the Earliest Stadium at Nemea." In *Olympia 1875–2000: 125 Jahre Deutsche Ausgrabungen*, ed. Helmut Kyrieleis, 239–50. Mainz am Rhein: Philipp von Zabern.

———. 2004a. *Ancient Greek Athletics*. New Haven, CT, and London: Yale University Press.

Miller, Stephen G., ed. 2004b. *Arete: Greek Sport from Ancient Sources*. 3rd ed. Berkeley: University of California Press.

Minetti, Alberto E., and Luca P. Ardigó, 2002. "Biomechanics: Halteres Used in Ancient Olympic Long Jump." *Nature* 420(14 Nov.):141–42.

Mitsopoulos-Leon, Veronica. 1998. "Elis." In *100 Jahre Österreichisches Archäologisches Institut, 1898–1998*, 182–85. Vienna: Österreichisches Archäologisches Institut.

Möller, Astrid. 2005. "Epoch-making Eratosthenes." *GRBS* 45:245–60.

Molyneux, John H. 1992. *Simonides: A Historical Study*. Wauconda, IL: Bolchazy-Carducci.

Montgomery, H.C. 1936. "The Controversy about the Origin of the Olympic Games: Did They Originate in 776 B.C.?" *Classical Weekly* 29:169–74.

Moraux, Paul. 1951. *Les listes anciennes des ouvrages d'Aristote*. Louvain: Éditions universitaires de Louvain.

Moreno, Paolo. 1998. *I bronzi di Riace: Il maestro di Olimpia e i Sette a Tebe*. Milan: Electa.

Moretti, Jean-Charles. 2001. "Kleroteria trouvés à Delos." *BCH* 125:133–43.

Moretti, Luigi. 1953. *Iscrizioni agonistiche greche*. Rome: Signorelli.

———. 1954. "Note sugli antichi periodonikai." *Athenaeum* 32:115–20.

———. 1957. *Olympionikai, i vincitori negli antiche olympici*. Rome: Accademia Nazionale dei Lincei.

Morgan, Catherine. 1990. *Athletes and Oracles: The Transformation of Olympia and Delphi in the Eighth Century B.C.* Cambridge: Cambridge University Press.

———. 1991. "Ethnicity and Early Greek States. Historical and Material Perspectives." *Proceedings of the Cambridge Philological Association* 37:131–63.

Morgan, Charles H., II. 1937. "Excavations at Corinth, 1936–37." *AJA* 41:539–52.

Morris, Ian. 1996. "The Strong Principle of Equality and the Origins of Greek Democracy." In *Demokratia,* ed. Josiah Ober and Charles Hedrick, 19–48. Princeton, NJ: Princeton University Press.

———. 1997. "The Art of Citizenship." In *New Light on a Dark Age,* ed. Susan Langdon, 9–43. Columbia: University of Missouri Press.

———. 2000. *Archaeology as Cultural History*. Oxford: Basil Blackwell.

Mosshammer, Alden A. 1979. *The Chronicle of Eusebius and Greek Chronographic Tradition*. Lewisburg, PA, and London: Bucknell University Press.

Mouratidis, Jannis. 1985. "The 776 B.C. Date and Some Problems Connected with It." *Canadian Journal of History of Sport* 16(2):1–14.

———. 1989. "Are There Minoan Influences on Mycenaean Sports, Games and Dances?" *Nikephoros* 2:43–63.

Müller, Stefan. 1995. *Das Volk der Athleten: Untersuchungen zur Ideologie und Kritik des Sports in der griechisch-römischen Antike*. Trier: Wissenschaftlicher Verlag.

Müller, Walter, and Ingo Pini. 1999. *Corpus der minoischen und mykenischen Siegel. Iraklion Archäologisches Museum,* Vol. 6: *Die Siegelabdrücke von Aj. Triada und Anderen Zentral- und Ostkretischen Fundorten*. Herakleion: Archaiologikon Mouseion Herakleiou.

Murray, Oswyn. 1983a. "The Greek Symposion in History." In *Tria Corda: Scritti in Onore di Arnaldo Momigliano,* ed. Emilio Gabba, 257–72. Como: New Press.

———. 1983b. "The Symposion as Social Organisation." In *The Greek Renaissance of the Eighth Century B.C.: Tradition and Innovation,* ed. Robin Hägg, 195–99. Stockholm: Paul Åströms.

———. 1990. "Sympotic History." In *Sympotica: A Symposium on the Symposion,* ed. Oswyn Murray, 3–13. Oxford: Clarendon.

Mussche, H.F. 1992. "Sport et Architecture." In *Le Sport dans la Grèce antique,* ed. Doris Vanhove, 43–55. Brussels: Palais des Beaux-Arts.

Nagy, Gregory. 1990. *Pindar's Homer: The Lyric Possession of an Epic Past*. Baltimore: Johns Hopkins University Press.

Nicolet-Pierre, Hélène. 1975. "Remarques sur la chronologie relative des plus anciennes séries de statères éléens." *Revue Numismatique*, ser. 6, 17, 7–18.

Nielsen, Thomas H. 1999. "The Concept of Arkadia—The People, Their Land, and Their Organisation." In *Defining Ancient Arkadia*, ed. Thomas H. Nielsen and James Roy, 16–79. *Acts of the Copenhagen Polis Centre 6*. Copenhagen: Copenhagen Polis Centre.

Nijf, Onno van. 1999. "Athletics, Festivals and Greek Identity in the Roman East." *PCPS* 45:176–200.

Nilsson. Martin P. 1968. *The Minoan-Mycenaean Religion and Its Survival in Greek Religion*. 2nd rev. ed. Lund: C.W.K. Gleerup.

Nisetich, Frank. 1980. *Pindar's Victory Songs*. Baltimore: Johns Hopkins University Press.

Oeconomides, Mando. 1993. "Recherches sur le monnayage d'Elis-Olympie à l'époque hellénistique." In *XIth International Congress of Numismatics*, ed. Mando Oeconomides and Hélène Nicolet-Pierre, 193–203. Brussels: Actes Louvain-la-Neuve.

Orlandos, Anastasios. 1924. "Ἀνασκαφαὶ ἐν Στυμφάλῳ." Πρακτικα: 117–23.

———. 1925. "Ἀνασκαφαὶ ἐν Στυμφάλῳ." Πρακτικα: 51–55; 131–39.

———. 1927. "Ἀνασκαφαὶ ἐν Στυμφάλῳ." Πρακτικα: 53–56.

———. 1928. "Ἀνασκαφαὶ ἐν Στυμφάλῳ." Πρακτικα: 120–23.

———. 1929. "Ἀνασκαφαὶ ἐν Στυμφάλῳ." Πρακτικα: 92.

———. 1930. "Ἀνασκαφαὶ ἐν Στυμφάλῳ." Πρακτικα: 88–91.

Osborne, Robin. 1990. "Competitive Festivals and the *Polis*: A Context for Dramatic Festivals at Athens." In *Tragedy, Comedy, and the Polis: Papers from the Greek Drama Conference, Nottingham, 18–20 July 1990*, ed. Alan H. Sommerstein et al., 21–37. Bari: Levante Editori.

Page, D.L. 1951. "Simonidea." *JHS* 71:133–42.

Palmer, L.R. 1956. "Military Arrangements for the Defense of Pylos." *Minos* 4: 120–45.

———. 1957. "A Mycenaean Tomb Inventory." *Minos* 5:58–92.

Papahatzis, Nikolaos D. 1979. Παυσανίου Ἑλλάδος Περιήγησις. Vol. 3. Athens: Ekdotike Athenon.

Patrucco, Roberto. 1972. *Lo sport nella Grecia antica*. Firenze: Leo S. Olschki.

Pauly, August F., Georg Wissowa, Wilhelm Kroll et al., eds. *Paulys Realencyclopädie der classischen Altertumswissenschaft, neue Bearbeitung*. Stuttgart: Metzler

Pausanias. 1971. *Guide to Greece*. Vol. 2, *Southern Greece*. Translated by Peter Levi. Harmondsworth, England: Penguin Books.

Peiser, Benny. 1990. "The Crime of Hippias of Elis: Zur Kontroverse um die Olympionikenliste." *Stadion* 16:37–65.

Perlman, Paula. 2000. *City and Sanctuary in Ancient Greece: The « Theorodokia » in the Peloponnese*. Göttingen: Vandenhoeck und Ruprecht.

Perlman, S. 1969. "Isocrates' *Philippus* and Panhellenism." *Historia* 18:370–74.

———. 1976. "Panhellenism, the Polis and Imperialism." *Historia* 25:1–30.

Pfaff, Christopher A. 2003. "Archaic Corinthian Architecture, ca. 600 to 480 B.C." In *Corinth XX: Corinth, the Centenary 1896–1996*, ed. Nancy Bookidis and Charles K. Williams II, 95–140. Princeton, NJ: Princeton University Press.

Pfeiffer, Rudolf. 1968. *History of Classical Scholarship: From the Beginnings to the End of the Hellenistic Age*. Oxford: Clarendon.

Philipp, G.B. 1984. "Herakles und die frühgriechische Dichtung." *Gymnasium* 91:327–40.

Phillips, David, and David Pritchard, eds. 2003. *Sport and Festival in the Ancient Greek World*. Swansea: Classical Press of Wales.

Picard, Charles. 1939. *Manuel d'archéologie grecque*. Vol. 2, *La sculpture*. Paris: Picard.

Pini, G. 1967. "Correzioni di miti in Pindaro." *Vichiana* 4:339–82.

Pini, Ingo. 1993. *Corpus der minoischen und mykenischen Siegel. Kleinere Griechische Sammlungen*. Vol. 5, Suppl. 1B. *Neufunde Teil 2*. Berlin: Mann.

Platon, Nicolas. 1978. "Τὸ χρυσὸ δακτυλίδι τοῦ Μίνωα." *Rotonda* 4:438.

———. 1984. "The Minoan Thalassocracy and the Golden Ring of Minos." In *The Minoan Thalassocracy: Myth and Reality. Proceedings of the Third International Symposium at the Swedish Institute in Athens, 31 May–5 June, 1982*, ed. Robin Hägg and Nanno Marinatos, 65–69. Stockholm: Svenska Institutet i Athen.

Pleket, Henri W. 1992. "The Participants in the Ancient Olympic Games: Social Background and Mentality." In *Proceedings of an International Symposium on the Olympic Games, 5–9 September 1988*, ed. William Coulson and Helmut Kyrieleis, 147–52. Athens: DAI.

———. 2001. "Zur Sociologie des antiken Sports." *Nikephoros* 14:157–212.

Pohlenz, Max. 1916. "Kronos und die Titanen." *Neue Jahrbücher für das klassiche Altertum* 37:569–72.

Poliakoff, Michael B. 1987. *Combat Sports in the Ancient World*. New Haven, CT, and London: Yale University Press.

Pomeroy, Sarah B. 2002. *Spartan Women*. Oxford: Oxford University Press.

Poursat, Jean-Claude. 1977. *Catalogue des ivoires mycéniens du Musée National d'Athènes*. Athens: École française d'Athènes.

Putnam, B.J. 1967. "Concepts of Sport in Minoan Art." Ph.D. diss., University of Southern California.

Quintilian. 1958. *The Institutio Oratoria*. Vol. 4. Translated by H.E. Butler. LCL. Cambridge, MA, and London: Harvard University Press and William Heinemann.

Rahn, Helmut, ed. and trans. 1995. *M. Fabii Quintiliani Institutionis Oratoriae Libri XII, Pars Posterior*. Darmstadt: Wissenschaftliche Buchgesellschaft.

Raschke, Wendy J., ed. 1988. *The Archaeology of the Olympics: The Olympics and Other Festivals in Antiquity*. Madison, WI: University of Wisconsin Press.

Raubitschek, Antony E. 1949. *Dedications from the Athenian Akropolis*. Cambridge, MA: Archaeological Institute of America.

———. 1988. "The Panhellenic Idea and the Olympic Games." In *The Archaeology of the Olympics: The Olympics and Other Festivals in Antiquity*, ed. Wendy J. Raschke, 35–37. Madison, WI: University of Wisconsin Press.

———. 1992. "Unity and Peace through the Olympic Games." In *Proceedings of an International Symposium on the Olympic Games, 5–9 September 1988*, ed. William Coulson and Helmut Kyrieleis, 185–86. Athens: DAI.

Rausch, Mario. 1998. "'Nach Olympia'—der Weg einer Waffe vom Schlachtfeld in das panhellenische Heiligtum." *ZPE* 123:126–28.

Renfrew, Colin. 1972. *The Emergence of Civilisation: The Cyclades and the Aegean in the Third Millennium B.C.* London: Methuen.

———. 1988. "The Minoan-Mycenaean Origins of the Panhellenic Games." In *The Archaeology of the Olympics: The Olympics and Other Festivals in Antiquity*, ed. Wendy J. Raschke, 13–25. Madison, WI: University of Wisconsin Press. 1988.

Rhodes, P.J. 1982. "Problems in Athenian *Eisphora* and Liturgies." *American Journal of Ancient History* 7:1–19.

Richardson, William Frank. 1985. *Numbering and Measuring in the Classical World: An Introductory Handbook*. Auckland: St. Leonards Publications.

Richter, Gisela M.A., and Marjorie J. Milne. 1935. *Shapes and Names of Athenian Vases*. New York: Metropolitan Museum of Art.

Ridgway, Brunilde Sismondo. 1970. *The Severe Style in Greek Sculpture*. Princeton, NJ: Princeton University Press.

———. 1984. "The Riace Bronzes: A Minority Viewpoint." In *Due Bronzi da Riace: Rinvenimento, restauro, analisi ed ipotesi di interpretazione (Bolletino d'arte*, Serie Speciale 3), 313–26. Rome: Istituto Poligrafico e Zecca dello Stato.

Ridington, William Robbins. 1935. "The Minoan-Mycenaean Background of Greek Athletics." Ph.D. diss., University of Pennsylvania.

Robbins, Emmet. 1982. "Heracles, the Hyperboreans, and the Hind: Pindar, Ol. 3," *Phoenix* 36:295–305.

Robert, Carl. 1893. "Sosipolis in Olympia." *MDAI(A)* 18:37–45.

———. 1900. "Die Ordnung der olympischen Spiele und die Sieger der 75.–83. Olympiade." *Hermes* 35:141–95.

Robert, Louis. 1974. "Les femmes théores à Éphèse." *Comptes rendus des séances de l'Académie des inscriptions et belles-lettres*, 176–81.

Robertson, Martin. 1992. *The Art of Vase-Painting in Classical Athens*. Cambridge: Cambridge University Press.

Robertson, Noel. 1988. "The Ancient Olympics: Sport, Spectacle, and Ritual." In *The Olympic Games in Transition*, ed. Jeffrey O. Segrave and Donald Chu, 11–25. Champaign, IL: Human Kinetics Books.

Robinson, Rachel Sargent. 1981. *Sources for the History of Greek Athletics*. 1995. Reprint. Chicago: Ares.

Rodenwaldt, Gerhart. 1911. "Fragmente mykenischer Wandgemälde." *MDAI* 36:237–78.

Roller, Lynn. 1981. "Funeral Games for Historical Persons." *Stadion* 7:1–18.

Romano, David G. 1981. "The Stadia of the Peloponnesos," Ph.D. diss., University of Pennsylvania.

———. 1982. "The Stadium of Eumenes II at Pergamon." *AJA* 86:586–89.

————. 1990. "Philip of Macedon, Alexander the Great, and the Ancient Olympic Games." In *The World of Philip and Alexander,* ed. Elin Danien, 63–79. Philadelphia: University of Pennsylvania Museum.

————. 1993. *Athletics and Mathematics in Archaic Corinth: The Origins of the Greek Stadion.* Philadelphia: American Philosophical Society.

————. 2004. "Multiple Victors at Olympia: Images, Portraits and Icons." In *The Olympic Games in Antiquity,* ed. M.A. Kaila, G. Thill, H. Theodoropoulou, Y. Xanthacou, and C. Lerounis, 94–133. Athens: Atrapos Editions.

Roos, Paavo. 1985. "Alexander I in Olympia." *Eranos* 83:162–68.

Rose, H.J. 1985. "The Greek Agones." *Arete* 3(1):163–82. Originally published 1922.

Ross, Ludwig. 1841. *Reisen und Reiserouten. Teil 1—Reisen im Peloponnes.* Berlin: Reimer.

Roy, James. 1998. "Thucydides 5.49.1–50.4: The Quarrel between Elis and Sparta in 420 B.C., and Elis' Exploitation of Olympia." *Klio* 80(2):360–68.

————. 2002. "The Synoikism of Elis." In *Even More Studies in the Ancient Greek "Polis,"* ed. T.H. Nielsen. Papers from the Copenhagen Polis Centre, 6, 249–64. Stuttgart: Steiner.

Runnels, Curtis N., and Julie M. Hansen. 1986. "The Olive in the Prehistoric Aegean: The Evidence for Domestication in the Early Bronze Age." *OJA* 5:299–308.

Rystedt, Eva. 1986. "The Foot-Race and Other Athletic Contests in the Mycenaean World." *Opuscula Atheniensia* 16:103–16.

Säflund, Marie-Louise. 1970. *The East Pediment of the Temple of Zeus at Olympia.* Göteborg: Paul Åströms.

Sansone, David. 1988. *Greek Athletics and the Genesis of Sport.* Berkeley and Los Angeles: University of California Press.

Scanlon, Thomas F. 1999. "Women, Bull Sports, Cults and Initiation in Minoan Crete." *Nikephoros* 12:33–70.

————. 2002. *Eros and Greek Athletics.* New York: Oxford University Press.

Schilbach, Jürgen. 1992. "Olympia: Die Entwicklungsphasen des Stadions." In *Proceedings of an International Symposium on the Olympic Games, 5–9 September 1988,* ed. William Coulson and Helmut Kyrieleis, 33–37. Athens: DAI.

————. 2000. "Massbecher aus Olympia." In *XI. Bericht über die Ausgrabungen in Olympia,* ed. Alfred Mallwitz, 323–37. Berlin: De Gruyter.

Schliemann, Heinrich. 1880. *Mycenae: A Narrative of Researches and Discoveries at Mycenae and Tiryns.* New York: Scribner's Sons.

————. 1885. *Tiryns: The Prehistoric Palace of the Kings of Tiryns.* New York: Scribner's Sons.

Schmemann, Serge. 2002. "Drama and Scandal Make the Olympics." *New York Times,* 19 February, D1.

Schmid, H. 1997. *Zur Technik des Weitsprungs in der griechischen Antike.* Dissertation. Hasselroth: Johannes Gutenberg-Universität Mainz.

Schmidt, M. 1967. "Dionysien." *Antike Kunst* 10:70–76.

Schmitt-Pantel, Pauline. 1990a. "Collective Activities and the Political in the Greek City." In *The Greek City from Homer to Alexander*, ed. Oswyn Murray and Simon Price, 199–213. Oxford: Clarendon.

———. 1990b. "Sacrificial Meal and Symposion: Two Models of Civic Institutions in the Archaic City?" In *Sympotica: A Symposium on the Symposion*, ed. Oswyn Murray, 14–33. Oxford: Clarendon.

Schrader, Hans. 1937. "Zur Chronologie der elischen Münzen." *Archaiologike Ephemeris:*208–16.

Schreier, Ulrich. 1972. *Olympia-Münzen, Einst und Jetzt.* 2nd ed. Baden-Baden: Victor Gadoury.

Schröder, Bruno. 1927. *Der Sport im Altertum.* Berlin: Schoetz.

Schultz, Sabine. 1979. "Griechische Münzen von der Peloponnes." *Numismatische Beiträge* 22(1):46–52.

Schwabacher, Willy. 1962. "Olympische Blitzschwinger." *Antike Kunst* 5(1):9–17.

Schwartz, Jacques. 1960. *Pseudo-Hesiodeia: Recherches sur la composition, la diffusion et la disparaison ancienne d' oeuvres attribuées à Hésiode.* Leiden: Brill.

Segal, Charles. 1985. "Archaic Choral Lyric." In *The Cambridge History of Classical Literature*, ed. P.E. Easterling and B.M.W. Knox, Vol. 1, 165–201. Cambridge: Cambridge University Press.

Seltman, Charles T. 1921. *The Temple Coins of Olympia.* Cambridge: Bowes and Bowes.

———. 1948. "Greek Sculpture and Some Festival Coins." *Hesperia* 17:71–85.

———. 1951. "The Katoche Hoard of Elean Coins." *Numismatic Chronicle* 111:40–55.

Semso, M. 1977. "Catalogue of Coins of the Montreal Games." *Olympic Review* 116/117:419–20.

Semso, M., and M. Ouellet. 1975. "Olympic Coins." *Olympic Review* 87/88:45–50.

Serwint, Nancy. 1993. "The Female Athletic Costume at the Heraia and Prenuptial Initiation Rites." *AJA* 97:403–22.

Shapiro, H.A. 2000. "Modest Athletes and Liberated Women: Etruscans on Attic Black-Figure Vases." In *Not the Classical Ideal: Athens and the Construction of the Other in Greek Art*, ed. Beth Cohen, 313–37. Leiden: Brill.

Shaw, Maria. 1996. "Bull-Leaping Fresco from Below the Ramp House at Mycenae: A Study in Iconography and Artistic Transmission." *ABSA* 91:167–90.

Shaw, Pamela-Jane. 2003. *Discrepancies in Olympiad Dating and Chronological Problems of Archaic Peloponnesian History. Historia Einzelschriften* 166. Stuttgart: Franz Steiner.

Shelmerdine, Cynthia W. 1985. *The Perfume Industry of Mycenaean Pylos.* Göteborg: Paul Åströms.

Shelmerdine, Susan C. 1987. "Pindaric Praise and the Third *Olympian*." *HSCP* 91:65–81.

Siewert, Peter. 1981."Eine Bronze-Urkunde mit elischen Urteilen." In *X. Bericht über die Ausgrabungen in Olympia*, ed. Alfred Mallwitz, 228–48. Berlin: De Gruyter.

———. 1992. "The Olympic Rules." In *Proceedings of an International Symposium on the Olympic Games, 5–9 September 1988*, ed. William Coulson and Helmut Kyrieleis, 113–17. Athens: DAI.

———. 1996. "Votivbarren und das Ende der Waffen—und Geräteweihungen in Olympia." *MDAI(A)* 111:141–48.

Simri, Uriel. 1980. "The Development of Female Participation in the Modern Olympic Games." *Stadion* 6:187–216.

Singor, H.W. 1995. "Eni Prôtoisi Machesthai." In *Homeric Questions*, ed. Jan Paul Crielaard, 183–200. Amsterdam: Gieben.

Sinn, Ulrich. 2000. *Olympia, Cult, Sport and Ancient Festival*. Translated by Thomas Thornton. Princeton, NJ: M. Wiener.

Slater, William J., ed. 1969. *Lexicon to Pindar*, s.v. "Ἀγησίας." Berlin: De Gruyter.

Slowikowski, Synthia. 1989. "The Symbolic Hellanodikai." *Aethlon* 7:133–41.

Snodgrass, Anthony. 1980. *Archaic Greece: The Age of Experiment*. Berkeley: University of California Press.

Sophocles. 1973. *Electra*. Edited by J.H. Kells. Cambridge: Cambridge University Press.

Sourvinou-Inwood, Christiane. 1973. "On the Lost 'Boat' Ring from Mochlos." *Kadmos* 12:149–58.

———. 1988. *Studies in Girls' Transitions: Aspects of the Arkteia and Age Representation in Attic Iconography*. Athens: Kardamitsa.

———. 1990. "What Is *Polis* Religion?" In *The Greek City from Homer to Alexander*, ed. Oswyn Murray and Simon Price, 295–322. Oxford: Clarendon.

Spears, Betty. 1984. "A Perspective of the History of Women's Sport in Ancient Greece." *JSH* 11:32–47.

Spivey, Nigel. 2004. *The Ancient Olympics*. Oxford: Oxford University Press.

Spyropoulos, Theodoros G. 1970. "Excavation at the Mycenaean Nekropolis of Tanagra." *Athens Annals of Archaeology* 2:184–97.

Starr, Chester. 1982. "Economic and Social Conditions in the Greek World." In *The Cambridge Ancient History*, 2nd ed., ed. John Boardman and N.G.L. Hammond, Vol. III, Part 3, 417–36. Cambridge: Cambridge University Press.

Steiner, Deborah. 1998. "Moving Images: Fifth-Century Victory Monuments and the Athlete's Allure." *Classical Antiquity* 17:123–49.

Stein-Hölkeskamp, Elke. 1989. *Adelskultur und Polisgesellschaft: Studien zum griechischen Adel in archaischer und klassischer Zeit*. Stuttgart: Franz Steiner.

Stewart, Andrew. 1997. *Art, Desire, and the Body in Ancient Greece*. Cambridge: Cambridge University Press.

Storch, Rudolph. 1998. "The Archaic Greek Phalanx, 750–650 B.C." *Ancient History Bulletin* 12:1–7.

Swaddling, Judith. 1980. *The Ancient Olympic Games*. London: British Museum Publications.

———. 1999. *The Ancient Olympic Games*. 2nd ed. Austin: University of Texas Press.

———. 2004. *The Ancient Olympic Games*. 3rd ed. London: British Museum.

Sweet, Waldo E. 1987. *Sport and Recreation in Ancient Greece: A Sourcebook with Translations.* New York and Oxford: Oxford University Press.

Talvio, Tuuka. 1979. "The First Modern Olympic Commemorative Coin." *Seaby's Coin and Medal Bulletin* 730:182–83.

———. 1984. "Det Finska Olympiamyntet och dess Forebilder [The Finnish Olympic Coin and Its Background]." *Myntkontakt* 7:180.

———. 1994. "Vapauden Jumaladar Seppeloi Nuoruuden—Felix Nylundin Ehdotus Olympiarahaksi [The Goddess Freedom Crowns Youth—Felix Nylund's Proposal for the Olympic Coin]." *Numismaatinen Aikakauslehti* 1:14–15.

Themelis, Petros. 1968. "Thyron—Epitalion." *Athens Annals of Archaeology* 1:201–204.

———. 1969. "Minoan Evidence in Olympia." *Athens Annals of Archaeology* 2:254–56.

Thompson, J.G. 1986. "The Location of Minoan Bull-Sports: A Consideration of the Problem." *JSH* 13:5–13.

———. 1989. "Clues to the Location of Minoan Bull-Jumping from the Palace at Knossos." *JSH* 16:62–69.

Thompson, Margaret, Otto Mørkholm, and Colin M. Kraay, eds. 1973. *An Inventory of Greek Coin Hoards.* New York: American Numismatic Society.

Tod, M.N. 1950. "The Alphabetic Numeral System Used in Attica," *ABSA* 45:126–39.

———. 1954. "Letter-labels in Greek Inscriptions." *ABSA* 49:1–8.

Tyrrell, William Blake. 2004. *The Smell of Sweat: Greek Athletics, Olympics, and Culture.* Wauconda, IL: Bolchazy-Carducci.

Ulf, Christoph. 1997. "Die Mythen um Olympia—politischer Gehalt und politische Intention." *Nikephoros* 10:9–51.

Ulf, Christoph, and Ingomar Weiler. 1980. "Der Ursprung der antiken Olympischen Spiele in der Forschung: Versuch eines kritischen Kommentars." *Stadion* 6:1–38.

Unz, R.K. 1986. "The Chronology of the Elean War." *GRBS* 27:29–42.

Valavanis, Panos. 1999. *Hysplex: The Starting Mechanism in Ancient Stadia.* Berkeley: University of California Press.

———. 2004. *Games and Sanctuaries in Ancient Greece: Olympia, Delphi, Isthmia, Nemea, Athens.* Translated by David Hardy. Los Angeles: Getty Publications.

Vallois, René. 1926. "Les origines des jeux olympiques." *Revue des études anciennes* 28:305–22.

Vegas-Sansalvador, A. 1991. "XAMYNH: An Elean Surname of Demeter." In *Achaia und Elis in der Antike*, ed. A. D. Rizakis, 145–50. Athens: Kentron Hellinikes kai Romaïkes Archaiotitos.

Vidal-Naquet, Pierre. 1968. "La tradition de l'hoplite athénien." In *Problèmes de la guerre en Grèce ancienne*, ed. Jean Pierre Vernant, 161–81. Paris: Mouton.

———. 1986. *The Black Hunter: Forms of Thought and Forms of Society in the Greek World.* Translated by Andrew Szegedy-Maszak. Baltimore: Johns Hopkins University Press.

, Hector, Gerald Schaus, Susan Marie Cronkite Price, Ben Gourley, and
s Hagerman. 1998. "Excavations at Ancient Stymphalos, 1997." *Echos du
de classique/Classical Views*, n.s., 17:261–319.

, Hector, Gerald Schaus, Susan Marie Cronkite Price, Ben Gourley, and
y Lutomsky. 1997. "Excavations at Ancient Stymphalos, 1996." *Echos
1onde classique/Classical Views*, n.s., 16:23–73.

ad, A.G. 1959. *The Study of Greek Inscriptions*. Cambridge: Cambridge
ersity Press.

udides, Stephanos. 1921. *The Vaulted Tombs of the Mesara*. Liverpool:
rpool University Press.

, Nikolaos. 1965. "Μυκηναϊκὸς τύμβος Σαμικού." Αρχαιολογικὸν
τίον 20A:6–40.

1976. *The Olympic Games*. Athens: Ekdotike Athenon S.A.

David C. 1984. *The Olympic Myth of Greek Amateur Athletics*. Chicago:
s.

1996a. *The Modern Olympics: A Struggle for Revival*. Baltimore and Lon-
1: Johns Hopkins University Press.

. 1996b. "First with the Most: Greek Athletic Records and 'Specializa-
1.'" *Nikephoros* 9:175–97.

. 2004. *A Brief History of the Olympic Games*. Malden, MA, Oxford, and
toria: Blackwell Publishing.

:r, John. 1995. "Bronze Age Representations of Aegean Bull-Games, III."
gaeum 12:507–45.

Visser, Marinus Willem de. 1903. *Die nicht mensc*
Griechen. Leiden: Brill.

Von Bothmer, Dietrich. 1975. "Two Bronze Hydrias
Museum Journal 1:15–22.

Wacker, Christian. 1998. "The Record of the Olympic
11:39–50.

Walbank, Frank W. 1979. *A Historical Commentary on*
Clarendon.

Warren, Jennifer A.W. 1962. "A Neglected Hoard of E
Chronicle 122:413–15.

Warren, Peter. 1987. "The Ring of Minos." In *ΕΙΛΑΠΙΝ*
τὸν Καθηγητὴ Νικολάο Πλάτωνα, ed. Lenia Kastr
and Nikos Giannadake. Heraklion: Demos Herakle

Weege, Fritz. 1911. "Einzelfunde von Olympia 1907–19

Wees, Hans van. 1992. *Status Warriors: War, Violence a*
History. Amsterdam: Gieben.

———. 1995. "Politics and the Battlefield: Ideology in
Greek World, ed. Anton Powell, 153–78. London: R

———. 2001. "The Myth of the Middle-Class Army: Mi
Ancient Athens." In *War as a Cultural and Social Fo*
Antiquity, ed. Tønnes Bekker-Nielsen and Lise Ha
hagen: Stougard Jensen Scantryk.

Weiler, Ingomar. 1985–86. "Der 'Niedergang' und das E
ischen Spiele in der Forschung." *Grazer Beiträge* 12(

———. 1997. "Olympia—jenseits der Agonistik: Kultur un
10:191–213.

Weir, Robert. 2004. *Roman Delphi and Its Pythian Games*

Weniger, Ludwig. 1895. *Der heilige Ölbaum in Olympia.*
buchdr.

———. 1919. *Altgriechischer Baumkultus.* Leipzig: Diete

Wiegand, Theodor. 1941. *Didyma.* Vol. 1.1. Berlin: Man

Wiegand, Theodor, and Hans Schrader. 1904. *Priene: Er*
gen und Untersuchungen in den Jahren 1895–1898. B

Willetts, R.F. 1955. *Aristocratic Society in Ancient Crete.*
Kegan Paul.

———. 1957. "A Neotas at Dreros?" *Hermes* 85:381–84.

———. 1962. *Cretan Cults and Festivals.* London: Routle

———. 1965. *Ancient Crete.* London: Routledge and Keg

Williams, Charles K., II, and Pamela Russell. 1981. "Corinth
Hesperia 50:1–44.

Williams, Hector, Susan Marie Cronkite Price, and Geral
vations at Stymphalos, 1995." *Echos du monde classiq*
15:75–88.

Williams, Hector, Gerald Schaus, Ben Gourley, Susan Mari
leen Donahue Sherwood, and Yannis Lolos. 2002. "Ex
los, 1999–2002." *Mouseion* 2:135–87.

PART II

THE MODERN OLYMPICS

The Olympic Games
in Modern Times

Robert K. Barney

In 1895, the Chinese government received, through its French embassy, an unusual invitation: to send athletes to Greece to compete in the new Olympic Games, planned for Athens in the spring of 1896. Chinese officials, who had no idea what this competition was all about, chose to ignore the invitation. Meanwhile, thousands of miles away in the United States, most citizens knew little more about this new phenomenon, with at least one exception—William Milligan Sloane, a history professor at Princeton University. Sloane gathered together a small group of Princeton students and sent them to Greece for the competitions. They returned with marvellous tales of a glorious event, staged in the splendour of a city imbued with antiquities and Greek hospitality. And so were born the modern Olympic Games. Over a hundred years later, in August 2004, the Games of the 28th Olympiad were presented to the world by another generation of Athenian hosts. On-site spectators and some four billion global television viewers were fascinated, thrilled, entertained, and indeed even inspired by all that took place in Greece's hallowed, antiquity-immersed landscape. Most looked forward to the next edition of the Games, those to be celebrated in Beijing in 2008 (or the Olympic Winter Games scheduled for Turin in 2006).

Over their now slightly more than one hundred years of history, the modern Summer Olympic Games have grown from a quaint *fin de siècle* festival involving thirteen countries and fewer than three hundred athletes to a movement that can now count slightly over two hundred of the world's countries as members of the Olympic family. Further, the Summer Games now showcase the sporting exploits of well over ten thousand athletes; the Winter Games, over two thousand. The Olympic festival has evolved into the modern world's foremost example of sport spectacle and extravagant cultural ritual. Finally, the Games have become a phenomenon that energizes nations the world over to mount elaborate financial and organizational efforts in order to be presented in a good light at these great quadrennial occasions. Political factions, ethnic groups, religious sects, economic cartels, media, artists, scholars, and "cause conscious" factions of almost every hue and design are both hypnotized and galvanized by what the Olympic Games can engender in the way of attention to cause, enhanced prestige, potentially huge profits, and opportunities for individual and group expression. No other regularly occurring world event casts such a penetrating global effervescence and, at the same time, such a tall shadow of frightening possibilities.

Origins

It took the modern world almost two thousand years to become aware of the illustrious sporting legacy achieved by the cornerstone of Western civilization—the Ancient Greeks. As nineteenth-century archaeologists began to discover remains of ancient stadiums, exercise gymnasiums, and statues and vase paintings by the thousands displaying scenes of athletic and sporting endeavour among Greeks, and as fragments of their preserved literature on sporting matters became known, the spirit of modern humankind was moved to attempt an emulation of such past glories. After all, health, fitness, physical education, competitive sporting prowess, and glorification of the body served Greece supremely during its golden eras of antiquity; why could such things not serve similarly in modern times? One individual who thought they could was a French aristocrat named Pierre de Frédy, the Baron de Coubertin (1863–1937).

Coubertin was born in Paris into an aristocratic and cultured family. As a young man he had witnessed the humiliating defeat of his country by the Germans in the Franco-Prussian War. A disinterested student of military science, and later a law school dropout, Coubertin instead devoted his attention to French history, social philosophy, and educational reform.

Concerned by the lack of a sporting ethic among his countrymen and an absence of physical education in the schools of France, Coubertin set about to initiate change. He travelled widely in England and the United States, and returned greatly impressed by what he viewed in the way of sport and physical education in England's so-called "public schools" and American colleges and universities. Though Coubertin wrote and lectured vigorously on themes involving needed changes in French education, he was largely rebuffed by his country's education authorities. As a result, Coubertin's sport-education ideas turned instead to international perspectives, one emerging theme of which was the reincarnation in modern context of the epitome of ancient Greek athletic expressions, the Olympic Games.

In June 1894, Coubertin convened a conference at the Sorbonne in Paris to debate both common eligibility standards for participation in international sporting competition and a possible revival of the Olympic Games. Although no meaningful conclusions were reached on the former, the latter was unanimously endorsed by the assembly of over two hundred delegates. An International Olympic Committee (IOC) was formed, and the first Games were awarded to Athens for the spring of 1896. Dimitrios Vikelas, a Greek intellectual, was elected first president of the IOC, and Pierre de Coubertin its secretary. The choice of Athens was questioned by Europeans, many of whom felt that Greece was too far removed from the mainstream of modern developments in athletics. In reality, however, the Greeks had previously staged attempts to re-establish the ancient Games in modern context. Through the beneficence of millionaire Evangelos Zappas, successful festivals were held in 1859 and 1870. Further attempts were less successful, but there is little doubt that by 1896 Greeks of the latter nineteenth century had experienced modest episodes of modern sport organization and performance.

With the energetic organizational efforts of Greece's royal family, particularly Crown Prince Constantine, and the financial contributions of Greeks worldwide, particularly millionaire Georges Averoff, the 1896 Games were a huge success. Over sixty thousand people attended the opening ceremonies in the grand marble stadium—restored specifically for the occasion, and certainly far outstripping a more modest restoration in wood, completed in advance of the 1870 Games, that had fallen into disrepair. A small band of American athletes dominated the track and field events, but the Greeks themselves performed worthily. Spiridon Loues, a modest "country worker" whose startling victory in the marathon event marked the only occasion in his lifetime that he competed in international sport, became the toast of all Greece and an eternal memory in Greek sport history.

Growing Pains

Vikelas retired from the IOC following the Athens festival, and Coubertin became president, a post he held continuously until his retirement in 1925 at the age of 62. The Games of the Second Olympiad were staged in France as part of the Paris World Exposition of 1900. Enveloped by the great fair, they failed miserably to capitalize on their auspicious beginning four years earlier. The Paris Olympics were reported in the world's newspapers as anything but Olympic in nature. Rather, they were most often referred to as "World University Championships" or "Exposition contests."

The demeaning of the Olympic Games caused by organizing them as a sideshow to a World's Fair was a lesson ignored in 1904. The American city of St. Louis organized the Games of the Third Olympiad as part of the Louisiana Exposition's physical culture exhibits and activities. Though athletic performance was superb, foreign participation was so scant that the track and field events, in particular, were reduced to being largely American championships. Coubertin was not pleased. But one positive impact of the 1904 Games being held for the first time outside Europe was the fact that the modern Olympic movement had "arrived" in the United States; indeed, the Olympics became an indelible dimension of America's early twentieth-century crusade for international sporting prominence.

Ensuing Olympic festivals were staged in London in 1908 and Stockholm in 1912. In the context of global culture, the culmination of the Stockholm festival signalled the arrival of the Olympic Games as the world's premier international sporting event. National Olympic committees from twenty-eight countries, located on five continents of the world, sent some 2,500 athletes to Sweden to compete in 102 events. Whereas local organizers had officiated at the sporting events of previous Olympic Games, officials of individual international sports federations governed the competitions in Stockholm, a phenomenon that became critical for the organization and execution of future Olympic competitions. In Stockholm, too, competitions were staged in sculpture, painting, literature, music, and town planning.

By 1914 Baron de Coubertin had much to celebrate as he hosted the twentieth anniversary celebration of the Olympic movement's founding in 1894. By 1914, too, the IOC had new symbols, the now famous five-ring logo and its motto, the Latin phrase, *citius, altius, fortius* (swifter, higher, stronger). For Coubertin, many of his expectations for the modern Olympic movement had begun to emerge. As expressed in 1908, Coubertin told the world that he had revived the Olympic Games in a modern context with several motivations in mind:

1. as a cornerstone for health and cultural progress;
2. for education and character-building;
3. for international understanding and peace;
4. for equal opportunity;
5. for fair and equal competition;
6. for cultural expression;
7. for beauty and excellence; and
8. for independence of sport as an instrument of social reform rather than government legislation.

Disillusion surrounded the Olympic movement between 1914 and 1918 as much of the world went to war. Coubertin, serving as a non-combatant in the French army, somehow found time to ensure that things Olympic did not die in the international sports psyche. He lectured often, corresponded in his usual energetic manner, soothed animosities aroused between IOC members fighting on opposite sides in the war, and, in 1915, established new Olympic headquarters in Lausanne, Switzerland, a safer and more receptive environment than wartime Paris.

The First World War put an end to the plans to hold the Games of the Sixth Olympiad in Berlin, but in 1920, with the world temporarily at peace, the Games unfolded in Antwerp. Prominent among members of the Belgium Organizing Committee was Count Henri Baillet-Latour, the IOC member who would succeed Coubertin as president five years later.

When Coubertin and his original International Olympic Committee convened in Paris in 1894 following the Sorbonne Conference, a number of sports were considered for inclusion in the Olympic program. One of them, oddly enough, was *patinage*, or ice skating. An indoor exhibition of figure skating was presented by London organizers in 1908. In Antwerp in 1920, Belgian officials organized figure skating events once again, together with an exhibition ice hockey tournament. It would take the departure of Coubertin, an opponent of the concept of separate Olympic Winter Games, before such a phenomenon became reality. A modest winter sports festival was arranged in 1924 in Chamonix, France, separate and distinct from the Summer Games in Paris. But the Chamonix festival did not become recorded as the first Olympic Winter Games until after the Baron's retirement in 1925. Beginning in 1928, Olympic Winter Games were organized every four years, mostly in Europe.

The Games Reach Maturity

Cities the world over mount energetic and elaborately detailed plans in order to win the IOC's approval to host the Olympic Games. Such campaigns are underpinned by various motivations, the most apparent of which are civic and national pride and prestige, political gain, and economic benefit. The quest by Los Angeles to host the Olympic Games provides an early example. Prompted by a desire to promote itself as a tourist and vacation mecca, with a healthful climate in which to live and an even healthier economic potential for those with capital to invest, the city made a bid for the Games of 1920. Coubertin's intent to hold the 1920 (Antwerp), 1924 (Paris), and 1928 (Amsterdam) Olympic festivals in Europe stalled the Los Angeles bid, but the persistence of William May Garland and his Los Angeles colleagues finally paid off and the city received the Games for 1932. By the eve of the Games of the Tenth Olympiad, America, indeed much of the world, was in the midst of a devastating economic Depression. Despite this, the Games went on, and—it might be argued—in glorious fashion. With funding for much of the festival coming from a $1 million state appropriation gained through a public referendum, the main events were held in the relatively new Los Angeles Memorial Coliseum. An innovative Olympic Village was built for the first time, but only for men; the women were accommodated at the Chapman Hotel in suburban Beverly Hills. Were the expectations of California's tourist and land speculators realized as a result of bringing the great world sporting spectacle to Los Angeles? One has only to gaze on the city of Los Angeles and the state of California today to arrive at the answer.

Largely a patriarchal expression in both organization and athletic participation during the first three decades of its history, the modern Olympic movement offered few opportunities for women. Through the pioneering efforts of an idealistic French woman, Alice Milliat, the International Federation for Women's Sport (the Fédération Sportive Féminine Internationale, or FSFI) was organized in 1921, and several successful editions of "Women's Olympic Games" occurred between 1921 and 1934. Though women competed in Olympic demonstration events in 1900 in tennis and golf, in swimming and diving beginning in 1912, and even in track and field in 1928, it would require female Olympic stars comparable to the status of Jim Thorpe, Paavo Nurmi, and Johnny Weissmuller before women's participation was taken seriously. In this regard, the startling performances of Sonja Henie, the youthful Norwegian skating beauty of the 1928, 1932, and 1936 Winter Games, and the track and field accomplishments of the tomboyish Mildred "Babe" Didrikson in 1932, initiated a trend that projected women into the limelight of the Olympic program.

Ominous signs of world discord permeated much of the 1930s, including the staging of the 1936 Games in Berlin. When the Games of the Eleventh Olympiad were awarded to Germany in 1931, the lingering vestiges of the Weimar Republic governed Germany. By the time the Olympic flame was lit in Berlin's magnificent Olympic stadium in the summer of 1936, the National Socialists—led by Adolf Hitler—were in power. Under IOC rules, host cities, not national governments, are directed to organize and stage the Games, but Hitler's representatives were everywhere, controlling and shaping the Olympic festival to serve Nazi interests. Though much of the two-week celebration was an expression of German nationalism, Nazi propaganda, and Teutonic military culture, it was also an extravaganza featuring German organizational precision. Many countries, including the United States, feared sending a team to compete. More than any other country, controversy in the extreme arose in America: "to go or not to go" became the question debated at length by various factions allied with, as well as completely divorced from, the amateur sport movement in the country. Many viewed it as immoral to support an "evil German regime" by taking part. Nazi postures on religion and race defied Christian principles and ran counter to Olympic moral codes. In the end, a U.S. Olympic team sailed to Europe in the summer of 1936. Superb athletic performances abounded in Berlin, but none were more spectacular than those of Jesse Owens, the black American sprinter. At first a curiosity and then a celebrity in the eyes of most German spectators, Owens won the 100- and 200-metre sprints and the long jump, and ran a leg on the winning 4 x 100 meter relay team—dispelling in graphic fashion the warped Nazi doctrine of Aryan supremacy. The epic 1936 Games were filmed by Leni Riefenstahl. Her film, entitled *Olympia*, premiered in 1938 and was judged the world's finest film for that year, winning the coveted Venice Golden Lion Award. Walt Disney's *Snow White* was a distant runner-up.

By 1940 the world was at war again. The 1940 Summer and Winter Games, which were awarded to Japan (Tokyo and Sapporo, respectively), were cancelled, as were the 1944 Summer Games set for Helsinki. In the middle of the war, IOC President Count Baillet-Latour died from a heart attack. He was succeeded by vice-president Sigfrid Edström of Sweden, who strove to hold the Olympic movement intact by issuing a steady stream of communications and newsletters to IOC members from countries aligned with both Allied and Axis powers.

Postwar Trials

With the conclusion of the Second World War in 1945, the IOC turned its attention to the re-establishment of the Olympics. In the summer of 1948, the Games of the Fourteenth Olympiad were staged in war-ravaged London. Germany, Italy, and Japan were missing—banned as the perpetrators of the war, just as Germany had been disallowed from competing in the Games of 1920 and 1924 for identical reasons after the First World War. The Summer Games of 1948 were preceded by the Winter Olympics, held in St. Moritz, Switzerland. Both the 1948 Winter and Summer Games were a far cry from those in 1932 and 1936 in terms of organization, facilities, and pomp; nevertheless, superb athletic endeavour more than compensated.

The results of the Second World War shaped a new world geography, creating vexing problems for leaders of the Olympic movement. The fracture of Europe into "east" and "west" spheres of political polarization, particularly the split of Germany into two countries, produced thorny consequences for the IOC. Germany returned to the Olympic Games in 1952 in Helsinki, where it was represented only by athletes from the Federal Republic. For the next four summer and winter Olympic festivals (Melbourne/Cortina d'Ampezzo in 1956, Rome/Squaw Valley in 1960, Tokyo/Innsbruck in 1964, and Mexico City/Grenoble in 1968), Germany was represented by a combined team of athletes from both East and West. The Soviet-controlled German Democratic Republic and the West-backed Federal Republic of Germany did not compete as individual nations until the Munich/Sapporo Games in 1972.

If the German problem was not enough to frustrate IOC members, the emergence of the Soviet Union as an Olympic nation to be reckoned with, the place of South Africa in the Games, and ultimatums from the People's Republic of China promoted a constant state of turmoil. The Soviet Union's first appearance in the Olympic Games, in Helsinki in 1952, served notice that they were the Olympic power of the future. Their medal count in Finland was barely eclipsed by the United States. An elaborate scheme of early identification of young athletes, specialized sports schools, application of scientific research to sport performance, and elaborate financial support at all levels within the nation's sport mechanism ensured consistent representation on Olympic victory podiums. The Soviet approach prompted constant debate by IOC authorities, particularly on the question of "state professionals." The proven success of the Soviet model, however, spurred many nations the world over to adopt various dimensions of the Russian blueprint for athletic success.

South Africa had been a valued Olympic family member since its first participation in 1908. For almost half a century no one questioned South Africa's ever-expanding policy of apartheid, a policy in direct confrontation with the Olympic code's principle that participation in the Games "shall not be denied for reasons of race." South Africa's Olympic team had always been lily white. With the disintegration of European colonial empires on the continent of Africa following the Second World War, and the commensurate evolution of new nations reflecting black pride and political power, the racial policy of South Africa came under censure and severe challenge, internally and externally. There were several political and economic measures that other African countries tried to exert in bringing about change. One of the political measures was a campaign aimed at forcing South African Olympic teams to be integrated, a first step in the dissolution of that nation's overall policy of discrimination towards people of colour. With the backing of the Soviet Union, whose support on the measure, in part, was underscored by the prospect of political and economic dividends to be gained in Africa, a steady campaign was waged. The threat of boycotting the Games by a unified bloc of African countries was the trump card played. Although Avery Brundage, Sigfrid Edström's successor as IOC president, tried every means to keep South Africa in the Olympic movement, the council rooms of the IOC increasingly echoed with a gathering storm of protest through the 1960s. After having its invitation to compete "withdrawn" in 1964 (Tokyo) and 1968 (Mexico City), South Africa was finally expelled from the family of Olympic nations in 1972. Black Africa had won the battle, but not the war. South Africa's apartheid policies remained entrenched for twenty more years. It was not until 1992 at the Barcelona Games that black and white athletes representing South Africa finally marched together as members of an Olympic team reunited with the modern Olympic movement.

With the triumph of Mao Zedong's Communists over the Nationalist followers of Chiang Kai-shek in China's drawn-out civil war of the 1930s and 1940s, still another perturbing Olympic problem presented itself. Which was the real China in the IOC's eyes? Mainland Communists? Or Nationalists who had retreated to Formosa, an island off China's coast that eventually became known as Taiwan? Because the pre-war national Chinese Olympic Committee had been in the hands of the Nationalists, the IOC recognized Taiwan, which, in turn, insisted upon being called the Republic of China. In a series of arguments and angry rebuffs, the People's Republic failed to move the IOC towards its point of view—that its population, fifty times that of Taiwan, and indeed nearly one third of the world's total, made "it" the real China. Taiwan, it argued, was but an obscure renegade offshore Chinese province. Stubbornly, the People's Republic remained aloof from the modern Olympic movement until changes in political times prompted its appearance at the 1984 Games in Los Angeles.

All this, and much more, caused the IOC presidency of Avery Brundage to be filled with controversy and crisis. Few could have been equal to the task of steering the Olympic schooner through such turbulent waters during the 1950s, 1960s, and early 1970s, but Brundage proved to be a capable captain. And, like a good captain, he demanded and received absolute obedience from his crew (IOC members). He remained consistent in proclaiming that sport should never be contaminated by politics; that the Olympic Games were for amateur athletes; that the Olympic movement should be insulated from the evils of commercialism; that women's competition should be reduced; that the Games should become smaller, not larger; and, indeed, that perhaps the Winter Games were a bad idea and ought to be eliminated altogether. During his tenure as president (1952–1972), he fought tenaciously against South Africa's expulsion. As well, he constantly monitored the sanctity of amateurism, protecting the hallowed Olympic precincts from encroachment by professionals. In most bastions of sports conservatism around the world, Brundage was held in high regard. In the chambers of liberalism and those forums arguing for change, he was vilified.

The 1968 Mexico City Games will always be noted for the emergence of African athletes as track and field giants in distance racing. True, Abebe Bikila from Ethiopia had won the gruelling marathon at Rome in 1960, and again at Tokyo in 1964, but these were isolated and opaque examples of what was to come in the form of African achievement. Between Kipchoge Keino, Naftali Temu, and Amos Biwott of Kenya, Mamo Wolde of Ethiopia, and Mohamed Gammoudi of Tunisia, Africans won every men's running event in Mexico City at distances over 800 metres. Sadly, a shocking episode that occurred shortly before the opening of the Mexico City Games cast a giant pall on the gala festival and demonstrated how the Olympic Games can at times be used to draw national and international attention to socio-political causes. Throughout the 1960s, costs associated with staging the Olympics spiralled to dizzying heights. In a relatively poor country like Mexico, where millions lived in poverty and squalor, huge expenditures for Olympic Games in place of funding for badly needed social welfare projects proved a bone of contention to many, especially left-wing political radicals and idealistic university students.

Protests and demonstrations on this point angered a Mexican government intent on ensuring a peaceful atmosphere during the nation's appearance before the world. Confrontations between military police and university students boiled over into violent reaction, resulting in what has become remembered as the massacre of Tlatelolco Square. Depending on whose story is believed, that of the Mexican government or that of its antagonists, some thirty to three hundred students were killed. And that was not all. There was still another controversial incident to disturb Mexico's Olympic peace. Almost a year before the Games began, U.S. civil rights activist Harry Edwards had attempted to rally black athletes to boycott the Games. This was an attempt to focus world attention on the often pitiful socio-economic and civil rights conditions of millions of black Americans. Black athletes were not unanimous in supporting the boycott. A few stayed home, but many left for Mexico City intent on making personal statements in order to focus attention on the issue. Tommie Smith and John Carlos, winners of gold and bronze medals in the 200 metres, mounted the victory podium, bowed their heads as the "Star Spangled Banner" was played, and thrust black glove-clad fists aloft. This symbolic act, graphically portrayed on television before the whole world and termed by an angry Avery Brundage as "disrespectful," prompted an IOC ultimatum to the U.S. Olympic Committee to expel Carlos and Smith from the Olympic Village and all further competition. Smith and Carlos returned home, but their gesture and the cause it represented remains even today a forceful suggestion to all of just what a powerful transmission device the Olympic forum can be.

For all Brundage's unyielding stance on most matters about which he felt strongly, one item succeeded in breaching his resolve—television. One fundamental fact had always stood in the way of the IOC realizing its ambitions—its poverty. There was hardly enough money to maintain its modest headquarters in Lausanne, let alone support the numerous initiatives it would have wished to mount. Though scorning any link to what he called "commercialism," Brundage recognized as early as the late 1940s the value of television in advertising the Olympic movement worldwide. At first Brundage was not cognizant of the fact that the Olympic Games were indeed an entertainment extravaganza, one that might be sold on the competitive market. However, as major sporting events in the United States increasingly began to penetrate television programming, he was led to consider the prospect of selling television rights for the Games. Stemming from a difference of opinion with television media in Melbourne at the 1956 Games, a confrontation prompted by arguments of whether the

Olympics were *news* or *entertainment*, the IOC moved resolutely towards framing constitutional statutes in the Olympic Charter for the protection of its product. Thus, the now famous Rule 49 came into being. Any television broadcasting of the Olympic Games longer than three-minute news briefs, aired a maximum of three times per day, would have to be purchased by television networks. The Winter Games of 1960 in Squaw Valley were the first to be sold to U.S. television under the new rights-fee statute. They went to CBS for $50,000. CBS also won the exclusive U.S. rights for the Summer Games in Rome. The fee negotiated was $394,000. As the television giants ABC, NBC, and CBS competed vigorously for the right to air each succeeding edition of the Winter and Summer Games, U.S. television rights fees reached beyond the $2 million mark in 1964, spiralled to over $100 million by 1980, and rose to $456 million for the Atlanta Games in 1996, with the European Broadcasting Union paying an additional $250 million for European rights. Recently, NBC paid a $2.1 billion fee package to the IOC for the American rights to televise the 2010 Winter Games in Vancouver and the 2012 Summer Games in London. The IOC, in a very short span of years, found itself rolling in money.

Brundage's twenty-year tenure as IOC president came to an end following a vote by the IOC at the 1972 Games in Munich. In more than one member's mind, twenty years of "Slavery Avery" were enough. Never in Brundage's tenure had his power and authority been under such severe challenge as they were by this time. At the Winter Games in Sapporo, Brundage tried to deny entry to a host of alpine skiers, many of whom he felt to be violators of the Olympic amateur code. Their flagrant disregard for Olympic rules greatly angered him, especially their acceptance of "cash and kind" from ski equipment manufacturers in return for orchestrated display of the company's equipment on television, and their acceptance of money far beyond "reasonable expenses" for appearances at major ski meets on the world circuit. Brundage, his influence badly eroded by 1972, had to settle for a token expulsion. The scapegoat was Karl Schranz, the gold medal favourite in the alpine events. Not permitted to compete, Schranz was sent home. He was greeted by thousands at the Vienna airport in his native Austria, a heroic martyr instead of a disgraced scapegoat.

The 1972 Munich Summer Games began in an atmosphere quite reversed from the last time Germany played host to the Olympics (1936). Instead of the red, black, and white colours identified with the Nazis, soft pastels were Munich's colour theme. Instead of the Nazi rank and file, cheery Bavarians greeted visitors. If, however, there was uncertainty in the minds of some that sport is devoid of politics, the events of Septem-

ber 5 and 6 obliterated such doubts. In Olympic history's most horrible incident, a group of Palestinian terrorists infiltrated the Olympic Village, took
members of the Israeli wrestling team hostage, and bargained for the
release of two hundred Palestinians incarcerated in Israeli jails. In a dramatic sequence of events at Munich's Fürstenfeldbruck Airbase, a shootout
occurred between the terrorists and German sharpshooters. Five of the eight
Palestinians were killed, but not before all of the Israeli hostages were
slain by the terrorists. Brundage, in his last public act as IOC czar, arranged
a huge memorial service in the Olympic stadium and then dictated that "the
Games must go on." The Olympics must never bow to "commercial, political, and now criminal pressure," the 84-year-old Brundage exclaimed.
With his exit from that forum, an Olympic career whose impact had
rivalled that of Coubertin came to an end. Brundage was succeeded in
office by Ireland's Michael Morris, the Lord Killanin.

Boycotts and Bucks

The horror of Munich dictated that complex security mechanisms be put
in place at all future Olympic festivals. At the Summer Games of 1976 in
Montreal, about $1 million was spent on security, including the support
of a 16,000-man militia force. Montreal struggled to meet preparation
deadlines for the Games. In the end, labour disputes, construction problems, cost overruns, and a host of other problems burdened Mayor Jean
Drapeau's city and *la belle province* with millions of dollars of debt. To this
day, the residue of financial embarrassment continues to be felt. At the same
time, politics escalated as a major problem area for the IOC and its Olympic
family members—host city organizers, national Olympic committees, and
the international sports federations. Continuing their quest to end South
Africa's racial policy, African countries argued that New Zealand should
be barred from competing in the Montreal Games because its national
rugby team, the famous All Blacks, played matches against South Africa's
nationals, the equally noted Springboks, thus violating an IOC ban on participating against South African sports teams. In turn, the IOC argued that
the rule applied only to Olympic sports, which rugby was not. The African
complaint was dismissed. Twenty-seven African countries and nations boycotted the Games, abandoning their Olympic quest: twenty withdrew and
seven refused to travel to Montreal. The long-brandished African threat
of boycott was finally implemented.

The 1980 Summer Games were awarded to Moscow. The Soviet state
prepared diligently for its chance to showcase "the triumph of Communism"

before the world, but, in December 1979, practically on the eve of the opening of the Lake Placid Winter Games, Soviet military forces marched into neighbouring Afghanistan to prop up a Communist-controlled government on the brink of being toppled by Islamic fundamentalist factions. In response to this act, U.S. President Jimmy Carter called for a world boycott of the Moscow Games. He didn't quite get "the world" to go along with him, but U.S. diplomatic pressures on the global community ultimately led sixty-two countries to boycott the Games. Eighty-one nations participated, the fewest number since the Melbourne Games twenty-five years earlier. The Moscow Games proceeded; Soviet and East German athletes dominated the sports contests. There was little doubt that the Soviet Union, which had poured millions of the State's precious rubles into preparing for the Games, was considerably angered by the boycott. It did not take them long to get revenge.

The historic city of Sarajevo in Yugoslavia hosted the Winter Games in 1984. In a spirit of unity and commitment, Muslims, Serbs, and Croats combined efforts to produce a well-organized and orchestrated festival. Seven years later they were at war with each other and much of the beautiful city that was host to a great world festival of sport, peace, and beauty lay in shambles, the bodies of thousands of its citizens buried in coffins made of wood torn from former Olympic sports buildings. After the financial debacle of Montreal in 1976, none but Los Angeles, California, presented a bid to host the 1984 Summer Games. In the end, the city tried to renege on its hosting responsibility; secondary planning pointed to a huge budget deficit, most of which would have to be paid by the taxpayer. Enter Peter Ueberroth and a group of associates, who laid a plan before the IOC to fund the Games by selling exclusive corporate sponsorships. The IOC's position was that only cities are awarded Olympic Games, not private corporations; that was the rule. In the end, however, it was faced with either Ueberroth's plan or no Games at all. The IOC buckled. World television rights generated $260 million. Another $130 million was raised from corporate sponsors pledged to pay at least $4 million each in return for rights to manufacture and market their products and services with the Olympic five-ring logo emblazoned on them. Furthermore, forty-three companies paid a premium to sell their products as the "official" Olympic drink (Coca-Cola), the "official" domestic beer (Schlitz), the "official" Olympic hamburger (McDonald's), and so on. By the time the Games had concluded, not only had they been carried off in solvent fashion, but they had made a profit for the organizers—close to $150 million, in fact. ABC television presented Olympic programming so blatantly nationalistic that even patriotic Americans cringed. The Soviets called the Games a farce; they weren't even there, having led a "tit for tat" seventeen-nation Eastern Bloc boycott for the embarrassment exacted on them in 1980.

The IOC was in an angry mood as it convened its general session meetings following the Los Angeles Games. Severe penalties were threatened to those who might pursue a boycott stance in the future. Large-scale boycotts ceased, but not because of IOC threats. In effect, boycotts simply did not work: the Soviets remained in Afghanistan for a sustained period, U.S. athletes won 174 medals in the absence of competitors from Eastern European countries, and a gathering storm of protest rose from those who had dedicated four years of their lives for a chance to become an Olympian only to see their chances obliterated by politicians. At the opening ceremonies of the 1988 Summer Games in Seoul, only Cuba and North Korea refused to attend. The Games of the 24th Olympiad, bathed in Korean culture and charm, once again celebrated athlete and spectator harmony.

Confrontations between Olympian gods in antiquity formed the basis for Greek mythology. Showdowns between athletes of supreme Olympian-like status provide a modern similarity. The 100-metre sprint final in Seoul, featuring rivals Carl Lewis of the United States and Ben Johnson of Canada was akin to Heracles wrestling the Nemean lion. Johnson won in the extraordinary time of 9.73 seconds—a world record. Two days later it was determined that his post-race urine sample was saturated with residuals of a performance-enhancing drug, Stanozolol. Johnson was disqualified; Lewis received the gold medal. The aftermath of all this produced a national inquiry in Canada, revealing that drug-taking to improve athletic performance was not limited solely to those whose fame and fortune depended on the outcome of a less-than-ten-second sprint. The female star of the Seoul Games was U.S. sprinter Florence Griffith Joyner, or "Flo Jo" as she was affectionately dubbed by the press. "Flo Jo" ran the 100 metres less than a half second slower than Ben Johnson's startling time. Her heavily muscled thighs and lightning-like reaction at the start raised questions in the minds of many as to what her pharmaceutical menu might have been in preparing for the Games. No charges were ever officially levied; Griffth-Joyner retired from competition immediately following the conclusion of the Korean Games. Her death a short time later was thought to be, in part, a consequence of her journey into the world of performance enhancement by artificial means.

In February 1988, Canada hosted its first Winter Games. Hoping to make a profit from them, Calgary pressed Ueberroth's 1984 financial model into place. An ABC television rights fee of $309 million, and corporate sponsorship on the order of what was seen in Los Angeles, ensured a profit and a lasting Calgary Olympic legacy in the form of sports facilities and a huge Olympic trust fund. Though a glorious festival by any standard of measurement, there was some distress for Canada; in Montreal, it had become the first country in Olympic history to host the Summer Games without winning a single gold medal, while in Calgary it became the fourth country to record this dubious distinction at a Winter Olympics.

Albertville, France, was the scene of the last Winter Games to be celebrated in the same year as the Summer Games. Shortly before the Games opened, Communist hardliners attempted to snuff out a Soviet flirtation with democracy sponsored by Premier Mikhail Gorbachev. Their failed coup sparked a series of events that disintegrated isolationist policies between East and West. In rapid order, down came the infamous Berlin Wall, symbol of separation between East and West Germany; down came the doctrine of Communism that had ruled Soviet lives for three quarters of a century, as well as those of most eastern Europeans since the Second World War. Up rose new countries from the remnant of the old Union of Soviet Socialist Republics; up rose the number of new nations in the Olympic family, many of them well-known former Soviet states, including Russia, Ukraine, Estonia, and Belarus. The political events occurred so rapidly that most of the newly-formed countries could not organize independent national Olympic committees in time for the Albertville Games. Rather than scuttle the hopes of so many prospective Olympic participants, the IOC allowed former Soviet state athletes to compete under a hastily contrived sobriquet, the Unified Team. Their flag-bearer marched into the stadium for the opening ceremonies holding aloft the Olympic flag.

In 1980, an ailing IOC President Lord Killanin was succeeded by a Catalonian Spaniard, Juan Antonio Samaranch. A one-time roller hockey goalie and former Spanish ambassador to the Soviet Union, Samaranch quickly asserted himself as an Olympic progressivist. Though Killanin had planted the seeds of reform following Brundage's lengthy conservative tenure as president, it was Samaranch who reaped the harvest. Under his leadership, the IOC elected women to its ranks for the first time ever. Samaranch also presided over new financial initiatives. Since the mid-1970s, the IOC had been restive about the fact that some 97 per cent of its operating revenue came from television. By the mid-1980s, a new IOC revenue source took its place beside television. It was called TOP (originally signifying "The Olympic Program," now "The Olympic Partners"). Contracting with the Swiss licensing and sports marketing firm International Sports and Leisure Marketing (ISL), the IOC sold the rights to market the five-ring logo to a dozen multinational manufacturing firms. Coca-Cola, Kodak, and Federal Express were among the first TOP clients to sign up. The exclusive use of the logo was sold for a period of four years, an Olympic quadrennial. TOP I (1985–1988) produced $97 million; TOP II (1989–1992) approached $175 million; TOP III (1993–1996), some $279 million. In its most recent complete iteration, TOP V (2001–2004), the program raised $603 million.

Under his presidency, too, Samaranch orchestrated a relaxation of eligibility rules that permitted a drift towards allowing the best athletes in the world to compete in the Games, irrespective of the fact that they might be professionals. Changes in Olympic eligibility rules prompted a sensational event to be orchestrated in Barcelona in 1992. With the concurrence of Samaranch, the International Basketball Federation (FIBA) relaxed all rules against professionals competing. To many, the result was a travesty of sporting justice. The United States sent its foremost stars of the National Basketball Association to perform against the rest of the world. Long-established professionals, whose salaries in all cases were in the multi-million dollar range, competed against outclassed neophytes from Angola, Lithuania, Croatia, and Puerto Rico. The results were predictable—lopsided wins in every contest on the way to winning the gold medal. Indeed, it often appeared that the aura of Michael Jordan, Magic Johnson, Larry Bird, Charles Barkley and company was greater than the Games themselves, or of host Barcelona, one of the world's most beautiful cities.

As both the winter and summer Olympic festivals grew larger and larger in terms of new sports, events added within sports disciplines, competing countries, athletes, and the administrative energy and resources needed to present them, the IOC was finally prompted to debate the merits of alternating the winter and summer festivals, holding each four years apart in even-numbered years. Cynics said that this plan was much ado about money. When the plan was implemented, one fact became evident right away; with the intervals between the Olympic years reduced to two years instead of four, the world's Olympic psyche was raised to a new level of awareness, creating all sorts of possibilities for those who benefit from selling or acquiring Olympic rights, whether in the form of television programming or Kodak film. Coubertin's original inspiration for what the Olympic Games might promote—international peace, harmony, brotherhood, education, beauty, joy, and sportsmanship—never came as close to being realized than at the Lillehammer Winter Games in 1994, the first edition of those Winter Games which stood apart from its summer counterpart by two years. The Norwegians dedicated their Games to a war-torn sister winter Olympic host city, Sarajevo. In his opening address, Samaranch called for an "Olympic truce," pleading for belligerent factions around the world to "put down your guns." The Norwegian speed skater Johann Olav Koss, winner of three gold medals, donated to the Olympic Relief Fund the entire monetary award bestowed on him by his grateful country for his astounding performances. Further, he donated the skates he wore in his events to an auction whose proceeds went to the same Relief Fund. The Koss episode was just one of many that inspired millions of people around the world who watched the events on television as they unfolded. In the end, the Lillehammer Games fully justified Samaranch's usual proclamation uttered after each Olympic Games (with the exception of Atlanta) held during his tenure—they were "the best ever."

The centennial Olympic Games of the modern era, those celebrated in Atlanta in 1996, will always be remembered as the "Commercial Games." To raise the necessary revenues, both the organizing committee and the city of Atlanta sold licences to hundreds upon hundreds of small entrepreneurs to sell goods of every description in stalls, kiosks, parking lots, tents, even huts. A blanket of crass commercialism enveloped the city's Olympic atmosphere. IOC members were "hand-wringing" bystanders to all this. In the end, the Games just about broke even financially, but they left a sour taste in many mouths.

The Winter Games returned once again to Japan in 1998. Nagano, a surprise winner over Salt Lake City for the right to host them, carried off the assignment with both precision and Asian panache. Two years later, the first Games of the new millennium were held in Sydney, which had beaten Beijing by two votes in the final accounting for the right to host them. By September 15, 2000, a glorious new Olympic precinct had been finished at Homebush, some twenty miles upriver from the heart of Sydney Harbour. By the time the Games closed, sixteen days later, the Aussies had achieved their "best ever" Olympic performance (fifty-eight medals, sixteen of them gold). They also incurred a debt of $1.7 billion, an imposition that New South Wales taxpayers were ultimately forced to pay, while the Greeks are dealing with an $11–14 billion debt from the 2004 Summer Olympics.

Refusing to give up all hope in a quest to host Olympic Winter Games, Salt Lake City, in the heartland of "Mormon America," was a landslide winner in the competition to host the 2002 festival. In late November 1998, with preparations in full swing, a scandal of Olympian proportions broke before the eyes of the world. Unveiled for all to ponder were the zealous machinations of bid committee members in their quest to curry favour with IOC members in return for their vote. Numerous visitations occurred, and an avalanche of gratuities was bestowed, including expensive gifts, business opportunities, college tuition for family members, health care, travel and accommodation far beyond reason—even attempts to provide "green card" immigration status to the son of Un Yong Kim, the IOC member in South Korea. The fault, of course, did not lie solely with Salt Lake's bid committee. IOC members themselves were culpable. After two IOC investigations, and independent examinations of the whole affair by the U.S. Olympic Committee, the State of Utah, and the United States Department of Justice, some twenty-one members of the IOC, almost one sixth of the organization, were found guilty to greater or lesser extent. The penalties finally invoked by the IOC led to the outright dismissal of six members, the resignation of four others, and "less serious" to "extremely serious" warnings levied on ten. Another implicated member died before the examination commenced. Tom Welch and Dave Johnson, president and vice-president of Salt Lake's bid committee, were brought to trial by the Department of Justice. In an at times sensational trial that culminated in December 2003, each was acquitted on all counts (fifteen in number), and set free. One of the two most important pieces of merchandise the modern Olympic movement had to sell the business world, *image* (the other is *exposure*), took a severe beating. In the end, the Boston venture capitalist Mitt Romney, a Mormon, took over the organization of the 2002 Games. They were peaceful, colourful, grand, and even spectacular at times. It was a significant achievement for Romney and his colleagues, whose task had become even more challenging in the wake of 9/11. Back home in Massachusetts, Romney rode his personal high profile and accrued popularity right into the Statehouse, winning the election for governor in November 2002. For the IOC, the experience was one of pain and upheaval. The IOC's response included the introduction of fifty new statutes into its Charter, many dealing with ethics, transparency, and accountability. IOC members would no longer be allowed to visit candidate cities to assess their worthiness as hosts for the Games. A special evaluation commission, funded entirely by the IOC, now performs the duty.

A Final Word

As the Olympic Games face the future, the pathways they must navigate are strewn with hazards. The IOC, currently under a new president, Jacques Rogge of Belgium, must grapple with problems related to the immense size of the Games, to maintenance of a fair playing field for athletes in the face of doping offences, to distribution of its wealth for worthy initiatives, and, perhaps most importantly, to sensitivity towards the underlying values of the modern Olympic movement: recognizing and encouraging cultural differences in the quest to develop a better world. It seeks to do this by presenting an Olympic philosophy it calls "Olympism," a belief that there is joy in sporting effort, educational value in the good example that sport most times portrays, and pursuit of ethical principles that know neither geographical nor cultural boundaries.

Bibliographical Notes

In the past quarter century there has been an explosion of serious scholarship on various aspects of the modern Olympic movement, much of it in English. The results of these endeavours have greatly benefited those who seek a deep understanding of this great global sporting phenomenon. Ignoring the multitude of journal articles on this subject, many of them indeed meritorious, I list only the major book-length sources of note.

For the best general survey-type works on Olympic history, see Allen Guttmann, *The Olympics* (1992); John Findling and Kimberly Pelle (eds.), *Historical Dictionary of the Modern Olympic Movement* (1996; second edition, 2004); and Jeffrey Seagrave and Donald Chu (eds.), *The Olympic Games in Transition* (1988).

For the most noted works on politics and the Olympic Games, the reader is referred to Alfred Senn, *Power, Politics, and the Olympic Games* (2001); David Kanin, *A Political History of the Olympic Games* (1981); and Richard Espy, *The Politics of the Olympic Games* (1979). For Olympic business and commercial history, see Robert K. Barney, Stephen R. Wenn, and Scott G. Martyn, *Selling the Five Rings: The International Olympic Committee and the Rise of Olympic Commercialism* (first edition, 2002; revised second edition, 2004).

For Avery Brundage's long Olympic career, see Allen Guttmann, *The Games Must Go On: Avery Brundage and The Modern Olympic Games* (1984). On Lord Killanin's tenure as IOC President, see his own *My Olympic Years* (1983). On Juan Antonio Samaranch's career as IOC President, see David Miller, *Olympic Revolution* (1992).

For the best works on the modern origins and early years of the Olympic Games, see David Young, *The Modern Olympics: A Struggle for Revival* (1996); John MacAloon, *This Great Symbol: Pierre de Coubertin and the Origins of the Modern Olympic Games* (1981); and Richard Mandell, *The First Modern Olympics* (1976). For classic works on the 1936 Berlin

Games, a singular festival on which more has been published than any other, see Richard Mandell, *The Nazi Olympics* (1971; second edition, 1987); and Duff Hart-Davis, *Hitler's Games* (1986). On the future of the Olympic Games, see John Lucas, *Future of the Olympic Games* (1992).

Duke Kahanamoku—Olympic Champion and Uncle Sam's Adopted Son: The Cultural Text of a Hawaiian Conqueror

Jim Nendel

On 12 July 1912, the *Pacific Commercial Advertiser* ran a cartoon depicting Duke Kahanamoku, Hawai'i's Olympic champion swimmer, wearing an olive wreath, surrounded by representatives of other nations over whom he towered. Included in the admiring horde was the figure of "Uncle Sam," who exclaimed: "My adopted son, you bet!"[1] Kahanamoku's participation in the 1912 and 1920 Olympic Games paved the way for Hawaiian dominance in swimming events. The Hawaiian Islands embraced him as their representative to the world, as did the mainland United States.[2] Remnants of the old *Ali'i* blood—the blood of ancient Hawaiian nobility—ran through his veins, yet he was a modern man in every sense. In essence, he was the perfect representation of a figurehead king, a symbolic figure who held no real power. In this way, Kahanamoku became a monarch who held no political or economic authority, but enjoyed worldwide renown for his athletic achievements. With the aid of the media, Kahanamoku accepted the role offered to him through sport to represent Hawai'i as a modern state.

Sport historian Michael Oriard has examined Muhammad Ali as a "cultural representation" through the "public images of Ali, and the power they had in the 1960s and 1970s."[3] Oriard shows the "extraordinary range" of those images in terms of Ali, noting that he was "the prettiest and the greatest: he was fighter and dancer, loudmouth and poet, exuberant child and heavyweight champion."[4] At a different time in history, Kahanamoku could also be viewed as a cultural text. He was Hawaiian and American, gentle native and modern man, Olympic champion swimmer and laid-back father of surfing. Kahanamoku projected many different images.

In one sense, he destroyed the preconceptions of Hawaiians that had preceded him in newspapers and magazines, and became one of their favourite subjects to cover. The *New York Times* referred to him as "one of the best-liked athletes who ever visited New York," even though they loved to see New Yorkers triumph over him.[5] Kahanamoku was welcomed as an example of the strength of the American "melting pot" ideal as presented by the media in the early twentieth century. The cartoon referred to above is a classic representation of the melting pot concept.

U.S. Olympic officials used Kahanamoku's celebrity as a symbol of American polyglot might, even though—in reality—Kahanamoku lived amidst racial prejudice both in Hawai'i and on the mainland. Nevertheless, he became a beloved Olympian, sought out by fellow athletes, royalty, and the doting masses for his representation of the *aloha* spirit.

In many ways, his complexity mirrors that of the word *aloha*, a term with many meanings. The most common are as a greeting, "hello," and "goodbye," yet *aloha* also means pity, mercy, and compassion, and has connotations of deep love and affection.[6] The intricacy of this simple, common Hawaiian word reflects the remarkable depth of a simple Hawaiian athlete whose personality served as a living example of *aloha*.

Kahanamoku was one of those rare athletes whose media representation seems extremely close to reality. The Olympic champion swimmer became a beloved figure of the worldwide press and of other athletes as well. Teammates and competitors alike showered praise on Kahanamoku, reflecting upon his gentle manner and grace. At the same time, however, Kahanamoku was seen as a non-threatening "native" by white society, the *haole* conquerors of his land—as was his 1912 Olympic teammate Jim Thorpe.

After his victories in the 1912 Olympic Games, Kahanamoku became the anointed king of swimming. But he admired and respected Jim Thorpe, whose greatness he recognized. While travelling to Sweden on the U.S.S. *Finland*, Kahanamoku reportedly asked Thorpe: "Jimmy, I've seen you run, jump, throw things and carry the ball. You do everything, so why don't you swim too?" Thorpe, showing his reciprocal respect for the champion swimmer, grinned at Kahanamoku and replied, "Duke, I saved that for you to take care of. I saved that for you."[7]

Thorpe and the other track and field athletes attracted the lion's share of media attention at the Olympic Games, and this hampered Kahanamoku's ability to claim his rightful place in the public eye. Track and field's grip on attention was so great that in its reporting of the 1920 Olympic Games in Antwerp, the *New York Times* only ran front-page stories on the Games until the track events were finished. Thereafter, reports on the Games and most of the articles found themselves deep in the sports pages. The majority of the swimming events fell on dates after the track and field portion of the competition had concluded and the public consciousness of the Olympics had waned. The smaller amount of attention directed towards Kahanamoku was, in part, due to swimming's status as a pastime in American sporting culture, especially compared to track and field at the Olympic Games.[8] Thorpe also factors in, considering that he was the story of the 1912 Games in Stockholm. Winner of the pentathlon and the decathlon, Thorpe was heralded as "the greatest athlete of the age."[9] Although Kahanamoku did not reap headlines, it would be incorrect to classify him as anything less than a celebrity. The American media and American Olympic Committee (AOC) officials utilized his abilities, as well as those of Thorpe and other minorities, to prove that American superiority did not rest solely in the leftover bloodlines of Englishmen. Kahanamoku and Thorpe became living proof of the superiority of the melting pot that was American culture, and were adored "sons" of Uncle Sam for the entire world to see.

The complexity of Kahanamoku as a cultural text is evidenced in the projection of his apparent native royal status. To his credit, regardless of the media slights and the exploitation of the AOC, Kahanamoku represented Hawai`i with grace and an easygoing manner. Those who questioned what Hawaiians were truly like would, once they had encountered the "Duke," be convinced that these had to be the most wonderful people on earth. Unsure about his true name, early accounts of Kahanamoku in mainland newspapers usually styled his name in quotation marks—"Duke"—due to the controversy surrounding his heritage.[10] People often wondered whether he was a duke by birthright in Hawai`i, since there were rumours that he was descended from the royal lineage of Kamehameha. Referring to him as a duke may have westernized his image to some extent, and reinforced the representation of the "good and civilized native." Olympic teammate and gold medallist Aileen Riggin recalled: "Of course, his name intrigued us. He wasn't really a duke, but I think the

Duke of Edinburgh, or someone, had visited the islands when he was an infant and his family thought that was a nice name."[11] Riggin's conjecture was not far off the mark. Kahanamoku had been named Duke after his father, who had been born during the Duke of Edinburgh's visit to the islands in 1869. In 1917, the *New York Times* sought to clarify the origins of the swimmer's first name. "There are a half a dozen important events in Hawaii's history which are still referred to by old-time Hawaiians as unusual incidents and one of these was the English peer's visit," the reporter revealed. "During his sojourn in the Hawaiian capital a son was born to a high chief, whose family was named Kahanamoku. The son was named Duke in honour of the visiting peer, who was sponsor at the christening. The son of the first Duke Kahanamoku is the present Duke."[12] Late in 1912, when reporters were well aware of Kahanamoku and learned about his heritage, they styled his name correctly, without quotation marks. In later years, some reporters referred to him as "The Duke," using the term as a nickname or term of endearment familiar to sportsmen of the period.[13] These terms of endearment were not surprising to those who knew Kahanamoku well and believed he embodied the *aloha* spirit of the islands. In some ways, this allowed for more of a common man image within the athletic fraternity while holding on to the vestiges of a royal past. As a result, he was accessible to all classes of society.

During the 1912 Olympics, Kahanamoku immediately became a favourite of the people in Stockholm thanks to his *aloha* spirit. The *New York Times* reported that he had "become one of the most popular characters at the Olympics," and "had a distinguished assembly to witness his predestined and easy triumph." King Gustav V of Sweden and most of the royal family, including the queen, who was in deep mourning for the late King of Denmark, crowded the triumph box to see Kahanamoku swim in the final heat of the 100-metre race. The American press also noted that the Crown Princess appeared "to be intensely interested."[14] King Gustav had taken notice of this young athlete and had actually shown up the day before to watch Kahanamoku swim during practice. The king asked to "see the famous swimmer in action so Kahanamoku gave an exhibition of his skill receiving the personal thanks and congratulations of the King."[15] After his victory in the 100-metre heat, the king rose and beckoned Kahanamoku to the royal box, where the Swedish monarch "clasped his hand and congratulated him heartily, declaring it was a pleasure to meet the man who had lowered the pride of the world's best swimmers." The king also introduced Kahanamoku to the rest of the royal family and dignitaries present.[16]

This was not the only time that Kahanamoku won the adoration of royalty. Throughout his life, Kahanamoku entertained royals and visited them. At the 1920 Antwerp Games, King Albert of Belgium made a point of seeing the great Hawaiian swim, and personally presented him with his medal. After the ceremony, the monarch also allowed the Olympic champion swimmer to come into the royal box to have his picture taken.[17] In 1920, the Prince of Wales—later Edward VIII—travelled to the Hawaiian Islands for the Hawaiian Missionary centennial, and was eager to meet the world-renowned swimmer. The prince asked Kahanamoku to teach him to surf, and Duke heartily agreed. Kahanamoku's coach, George "Dad" Center, made the arrangements. Kahanamoku and the heir to the throne of England spent the day surfing, first in an outrigger canoe and then on surfboards. Kahanamoku later told Center, "Dad, I never felt so comfortable with a man. We have a big aloha for each other." Center replied, "Why not? You're both right guys." The prince enjoyed his visit so much that he made another unplanned stop later in the year to surf with the Olympic champion.[18] A man on equal terms with royals became a potent representation of this Hawaiian champion.

While the image of Kahanamoku cavorting with royalty was powerful, he also became the champion of the masses. At the 1912 Stockholm Games, after one of his preliminary heats, "the vast throng of more than ten thousand people cheered and yelled and gave him an ovation that he will remember as long as he lives."[19] At the 1920 Antwerp Olympics, the *New York Times* reported that as Kahanamoku practised, "a large crowd" came out to see him perform.[20] For Kahanamoku this was nothing new. Since his astounding victory in Stockholm, flocks of tourists had come to Waikiki to watch him surf and swim and to get pictures with him. And Kahanamoku was unfailingly cordial and welcoming. From tourists and fans to beach boys and royals, the masses flocked to this Waikiki legend.[21]

Spectators were not the only fans attracted to Kahanamoku. Fellow athletes also enjoyed being around this ukulele-playing Hawaiian, and he developed many friendships through his international competitions. His graciousness with competitors extended even into the pool itself. Due in part to a community spirit inherent in his native Hawaiian culture, Kahanamoku found it "painful to embarrass an opponent" by beating him overwhelmingly.[22] This is evident in the preliminary heat he swam at Stockholm. In this 100-metre race, he jumped out to a commanding lead and "half way down the tank turned to survey the rest of the field. His nearest rival was ten feet behind. Kahanamoku slowed down after that and seemed to swim leisurely." Kahanamoku still won the race easily, but all the swimmers were "so close to one another that none of them had reason to be ashamed of the performance." As Kahanamoku exited the pool to a great ovation, "men of various nationalities" were "slapping him on the back and shaking hands."[23]

One of the men he beat in this race, Cecil Healy, would become a good friend of Duke's and would be instrumental in inviting Kahanamoku to Australia in the winter of 1914–1915. While there, Kahanamoku introduced surfing to the Australians, and made such an impression that even today there is a statue of Kahanamoku and a beach named after the Hawaiian surfer and swimmer.[24]

In fact, Healy revealed the respect he had for his competitor during a pivotal event in the Stockholm Games. Due to a mix-up concerning starting times for the 100-metre semifinal, Kahanamoku and the other Americans were sleeping aboard the U.S.S. *Finland* at the time of the race. This was the second time Duke had been late to a race at these Games. In the first instance, Michael "Turk" McDermott, one of Duke's teammates, ran back to the ship and alerted Kahanamoku that his race was about to start. They sprinted to the swimming arena, and Duke asked the starter to delay the race long enough to allow him to don his bathing suit. The officials assented after scolding the young Hawaiian, and Kahanamoku won his heat easily.[25]

A few days later, a second mix-up concerning the semifinal start time once again caught Kahanamoku sleeping along with the rest of the American swimmers. When they failed to appear, Olympic officials disqualified the apparently sleep-deprived athletes. The Americans protested and asked for the race to be re-swum. Healy, who had won the semifinal and would have been the favourite to win the gold medal with the Americans out of the picture, stood up for Kahanamoku. He refused to race in the final if the Americans could not swim. The officials decided that the Americans would swim in an independent heat and the winner would qualify for the finals. Kahanamoku won that heat. The Hawaiian then triumphed in the final, thanks in no small part to Cecil Healy.[26]

Undeterred, Kahanamoku continued his practice of napping at the Olympic Games. In 1920, he again fell asleep prior to the start of the relay race. Fortunately, this time he was in the arena behind the bleachers, and one of his teammates found him in time for the bleary-eyed champion to swim and set a new world record.[27]

The image of an athlete so relaxed that he could sleep through the start of Olympic races spoke to perceived stereotypes of a laid-back Hawaiian. In fact, champion surfer George "Keoki" Downing told a story that

Kahanamoku had recounted to him in which Kahanamoku had fallen asleep while working in the Honolulu harbour doing scuba diving work. He was waiting for some work to be done by others top-side and took advantage of the opportunity to have a nap on the harbour seabed. He gave everyone quite a scare when he failed to respond until divers went down and found him sleeping peacefully.[28] This story further illuminated the image of a kind native untouched by the fast pace of the urbanized industrial world he had entered.

Kahanamoku's calm and welcoming nature also scored points among his teammates. Aileen Riggin, the gold medallist in springboard diving at the 1920 Olympic Games, remembers that on the boat to Antwerp "the Hawaiians would entertain us." Kahanamoku was the leader of the eleven Hawaiians on the trip, and she remembers him as "a magnificent looking man, he had a marvelous build, and he was just as nice as he looked. They played at night, they all brought their ukuleles and guitars and they all had beautiful voices."[29]

Charlie Paddock, the revered American Olympic sprinter of the 1920s, remembered "the Duke" in his autobiography. On his visit to the islands in 1922, Kahanamoku came out to greet his boat in a tiny launch. "The same strength that marked Kamehameha," Paddock wrote, "belongs to Kahanamoku. No other Hawaiian possesses so much sheer power. He can launch an outrigger alone; he can ride the waves on his great board, and he can out swim all his countrymen." Coming from Paddock, a tireless self-promoter, this was indeed high praise.[30]

The image of Kahanamoku as the second coming of Kamehameha was not unique to Paddock. Many others saw the similarities, and, utilizing the notion of royal blood running throughout his veins, Kahanamoku became an unofficial king of Hawai'i. Paddock alluded to a prophecy uttered by Kamehameha, which stated that "some day my people will lose their freedom; some day they will have been so stricken that only a handful shall remain. In that time will come a man, strong like myself, who can launch an outrigger, throw a spear and ride the surf as I. The fame of that man shall go throughout the world, and the name of my people will not be forgotten."[31] In Paddock's mind, as well as in the minds of others, the person of Duke Paoa Kahanamoku fulfilled this prophecy. As a result, Kahanamoku was revered by many as a member of the *Ali'i*, or ancient Hawaiian chiefs, and assumed the role as the spokesman for Hawai'i around the world and at home. He represented Hawai'i at the Panama Pacific International Exposition in San Francisco in 1915 as a swimmer in the athletic events, and also appeared in traditional dress and danced the hula at the Hawaiian exhibition hall. Kahanamoku loved the hula and surfing, and he spoke Hawaiian, all of which were activities banned at one time or another through *haole* influence.[32]

Kahanamoku destroyed media preconceptions of Hawaiians and became a favourite subject of newspaper and magazine coverage. In later decades, he would become a movie actor, sheriff, and life-saving hero, adding to his fame.[33] At his funeral on 27 January 1968, the media and friends once again connected him to the ancient *Ali`i*. Tradition has it that when an *Ali`i* dies, it always rains on the funeral. True to form, the tears shed that day were not only those of the people who loved him here on earth, but also those of the heavens as the monarch who provided a bridge between the old and new Hawai`i had his ashes scattered at sea.[34]

Even in death, the legend of Duke Kahanamoku grew, and the cultural text of the Hawaiian struggle he embodied continued. The success of the media representation of Kahanamoku, which began in the early years of his career and which he utilized to transcend racial and cultural barriers, is evident in the inscription on a plaque dedicated to him at Huntington Beach, California. It concludes: "The image he created, the principle of fair play and good sportsmanship he advocated should be preserved for all time. Although mortal man has lost this rare human being, he will be remembered for his long aloha."[35]

Notes

1 "Everybody's Doing It Now," *Pacific Commercial Advertiser*, 12 July 1912, p. 1.
2 "Many Chip in for Kahanamoku Fund," *Pacific Commercial Advertiser*, 16 July 1912, p. 2.
3 Oriard 1997, 390–91.
4 Oriard 1997, 392.
5 "Vollmer to Clash with Kahanamoku," *New York Times*, 9 April 1916, p. 53.
6 Pukui and Elbert 1992, 10.
7 Hall and Ambrose 1995, 4.
8 It is abundantly clear that track and field was the focus of the American public and press in the Olympic Games. In both previews and wrap-ups of the Games, the focus of attention is solely on track and field. Examples of this are: Moss 1912, 11–12; Camp 1912, 22–26.
9 "Sullivan Praises Thorpe," *New York Times*, 4 August 1912, sec. 4, p. 18.
10 "Cyclists and Runners Out," *New York Times*, 26 June 1912, p. 11. Most writers would use the form "Duke" Kahanamoku when writing his name.
11 Riggin 2000, 21.
12 "Story of Kahanamoku," *New York Times*, 23 September 1917, p. 22.
13 "Kahanamoku Is Defeated in Hundred by McGillivray," *The Pittsburgh Post*, 9 July 1916, sec. S, p. 1.
14 "Briton Outraces American Runners," *New York Times*, 11 July 1912, p. 3.
15 "American Runners Win Olympic Heats," *New York Times*, 10 July 1912, p. 1.

16 "Swedish Royalty Congratulates Duke before Crowds in Stadium," *Pacific Commercial Advertiser*, 11 July 1912, p. 1 [hereinafter "Swedish Royalty"].
17 Brennan 1994, 135–36.
18 Hall and Ambrose 1995, 65; Brennan 1994, 127–34; *Honolulu Advertiser*, 14 April 1920 and 30 August 1912.
19 "Swedish Royalty," p. 1.
20 "U.S. Athletes in Olympic Quarters," *New York Times*, 9 August 1920, p. 14.
21 "How It Feels to be the World's Champion Swimmer," *Sunday Advertiser*, 20 August 1911, sec. F, p. 1.
22 Brennan 1994, p. 5.
23 "Briton Outraces American Runners," p. 3.
24 Bob Krauss, "Australia's Salute to Duke," *Honolulu Advertiser*, 19 January 1994, p. 17; Hall and Ambrose 1995, p. 44.
25 Brennan 1994, p. 52.
26 Hall and Ambrose 1995, p. 6.
27 Hall and Ambrose 1995, p. 19.
28 Hall and Ambrose 1995, p. 98.
29 Riggin 2000, p. 21.
30 Paddock 1932, pp. 139–40.
31 Paddock 1932, p. 139.
32 Trask 1993, p. 16.
33 "Passings," 1968, 8.
34 Hall and Ambrose 1995, p. 132.
35 Hall and Ambrose 1995, p. 134.

Carl Diem's Inspiration for the Torch Relay? Jan Wils, Amsterdam 1928, and the Origin of the Olympic Flame

Robert K. Barney
Anthony Th. Bijkerk

In the striking world of contemporary sport, one can hardly argue against the fact that the Olympic Games present the most elaborate and glorious sport spectacle known to us in modern times—indeed, as the erudite Olympic anthropologist John MacAloon tells us, a spectacle *par excellence*.[1] Dwell for a moment on those things reflective of an Olympic festival experience: protracted rectangles of human action attendant to the Games: huge crowds streaming en masse towards stadium and course venues; hawkers of Olympic memorabilia and scalpers of Olympic events tickets; thousands of uniformed Olympic volunteers; masses of humanity clothed in costumes of every imaginable distinction, conversing in dozens of languages, all negotiating the environs of a city clothed in banners, pennants, and the trappings of multiple hue and design. Watching all this on television from the near and far corners of the global village are some three billion folks. Exciting? You bet, as anyone who has ever attended an Olympic Games, winter or summer, will tell you—a once-in-a-lifetime experience!

A bit more solemn, but nevertheless just as spectacular, are the celebratory Olympic rituals and institutions that normally unfold during the course of the great festival. One of the central components of the Olympic celebration is the now universally familiar final interval of the torch relay and ensuing spectacular lighting of the Olympic flame. Both episodes—the torch relay and lighting of the flame—are now firmly institutionalized in Olympic Games protocol.

Most Olympic historians and pundits know that the idea of a torch relay—unfolding from Olympia, the site of the historical birth of the Olympic Games, to the stadium-site of the global host city in modern times—was the inspiration of Germany's Carl Diem, secretary-general of the organizing committee for the Berlin Games in 1936. Diem's conceptual inspiration for organizing a torch relay in the Olympic context, we are told, had two origins: his knowledge of sport in antiquity, where a somewhat similar exercise at ancient Olympia may have occurred in religious-ceremonial perspective, and his witnessing of a torch relay organized in 1922 by students at the Deutsche Hochschule für Leibesübungen (German National Sport Institute) to commemorate the opening of the Deutsche Kampfspiele and at the same time celebrate Diem's fortieth birthday.[2] It is not likely that the torch relay event in 1922 was Diem's idea. If, in part, the relay served to celebrate his birthday, he would hardly have played a role dedicated to his own self-glorification. And, the torch relay aside, it was certainly not Diem's spirit and action that resulted in an "Olympic flame" presiding over the site of an Olympic Games for the first time. There is nothing to suggest that when Diem, chef de mission of the German Olympic team, witnessed Olympic history's first cauldron flame perched atop the Marathon Tower of the Amsterdam stadium in the summer of 1928, he had previously harboured any thoughts about a linkage between sacred fire and the modern Olympic Games.

It is the premise of this essay that the 1928 Amsterdam flame experience served as the primary prompter of Diem's torch relay concept. After all, without a flame to light at the end of the torch relay, what reason could one give for executing a relay exercise at all? We do not denigrate the value of Diem's contribution to Olympic ritual, which has been deservedly recognized and celebrated. Little known, however, is the fact that the Olympic flame idea sprang from the mind of the designer of the Amsterdam stadium, the celebrated Dutch architect Jan Wils. This paper takes a look at Jan Wils, his inspiration for conceiving the flame event, his shift from the idea of a searchlight to a flame, and what impact, if any, the flame might have had on Diem for thinking up the concept of the torch relay in 1931.

Jan Wils

The name Jan Wils is prominent in the history of Dutch architecture. Wils was infinitely suited to execute the most important task in Amsterdam's preparation for the 1928 Olympic Games, designing and supervising the construction of the main stadium venue and vast Olympic facility precinct. Jan Wils was born in Alkmaar on 22 February 1891. His father owned and operated a construction contracting firm, exposing him very early in life to the intricacies of engineering and the building of various types of edifices. Almost from the start of his high school days in Alkmaar, he was convinced that his future lay in architecture. At the age of 18, he won his first competition in architecture. After high school, he studied architecture at the Technical University in Delft. His first professional experience was in the municipal office of the city of Alkmaar, where he worked for two years. Moving to The Hague, Wils secured a position as a draughtsman in the offices of the famous Dutch architect H.P. Berlage. There is little doubt that the influence of Berlage on Wils and his career was significant. In effect, Berlage was Wils's mentor, a fact that Wils himself proudly substantiated throughout his life.

In 1915, the 25-year-old Wils opened his own architectural firm in the city of Voorburg. From the outset of this venture, Wils had little trouble securing commissions, designing structures that ranged from villas for the rich to farmhouses for folks less wealthy. Shortly after opening his own business, Wils met Piet Mondrian, the famous painter, as well as Vilmos Huszár and Theo van Doesburg, co-founders of the periodical *De Stijl*, a journal that garnered its name from the radically distinctive architectural movement of the 1920s.[3] Wils became an active author and critic, writing in both *De Stijl* and *Wendigen*, the publication of the expressionist Amsterdam School. He was also a prominent member of the Hague Art Circle. Even though Wils left the *De Stijl* Movement in 1919, his most innovative works continued to be influenced by its principles. His complex of townhouses built in Alkmaar in 1919, a project designed in accordance with *De Stijl* principles and which enlisted Vilmos Huszár as colour consultant, were his first buildings to incorporate flat roofs. In time, Wils became known as "Frank Lloyd Wils" because of his admiration for—and sometime imitation of—the work of Frank Lloyd Wright. Although most of his designs were too original to be judged derivative, one of his earliest and most successful commissions—a housing development in Daal en Berg, built in The Hague in 1920—echoed work by Wright.

In the early 1920s, Wils's business experienced a quiescent period—commissions were scarce. Nevertheless, he developed several concepts during this period that would later buttress his eventual Olympic designs. Chief among them were designs featuring horizontal, flat-roofed buildings with large steel-framed windows and detailed ornamentation. His later works, particularly those designed between 1925 and 1935, reflected the influence of functionalism. The eventual design for the Amsterdam stadium, with its heavily walled appearance, was an example of functionalism, as were Wils's Citroen Buildings in Amsterdam—the first completed in 1931 and the second completed in 1959—and City Theater (Amsterdam, 1935).

There was little activity in either building design or construction during the Second World War, as all of Holland suffered under German occupation. Most Dutch citizens struggled just to survive, reduced to a daily food consumption of less than 1,500 calories and in some cases as low as 900. Following the war, however, as the economy started to recover and construction began anew, Wils received several design commissions, among the most prominent of which were the Hotel Bouwes in Zandvoort (1952) and the Chamber of Commerce Building in The Hague (1956). Wils passed away in Voorburg on 11 February 1972.[4]

Jan Wils and the Olympic Games

Of inestimable importance to Jan Wils and his architectural designs for athletic facilities was the fact that he himself had been a keen athlete in his youth, particularly in the sports of yachting, fencing, rowing, and gymnastics. He remained an enthusiastic yachtsman for most of his life, not at all unusual for men and women of the sea-oriented Netherlands.

Wils's first brush with "matters Olympic" occurred in 1923. His visits to some of the leading cities in Europe, where he studied modern forms of "city-building," including the provision of sports facilities, led him to write a book. *Gebouwen en Terreinen voor Gymnastiek, Spel en Sport* [Buildings and Grounds for Gymnastics, Games, and Sports], co-authored with P.W. (Pieter) Scharroo, was greeted with critical acclaim and translated into German. Could this book have been instructive in preparing Berlin for the Olympic Games staged more than a decade later? We shall probably never know the definitive answer to that question.

But from the publication of this important book sprang Wils's first steps on a five-year journey into the realm of the modern Olympic Games. Pieter Scharroo, Wils's co-author, was a distinguished member of the Netherlands Olympic Committee (NOC), on which he served as acting president in 1924. He was a member of the International Olympic Committee from 25 June 1924 to 23 September 1957, as well as a member of the IOC executive board from 1946 to 1953. For many years he served as president of the Dutch Athletic Federation; he was also a colonel in the Corps of Royal Engineers. Chiefly because of Scharroo's influence, Wils's name and architectural reputation were placed before the attention of the Dutch NOC, which subsequently appointed him to represent the Netherlands on the International Jury for Architecture in the Arts Competitions associated with the Games of the Eighth Olympiad in Paris in 1924. In fact, Wils became somewhat of a fixture on the international juries judging the architecture competitions at Olympic Games held in Europe. Beyond Paris in 1924, he served in Berlin (1936, where he chaired the jury council), and London (1948).[5]

In 1922, Amsterdam was awarded the Olympic Games for 1928. It was only natural that Wils eventually be considered to steer the design of Olympic facilities. Through Scharroo, both George van Rossem, secretary-general of the organizing committee for the Amsterdam Games, and his top deputy, Westerouwen van Meeteren, knew of Wils. Following a discussion between Wils and NOC officials, in which the architect convinced the committee of the necessary requirements for an Olympic stadium and other supporting facilities needed to organize the Games, Wils was given the sole responsibility for designing the Olympic venues. By 1926 he had executed some 1,200 technical drawings on which building contractors might base their construction calculations.[6]

Wils's initial design for the Amsterdam Olympic stadium was completed in September 1925. One of the central features of the original design was the stadium's entrance, the so-called Marathon Gate, an entry between two towers of modest dimensions. There was, however, a problem. The Dutch NOC wanted to erect a monument of noteworthy size dedicated to the Netherlands' most storied early Olympic figure, IOC member F.W.C.H. "Frits" van Tuijll van Serooskerken. Besides being the first Dutch member of the IOC, van Tuijll had initiated Amsterdam's bid to host the 1928 Games. The monument's location was planned for a spot adjacent to and slightly to the right side of the stadium's main entrance. With the monument partially superimposed against the entrance, Wils thought the resulting perspective unpleasant. To put it bluntly, it was in the way of entry traffic.

The van Tuijll monument would have to be relocated. In the May 1926 issue of the official magazine *De Olympiade*, Jan Wils (and the editors of the magazine) presented a new plan, with a completely new element, to solve the problem. The stadium's entrance would not feature the original modest twin towers, but rather one great Marathon Tower, a minaret-like concrete and brick structure some 40 metres high featuring a huge cauldron (3.5 metres in diameter) on top, from which a searchlight lit up at night would cast a giant beam heavenward into the darkness. A winding staircase inside the tower led from the base to the top. Finally, two vertical shafts of electric light arranged on each side of the tower itself would be illuminated in such a way that the entire effect (tower and searchlight beam together) would appear at night as one continuous skyscraping pillar of light. Indeed, the finished result of this thinking was everything Wils had hoped it would be. And the van Tuijll monument? Wils moved it to a position to the left of the Marathon Gate and opposite the Marathon Tower, out of the way of foot traffic.

In May 1926 the design of the Olympic stadium was approved by the city council of Amsterdam. Immediately, steps were taken to invite tenders from building contractors. It was at that precise point that Olympic history took a noteworthy turn. Sometime between 5 May and 30 June 1926, the date when Wils presented a once again modified tower design to city council, one basic feature of his Marathon Tower plan had changed. No longer would the great basin atop the tower emit a searchlight beam. Instead, a great flame, an Olympic flame, if you will, would rise from the depths of the cauldron to cast its brilliance over the stadium. There is no doubt that Wils conceived the idea and produced the sketch. Wils personally presided over every little design and construction detail of the entire Olympic precinct. Indeed, his confirming signature appeared on the bottom right-hand margin of the design.

Why and how did the idea of an "Olympic flame" rise in the mind's eye of Jan Wils? There are scarce notations in modern Olympic history to prompt such a concept. One of the very few references that linked the Olympic Games with fire came from Pierre de Coubertin. In his speech closing the Stockholm Games of the Fifth Olympiad in 1912, the baron opened his remarks with the following: "And now, gentlemen, see how a great people [the Swedes] has, by our arrangement [IOC], received from your hands the Olympic flame and has undertaken to protect it and, if possible, enhance the radiance of the precious flame."[7] It is extremely doubtful that Wils heard these words (he was not present in Stockholm for the Games), much less ever read them. Nevertheless, a point of reference had been enunciated: that the last act culminating the evening of the Olympic Games closing is one that will in time greet the dawn of the next Games. From this one might grasp the concept of a flame lit to open the Games and extinguished to close them, exactly the case in modern circumstance.

Notes

1 MacAloon 1984, 252.

2 Borgers 1996, 16. The Deutsche Kampfspiele, the so-called "German National Games," were designed to fill the void caused by Germany's temporary disqualification from the Olympic Games following its defeat in the First World War. Excluded from the Antwerp Games in 1920 and the Paris Games in 1924, Germany returned to Olympic participation in Amsterdam in 1928.

3 One of the goals of the *De Stijl* movement was to establish a working collaboration between painters and architects, a collaboration that Wils himself consistently put into practice. For example, van Doesburg acted as colour consultant for Wils in his design of the De Lange House, built in Alkmaar in 1917, and his Hotel De Dubbele Sleutel, built in Woerden in 1918. See the *Grove Dictionary of Art*, http://www.groveart.com.

4 For biographical information on the life and career of Jan Wils, see *De Olympiade* (the newsletter of the Dutch Organizing Committee for the 1928 Olympic Games), February 1926 (in English) and May 1926 (in Dutch), as well as the *Grove Dictionary of Art*, http://www.groveart.com.

5 See Stanton (2000) for confirmation of Wils's membership on Olympic Games International Juries for Architecture, as well as for an exhaustive study of the history of Olympic art contests.

6 See the addendum to *De Olympiade*, February 1926, with an article in four languages on "The Architect of the New Stadium at Amsterdam, Jan Wils."

7 In its original French: "Et maintenant, Messieurs, voici qu'un grand peuple a, par notre entremise, reçu de vos mains *le flambeau des Olympiades* et s'est engagé par là à en préserver et, si possible, à en aviver la flamme précieuse. Une coûtume s'est établie que la dernière parole dite au soir des Jeux Olympiques fût pour saleur *l'aurore de Jeux suivants*." (Brackets and italics ours.) "Closing Words," 1966, 39; Mallon and Widlund 2002, 25.

The Great Progression: A Content Analysis of the *Lake Placid News* and the *Los Angeles Times'* Treatment of the 1932 Olympics

Jonathan Paul

In the past twenty-five years the Olympic Games have been transformed into big business, with the host city expecting to accrue billions of dollars in revenues and incur at least the same in terms of costs. Decisions related to the distribution and allocation of economic resources, controlled by an organizing committee, are a significant predictor to hosting a successful event. A secure financial framework is of course a necessity for success. Given the complexity of the Olympic Games, however, there are other equally important contributors to their success. This expanding list includes the mass media and the coverage provided by media organizations. Given the greater than 17,000 media personnel present at the Olympic Summer Games in Sydney, the need to inform the public has become an influential force in the Olympic movement.[1] As stated in the *Olympic Review*:

> (t)he enormous, almost universal appeal of the event and the concomitant potential for generating advertising revenue, combined with the Olympics' ability to provide wonderfully striking images...has resulted in tremendous growth in media attention in recent years.[2]

As the number of media representatives increases with each quadrennial festival, a properly cultivated relationship between organizers and all types of media is essential. This relationship is accomplished by allowing the media reasonable access to the operations and plans for the event. When these accommodations are not provided, the manner in which the event is reported is often adversely affected. Such was the case with the 1996 Summer Games in Atlanta, Georgia. A poorly conceived plan for dealing with the media contributed to the lasting legacy of an over-commercialized and crowded Olympic Games. Members of the media were housed in forty different venues, causing traffic jams and inconveniences, as buses were the only form of transportation to the events.[3] In addition to the travel problems, problems with electronic communications hampered the media in sending news stories back to their respective outlets.[4] Given that the journalist's most important priority while covering an event is "good communications," the inability of organizers to accommodate this group negatively contributed to the public perception of the Games.[5]

In addition to accommodating the media, the amount of public funds currently needed to finance a bid stimulates debate concerning the necessity of the mega-event itself. Opposition from scholars such as Helen Lenskyj, organizations such as Bread Not Circuses, and journalists such as Stephen Brunt of the *Globe and Mail* and British investigative reporter Andrew Jennings, has questioned the importance and value of staging the Olympics in the current economic environment.[6] As a result of concerns raised by these parties concerning the Olympic Games in Atlanta, Sydney, and Salt Lake City, and the successful bids of Beijing and Vancouver, current public opinion is quite polarized about the value of hosting the event. From headlines exclaiming "Burn the Olympics" and "Games Hurt the Area's Needy," a strong resistant culture has emerged.[7] This critical analysis has consistently challenged the advantages, particularly economic, of hosting the event. Today, Olympic bids and the Games themselves should not expect anything more than a polarized stance from the print media.

While the media culture is one of scepticism, one must wonder if this opinion has been present throughout the history of the Olympic movement. The 1932 Olympic Winter Games in Lake Placid, New York, and Summer Games in Los Angeles, California, offer historians a distinct opportunity to evaluate the media's stance towards the economic costs of hosting the global festival, given their shared U.S. location and time of occurrence.

In order to understand the uniqueness of both 1932 Olympic Games within the modern Olympic movement, it is necessary to provide a brief overview. Bid and organizing committee president Dr. Godfrey Dewey secured the rights to the Third Olympic Winter Games for Lake Placid at the IOC's April General Session in 1929.[8] Despite strong protests from a California contingent within the American Olympic Committee about the feasibility of hosting the event in a small community, Lake Placid delivered the event effectively. The most contentious issue during the hosting process was the construction of the bobsleigh run. Initially slated for public land, the Organizing Committee for the Olympic Games (OCOG) had to seek a site on private land after a lawsuit filed by the Association for the Protection of the Adirondacks was issued.[9] Citing New York State law, the association noted that the construction of the run violated state law because of the removal of some two thousand trees.[10] The judge agreed with the association's argument and ruled against the OCOG. As a result, the OCOG explored alternative sites and the bob run was finally built.

Although this issue caused a two- to three-month delay, the event still occurred from 4 to 13 February 1932, with approximately 58,000 paid spectators and 252 athletes attending.[11] The organizing committee expected more athletes, but as a result of the international effects of the Great Depression, the number of countries decreased from the originally estimated twenty-five to seventeen, resulting in a $75,000 deficit.[12]

As opposed to the rapid preparations of the Lake Placid OCOG, Los Angeles secured the rights to the Games of the Tenth Olympiad in 1923. With this extended period, a large majority of the finances were secured prior to the onset of the Great Depression in 1929. As many of the facilities, including the Los Angeles Memorial Coliseum, were finished or required only minor renovations, the OCOG was able to use the finances from the Olympiad Bond Act for other purposes.[13] This included a strong advertising and ticket strategy, construction of the first Olympic Village, and protecting the Olympic symbols. This aggressive approach to the delivery of the Games minimized potential problems for the OCOG and helped deliver a successful event. Despite the apparent financial stability of its operations in Los Angeles, similar to its winter counterpart, the number of participating countries dropped with the onset of the Great Depression. The event occurred from 30 July to 14 August, with 1,400 athletes representing thirty-seven countries.

Both OCOGs encountered Great Depression–related problems that restricted budgets of foreign national Olympic committees (NOCs) and caused the organizations to re-evaluate the merits of sending their athletes to the Pacific coast. Beginning with unpaid foreign debts, the Great Depression began in the United States when the economy weakened and could no longer afford to lend money internationally.[14] As a result, the stock market fell to its lowest level on 24 October 1929. Given the dwindling economy of the United States, and the needs of ordinary citizens, resistance from the media towards the big budgets of the Olympic Games could have occurred.

The potential for resistance in the print media towards the astronomical budgets of both of the mega-events, given the realities of the Great Depression, provided the focus for a content analysis of the Friday edition of the *Lake Placid News* and the Saturday edition of the *Los Angeles Times*.[15] Each article (during the course of the 1929–1932 period) was coded in support of or against the staging of the Olympic Games. Articles with no obvious stance were coded as neutral. Data were analyzed using keywords concerning the financial aspect of hosting the games. The keywords included: Olympic Games; sponsorship; funding; government; the Great Depression; and facility construction. The terms sponsorship, funding, government, and facility construction are secondary keywords that were coded only if they were found in the same document as the Olympic Games. The use of general terms was geared to allow for the compilation of a large data pool that could be further restricted after data collection.

With the varying methods of delivery, it was hypothesized that differing moods would emerge in the print media coverage of the two events. For Lake Placid, the size of the town (approximately 1,800), coupled with the crippling effects of the Depression, was hypothesized by the researcher to cause a substantial shift in the media coverage of the Games from positive to negative.[16] Furthermore, it was suggested that the pressures of securing finances during a period of economic crisis would be difficult and, as a result, a groundswell of negative reporting would occur. For Los Angeles, the extra time to prepare and secure finances ensured continued positive media coverage. In addition to these factors, it was suggested that the five newspapers of the region agreed to positively endorse the event. With the presence of *Los Angeles Times* publisher Harry Chandler on the organizing committee, a positive endorsement of the event was expected. Therefore, it was expected that the *Lake Placid News* would have the only shift of mood in print.

Results

The results indicate a general neutral stance in both newspapers. Therefore, this discussion will analyze the articles deemed neutral before discussing the few positively and negatively coded articles.

Lake Placid

For Lake Placid, thirty-four articles were coded neutral in 1929, as no obvious stance was taken by the *Lake Placid News* in the data. Of the four years analyzed in this investigation, 1929 would seem the most appropriate time to question the merits of hosting such a mega-event in the small town. While the crash of the stock market in October 1929 marked the official beginning of the Great Depression, the national economy had struggled for the previous year due to other international economic markets slumping, as well as an overproduction of goods.[17] With the global economy struggling, the lack of criticism towards the substantial commitment of public monies reflects the stance of the *Lake Placid News*. Considering that the passing of the $250,000 public bond and a state government bill declaring official support for the event were both reported neutrally, the lack of criticism reveals a positive position in the paper directed towards the staging of the event.

Of the remaining 107 articles identified from 1930 to 1932, 97 were coded neutrally. Over this two-year period (1930 to the start of the Games), there were many potentially explosive events that were reported neutrally. These events included two lawsuits filed in 1930 against the OCOG. The first, filed by the Association for the Protection of the Adirondacks, stated that the organizing committee could not alter any of the physical environment on the publicly protected land slated for the Olympic bob run.[18] The result was further investigation of a new site by the organizing committee and a need for additional funds.[19] The second lawsuit, filed by the editor of the *Jewish Tribune*, David Mosesohn, questioned the use of public money for the benefit of Olympic athletes when Jewish people were not allowed to join OCOG president Dr. Godfrey Dewey's own Lake Placid Club.[20] Initially dismissed by members of the OCOG as a publicity stunt, the lawsuit gained further momentum when, one week later, other Jewish media outlets across the country supported the lawsuit.[21] While a settlement was reached weeks later, the media had an opportunity to be more subjective in its analysis given the controversial nature of the subject. Both stories were reported in a factual manner, however, and direct quoting dominated each article.

With both of the previously identified controversies reported neutrally and unable to alter the procedures of the Lake Placid OCOG in 1930, it is not surprising that other seemingly less controversial events did not disrupt the process of staging the Olympic Games. Important funding initiatives, such as the passing of two bond issues for additional funding, the official endorsement of the event from the state government, the construction of a new arena in the middle of the town, and the reluctance of the OCOG to rely on sponsorship revenue, were reported with no supplementary analysis. Given the overwhelming support by the public for the two public bond issues and the desire of gubernatorial candidate Franklin D. Roosevelt to use the positive economic impact of the event, the *Lake Placid News* may not have wanted to inject analysis that would be counterproductive to the overall success of the event.

While there were no negative articles in the data set analyzed, there were ten positively coded articles. The first positively coded article, which appeared on 28 February 1929, described how the county was going to cooperate with Olympic plans, ensuring no barriers to delivery. It was coded positively because the article begins with the line "One of the best bits of news" when describing the new partnership. The other nine coded articles in editions of the paper from 19 December 1930 to 20 February 1931 marked the only true evidence of positive support. A column entitled "Olympic Sidelights" was created, enabling the organizing committee and members of the newspaper's editorial staff to communicate information and opinions on the Games. This direct partnership indicates an excellent relationship between the two parties. For example, the January 9 column suggests that "this is the most important event in the history of Lake Placid," and that the event would leave a "positive legacy in the area."[22] Given the positive subject matter of the column and the partnership it represented, it is surprising that without written explanation, the column disappears after the month of February. As there were no dramatic events which occurred during this time period, it is difficult to hypothesize a potential reason for its removal. The other forty articles took a neutral stance on the reporting of information. Events such as the creation of the publicity committee, the lawsuit filed against construction of the bob run on public land, and the release of the publicity plan were all published with no critical analysis.

While it was hypothesized that there would be a more negative stance in the *Lake Placid News*, the results of this section are not as surprising as they might seem. Even though 10 of the 141 articles were coded positively, the lack of negative spin in the remaining articles also indicates a positive stance, even though it is not evident in the wording. The short amount of time from the awarding to the delivery, and the small size of the town, caused a more monolithic outlook on the event. In addition, organizing committee president Godfrey Dewey was a constant influence in various Olympic committees and public forums. As a result of this accessibility, in addition to his successful years as president of the Lake Placid Club, Dewey positively influenced the media and thus the public's perception of the event.

Los Angeles

For the Los Angeles Organizing Committee, the Great Depression came at a more secure time during the hosting process. While drastic budget cuts were occurring and Depression remedies were being sought throughout the country, the coverage of the Games of the Tenth Olympiad in the *Los Angeles Times* was generally unaffected by the collapsing economy. This disposition is reflected in the results of this study. As the Great Depression occurred much later in the organizational phase for the Los Angeles Organizing Committee, and because of the *Los Angeles Times'* status as a daily newspaper with many additional issues not within the limits of this investigation, there are considerably fewer relevant data in this section.

For the first two years of the period selected (1929 and 1930), there was only neutrally coded data. The articles in this group include a report on organizing committee president William May Garland's trip to Europe, reassurance that Los Angeles would remain the host city for the event, plans to renovate the Olympic Coliseum, a continuation of the national advertising campaign, early discussions about the issue of travel to Los Angeles for the foreign NOCs, and continued preparations by the local community for the Games.

The 1931 data reveals twenty-one coded articles, twenty neutral, and one that was coded positively. With the Olympic Games approaching, most of the twenty neutral articles deal with the release of the Olympic ticketing program in late June, and the construction of the rowing bleachers and various inspections of the facilities by professionals and athletes. The one positively coded article is in the special fiftieth anniversary edition of the *Los Angeles Times*. As it was a special issue, a section of the paper was devoted to the history of Los Angeles, with ten pages of it devoted to the Olympic Games. Written by Maynard McFie, vice-president of the organizing committee, the article discussed the upcoming Olympic Games, mostly describing the history of the ancient and modern Olympic Games and the schedule for upcoming events. The article describes the positive relationship the organizing committee had with the *Los Angeles Times*, and how the newspaper would continue to contribute positively to the overall success of the Games.

The 1932 data reveals twenty-one total articles to the end of the event. Of these articles, two were positive, eighteen neutral, and one negative. The subjects of the neutrally coded articles include the release of the ticket plan, endorsements from foreign athletes and dignitaries about the readiness of Los Angeles for the event, reactions as the event was occurring, and some of the ingenious ways gate crashers tried to enter the event. The two articles coded positively were identified for different reasons. In an article of 2 July entitled "Olympic Fashion Plate," a comparison is made between Palm Beach, Florida, and Los Angeles.[23] In describing the influx of tourists expected and the fashion scene in Palm Beach, the article mentions that as citizens of Los Angeles "we ought to have a brand of light summer wear named for Los Angeles." The other article was in the final Saturday edition of the paper during the Games. It provided a synopsis of the Games and discussion of the legacy that would be left behind. The article credited those who had made the Games "the best ever," and described how Los Angeles was a better city for having hosted the Games. Although coded negatively, an article of 9 July on the potential economic impact of the Games can be better termed as cautious. The Los Angeles Times questions the validity of the published projections from the All Year club, and warns the readership not to be overly optimistic, suggesting it would be better to wait until after the event to calculate the economic impact.

As a whole, the data from the Los Angeles section reveals a generally neutral stance, as only four out of seventy-four total articles were positively or negatively coded. It is clear that the paper adopted a hands-off approach to reporting on the event. Eleven years had passed between the time when the idea of hosting was first proposed and the completion of the event.[24] The long period prior to hosting, and a secure financial framework before the Great Depression, contributed to the small amount of reported debate in the papers.

Conclusions

Compared with the divisive media coverage of the past ten years about the importance of the Olympic Games, little to no debate occurred in either of the two selected papers during the period of 1924 to 1932. There are many potential explanations for this finding. One of the most plausible arguments suggests that this is the way both newspapers wanted it. Of the 215 articles from both papers, only ten articles had a specific author attached. By not attaching an author to the articles, the paper appears to be more objective by maintaining a neutral position while still controlling the flow of information. Michael Young, in his article "The Melbourne Press and the 1980 Moscow Olympic Boycott Controversy," states that "to criticize the press purely on the basis that it does not print all the news is both impractical and pointless."[25] Don Morrow and Janice Waters, in their article "Method in Sport History: A Content Analysis Approach," elaborate further by mentioning that newspapers were "never published as historical documents."[26] As a result, even though the lack of name attachment in both of the selected newspapers appears to indicate a more neutral approach, the lack of negative reporting indicates a more positive and subjective position in the *Lake Placid News*.

In addition to the lack of author attachment, many articles contained directly quoted information rather than a synthesized version in the paper's own words. For example, all of Godfrey Dewey's speeches, coverage of IOC president Henri Baillet-Latour's press conference following a visit to the Los Angeles facilities, and several bills from the state legislatures were printed verbatim. The majority of these articles were printed with no wrap-up or analysis. The articles begin with a brief contextualized description of the parties involved, with the verbatim transcript to follow. As a result, there was no summary at the end of the articles highlighting the important elements of the story.

Finally, and most plausibly, while the wording is neutral, an examination of the positive or negative nature of the subject of the articles reveals the position of both papers. Of the *Lake Placid News* articles, only ten of 131 report negatively, and seven of those concerned the change of site for the bob run. Of the *Los Angeles Times* articles, only seven of seventy-four report negative news, with five of those concerned with travel problems for European NOCs and potentially reduced funding for the Games from the American Olympic Committee.

There are two potential interpretations of this data. First, it can be said that little to no negative news occurred at all during the hosting of both Games. More plausible, however, is the interpretation that the newspapers may have chosen not to publish, or were not aware of, all of the negativity and potential barriers. As the results indicate a neutral to positive approach, it is clear that both of the selected newspapers did not publish all of the negative news.

It can thus be concluded that the Great Depression did not sway the media coverage as much as originally hypothesized. The two selected papers refused to allow the economic effects of the global economic collapse to negatively alter the staging of an important event for the two areas. For the two papers, the potential economic impact of the Games influenced their coverage. The small community of Lake Placid championed the mega-event, and this spirit infused the reporting style. In Los

Angeles, the firm financial framework and the boosterism inherent in the area combated the crippling effects of the Depression. As a result of these positive forces, both of the selected newspapers served as more of a source for Olympic information than for public debate.

Future research should focus on comparing the two selected newspapers with counterparts in their states. For example, given the lawsuit filed by its editor against the OCOG, the *Jewish Tribune* most likely covered the Third Olympic Winter Games with a different approach than that of the *Lake Placid News*. By comparing regionalized newspapers, stronger conclusions could be made regarding the overall coverage of the event in each region. As each local newspaper has a different target market, a unique perspective on the coverage of the event should be expected. By applying the same parameters to a group of local newspapers in the Lake Placid and Los Angeles regions, a better understanding of the effects of the Great Depression on the local hosting areas would be understood.

Because of the uniqueness of the media coverage between 1929 and 1932, a different label should be used. As there was an unyielding persistence by the contributing parties to deliver the Olympic Games regardless of the overwhelming obstacles, the time period of 1929–1932 relative to the staging and hosting of the Games should be titled the Great Progression, not the Great Depression.

Notes

1   "How Does the Media Cover the Games?," 60.
2   "How Does the Media Cover the Games?," 60.
3   Gratton 1999, 124.
4   Gratton 1999, 124.
5   Gratton 1999, 124.
6   For examples of criticism of the Olympic Games, see Lenskyj 2000; Simson and Jennings 1992; Jennings 1996.
7   IOC press clippings, International Centre of Olympic Studies (ICOS), London, ON: University of Western Ontario.
8   Fea 1996, 234.
9   "North Elba Citizens Have Keen Interest in Decision Concerning Olympic Bob Run on State Land," *Lake Placid News*, 6 December 1929, p. 1, Lake Placid Library, Reel 8 [hereinafter "North Elba Citizens"].
10 "North Elba Citizens."
11 Organizing Committee for the Olympic Winter Games, *Official Report for the III Winter Olympic Games* [hereinafer *Official Report*], 1932, 123–24.
12 *Official Report*, 270.
13 The Olympiad Bond Act was passed by voters on 6 November 1928.
14 Fearon 1979, 16.
15 A content analysis can reveal many patterns and themes about the media, particularly print media. Newspapers are often treated as objective forms of information, but it is

important to accept the form as a method designed to sell papers. See Morrow and Waters 1982, 31.

16 Personal communication with Barbara Whitney, town clerk of Lake Placid, 16 September 2003. She suggested an approximate population of 1,800 in 1932.

17 Personal communication with Barbara Whitney.

18 "North Elba Citizens."

19 "North Elba Citizens."

20 "Jewish Protest against Olympics Starts Action," *Lake Placid News,* 14 November 1930, Lake Placid Library, Reel 9.

21 "Jewish Protest against Olympics Starts Action."

22 "Olympic Sidelights," *Lake Placid News,* 9 January 1931, p. 4, Lake Placid Library, Reel 9.

23 "Olympic Fashion Plate," *Los Angeles Times,* 2 July 1932, Section II, p. 8, Purdy-Kresge Library, Wayne State University, Detroit.

24 In late 1919, the Community Development Association, a group of wealthy businessmen who wanted to promote the Los Angeles region internationally, first discussed the idea for the event. At the time, California was an escapist paradise undergoing an economic boom, and the Olympics were an optimal event to maximize interest in the Los Angeles region. For a more detailed analysis of the Community Development Association, see White 2002; Riess 1981.

25 Young 1988, 195.

26 Morrow and Waters 1982, 31.

Womanizing Olympic Athletes: Policy and Practice during the Avery Brundage Era

Kevin B. Wamsley

When America's Stacy Dragila soared over the bar in Sydney at the 2000 Olympic Games, the leap was as significant symbolically for women's sport as it was in the literal sense for securing her gold medal. She pole-vaulted over a bar set in excess of 4 metres,[1] and over a line that for 104 years was crossed only by men in the Olympic Games. Defenders of male physical superiority will inform us that she didn't come close to the men's grade, but, then again, as R.W. Connell reminds us, one of the hallmarks of modern sport, indeed in most aspects of the societies in which they are situated, is the common social understanding that men are better than women.[2] And sport has always been one of those institutions. The complicated issue of women's participation in the Olympic Games has been addressed to a certain extent, from the intricacies of the early debates and personalities, to the participation of organizations including the International Olympic Committee (IOC), la Fédération Sportive Féminine Internationale (FSFI), and the International Amateur Athletics Federation (now the International Association of Athletics Federations—IAAF), to the votes, the arguments, the doomed 800-metre race in 1928, and the residual Victorian rhetoric that typically accompanied the critics' indignation. But the long-term significance of participation for women and men has yet to be fully dissected by historians and sociologists.

Studies have examined the basic premises of men's and some women's opposition to women's participation, and the lobbying efforts of women and supportive men to include official women's events, particularly athletics or track and field. But the idea of inclusion per se, or equality through numbers of athletes or numbers of events, is not at issue here; rather, this research focuses on the deeper structuring of behaviours and values entailed in the consumption of Olympic culture through participation and spectatorship, or the spread of specific information where distinct behavioural attributes are normalized or naturalized.

Without question, there is no other social institution in modern history that has provided more opportunities for female athletes to participate in elite sport, and promoted women's sport to audiences around the world, than the Olympic Games. However, the main impetus or driving force behind the significant increases in women's events—indeed, female participants in the Olympics—was the Cold War context of competition, announced by the arrival of the Soviet Union in 1952 and exacerbated in the subsequent heated international rivalry played out most prominently through Olympic sport for more than thirty years. On the other hand, no institution has been so powerful as to structure both the nature of participation and performance, and to influence the consumption of women's sport, to such a degree. It was an Olympic culture (one consisting, for our purposes in this instance, of Olympic, national, and international sport leaders, and the emerging global media complex) that actively promoted the feminized athlete, while tolerating but systematically criticizing those who participated in traditional men's events or who did not exude the typically expected feminine physical traits. The Olympic Games taught us about being men and women. The Olympic Games sustained a historically specific gender order that went far beyond the stadium to households around the world. As Olympic culture had normalized the class hierarchies of the gentleman amateur earlier in the century, so too did it normalize a hierarchy of social differences between men and women, including the long-term access and trade in symbolic and economic capital.

From examinations of the primary materials of IOC executive meetings and in the personal writings and correspondence of Olympic presidents such as Pierre de Coubertin, Sigfrid Edstrøm, Henri Baillet-Latour, and Avery Brundage, it is plainly evident that the promotion of women's participation was not one of the heralded Olympic ideals; rather, the impetus came from nations such as the United States, responding immediately to the challenges posed by massive Soviet teams that fielded a nearly full women's complement.[3] We now recognize that it was Sigfrid Edstrøm who, on a course of political expediency, steered the entrance of women into athletics or track and field events to manage the tide of female participation in traditionally men's events at the Olympic Games.[4]

Further research on the issue of women's participation has focused on the sexualization of female athletes by the world press, in addition to the imposition of standards of femininity by international sport federations,[5] and, to a lesser extent, the beauty complex of the starlet athlete, which must arguably be connected to emergence of Hollywood's early female icons of film.[6] How the early IOC presidents addressed the issue of women's participation has been studied to a limited extent,[7] but, certainly, more work is warranted. The issue is much more complicated than just simple opposition, concessions to fervent lobbying, or even a promotion of competitions for women. Guttmann has argued, in his biographical treatment of Avery Brundage, that "the extent of his opposition to women's athletics has been exaggerated."[8] Guttmann reached this conclusion after assessing Brundage's early opposition and his later support for events such as mixed yachting, and then his glowing and sexually charged descriptions of the Dutch runner Fanny Blankers-Koen's victories in 1948. Guttmann is correct insofar as Brundage was a minor player initially, relative to Edstrøm, who gradually came to accept that women's participation was inevitable for the IOC if it was to promote itself as the first body of world sport. Edstrøm didn't favour women's participation either, but he had more political savvy and a broader perspective on the issue at the time than either Baillet-Latour or Brundage. Call it exaggeration or not—none of them wanted women to participate in Coubertin's Olympic Games, but that was simply not an option.

The focus on the Brundage era is important for a number of reasons. In the first instance, the arrival of women to the Games en masse in the public eye occurred between 1932 and 1972 against the backdrop of Cold War competition; in the second instance, following the reaffirmation of women's athletics on the 1932 program in Los Angeles, we get a sense of how sport leaders and the press began to handle, manage, and represent the presence of women on the podiums that were supposed to celebrate male achievements. Finally, it is interesting to note the reactions of Brundage himself, one of the most influential sport leaders of the twentieth century, and the grounds on which he was able to accept women's participation. IOC members, individuals who knew him, and some scholars argue that Brundage alone saved the Olympic Games from extinction during times of extreme turmoil[9]—although few scholars have unearthed what it was that he saved. And part of that answer rests in how the Olympic Games influenced people's lives during this era. The Brundage years featured some of the residual values of the Coubertin era.

Newspaper reports on the Olympic Games in the 1920s, for example, tended to sexualize female athletes. In their assessments, writers focused on facial beauty and the feminine figure first, followed by personal behaviour. Athletic performance remained a distant third. This was not unusual for female athletes of the 1920s, whose sporting exploits often appeared on the society page instead of the sports page.[10] For men, who were perceived as the real "athletic missionaries"[11] of the modern era for many countries, performance came first, followed by personal behaviour, with looks and form following third—unless, of course, as in the cases of Jesse Owens or Paavo Nurmi, unruly behaviour was cited as a distinguishing factor.[12] In many respects, the media linked readings of the female athlete in the 1930s and 1940s to the creation of Hollywood film star icons. Indeed, many of the social events of the 1932 Los Angeles Olympics mingled Hollywood icons and athletic champions, as the stocks of symbolic capital continued to rise for Olympic celebrities of the right sort. Hollywood even hand-picked athletic men, including Johnny Weissmuller, for epic roles. For the movies, magazines, and the Olympic Games, there were clear distinctions on the masculine and feminine, lines that could not be crossed without social repercussions. For women, sexualized representations and the focus on beauty and grace offset period fears of the masculinization process supposedly engendered through participation in sport. If female athletes could be beautiful, graceful, and heterosexual, participate in gender-appropriate sports, and eventually be good wives and mothers, then their participation in sport did not compromise the traditionally accepted gender orders—at least in the countries examined here, including Britain, the United States, and Canada. A feminized athlete could not challenge the celebration of manhood through sport, and thus did not displace men as the "real" athletes of the era.

The new leaders of Coubertin's Olympic Games, Baillet-Latour, Edstrøm, and Brundage, eventually accepted the basic premise of women's participation—provided, they argued, that it was in events such as swimming, fencing, and tennis, but not in strenuous masculine sports such as shot putting.[13] The shot put event for women was not introduced until 1948.[14] Although the IOC and IAAF policies on women's participation, and the decision-making processes therein, appeared linear and progressive, the minutes reveal several attempts to eliminate women's track and field, cited a few times as a method of reducing the program, and a few attempts by women's sport organizations to have women's events struck from the Olympics.[15] The issue was rather uneven, to say the least.

On the part of sport leaders such as Brundage, politically astute commentaries were delivered when necessary, as in the official reports of his national Olympic committee, but occasional outbursts belied any notions that women's participation was promoted. For example, after the Berlin Olympics, arguably a period of time when Brundage wore his politics on his sleeve, he commented on female athletes: "I am fed up to the ears with women as track and field competitors...her charms sink to something less than zero. As swimmers and divers, girls are beautiful and adroit, as they are ineffective and unpleasing on the track."[16] Following the 1936 Games, the United States Olympic Committee sent a letter, signed by Brundage, to the IOC, requesting that the international federations be alerted to the "abnormal woman athletes," an early call for sex testing.[17] Brundage's letter to Baillet-Latour about a particular United States athlete demonstrated unequivocally his views on the female body image:

> As an interested sport fan and one who upholds the participation of feminine athletes in athletics I feel _____ has been allowed to take part in a field where she (?) doesn't belong. I saw and spoke to her when she took part in an exhibition meet here. Her deep bass voice, her height and 10½ inch shoes surely proclaim her a border-line case if there ever was one. I feel she has never put forth her best efforts in the events because if she did, the entire public would take a great deal more notice. Judging from her past performances she will, without a doubt, be a member of the United States team and if this is permitted the normal American girl will certainly be misrepresented. Something should be done to prevent this and rules should be made to keep the competitive games for normal feminine girls and not monstrosities.[18]

Even for appropriately feminine athletes, such as champion swimmer Eleanor Holm, and for male athletes, appropriate behaviour was of paramount importance for Brundage. Holm was suspended for excessive drinking and what the United States Olympic Committee termed "insubordination."[19] For a man concerned with shielding his own behaviour—girlfriends, children out of wedlock, really the breaking of American social codes—during his ascendancy to the throne, he was very animated about the proper decorum of others.

One might consider the IOC and Brundage himself seemingly ambivalent on the issue of women's participation. In some cases, he considered removing them; in others, he supported their continued participation. He supported the addition of the 200-metre event and later the return of the 800-metre race in 1960. However, the terms under which Brundage, his contemporaries, and the press accepted women's participation were more significant than the events themselves. It was during the post-1932 era that women were actively channelled into what were commonly referred to as "feminine" sports, including swimming, gymnastics, figure skating, fencing, and tennis. How could the press not respond to the various commentaries provided by the most influential personalities in sport? And of course these leaders were influenced by the popular imagination of the day. That is to say, it was primarily a network of supporting influences and social forces of the era that created female sporting icons from the aesthetic sports, with a few exceptions. Sporting women of these sorts, like glamorous Hollywood stars, became the cultural icons of femininity, since the most positive commentaries by sportspeople and more generally in the press were directed to figure skaters and swimmers. Figure skater Barbara Ann Scott, winner of world championships and the 1948 Olympic gold medal, became *the* icon of exemplary femininity in Canada, even though she was chided for indiscretions by the amateur watchdog, Brundage himself.[20]

Active criticism against women who did not appear feminine by Western standards, particularly from eastern European countries, was rampant in the press from the mid-Brundage era even to the present day, and this ultimately led to the implementation of sex testing in Mexico City in 1968. Brundage himself attacked Communist female athletes for their appearances in 1960: "Those are a different type of women anyway. They carry bricks, labor in fields, clean the streets and do hard manual labor in their daily life. What do these Olympic lassies look like? Get a picture for yourself."[21] This commentary spoke as much to Brundage's periodic disdain for Communism as it did to his notions of appropriate femininity. Other commentators were willing to put traditional notions of femininity aside to face the onslaught of Communist athletes with America's best. New York lawyer George Gray Zabriskie wrote to Brundage: "woman athletes of the free world need not yield to regimented peasants from behind the Iron Curtain....What the AAU and similar bodies in other Western Countries [o]ught to do is have their local committees go out and beat the bushes for husky, athletic girls with competitive spirit in schools, colleges, farms and factories."[22] Others, including doctors, retorted that for female athletes, "The incidental exhaustive training tends to toughen a woman's body, rob her of her natural grace and ultimately make her not only unattractive but actually ugly."[23] But what if a superstar emerged who fit the bill of appropriate nation but not in traditional events? In the case of multiple gold-medal winner Fanny Blankers-Koen of the Netherlands in 1948, the press called her the "flying Dutch housewife" and Olympic "mama." It was true that she was married with two children—but, of course, this was a distinction reserved for a woman. In postwar Canada and the United States, the pressure to return to the household and raise families was brought to bear upon young women through media channels, magazines, and educational materials. Affectionate labelling was an important aspect of the media-related feminization process from the 1930s onward. Olympic Games delivered pixies, mermaids, and darlings to newspaper, then television audiences, reinforcing a gendered distinction of appropriate and exemplary femininity.[24] The reaction of Brundage—a reluctant supporter of the addition of the women's shot put to the program of 1948—to the star athlete from the Netherlands typified the incorporative powers of influential people and organizations when challenged by resistive or unusual circumstances. The powerful tended to embrace the challengers somewhat, delicately reshaping them and recasting them to suit their own purposes. Women were making inroads in non-traditional events, but these freedoms, in turn, had to be rationalized and recast so as not to disrupt the gender hierarchy. Brundage enthusiastically responded in retrospect to the gold-medal performances of Blankers-Koen: "A new type of woman is appearing—lithe, supple, physically disciplined, strong, slender, and efficient, like the Goddesses of ancient Greece. It is the day of the bikini and the mini skirt."[25] One didn't read in the press about Bob Mathias or Emil Zátopek in such terms. Allen Guttmann suggests that the 61-year-old Brundage's rather steamy comments might be related to his passionate affections for 29-year-old Lilian Dresden.[26]

Reducing the number of women's events or eliminating them remained part of IOC discussions after Brundage ascended to the presidency in 1952. Writing for the *New York Times*, Arthur Daley applauded Brundage's proposition to reduce the Olympic program: "He [Brundage] made the magnificent suggestion that women competitors be eliminated from the Olympics. It's a great idea. Don't get me wrong, please. Women are wonderful. But when these delightful creatures begin to toss the discus or put the shot—well, it does something to a guy. And it ain't love, Buster."[27] Evidently, Brundage's concerns about appropriate body image continued until his retirement. He responded to a letter from Syracuse University's Clifford "Tip" Goes. Goes wrote: "With your retirement, it is my hope that you will leave a permanent policy, formally expressed, reassuring that women's rowing will never be included in the Olympic Program." He followed up with the question, "Do the other women's teams undergo a sex test?"[28] Brundage responded, "I note your position on rowing for women. We have resisted the application...but more and more pressure comes from President Tom Keller of the Rowing Federation. They claim that this has become a very popular sport in Europe. I wonder why?" Brundage assured him, "All women's teams are subject to a sex test."[29]

A report studying women's participation in sport, the Olympic Games in particular, was presented to the Study and Co-ordinating Committee of the National Olympic Committees in 1968 in Grenoble, France. The extensive study documented a history of women's participation in the Games, traced the numbers of participants in each Games and the events, and provided social commentary based on documented sources on such topics as "Self Expression," "Fear of Musculation," "Sports for the Improvement of Working Capacity," "Sport Helping the Mother in Her Educational Duties," and "Sport as a Prophylactic Against Social Evils." It was argued that "mothers who have a personal interest in sports will be able to direct correctly the motory habits of their children," and that "the mother's example of a healthy life always has a marked favourable effect on children." Further, the report suggested that sport could be utilized to educate youth and combat social evils such as juvenile delinquency, use of alcohol and narcotics, and prostitution.[30] For sport leaders and social commentators of the late 1940s, '50s, and '60s, attending to the "natural" calling of motherhood first helped to rationalize women's participation in sport—sustaining a gender order.

As in the case of sex testing, and the question of appropriate body images for female athletes, the feminization process had a much more profound effect on female athletes and the consuming public than labelling, sexualizing, and general ogling. During the latter part of Brundage's tenure, two feminized sports attracted significant attention among the programmed events for women—figure skating and gymnastics. Indeed, it was the feminization process, synchronous with the march of progress, and the quest for Cold War medals that brought the arrival of the child athlete to the Olympic Games in the last year of Brundage's presidency. The deeper consequences of appropriate female sport, and all artistic sports, ran into crisis when compared to the easily measured events marked by stopwatch, scale, and measuring tape. World records and the improvement of human performance fascinated people. What then for the judged sports? The only palatable answer was to deliver more excitement in the form of risk, and more complicated patterns of movement—more twists, more somersaults. These sorts of movements required certain sizes, body types, and, biomechanically, an efficient body weight to strength ratio—and ultimately the most efficient equation was to be found in little girls. These were the long-term waves created by the first ripples of channelling women into feminine-appropriate sports. Brundage himself recognized that the idea of progress was fundamental to the popularity of the Games. He wrote to Arthur Gander, president of the Fédération Internationale de Gymnastique in 1971 after the Pan American Games were held in Colombia: "there is something seriously wrong with the gymnastic program. If one man can win eight medals in an international set of Games, the events must be altogether too simple—and it certainly detracts from the importance of the sport."[31] Coaches, athletes, parents, and sport federations responded to the calls for progress, initiating athletes into elite training programs at early ages. Training hours for children reached new heights. The Olympic Games brought these images and performances of girl athletes to living rooms, to newspaper headlines of perfect "10s," to magazine covers, and to governments and parents who had bought the symbolic value of the Olympic pedestal lock, stock, and barrel.

Consequences of increasing risk and difficulty in the qualitative sports were devastating. Synchronous to the period fashion emphasis on thinness, and the importance of a new body image, eating disorders and body image problems became endemic, particularly in women's gymnastics. The eating disorders, in part a result of the call for "pixies" and "darlings" to turn more somersaults, created health problems, even death, for some female gymnasts.[32] The sport is still riddled with these problems. While the gender order of female athletes represented and reproduced most prominently through the Olympic Games obviously influenced the lives of these athletes, its representational influence was also significant for spectators and consumers who learned directly from television and the press.

Notes

1 "Dragila Vaults into History," BBC Sport coverage of the 2000 Olympics in Sydney, accessed online at http://news.bbc.co.uk/sport1/hi/olympics2000/athletics-field/941289.stm.
2 Connell 1995.
3 Wamsley 2002.
4 Wamsley and Schultz 2000; Wamsley 2000b; Morrow and Wamsley 2005.
5 Schweinbenz 2001.
6 Schweinbenz and Wamsley 2001; Morrow 1987, 36–54.
7 Coubertin 2000; Guttmann 1984; Wamsley 2002; Wamsley and Schultz 2000.
8 Guttmann 1984, 108.
9 Pound 2001.
10 Wamsley 1997, 146–55.

11 See Dyreson 1998a; Dyreson 1992.
12 From surveys of the *New York Times, Times* of London, and *Los Angeles Examiner* during pre– and post–Olympic Games months, and articles written during the Games.
13 Wamsley 2000a.
14 *Official Report of the Organising Committee for the XIV Olympiad*, 1951, 235–36, 284.
15 IOC Sessions, Cairo, 13 March, 15–18 March 1938, 209.
16 Simri 1977, 22.
17 Lyberg 1996, 365.
18 Avery Brundage Collection (ABC), International Centre for Olympic Studies (ICOS), (London, ON), Box 42, 23 June 1936.
19 *Report of the American Olympic Committee, Games of the XIth Olympiad, Berlin, Germany*, 33.
20 Morrow 1987; Wenn 1991.
21 Guttmann 1984, 195, from the *San Francisco Examiner*, 11 May 1960.
22 George G. Zabriskie to Avery Brundage, 5 April 1955, ABC, ICOS, Box 155, Reel 63.
23 Newspaper clipping by S.E. Bilik, M.D., no date, ABC, ICOS, Box 155, Reel 63.
24 Schweinbenz and Wamsley 2001.
25 Guttmann 1984, 108, citing "The Olympic Story," Chapter X, 10, ABC, Boxes 330–31.
26 Guttmann 1984, 108, citing "The Olympic Story," 194, ABC, Boxes 330–31.
27 Arthur Daley, "More Deadly than the Male," *New York Times*, 8 February 1953.
28 Clifford "Tip" Goes to Avery Brundage, 19 July 1972, ABC, ICOS, Box 217, Reel 126.
29 Avery Brundage to Clifford "Tip" Goes, 5 August 1972, ABC, ICOS, Box 217, Reel 126.
30 "Participation Féminine aux Jeux Olympiques," Meeting of the Study and Co-ordinating Committee of NOCs, Grenoble, 31 January and 1 February 1968, Part II, 6–14, ICOS.
31 Avery Brundage to Arthur Gander, 26 October 1971, ABC, ICOS, Box 215, Reel 125.
32 Ryan 1995; Wamsley 2000b.

The Bridge to Change: The 1976 Montreal Olympic Games, South African Apartheid Policy, and the Olympic Boycott Paradigm

Courtney W. Mason

A mere forty-eight hours prior to the opening ceremonies of the 1976 Montreal Olympic Games, thirteen African nations sent a letter to Lord Killanin, president of the International Olympic Committee (IOC). The short message demanded the exclusion of New Zealand from the Olympic Games if they did not withdraw their rugby team from South Africa. In total, twenty-six African nations would leave Montreal in protest against the apartheid policy in South Africa. This pronouncement kept more than one hundred world-class African athletes from participating in what was for many of them the most significant competition of their lives.[1]

The African boycott of the Montreal Olympics signified the pinnacle of a prolonged and weary battle waged between the IOC and international anti-apartheid supporters. Although the antecedents of this mêlée had their roots in early South African culture and government policy, the struggle of black South Africa against apartheid policy was, at least partly, conducted through twentieth-century sport.[2] The ramifications of the African Olympic boycott in Montreal extended much further than the black African unified anti-apartheid proclamation. The 1976 boycott not only generated international consciousness for the anti-apartheid movement against South Africa, but also indirectly induced social and political change.

The chronicle of the apartheid issue in the modern Olympic Movement demonstrates how political and social agendas can overshadow the realm of international sport. In an effort to emphasize the importance of the events leading up to the Montreal Olympic Games, this essay will trace the history of apartheid policy within South African government and sport, including the 1968 and 1972 Olympics. The influence of the African boycott at Montreal, the emergence of black African unity, and the rising momentum of the anti-apartheid movement will be covered in detail. In order to properly evaluate apartheid policy in South African society, it is also crucial to have a fundamental historical knowledge of the origins of this unique culture.

Colonization of the Cape

Apartheid policy in South African culture originates deep in colonial history. In direct contrast to other European colonies, the whites who settled South Africa over three hundred years ago never returned home. They founded a white nation on the tip of a black continent.[3]

In April 1652, the Dutch East India Company first established a small outpost near the Cape of Good Hope, in what is today the city of Cape Town, South Africa. The outpost provided supplies for Company ships travelling to and from the east. Over time the Dutch population would increase, and these settlers would become the founders of white South Africa. At the time of settlement, the Bantu tribes, which would by 1910 form 70 per cent of the population of South Africa, were over a thousand kilometres away on the east coast of the subcontinent.[4]

The colony of a few farms became insufficient for the demands of the ships, so larger plantations were created and slaves were imported from the west coast of Africa to meet the labour demands in 1658. Slaves from the East Indies, East Africa, and Madagascar added to the diversity of the population in the twentieth century. From 1650 to 1700, immigration encouraged from Europe also changed the cultural distribution, as French and German settlers arrived on the Cape. The newcomers were rapidly absorbed into the community, whose inhabitants came to be known as Boers (from the Dutch word for "farmers")—the culture later to be referred to as the Afrikaners.[5]

The Boer War: Differing Race Policies

In 1795, the British seized control of the Cape to protect its commercial interests in the East Indies.[6] The arrival of over five thousand British settlers in the 1820s created conflicts between the established Afrikaner population and the new settlers. As the British continued to alter government policy,[7] Afrikaners became increasingly more resentful and began to migrate out of the colony on the Cape and establish colonies in the interior. By 1834, some ten thousand Afrikaners had taken their departure in an exodus known as the Great Trek.[8] The newly established Boer colonies of the interior functioned on the principle of racial inequality, where whites sat upon the throne of the cultural hierarchy. In contrast to the Boer colonies, the British colonies on the Cape were adapting a liberal approach to the traditional colour bar. The foremost cause of the Boer War (1899–1902) was the difference in policies to which Boer and British colonies adhered regarding racial segregation and equality. At this time, the major ethnic dispute in South Africa was that of the Afrikaners and the British, and not the colour conflict that would overshadow the next century.[9]

White Privilege as the Corollary of Apartheid Policy

As a result of the British victory in the Boer War, four British colonies were created in 1902. In an effort to assimilate the two republics, it was assumed that major changes in policy would result from British control, but the race policy question was addressed with little resolve.[10]

In 1910, the South Africa Act created a union of government and the first union cabinet. There were ten members included, six of Afrikaner descent and four of British lineage. Although whites in South Africa were outnumbered nearly three and a half to one, no non-whites were incorporated into the cabinet.[11] The union cabinet perpetuated the paradigm of white privilege, as it represented solely the interests of the white minority group. The policy of racial segregation that later became known as apartheid would continue to dominate South African politics and culture throughout most of the twentieth century.[12]

Permeation of Apartheid into Sport

Even though Afrikaner and British South African tensions characterized South African politics, sport as a whole, but especially rugby, was used to manufacture a common solidarity among white South Africans.[13] A shared identity was constructed using rugby as the focal point. Despite attempts to unite whites around sport and the encouragement of participation, no efforts were made to consolidate black and white sport. In reality, the government austerely inhibited black sport.[14]

Prior to the 1950s, black sport suffered immensely from neglect. Lack of access to facilities and severe poverty ensured low participation rates. No financial support or moral encouragement came from the Department of Education or any other governing body.[15] White sports administrators accepted apartheid policy without objection, and national sporting bodies, including the South African National Olympic Committee (SANOC), endorsed the inequitable policies. The poor nutrition of blacks also reduced their interest in recreation. "In addition to racial ideology and material deprivation, another symptom mitigated against black participation in sport— ill-health."[16] As noted by Douglas Booth, even more insidious was the popular contention among white South Africans that blacks were not interested in sport, or that they did not possess the necessary ability to master the technique for most sporting practices.[17]

The all-encompassing nature of apartheid legislation ensured that all aspects of South African society were fully segregated. Even though apartheid government policy was well established by the 1950s, it was not until 1956, when a number of integrated sport incidents were discovered, that official guidelines for sport were formed. This policy perpetuated the inequitable treatment of blacks and effectively linked South African sport to the social and racial policies of the regime.[18]

South African International Sport Participation

South Africa's racial discrimination in its sport policy soon led to the formation of domestic and international oppositional organizations. The South African Sport Association (SASA) and the South African Non-Racial Olympic Committee (SANROC) made efforts to challenge the all-white South African presence in international sport.[19] The anti-apartheid movement progressed rapidly in the international sport community, mostly because the peripheral nature of sport made it the easiest way for many nations to express their dissent. By conveying their objections to South African sport policy, governments could show their commitment to civil rights and—most importantly—avoid breaking significant political and economic ties with South Africa.[20]

In the 1960s, the conflict over South African sport participation began to develop throughout international sporting bodies.[21] In May 1959, at a meeting between the IOC and the NOCs, IOC president Avery Brundage first raised the issue of apartheid in the Olympic movement, but dissatisfaction with the IOC's efforts to address the issue resonated throughout the international sporting community. Given the political nature of the Olympic movement, numerous NOCs viewed South Africa's participation in the Olympic Games as the IOC's affirmation of Pretoria's legitimacy.[22] In 1961, South Africa became a republic and officially left the Commonwealth. This isolated South Africa from Commonwealth states and ensured that Pretoria had to organize sport exchange on an ad hoc basis.[23] This was a significant development that adversely influenced South Africa's struggle for sporting legitimacy. As a result of South Africa's isolation, protestors against apartheid sport policy could now concentrate on individual events rather than attacking the policies of large organizations similar to the IOC.[24] In June 1962, at the 59th Session in Moscow, the Soviet NOC proposed that SANOC be expelled from the IOC, but SANOC was given only a stern warning. If they did not eliminate racial discrimination from sport, they would face repercussions by October 1963. After another extension given at Baden-Baden in 1963, appropriate changes were not instituted and SANOC's invitation to Tokyo was revoked.[25]

The 1968 Mexico City Olympic Games: A Platform of Human Rights

At the 1966 meeting of the IOC in Rome, Brundage's pro-SANOC position was clearly demonstrated when he postponed any decision to permanently expel SANOC.[26] As the IOC position was left unresolved, international dissent was on the rise. A few months later, the Supreme Council for Sports in Africa (SCSA) was created, and it soon became SANOC's principal critic.[27] The SCSA began to co-ordinate various movements against South African sport. In February 1968, after IOC vice-president Lord Killanin evaluated racial equality in South African sport, the IOC voted to rescind the suspension and readmit SANOC. "This decision," writes Shayne P. Quick, "stunned the sporting world."[28] As if in disbelief, many NOCs delayed a response while the SCSA quickly organized a massive boycott campaign for the Mexico City Games. "Boycott leaders were torn between the desire of African states to show off their physical prowess and the perceived necessity to oppose apartheid."[29] Despite the deliberation, only twelve days after the IOC decided to readmit South Africa, thirty-four African nations under Kenyan leadership announced their intention to boycott Mexico City. The SCSA also found support from the Islamic world, the Caribbean, and the Communist bloc. The boycott campaign became very persuasive; the IOC subsequently reversed its decision to readmit South Africa, and barred them from participating.[30]

The boycott of Mexico City was very complex in comparison to the simple rejection of South Africa prior to Tokyo in 1964. In addition to black Africa's difficult decision between the denunciation of apartheid policy or Olympic success, other issues clouded the campaign. The corresponding civil rights movement in the United States, led by professor and prolific black writer Harry Edwards, complicated the perspective of the United States Olympic Committee (USOC).[31] Issues were further convoluted with the banning of Rhodesia from the 1968 Games. Avery Brundage had always lobbied against the inclusion of politics within the Olympic Movement, and consequently became especially bitter regarding the Rhodesian matter in Mexico City. Given that Rhodesia had met all of the criteria for IOC participation, Brundage resented its being barred from participation in Mexico City. Unlike South Africa and its strict apartheid sport policy, Rhodesia was barred because of its white minority government.[32] The Mexican government yielded to international pressure and acted independently of the IOC to prevent Rhodesia's participation by refusing to accept its national passports. Even though both South Africa and Rhodesia were barred from participating in 1968, the chaos revolving around racial politics persisted shortly after the Games. At the IOC meeting in Warsaw in June 1969, the apartheid issue was again on the agenda. Should South Africa's suspension become an expulsion? Once again the IOC postponed its decision until the IOC meeting in Amsterdam in May 1970, at which point South Africa was expelled by a 35–28 vote.[33] The efforts of the SCSA were beginning to have significant consequence for South African sport. Between 1968 and 1970, South Africa was also suspended from the international sport federations of judo, boxing, pentathlon, weightlifting, and gymnastics.[34]

The 1972 Munich Olympic Games: The Boycott Paradigm

The South African issue was allegedly solved by the IOC expulsion of SANOC, but the Rhodesian question remained unresolved. According to a special investigation conducted in 1971 by the International Amateur Athletic Federation (IAAF), Rhodesian sport revealed no evidence of apartheid sport policy. The issue for the SCSA was not sport discrimination, but the white minority government that had recently proclaimed its independence from Britain. Again Brundage and the IOC failed to address SCSA dissension in advance of the Olympic Games. By August 1972, eight African nations had withdrawn from Munich in protest of Rhodesian participation.

Rhodesian athletes shocked Munich organizers when they arrived a few days before the Games. Their arrival prompted twenty-one African nations to signal their intent to boycott the Games if the Rhodesians were permitted to participate. Brundage characterized the threat as "naked political blackmail" and "a savage attack on basic principles."[35] Much to his chagrin, the IOC voted to oust Rhodesia from Munich and expel it from the Olympic movement.[36]

The paradigm of the black African boycott was perpetuated at Munich, and it was as successful as the preceding campaign in Mexico City. In essence, the success of the black African boycott paradigm in 1968 and 1972 acted as a prelude to the pandemonium that would be witnessed at the 1976 Olympic Games in Montreal.

The Chinese Boycott: The Premonition of Political Agendas

In 1975, aided by "ping-pong diplomacy," the People's Republic of China (PRC) reorganized its NOC and applied for readmission to the Olympic Movement.[37] Initiated in 1972, a diplomatic policy ensured that the Canadian government recognized only the PRC. In the midst of a major grain deal with the PRC in 1976, Beijing requested that Canada bar the Republic of China (ROC) from Olympic participation. Canadian Prime Minister Pierre Trudeau complied, and the Taiwanese or ROC passports were to be denied. The IOC, the IAAF, the USOC, and the Canadian Olympic Association (COA) immediately objected to Trudeau's actions. Killanin's ability as a diplomat momentarily prevailed, and a compromise was made with Trudeau. The ROC was permitted to participate under its own flag, but it would have to utilize the name Taiwan.[38] Despite these diplomatic efforts, however, a solution was not reached; the ROC refused to participate under the established conditions, and accordingly did not attend.[39] Although Killanin, the IOC, the COA, and Montreal organizers must have been relieved that the two-Chinas predicament did not flare up into a major boycott campaign, the Games were just beginning, and inevitably other political dilemmas would soon emerge.

The All Blacks as the New Target of the Anti-Apartheid Movement

The New Zealand Rugby and Football Union's (NZRFU) consideration of South African racial attitudes began in the 1920s. Throughout the century, many concessions would be made by the NZRFU, including the exclusion of Maori players,[40] in order to maintain the rugby rivalry that was so significant to both cultures.[41] In 1960, New Zealanders began to protest the compromises made by the NZRFU to continue rugby competition with South Africa. In 1965, New Zealand's rugby tour of South Africa was cancelled. Although South African president John Vorster allowed New Zealand to send coloured players on their 1970 tour, New Zealanders continued to protest, and the 1973–1974 tours were also cancelled.[42] It is generally contended that the cancelled tours hurt the Labour Party's position, and in 1975 the National Party of New Zealand was elected based partly on a campaign to renew rugby rivalries with South Africa. The All Blacks' tour of South Africa in 1976 set the stage for the international conflict that was conducted within the Olympic Movement.[43]

Throughout the 1960s and 1970s, the SCSA and other anti-apartheid organizations had become increasingly aggravated by the lack of involvement from the International Rugby Board (IRB) in any anti-apartheid endeavours to isolate South Africa athletically.[44] It was well known that rugby was the lifeblood of white South African sport. After South Africa was expelled from the Olympic movement, the continuation of international rugby competition became even more important to South African whites. Rugby soon became the principal focus of the anti-apartheid movement. New Zealand's status as a rugby world power and its history of competition with South Africa made it the primary target of opposition to rugby and apartheid policy.[45]

Triumph and Dismay: The Evolution of the African Boycott

After the expulsion of both South Africa (1970) and Rhodesia (1972) from the Olympic movement following the Munich Games, the IOC did not anticipate having to contend with apartheid or any other racial political issue at the 1976 Olympic Games in Montreal.[46] In June 1976, the All Blacks aroused dissent in the SCSA and other anti-apartheid organizations when they began a rugby tour of South Africa only days after the tragedy at Soweto, in which many black youths were killed.[47] The SCSA decided to try and utilize its newly found power in the form of black African unity to make a stand against apartheid and the sport that was most valued by white South Africans.

Only days before the opening ceremonies in Montreal, the scsa demanded that the ioc bar New Zealand from the Games. Even though ioc vice-president Mohammed Mzali of Tunisia identified twenty-six other nations that had sporting ties with South Africa, the scsa was determined to oust New Zealand from Montreal. Lord Killanin, who became president of the ioc in 1970, asserted that rugby was not an Olympic sport and that the ioc subsequently had no jurisdiction over test matches and tours.[48] Jean Claude Ganga, president of the scsa, approached the New Zealand delegation and requested the recall of its rugby team from competition in South Africa. The delegation informed Ganga that neither the New Zealand Olympic delegation nor the New Zealand government had control over the All Blacks. Ganga then requested that both the ioc and the New Zealand Olympic Committee make a joint condemnation of apartheid policy and the All Blacks' tour.[49] The proposal was rejected, and Killanin's original assertion was reiterated—rugby was not an Olympic sport. There was little left for the scsa to do except follow through on the boycott threat. The efforts of Ganga and Killanin were to no avail, and twenty-two black African nations departed Montreal.[50]

In total, twenty-six African nations boycotted the 1976 Olympic Games. The African boycott of Montreal saw more than a hundred African athletes depart in disappointment as their athletic aspirations were left shattered by the political agendas of their nocs and the scsa. The black African boycott also failed to achieve its two immediate objectives: the cancellation of the All Blacks' rugby tour of South Africa, and the expulsion of New Zealand from the Olympic movement.[51] Why would African nocs use their athletes and risk their Olympic involvement to forward political agendas? The answer to this question is certainly multi-faceted. The African Olympic delegations chose the Olympic boycott as their political weapon against South African apartheid for mainly one reason—the threat of the boycott had worked in the past. The threats to boycott in Mexico City and Munich were very effective. Not only was black Africa able to reveal its athletic ability on an international stage by competing in 1968 and 1972, its diplomatic power was also demonstrated, as it succeeded in ousting both South Africa and Rhodesia.[52] Even though the 1976 Olympic boycott is largely regarded as a costly tactical misjudgment, black Africa's attempt to manipulate the ioc into barring New Zealand and endorsing the anti-apartheid movement would have immediate and forthcoming ramifications.

Implications of the African Boycott:
New Zealand and South Africa

The trend of political involvement in the Olympic movement and the boycott paradigms that were established in Mexico City and Munich were perpetuated in Montreal. Although the 1976 African boycott failed to achieve its immediate objectives, it did not pass without repercussions in New Zealand. The nation's politics would become polarized over the issue of whether or not to continue sport relations with South Africa. Although the majority of New Zealanders supported the All Blacks' rugby tour, pro-testors began to organize large demonstrations against apartheid.[53] The 1981 tour of New Zealand by South Africa's national rugby team, the Springboks, would be the last for over a decade. As anti-apartheid protes-tors occupied the stadium, the tour's second match was suspended and the Springboks were sent home. No official rugby tours took place between 1981 and 1992.[54] The Montreal African boycott did have an impact on New Zealand's sport policy, as the government eventually took initiatives to end sporting ties with their long-time rugby rival.

Although the South African government and sport policy was not directly altered by the African boycott of the Montreal Olympic Games, two very important implications resulted from black Africa's unified anti-apartheid proclamation. First, the high profile of the Olympic Games ensured that the word "apartheid" appeared in many newspapers and on television broadcasts worldwide. This was significant in forming interna-tional consciousness regarding the anti-apartheid movement. As the world awakened to apartheid policy, opposition was the general response. Anti-apartheid campaigns began to evolve, and sport sanctions became an inte-gral component. Most notably, South Africa's isolation from international rugby became a major catalyst of change. In essence, "rugby was too important in the lives of too many white South Africans to be sacrificed completely."[55] The 1976 Olympic African boycott generated considerable international interest in the South African apartheid policy, and contributed to the evolving campaigns of opposition to it.

Second, the African-led boycott may have had a more direct implica-tion on the anti-apartheid campaign in South Africa. The united stand of black Africa was seen throughout the world. The perception of black Africa's willingness to sacrifice for the anti-apartheid cause in South Africa significantly raised the morale of the black youth protestors.[56] Even after the numerous devastating campaigns and rising fatalities, the show of sup-port from black Africa encouraged the non-white youth of the segregated townships to revive their protests. Anti-apartheid demonstrations by non-white youth did ensue after the Games, and the movement against apartheid policy was continued both within South Africa and around the globe.[57] The black African boycott of Montreal acted as an impetus for opposition against apartheid policy.

The history of sport sanctions against South Africa is complex and extensive. The very notion of South Africa's reluctance to change even under increasing pressure and international condemnation clearly illustrates how deep-rooted apartheid policy was in all aspects of the South African way of life. Even though the apartheid regime in South Africa was not dismantled until 1990, sport boycotts became effectual tools to isolate South African culture and encourage policy amendment. As noted by Douglas Booth, although it was evident that South African sport could not be depoliticized without fundamental governmental change,[58] the African boycott of Montreal and the sport sanctions that ensued were efforts to utilize sport as a means of changing government policy.

The constant struggle of South Africa to maintain links with the sporting world has been well documented throughout sport history. According to Shayne Quick, South Africa's struggle represents the most bitter conflict in Olympic history.[59] The period between the 1964 Tokyo Olympics and the 1976 Montreal Olympics was critical in the political and social battle against apartheid. The African boycott of the Montreal Olympic Games became much more than a symbol of black African unity. The implications of this unified stance extended much further than most predicted. The African boycott proclamation in Montreal clearly generated international consciousness for the anti-apartheid movement, and indirectly induced political and social change.

Apartheid policy was relinquished in the early 1990s, and South Africa subsequently returned to the Olympic Movement and other international sport competition. Unfortunately, dismantling apartheid did not create a racial panacea for South Africans. As a consequence of its own antecedents, South Africa remains very much a nation existing on the racial divide.[60] Negotiating the new South Africa is a daunting task, given that 350 years of history cannot be erased by any type of amendment—reminding us all that policy will always be easier to change than people.

Notes

1 Senn 1999, 165–67.
2 Booth 1998.
3 Neame 1962, 8.

4 Neame 1962, 11.

5 Neame 1962, 12.

6 Neame 1962, 14–15. At the end of the seventeenth century a rift developed between the individuals born on the Cape and monopolistic Dutch officials. Resentment grew as the Dutch officials began to enforce their authority over the colonizers. The Boers became both socially and geographically isolated from the Netherlands, and resented the constant influence on their daily lives. The Dutch, moreover, were preoccupied not just with this internal unrest, but with the invasion of the Netherlands by French Revolutionary armies. British forces utilized the timely circumstances to overrun the Dutch colony. Britain intended to use the colony for the same purposes as the Dutch, but, more importantly, wanted to discourage any Dutch presence in the East Indies.

7 Neame 1962, 17. With the increasing number of black slaves being integrated into the colony, regulations were established in 1685 forbidding interracial marriage. In the middle of the eighteenth century, as the Boers pressed further into the interior and Bantu tribes continued to migrate south, numerous altercations were recorded that later became known as the Kafir Wars. As a consequence, anti-intercourse laws were established that prohibited interaction between whites and any blacks that were not slaves.

8 Neame 1962, 19. This mass exodus of Afrikaners into the interior of South Africa changed the history of the nation. A number of reasons may have initiated the mass migration: insecurity of life, inadequate compensation for the loss of slaves, and the increasing British presence in government and culture. The division between the two white populations widened the gap that later would result in the Boer War (1899–1902).

9 Fatton, Jr., 1986, 47.

10 Neame 1962, 26. The Treaty of Vereeniging was signed on 31 May 1902. The treaty officially documented the annexation of the Transvaal and the Orange Free State (the two Boer republics), but failed to address the race policy question.

11 Neame 1962, 30. In a 1910 census, South Africa's population was 5,973,394, made up of 1,276,242 whites and 4,697,152 non-whites (4,019,006 Bantus, 152,203 Asians, and 525,943 Coloureds).

12 Booth 1998, 42. In 1924, General James Hertzog became prime minister as leader of the National Party, and reinforced a strict apartheid policy. Dr. D.F. Malan, Hertzog's Minister of the Interior, Education and Public Health, became prime minister in 1948 and perpetuated Nationalist Party apartheid—a word he had first used in 1947 to describe racial segregation policy. Both the United Party (official opposition) and the Labour Party also practised varying degrees of apartheid.

13 Booth 1998, 57.

14 Booth 1990.

15 Booth 1990, 157. See this source for further information regarding South African education, including legislative and administrative tactics to secure discriminatory sport.

16 Booth 1998, 71.

17 Booth 1998, 75.

18 Booth 1998, 58. In the early 1950s, the discovery of some examples of interracial sport forced the government to strictly reinforce apartheid in sport by creating specific legislation. A number of interracial soccer matches, and the medical determination that Ronnie van der Walt (the pride of South African boxing) was actually of coloured descent, acted as catalysts for the new legislation. The government sport policy reinforced in 1956 had a number of critical components: white and non-white athletes were to be separately organized; no mixed sport was allowed in South Africa; no mixed teams would be sent abroad; no mixed teams were to visit from abroad; non-white sport organizations were to seek recognition through white organizations; and the government could refuse travel visas to anyone who might campaign against South African sport policy. See Kanin 97.

19 Kanin 1981, 88. The South African Non-Racial Olympic Committee (SANROC) was established in 1962. Its intention was to eventually replace SANOC in the IOC. SANROC was accused of being involved with political matters outside of sport and the Olympics and consequently never achieved its objectives, but was successful at using sport to gain public awareness and international recognition. When SANROC president Dennis Brutus was shot in 1963 by the South African special police, it was widely suggested that the government wanted to silence any anti-apartheid sentiment. See Quick 1990, 27.

20 Kanin 1981, 99.

21 Quick 1990, 21. The IOC took notice of the South African sport issue well before 1960, as numerous National Olympic Committees (NOCs), including those of Norway and the Union of Soviet Socialist Republics (USSR), expressed their discontent with SANOC over its sport policy. The IOC's lack of appropriate action on the issue exasperated the concerned NOCs.

22 Kanin 1981, 99. Pretoria is South Africa's capital city and is often referred to when addressing issues of government national policy.

23 Kanin 1981, 99.

24 Booth 1998.

25 Quick 1990, 25.

26 Quick 1990, 23.

27 Quick 1990, 26. The SCSA was created as the sporting arm of the Organization of African Unity, which addressed any African concerns. The SCSA comprised thirty-two African nations and would have major significance in the development of African unity and the direction of the anti-apartheid movement through sport.

28 Quick 1990, 28.

29 Kanin 1981, 100.

30 Guttmann 1992, 132.

31 Harry Edwards's activities and events concerning the civil rights movement prior to Mexico City are more thoroughly documented in Wiggins (1989). The civil rights movement of black Americans was exemplified during the medal presentation for the 200-metre race at Mexico City, when two black Americans, Tommie Smith and John Carlos, displayed the Black Power symbol (raised gloved fist, bowed head) on the podium during the American anthem.

32 Guttmann 1984.

33 Guttmann 1992, 134.

34 Kanin 1981, 101.

35 Guttmann 1992, 135.

36 Kanin 1981, 102.

37 Senn 1999, 166. "Ping-pong diplomacy" refers to the 1971 visit of American table tennis athletes to mainland China in the hope that more important economic and political relations might be established as a result.

38 Macintosh and Hawes 1994, 68.

39 Kidd 1992, 158.

40 Nauright and Black 1999, 73. The Maori are the original Polynesian migrants who first settled in New Zealand. Through a number of successive waves of immigration between 1200 and 800 BCE, a large population was established. Although European settlement decreased their numbers through war and disease, Maoris represented approximately 12 per cent of the island's population in the 1960s.

41 Nauright and Black 1999, 74–75. The first sign of South Africa's divergent sport policy in international rugby competition with New Zealand was documented in the 1920s. New Zealand's national rugby team (known as the All Blacks because of the colour of their jerseys, not their skin), toured South Africa in 1928. The best All Black player of the 1920s, George Nepia, was excluded from the tour because of his Maori lineage.

42 Nauright and Black 1999, 76–79. Few objections arose to excluding Maoris from All Black
    tours of South Africa until 1960. At this point, the NZRFU's compliance with the South
    African requests of excluding Maoris from the tour became more difficult, as thousands
    of New Zealanders objected to the 1960 tour. The proposed All Black tour of 1965 was
    cancelled by the NZRFU following prime minister Keith Holyoake's announcement in Par-
    liament that New Zealand could not be "fully represented by a team chosen on racial
    lines." In 1966, after South African prime minister Hendrik Verwoerd was assassinated,
    John Vorster took over leadership. Vorster understood the importance of international
    rugby competition to the morale of white South Africans, so he made the decision to allow
    New Zealand to send three Maoris and a Samoan on the 1970 All Blacks' tour. Despite
    Vorster's decision, some New Zealanders continued to protest, and the 1973 and 1974
    tours were cancelled as a consequence.

43 Nauright and Black 1999, 75. The name All Blacks was coined by a reporter in 1905 dur-
    ing New Zealand's first official rugby tour of the British Isles. He thought the New
    Zealanders were so fast that they "appeared to be all blacks." The editor figured he
    was referring to their black uniforms, and so the name was created. For a detailed exam-
    ination of this tour, see Nauright 1991.

44 Nauright and Black 1999, 78. Throughout the 1960s and 1970s, the IRB failed to get
    involved in any anti-apartheid efforts to isolate South Africa athletically. The IRB con-
    sisted mainly of white-dominated societies: New Zealand, Australia, England, Scotland,
    Wales, Ireland, South Africa, and France.

45 Booth 1990, 163.

46 Booth 1990, 163.

47 Shearman 1977, 222. Scores of black youths, including children, were killed when a
    peaceful student march to protest education language policy turned into a violent con-
    frontation with police.

48 Macintosh, Cantelon, and McDermott 1993, 387.

49 Shearman 1977, 225.

50 Guttmann 1992, 145. A few days into the Games, and after already competing in some
    events, Cameroon, Egypt, Morocco, and Tunisia announced their intention to boycott
    and left the Games accordingly.

51 Kidd 1992, 164.

52 Quick 1990, 29.

53 Nauright and Black 1999, 83.

54 Booth 1990, 161. The actions of the Commonwealth heads of government also strongly
    encouraged New Zealand's government to discontinue sport relations with South Africa.
    In order to prevent any further boycotts of Canadian sport festivals, the Canadian gov-
    ernment, in conjunction with the Commonwealth governments, created the Gleneagles
    Agreement on apartheid and sport prior to the 1978 Commonwealth Games to be held
    in Edmonton. This declaration asked Commonwealth governments to discourage sport-
    ing contacts with South Africa. It became very effective at unifying Commonwealth
    nations in a collective anti-apartheid stance. The Gleneagles declaration was instrumen-
    tal in isolating South Africa from its traditional sporting opponents in the Commonwealth.
    See Macintosh, Greenhorn, and Black 38.

55 Nauright 1993, 73.

56 Shearman 1977, 228.

57 Fatton, Jr., 1986.

58 Booth 1990, 89.

59 Quick 1990, 29.

60 Merrett 2003.

Splitting Hairs: The Struggle between the Canadian Federal Government and the Organizing Committee of the 1976 Torontolympiad concerning South African Participation

David A. Greig

The hosting of the 1976 Olympiad for the Physically Disabled was awarded to Canada in 1972 at the Paralympic Games held in Heidelberg, Germany.[1] Four years later, 1,560 athletes representing 39 countries participated in the parade of nations at Woodbine Racetrack during the opening ceremonies of the Torontolympiad hosted by the Borough of Etobicoke in Toronto, Canada. The organizing committee, consisting of various volunteers and paid staff from the disabled sport system, as well as various levels of the provincial and municipal government, managed to deal with the logistical challenges posed by the world's largest disabled sports competition to date. With a budget of $2.5 million CDN, and the most accessible sports facilities in the world, the problems for the organizing committee did not result from the competitors' physical limitations, but from the Canadian federal government's foreign policy and the participation of a team from South Africa.

This chapter explores the struggle between the Canadian federal government and the organizing committee during the four years leading up to the staging of the 1976 Torontolympiad. Utilizing a historical narrative approach, a chronology of events and their key agents will unfold surrounding this critical period in the development of Canadian disabled sports. The sources utilized in this paper include primary documents found within the National Archives of Canada, the Province of Ontario Archives, and the personal archives of an organizing committee member, as well as an analysis of various newspaper archives, including the *Toronto Star* and *The Globe and Mail*.

In 1960, the International Stoke Mandeville Games (ISMG), a multi-sport festival for individuals with spinal cord injuries traditionally held in Stoke Mandeville, England, was moved to the site of the Olympic Games in Rome. The relocation of the ISMG signified the beginning of a parallel movement to the Olympic Games, now known as the Paralympics. The Rome Games were the first to take place in the same country and city as the Olympic Games—a practice that would eventually become standard. The Games saw four hundred disabled competitors from twenty-three nations participate in various events.[2] In 1964, Tokyo hosted the Games and used the Paralympic name for the first time, although at this time "para" stood for paraplegic, not parallel.[3]

Continuing with this pattern, the Paralympic Games should have been held in Mexico City in 1968, but the inability of the organizers to secure the support of their government, and the subsequent health concerns regarding the altitude of the venue, saw the games staged in Ramat Gan, near Tel Aviv, Israel.[4] At the games in Israel, 750 athletes from 29 countries gathered for the competition. Due to a lack of accessibility in the athletes' village, the 1972 Games were held not in the Olympic host city of Munich but in Heidelberg, Germany, in the weeks preceding the able-bodied Olympic Games. The event marked the first time the count reached one thousand participants, representing the combined total of participants from forty-four countries. With the Games of the Fifth Paralympiad awarded to Canada, organizers had their sights set on hosting the most inclusive and largest Games ever.

In Canada, the first organized disabled sports competition occurred in 1947 at the Deer Lodge Hospital in Winnipeg, Manitoba.[5] The first disabled sport, wheelchair basketball, began its development in 1951. In 1956 the Montreal Wheelchair Wonders travelled to England to compete in the ISMG, becoming the first Canadian disabled sport team to compete at an international multi-sport festival.[6] The 1950s and '60s can be characterized as a period of rapid growth as wheelchair clubs began to pop up in major Canadian centres, including Saskatoon, Edmonton, and Toronto. Despite the rapid development, most clubs during the mid-1950s were quick to dissolve due to a lack of transportation and administration.[7]

The 1960s witnessed an increase in competitive opportunities for individuals with disabilities with the first interprovincial games in Saskatoon in 1962 and the first Canadian athlete sent to the Second Commonwealth Games for the Physically Disabled in Jamaica in 1966.[8] In 1967, building upon this growth, Winnipeg hosted six other countries at the inaugural Pan-American Wheelchair Games. That year also marked the birth of the Canadian Wheelchair Sports Association, Canada's first national disabled sport organization. The beginning of what would become the annual Canadian National Wheelchair Games took place the following year. The wheelchair festival was hosted by cities across Canada until 1976, when it was renamed the Canada Games for the Physically Disabled. Along with the new name, the competition was opened up to athletes with various disabilities.[9]

The individual credited with bringing the Paralympic Games to Canada was Dr. Robert Jackson, a surgeon living in Toronto, Ontario. Serving as the chairman of the organizing committee, Jackson had a significant impact on the Games and fought to ensure the participation of as many countries as possible. As he assembled his organizing committee, he also sought support from the municipal, provincial, and federal levels of government. Skepticism by government officials towards the legitimacy of the games was evident upon initial receipt of the idea, due in part to the fact that Jackson had neither contacted Sport Canada nor arranged a bid proposal prior to committing Canada as a potential host country.[10] As a result of further meetings and debate in 1974, $500,000 in funding was first committed by the Municipality of Metropolitan Toronto on 18 July, followed by the federal government on 18 October, and lastly by the Ontario provincial government on 23 December 1974.[11] With commitments from all three levels of government, the total contributions towards the staging of the Torontolympiad reached $1.5 million CDN.

Despite the initial support, it became apparent—only a few years after Canada was awarded the Olympiad for the Physically Disabled—that the hosting of the Games was not going to be an easy task. A statement on 27 May 1974 by the Minister of Health and Welfare, Marc Lalonde, was released by the federal government, informing all sport federations that the government would not fund athletes travelling to South Africa due to its apartheid practices. This statement raised concern for the Torontolympiad organizing committee. Apartheid in South Africa had been a point of contention since the 1950s. With its practices of racial segregation and discrimination, the country was seen as being "possessed by the cancer of apartheid."[12] Governed by a white minority whose power resided in their command of resources and the subordination of the black majority, sport in South Africa was organized along multinational rather than multi-racial lines. According to South African Prime Minister John Vorster, South Africa was a country containing separate nations–white, coloured, Zulu, Xhosa, Tswana, and Shangaan, among others—which were to develop separately and in isolation from one another.[13] This approach was strongly condemned by the international community. When the attention of the United Nations (UN) focused on South Africa in the early 1970s, Canada, predictably, as a result of its UN membership, reinforced the stance of disapproval of the apartheid practices.[14]

With the hosting of the upcoming 1976 Olympic Games and the 1978 Commonwealth Games, the Canadian government was feeling the pressure to develop some type of official policy that it could fall back upon when questioned about the South African issue. The policy of not tolerating any form of racial bias was being scrutinized in the House of Commons, given the widespread belief that "the sooner apartheid ends in South Africa the better the world will be."[15]

Discussion at a Torontolympiad organizing committee executive meeting on 9 August 1974 focused on the expulsion of South Africa by the International Olympic Committee and the fact that South Africa was not barred by the International Stoke Mandeville Games Federation (ISMGF), the international sanctioning body for the Torontolympiad. The result was an inquiry regarding South African participation at the Games in Etobicoke.[16] Recognizing a potential for conflict, Jackson contacted Marc Lalonde, asking whether the federal government policy would apply to the Torontolympiad.[17] A reply in writing came from Lalonde on 21 November 1974, informing Jackson that the presence of a South African team at the Olympiad for the Physically Disabled would have embarrassing repercussions for the Torontolympiad. Lalonde urged the organizing committee not to invite the South Africans.[18] In turn, at a management committee meeting of the Torontolympiad organizing committee on 9 December 1974, it was decided that "no invitations...shall be sent out to countries until certain political problems and problems concerning the parent body of the 1976 Olympiad for the Physically Disabled are resolved."[19]

There would be no new progress regarding the issue until an Olympiad organizing committee management meeting on 7 April 1975. At this meeting, discussion resulted in the scheduling of a special meeting between Jackson, Torontolympiad executive director Richard Loiselle, and the Canadian Department of External Affairs.[20] From an External Affairs point of view, Jackson was informed that an invitation to South Africa would not reflect the stance of the federal government.[21] At a subsequent management committee meeting on 5 May 1975, however, the report brought forth from the meeting with External Affairs indicated that "after some discussions, it was agreed that an invitation be sent to South Africa stating they would be most welcome provided they had integrated trials and sent an integrated team to Canada," a position that seemed to differ from that stated by the federal government.[22]

On 20 June 1975, a letter sent by Dr. Jackson to South African officials informed their disabled sport governing body that if they were prepared to send an integrated team to the Torontolympiad, the Department of External Affairs would make a decision on whether or not to issue visas to the team. This decision depended upon the selection procedure and makeup of the team—if it was not selected on a totally integrated basis, then visas might not be issued.[23] In response to Dr. Jackson's letter, officials from External Affairs informed the organizing committee of the potential for a withdrawal of Canadian government funding if a South African team were included in the Torontolympiad.[24]

In order to bring about greater consistency in the policy regarding sporting contacts with South Africa, the government formally took the position that it could not fund events in Canada to which South African participants were invited. Lalonde reaffirmed the federal government's policy through letters to all sports federations, including the Torontolympiad. On 25 September 1975, Dr. Jackson wrote Lalonde, seeking a direct audience to request that the Torontolympiad be exempted from the policy.[25] Dr. Jackson's logic behind such a claim lay in his belief that the South African team was fully integrated. Jackson had written proof from the South African Minister of Sport, and the full support of Sir Ludwig Guttmann, president of both the ISMGF and the International Sports Organization for the Disabled (ISOD). Guttmann happened to be in Canada touring Centennial Park, the host site in Etobicoke, at the time. In a letter of reply, Lalonde claimed that evidence presented did not warrant modification to the policy, citing that the integration of a single federation was not "indicative of any fundamental change in the policy and practice of racial discrimination in South African sports."[26] The position taken by the federal government was further solidified on 28 November 1975, when Canada co-sponsored a United Nations resolution against apartheid in sport. The UN resolution called upon all governments, sports bodies and other organizations "to refrain from all contacts with sports bodies established on the basis of apartheid or racially selected sports teams from South Africa." The resolution also stated in section 4 that it "commends all sports bodies and sportsmen in South Africa which have been struggling against racism in sports."[27] Jackson claimed that the organizers fully agreed with the resolution, but the problem lay in the attempt of the organizing committees to implement section 4 by including an integrated team of black and white athletes at the Torontolympiad.

A series of letters sent by Jackson on 17 December 1975 outlined the position of the Torontolympiad in relation to that of the Canadian federal government. In one letter addressed to the Department of National Health and Welfare, he indicated that "the organizing committee for the 1976 Torontolympiad will accept the government's posture regarding South Africa's participation and will proceed to inform the South African organizers that, as of the present time, they will be unable to participate in the Olympiad."[28] A similar letter to the Department of External Affairs indicated that South African officials were being notified that their athletes would not be able to participate, yet still continuing with his belief that the South African team had broken through the barriers of apartheid, Dr. Jackson requested special consideration for the sportsmen and women of South Africa.[29] A final letter from Jackson to the South African representative, Mike Marcus, outlined the reasons why the South Africans could not compete at the Torontolympiad.[30]

Wanting to put an end to the South African ordeal, Secretary of State for External Affairs Allan J. MacEachen replied to Dr. Jackson's letter on 8 January 1976, stating that upon careful examination of the material presented, "I do not consider that the material represents sufficient evidence to justify a modification of this Government's policy in your case."[31] Lalonde also replied to Dr. Jackson's letter and set a deadline of 15 April 1976 for the organizing committee to indicate that the South African team was formally uninvited—or else, he warned, federal funding would be withdrawn.[32] Upon receipt of the South African entries on 28 January 1976, Jackson replied to Menzo Barrish, national vice-chairman and administrative manager of disabled sports in South Africa, stating that "we are prevented from accepting your entries, and are returning them."[33] At this juncture, there was to be no South African participation at the 1976 Olympiad for the Physically Disabled.

Support for the pro-South Africa position of the Torontolympiad organizing committee was growing as Dr. Philip Jones, chairman of Sport Ontario, brought to light his concerns in a letter sent to Prime Minister Pierre Elliott Trudeau. Another letter of concern was addressed to the Prime Minister by Donald E. Corren, executive director of the Canadian Paraplegia Association.[34]

As the debate concerning South African acceptance raged between the organizing committee and the federal government, the municipal and provincial levels of government prepared for the worst-case scenario. On 6 April 1976, a recommendation was presented at Metro Toronto Council to alter their original agreement, since the federal government had indicated that it did not wish to continue its funding.[35] At the provincial level, a letter of 9 April 1976 from the Minister of Culture and Recreation, Robert Welch, to Dr. Jackson regarding the Province of Ontario's financial contribution showed the support of the government. The province's contribution, at that time totalling $465,000, indicated its "continued support of this most worthwhile event." Welch went on: "I can appreciate your wishes to see an integrated South African team, and will await with interest news of any further developments on this subject."[36]

The 15 April deadline set by Lalonde passed without any incident or indication of the position of either side. On 6 May 1976, Lalonde gave Dr. Jackson a final deadline of 15 May to confirm that there would be no team from South Africa invited in order to maintain federal financing. As a result of Dr. Jackson's persuasion, the deadline was pushed back to wait for a decision until after the 27–29 April meeting of the Supreme Council for Sport in Africa, where it was to be determined whether the South African team was integrated or not. Despite Dr. Jackson's hope, this issue never came to light at the meeting.

On 11 May 1976, M.P. Otto Jelinek, "referring to the obviously abrupt attitude the Department of National Health and Welfare has taken in respect of the 1976 Olympiad for the Physically Disabled," placed pressure on Lalonde during House of Commons debate.[37] It was "a hypocritically double standard position," asserted Jelinek, since the government was refusing funding to athletes and events with South Africans present, yet at the same time it had "[allowed] Canadian businessmen to import approximately $180 million worth of South African goods" in the previous year, which "nobody has complained about."[38] Jelinek concluded by offering thanks "to this two-faced government for jeopardizing the dreams and hopes of nearly 2000 wheelchair, blind, and amputee athletes from around the world."[39] The response from Lalonde failed to deny or even address the double standard. Claiming that the federal government had thrown its support behind the Torontolympiad from the beginning and that the organizing committee was aware of the position held by the government, Lalonde broached the Canadian policies regarding apartheid and sport presented over the past two years, revealing that "the government has reviewed on a continuing basis reports from our mission in South Africa on apartheid in sports. We do not believe that circumstances in this country have changed materially, even though the South African government may allow modification in a particular case."[40] In short, the only way the federal government would support the Torontolympiad would be if there were no South African team participating. The view of the government towards the integrated team put forth by South Africa was that it was a mere show of tokenism.

An Olympiad management committee meeting on 12 May 1976 was the site of the monumental decision that would solidify the stance of the Torontolympiad organizing committee once and for all. At first, Tom Riley moved for the committee to inform the federal government that the Torontolympiad would go it alone, without their support. After some discussion this motion was withdrawn. It was then moved by executive committee member and Torontolympiad legal advisor Steve Posen that the entry forms of the integrated South African team be accepted. Management committee member and chair of finance Jim McMahon seconded this motion.[41] This decision ensured the withdrawal of Canadian federal government moral and financial support from the Games, thus placing Ontario as the senior level of government involved as sponsor of the Games.

"To hell with the federal government!" was the rallying statement by Jim McMahon at a 19 May 1976 press conference held by the Torontolympiad organizing committee.[42] Dr. Jackson also voiced his opinion: "If the government seeks to effect changes [in South Africa], surely this can be done through business, not through people. It's a form of financial blackmail."[43] Now $500,000 short of their fundraising goal, organizers turned to the public for funding assistance. The organizing committee had hopes of selling three thousand executive passes at $100 apiece, plus a myriad of souvenir products, including T-shirts, pens, and pins sold prior to and at the Games.[44] An optimistic Jim McMahon claimed that "all it will take is $10.00 from 50,000 Canadians and Canada will support the games without the feds."[45] The organizing committee was assured that the Games would go on by the executive of the ISOD and that any deficit would be assumed by its richer member nations.[46]

Days prior to the opening of the Torontolympiad, a news release on 28 July 1976 from Health and Welfare Canada outlined the intentions of the federal government to devote the funds destined for the 1976 Olympiad to sports and physical recreation activities for Canada's handicapped. Due to the withdrawal of Canadian government funds, the 1976 Olympiad for the Physically Disabled was the first Paralympic festival to be affected by political pressures. Although the Canadian federal government withdrew its funding, it did not deny the South African team visas. As a result of the decision to accept the South African team, many countries expressed their displeasure by participating in a formal boycott of the Games. Teams from Jamaica, India, Hungary, Poland, Yugoslavia, Sudan, Uganda, and Kenya withdrew from the games.[47] At an international level, Sir Ludwig Guttmann, the ISMGF, and ISOD viewed the South Africa issue and boycott as political blackmail.[48] Although the South African issue resulted in both positive and negative media attention to the Games, it drew in the support of the community in the form of donations and spectators.

The differences between the Torontolympiad organizing committee and the Canadian federal government were seen as unjustified by Jackson. He felt that the inability of the federal government to see that the South African team was integrated as early as two years prior to the UN resolution, and its failure to send an observer to the multi-racial trials, facilitated a lack of complete and thorough understanding of the situation. The federal government also conceded that although disabled sports might be integrated, this really did not represent a significant change in the outlook of the country. A lack of vision in recognizing the greater significance of the Torontolympiad in terms of rehabilitation for the disabled, and the opportunity to demonstrate the abilities of its participants, was apparent on the part of the federal government. Lastly, Jackson claimed that the commendation towards groups fighting to break apartheid, as outlined in the UN resolution of 1975, seemed to be only a verbal commendation; those who had succeeded in fighting apartheid were still denied the opportunity to participate by the federal government.[49] The federal government viewed the integration of the South African team as a cosmetic manoeuvre, and not indicative of any fundamental change in the application of apartheid policies and practices. Due to "overwhelming evidence" that South African sport was still fraught with racially discriminatory policies and practices, the federal government felt that the isolated instance of the 1976 Olympiad for the Physically Disabled did not justify any alteration of Canadian policy.[50] In hindsight, the boycott issue, although causing great stress and tension between the Torontolympiad organizing committee and the Canadian government, generated substantial interest in the Games, and was far more helpful than harmful to the 1976 Olympiad for the Physically Disabled.[51]

Notes

1   Memo to Dr. J.D. Plock, chief executive officer, Office of the Premier of Ontario, from D.R. Martyn, executive director, Community Services Division, regarding communication to the Premier of Ontario from G.J. Way, executive director of the International Stoke Mandeville Games, concerning the support of the provincial government and outlining

the games, 9 February 1973, Archives of Ontario, *1976 Olympiad for the Disabled*, RG 65–16, Box 10, File: '76 *Olympiad for Phys/Disabled 1972–1974* [hereinafter Memo to Dr. J.D. Plock from D.R. Martyn].

2 International Paralympic Committee, "Paralympic Summer Games," Bonn, Germany, 2002, retrieved from http://www.paralympic.org 4 February 2003.

3 Although utilizing the name Paralympics for the first time in 1964, when the ISMG was hosted by Tokyo, the Paralympic name, as used today, was not adopted until 1985. See Jackson and Fredrickson 1979, 293–96.

4 There is conflict in the literature regarding the reasons that Mexico did not host the Games. Jackson and Fredrickson note that there was a lack of governmental support, whereas Allan Ryan and David Legg claim altitude as the reason for Mexico's inability to host the 1968 Games. Sir Ludwig Guttmann cites a lack of ability to accommodate individuals with disabilities. See Ryan 1976, 133,135,137; Legg 2000, 265; Guttmann 1976, 34.

5 Legg 2000, 260; Gregson 1999, 108; Loiselle 1973, 12. Loiselle cites the *Winnipeg Free Press*, June 12, 1947, as providing reference for this event.

6 Loiselle 1973, 15. In 1954, organized competition came into being as a demand for the organization of programs and coaching increased. Wheelchair basketball was the first sport focused on the participation of individuals with spinal cord injuries to catch on in Canada. In 1951, a Vancouver automobile dealer, Dueck Chevrolet Oldsmobile, sponsored a wheelchair basketball team called the Dueck Powerglides. Douglas Mowat, a quadriplegic himself, managed the team, which was coached by Norman Watt of the University of British Columbia. Along with another team from Victoria, and two American teams, the Powerglides formed the Pacific Northwest Wheelchair Basketball league. Meanwhile, across the country, organizer William Hepburn and coach Harold Rabin took the initiative to formalize a group of war veterans and created a team called the Montreal Wheelchair Wonders. The Wonders participated in the U.S. National Wheelchair Basketball Tournament in New York, and subsequently became aware of the Stoke Mandeville Games. In 1956, they travelled to England to compete in the Games against teams from England, France, Finland, Israel, and the Netherlands.

7 Loiselle 1973, 15.

8 Loiselle 1973, 79.

9 An exception to the annual nature of these Games occurred in 1970, when a lack of funds on the part of the CWSA resulted in two regional festivals, not one national championship.

10 Memo to Dr. J.D. Plock from D.R. Martyn.

11 Archives of Ontario, *1976 Olympiad for the Disabled*, RG 65–16, Box 10, File: '76 *Olympiad for Phys/Disabled 1972–1974*.

12 Information Canada, *United Nations, Foreign Policy for Canadians* (Ottawa, 1970), p. 18.

13 National Archives of Canada, MG 32, Box 35, Vol 175, File 10: *Handicapped Sports and Recreation 1976–1979* [hereinafter National Archives of Canada, File 10].

14 See Information Canada, *United Nations, Foreign Policy for Canadians* (Ottawa, 1970), p. 18; Information Canada, *Report of the Department of External Affairs* (Ottawa, 1959), p. 3.

15 Canada, *House of Commons Debates*, Third Session, 25 November 1971, p. 9912.

16 Minutes—executive committee meeting, 9 August 1974. Archives of Ontario, RG 65–16, Box 10, File: '76 *Olympiad for the Phys/Disabled 1972–1974*.

17 National Archives of Canada, File 10.

18 National Archives of Canada, File 10.

19 Archives of Ontario, RG 65–16, Box 10, File: *1975 Correspondence 76 Olympiad for the Disabled* [hereinafter Archives of Ontario, File: *1975 Correspondence*].

20 Archives of Ontario, File: *1975 Correspondence.*

21 National Archives of Canada, File 10.

22 Minutes—Management Committee meeting, 5 May 1975, Archives of Ontario, RG 65–16, Box 10, File: *1975 Correspondence 76 Olympiad for the Disabled.*

23 Minutes—Management Committee meeting, 2 July 1975, Archives of Ontario, RG 65–16, Box 10, File: *1975 Correspondence Olympiad for the Disabled.* See also Memorandum to Prime Minister Pierre Elliott Trudeau and all Cabinet ministers and members of Caucus from Norm Cafik, M.P., 29 June 1976, National Archives of Canada, MG 32 B 35 Vol 175 File 10: *Handicapped Sports and Recreation 1976–1979* [hereinafter Cafik memo, National Archives of Canada, File 10].

24 National Archives of Canada, File 10.

25 Cafik memo, National Archives of Canada, File 10.

26 National Archives of Canada, File 10.

27 Press release by the 1976 Olympiad for the Physically Disabled, 19 May 1976, Archives of Ontario, RG 65–16 Box 10, *1976 Olympiad for the Physically Disabled, August 3–11, 1976 Information Kit.*

28 Cafik memo, National Archives of Canada, File 10.

29 Cafik memo, National Archives of Canada, File 10.

30 Archives of Ontario, File: *1975 Correspondence.*

31 Letter to Dr. Jackson from Allan J. MacEachen, 8 January 1976, Archives of Ontario. RG 65–16, Box 10, File: *Olympiad for the Physically Disabled.*

32 Cafik memo, National Archives of Canada, File 10.

33 Letter to Mr. Barrish from Dr. Jackson, 9 February 1976, Archives of Ontario, RG 65–16, Box 10, File: *Olympiad for the Physically Disabled.*

34 Pro-South African letters of support were sent by Dr. Philip Jones, chairman of Sport Ontario, on 10 March 1976, and by Donald E. Corren, executive director of the Canadian Paraplegia Association, on 5 July 1976.

35 Municipality of Metropolitan Toronto council minutes, 6 April 1976, Appendix A, p. 123.

36 Letter from Robert Welch to Dr. Jackson, 9 April 1976, Archives of Ontario, RG 65–16, Box 10, File: *Olympiad for the Physically Disabled.*

37 Canada, *House of Commons Debates*, 11 May 1976, p. 13427.

38 Canada, *House of Commons Debates*, 11 May 1976, p. 13427. Brackets mine.

39 Canada, *House of Commons Debates*, 11 May 1976, p. 13427.

40 Canada, *House of Commons Debates*, 11 May 1976, 13428.

41 Minutes—Management committee meeting, 12 May 1976, Archives of Ontario, RG 65–16, Box 10, File: *Olympiad for the Physically Disabled.*

42 Jim Kernaghan, "Olympiad officials go to public to obtain much-needed funds," *Toronto Star*, 20 May 1976, p. C2; Nora McCabe, "Organizers of Disabled Olympiad defy Ottawa," *Globe and Mail*, 20 May 1976, p. 50.

43 Kernaghan 1976.

44 Kernaghan 1976.

45 McCabe 1976.

46 McCabe 1976; Kernaghan 1976.

47 Legg 2000, 214.

48 Guttmann 1976, 234.

49 Archives of Ontario, RG 65–16, Box 10, File: *1976 Olympiad for Physically Disabled, August 3–11, 1976, Information Kit.*

50 Cafik memo, National Archives of Canada, File 10.

51 Jackson 1977, 69; Organizing Committee, Torontolympiad 1976, 1977.

Juan Antonio Samaranch's Score Sheet: Revenue Generation and the Olympic Movement, 1980-2001

Stephen R. Wenn
Scott G. Martyn

In July 2001, Jacques Rogge, an orthopaedic surgeon and three-time Olympian from Belgium, contemplated the path before him. At the Moscow session of the International Olympic Committee (IOC), Rogge emerged victorious in a five-person contest for the right to succeed Spain's Juan Antonio Samaranch as president of the IOC. Numerous challenges deserved a place on his presidential agenda. Doping, gigantism, elevating the involvement of women in Olympic decision-making, recovering some of the organization's lustre lost as a result of the Salt Lake City scandal, and pushing Greek organizers to implement an aggressive timetable concerning the construction of needed facilities for the 2004 Summer Olympics—all of these required attention. One thing that Rogge did not have to concern himself with, however, was the development of a revenue generation program to support the rapidly expanding Olympic movement. His predecessor, with a push from Horst Dassler, head of the worldwide Adidas empire, and assistance from Canada's Richard Pound and the IOC's marketing director, Michael Payne, had addressed that matter in the 1980s and 1990s.[1]

This chapter, based on IOC archival records, examines Samaranch's approach to generating revenue from television rights sales and a worldwide corporate sponsorship program. Samaranch's policies and methods assisted in underwriting the financial needs of the IOC, Olympic Games organizing committees (OCOGs), and the IOC's Olympic tripartite partners, the international sport federations (ISFs) and national Olympic committees (NOCs). This analysis will be buttressed by an exploration of developments in the Olympic world, some positive, some negative, that Samaranch's revenue generation program wrought. In short, Samaranch's efforts to expand both the IOC's revenue base and the Olympic movement's profile proved wildly successful. Managing this success posed a greater challenge.

Television

The IOC experienced a steep learning curve on television negotiations protocol and execution during the latter years of Avery Brundage's presidency and throughout Lord Killanin's tenure in the 1970s. Successive organizing committees, faced with the challenge of staging Olympic festivals with increasing numbers of events and athletes, and consumed by a desire to outdo their immediate predecessors, eyed television revenue as a means of offsetting burgeoning capital expenses. Brundage avoided conflict with the organizing committees by ceding the vast majority of television money to them.[2] However, the fiscal designs of the ISFs and NOCs forced Brundage and the IOC to establish a formal distribution method. The "Rome Formula," the organization's first formal policy for disbursing television revenue, was approved by the IOC's General Session in 1966 and provided organizing committees with two thirds of accrued television revenue.[3] The remaining money was shared by the IOC, ISFs, and NOCs. The policy satisfied few, and left Lord Killanin to deal with organizing committees that flouted IOC regulations in the 1970s in their search for more money. Killanin concluded accurately that averting this aggravation in the future necessitated taking a "hands on" approach in the negotiations process, rather than ceding the privilege of negotiating the contracts to the organizing committees, as had been Brundage's practice.[4]

Juan Antonio Samaranch inherited three problems related to the television portfolio. Monique Berlioux was acting as the IOC's point person in negotiations upon his arrival in Lausanne. While she provided valuable service in this area in the 1970s, the negotiations environment evolved beyond her level of expertise. Yet this reality represented only one reason for his decision to replace her with Canada's Richard Pound in 1983. Samaranch concluded that Berlioux's power base in Lausanne extended too far.[5] Second, he inherited Killanin's policy of joint negotiation of television contracts. This policy mandated that the IOC and organizing committees collaborate on the negotiation of television contracts with television network executives.[6] Organizing committees proved less than willing to concede any measure of authority previously granted to them in the negotiations arena. Samaranch, along with his new right hand in television matters, Pound, soon abandoned joint negotiation in favour of complete IOC control of television negotiations (a policy first employed for the 1992 Albertville/Barcelona cycle).[7] Third, the IOC's dependence on television revenue for more than 90 per cent of its yearly operating budget concerned the new president.[8] He explored the possibility of marketing the Olympic rings and the Olympic mystique for financial gain via an additional revenue stream—corporate sponsorship.

One driving thought guided Samaranch in his approach to Olympic television matters throughout the 1980s—how could the status of the Olympic Games as the pre-eminent sport spectacle in the world be secured and maintained? In terms of securing this status, Samaranch and the IOC required an attractive and marketable commodity. Yet he was confronted by world geopolitical baggage and boycotts of the 1970s and early 1980s, and persistent questions about the relevance and purpose of the Games from sizable segments of the world's media. Both the growing profiles of the World Cup (soccer) and the World Track and Field Championships, and the challenge to the status of the IOC's principal sport commodity from U.S. media tycoon Ted Turner and his Goodwill Games project in the mid-1980s, concerned him.[9] His desire to "grow" the Olympic movement and assist with the financial needs of member organizations also contributed to his policy approach.

How could Samaranch realize his desire for an attractive and marketable commodity? First, with diplomatic aplomb and patience, reflecting his past position as Spain's ambassador to the Soviet Union, he cajoled his IOC colleagues into opening up the Olympic Games to professional athletes. He reasoned that professional athletes competing in the Olympic arena, especially U.S. athletes, would drive the value of the Olympics as a television sports property even higher in the U.S. marketplace, enhance viewership, and further the Games' reputation as the pinnacle of sporting competition. Second, the IOC's ability to manage its growing responsibilities in overseeing two Olympic festivals on a quadrennial basis pushed IOC officials to stagger the two festivals on a biennial basis.[10] This decision had three positive results. Television money flowed into the Olympic movement's coffers on a steady basis, and Olympic media coverage occurred on a more regular basis. Media attention was not limited to the saturated coverage seen in previous Olympic years. It also freed up major television networks to focus on covering one festival rather than possibly stretching their resources and personnel to televise two mega-events in one year.

There is little doubt that Samaranch's agenda paid dividends. The Olympics emerged as an attractive and marketable commodity. The value of Olympic television rights soared, especially in the United States, and the number of countries whose citizens could view the Olympic spectacle increased. These positive developments created a significant opportunity on the television front for Samaranch in the 1990s.

The American Broadcasting Corporation (ABC), through the vision and commitment of its president of sports, the late Roone Arledge, established its reputation as "America's Olympic Network" in the 1960s, a reputation that extended through the 1970s and 1980s.[11] ABC's interest in the Olympics as a television property waned following the negotiations for the U.S. television rights to the 1988 Calgary Olympic Winter Games. ABC outbid its rivals, the National Broadcasting Company (NBC) and the Columbia Broadcasting System (CBS), with an offer of $309 million, but its representatives resented the negotiations process devised by Pound and Calgary organizers.[12] Arledge and other U.S. network officials charged that they were being asked "top dollar" for Olympic television rights, while their European counterparts, representing the European Broadcasting Union (EBU), were protected by Samaranch, who maintained control of the European negotiations and refused to consider rival bids from emerging private networks.

The charge had merit. Samaranch did not exact maximum payment from EBU. He defended this approach by highlighting its government-sponsored status, and the fact that no other television entity could provide blanket coverage on the European continent.[13] ABC's loss of more than $60 million on the Calgary project, and the company's sale to Capital Cities Communications, opened the exit door for ABC from the U.S. Olympic television negotiations environment. For a number of years in the late 1980s and early 1990s, CBS (Albertville/Lillehammer/Nagano) and NBC (Seoul/Barcelona/Atlanta) acquired successive Winter and Summer Olympics television properties. Then, in 1995, NBC's president of sports, Dick Ebersol, presented Samaranch with a proposal that he could not refuse.

Ebersol offered the IOC $1.25 billion for the U.S. rights to the 2000 Sydney and 2002 Salt Lake City festivals, but the offer was time sensitive and could not be discussed with either ABC, CBS, or the new player on the U.S. scene, FOX Television. Would the IOC be better advised to "go to the market" for each Olympic festival or look at a package deal that might provide a measure of financial security for the Olympic movement? Samaranch and Pound concluded that Ebersol's offer was too good to pass up.[14] Within months, Pound and Ebersol concluded a second set of discussions on a plan to sell the U.S. Olympic television rights for 2004, 2006, and 2008 to NBC.

Labelled by the two parties as the "Sunset Project," this dialogue resulted in a $2.3 billion agreement.[15] With this negotiations template in place, the IOC secured similar long-term television agreements in the world's other major television markets in 1996 and 1997. While NBC's rivals were not pleased, the IOC's decision proved wise. First, television money available to future organizing committees (through 2008) was known, and bid committees could employ this information in a more realistic cost planning process during bid competitions. Second, the IOC's budgeting process was assisted because the planners fully understood available revenue from television in the medium term. Third, when the Salt Lake City scandal burst forth on the Olympic scene in late 1998, television contracts were in place, and IOC officials were not forced to deal with a compromised negotiating environment for upcoming festivals.

The Sunset Project also brought a simmering dispute between the IOC and the United States Olympic Committee (USOC) concerning television revenue to a conclusion. In 1985, the USOC claimed a 20 per cent share of U.S. television revenue in light of its exclusive authority over the use of the Olympic five-ring logo in U.S. territory.[16] The U.S. government granted ownership of this logo to the USOC in 1978 via federal statute (the Amateur Sports Act). If the USOC did not receive a 20 per cent share of future Olympic television revenue, officials threatened to preclude the use of the five-ring logo by commercial advertisers on Olympic television broadcasts in 1988, and would prevent the U.S. Olympic television network(s) from using the rings in a promotional composite logo. Without these heretofore assigned privileges, the U.S. networks would submit reduced bids for future Olympic television rights.

Samaranch delegated Pound to deal with the USOC, and within a few months, an agreement was reached. The Broadcast Marketing Agreement (BMA), signed by the IOC and the USOC in March 1986, provided $15 million to the USOC for 1988 (a payment shared equally by the IOC and the Calgary and Seoul organizing committees), and 10 per cent of all future U.S. Olympic television contracts, in exchange for the USOC waiving its exclusive use of the logo in U.S. territory.[17] The USOC settled for this arrangement, but did not dispense with its desire for a 20 per cent share in the late 1980s. Pound was not inclined to shift the percentage, and these discussions ended in stalemate.

In 1990, and again on the heels of the Sunset Project negotiations, the USOC attempted to gain control of U.S. Olympic television negotiations via legislation on Capitol Hill.[18] The USOC grew restive as a result of Pound's unwillingness to review the USOC's 10 per cent share. While the 1990 episode could be interpreted as a "shot across the bow" for the IOC, the USOC's efforts in 1996 posed more of a threat. One of the reasons Pound supported moving forward with the Sunset Project initiative was that in 1995, at the time of his discussions with Ebersol, the USOC was still restricted to a 10 per cent share. When the USOC learned of the IOC's activities, it threatened to withhold USOC approval of the second contract until its percentage share had been altered. Pound was unmoved. USOC officials approached Samaranch for redress. While he appeared amenable to shifting the USOC's share to 15 per cent, the USOC, in clandestine fashion, moved forward through a proposed Senate bill to assume control of U.S. Olympic television rights negotiations. If the USOC controlled negotiations, it could establish its own percentage share. The USOC's activities were noticed by an NBC official in Washington, and were duly reported to Lausanne.[19]

In Samaranch's mind, it was one thing for the USOC to tangle with Richard Pound; it was something else for the USOC to work behind *his* back during face-to-face negotiations. Samaranch convened a meeting of senior IOC officials and representatives of the USOC in Mexico in October 1996 as a means of reining in the USOC and settling the issue. The USOC was granted 12.75 per cent of the U.S. television contract beginning in 2004, an arrangement covering the Sunset Project negotiations, phased in at the same time that the Olympic movement's share of Olympic television revenue shifted from 40 per cent to 51 per cent.[20] While the USOC's tactics failed to generate its desired 20 per cent, or even 15 per cent, the organization did get something more than 10 per cent. On television matters, with the USOC's share reviewed and altered, and contract negotiations completed through 2008, this troubling aspect of IOC/USOC relations could be set aside.

Corporate Sponsorship

In the commercial history of the Olympic movement, the Samaranch presidency represents a critical chapter. The IOC not only became wealthier beyond its most optimistic expectations, but extraordinarily more powerful in the context of international sport. Fuelled by the revenues generated from television rights, the activities commonly associated with corporate enterprise flourished inside the halls of power of the organization's Lausanne headquarters. Television matters aside, it was in the areas of product advertising and consumer sales, often identified as *marketing*, that the IOC became linked to what is commonly referred to as *commercialism*. Mistakenly branded a relatively recent phenomenon, the corporate sponsorship link with the Olympic movement has been modestly exploited by OCOGs dating from the earliest history of the modern Olympic Games. And conventional wisdom holds that Los Angeles' Peter Ueberroth "wrote the book" on how an OCOG should approach the task of securing funds needed for staging an Olympic festival. Ueberroth provided a workable financial blueprint for future OCOGs and energized previously reluctant civic leaders in some of the world's major cities to pursue host city privileges as a result of Los Angeles' financial success (especially given the financial and political problems surrounding recent festivals in Montreal and Moscow). He did not, however, lead the IOC and Samaranch into the world of corporate sponsorship. It was in fact an earlier sports marketing executive who had provided the impetus and means for the IOC to become inextricably wedded to the marketing of its five-ring symbol. That individual was Horst Dassler, son of Adi Dassler, founder of the global sporting goods empire known as Adidas. The influence of Horst Dassler on Juan Antonio Samaranch, and his expertise in the sector of innovations and sports marketing, has been underestimated by historians. Their dialogue on the commercial sponsorship of sport, and the potential linkage with the Olympic Games, commenced shortly after Samaranch's election to the presidency of the IOC in 1980. Despite the informal nature of these discussions, they were a critical factor in forging the now well-developed and highly visible link between the Olympic Games and corporate sponsorship.

Well before Samaranch acted on the discussion with Dassler and formed a commission to investigate new sources of revenue generation, the subject had engendered discussion inside the halls of IOC decision-making. The organization's dependence on the whim of television executives to continue to pay millions of dollars for television rights made many nervous. Adding to the uneasiness within the IOC was the prediction by some pundits of a gradual levelling of the spiralling rights fees, if not a decline. In response, the IOC, under Lord Killanin's direction, experimented with the international marketing of its symbols. Though educational in value, this first effort is commonly regarded as a dismal failure.[21]

In early December 1982, four months after soccer's World Cup tournament concluded in Madrid, a courier departed the newly created offices of International Sports and Leisure Marketing (ISL) in Lucerne, Switzerland, bearing a package addressed to Juan Antonio Samaranch at the IOC headquarters in Lausanne.[22] Accompanying the package was a letter from Klaus Jürgen Hempel, managing director of ISL, who had been entrusted by the Dassler family with the future development of ISL. Hempel's letter and Christmas gift were designed to capitalize on the informal talks held between Samaranch and ISL's founder/owner, Horst Dassler. An appreciative Samaranch quickly responded to Hempel, thanking him for "the nice lithograph," and offering his personal salutations and best wishes for "a happy and fruitful new year."[23] Indeed, 1983 proved to be fruitful beyond any prediction. In point of fact, 1983 ushered in an era of lucrative Olympic commercialism tied to the affairs of business marketing.

ISL, created by Horst Dassler shortly after the finals of the 1982 soccer World Cup, specialized in sports sponsorship marketing, and developed its reputation through exclusive contracts with the International Football (Soccer) Federation (FIFA) and two of its continental sub-federations, the European and South American Football Unions.[24] In an effort to expand its global operations, ISL identified the modern Olympic movement's five-ring symbol as "the most powerful and visible symbol in the world of sport."[25] ISL envisioned a worldwide sponsorship marketing program involving various multinational corporations that would generate sufficient money to provide a second revenue source for the Olympic family, and of course enhance its own company resources and power in the world of sport business.[26]

Samaranch's increasing anxiety over the IOC's nearly sole reliance on revenues generated from the sale of television rights, a legacy inherited from the previous administration, and the need for financial reform, prodded his support for ISL's vision of Olympic marketing.[27] Having already planted the seed with Dassler's assistance, Samaranch urged the organization of a new IOC commission responsible for identifying areas of opportunity for the generation of revenues and for recommending a strategic direction for their acquisition. The newly formed Commission of New Sources of Financing wasted little time and set to work on its mandate. At its second meeting in New Delhi in late March 1983, it approved in principle the concept of a worldwide sponsorship program along the lines of a plan forwarded to the IOC by ISL's team of marketing experts.[28]

If the revenues generated by the sale of television rights rescued the IOC from virtual insolvency in the 1970s, then the income derived from the TOP program (The Olympic Programme, now The Olympic Partner Programme) has eliminated the dependence on a single revenue stream. The TOP Program was originally created for the purpose of establishing a more diversified revenue base for the Games and the modern Olympic movement. As TOP participants, multinational corporations (1) are permitted to advertise themselves as the exclusive worldwide Olympic sponsors and to associate the Olympic words and emblems with their product on a worldwide basis; (2) receive exclusive marketing rights and opportunities within their designated product category; and (3) receive preferential treatment in the development of marketing programs with the IOC. In addition, each TOP sponsor receives exclusive hospitality opportunities at the Games, direct advertising opportunities and preferential access to broadcast advertising, and on-site concession/franchise and product sale/showcase opportunities, as well as ongoing ambush marketing protection through a global advertising and public relations support program in international print and electronic media.

Some two and a half years after the IOC commission's approval, following a long and often vitriolic dialogue with the USOC, the first TOP agreement (TOP I) was signed by Samaranch, representing the IOC, and Dassler, representing ISL, at the 148th meeting of the IOC executive session in Lausanne on 28 May 1985.[29] Although Dassler's team of experts did not create the concept of sponsorship, it was ISL that developed the structure of sponsorship as an orderly tool of marketing communications. Through its marketing, advertising, and communications experts, ISL was able to introduce, develop, negotiate, and implement this program, which, at this time, is in its fifth quadrennium.

In the late 1980s and early 1990s, the IOC, headed by Samaranch, and its partner, ISL, collaborated successfully as the TOP program generated impressive revenue for successive organizing committees in Barcelona, Albertville, Lillehammer, and Atlanta. The TOP I Program (1985–1988) attracted the support of nine multinational corporations and generated approximately $97 million US for the Olympic movement. Twelve corporations comprised the TOP II Program (1989–1992), including eight of the original TOP I sponsors. TOP II built upon the success of TOP I by generating in excess of $175 million US. TOP III (1993–1996) included ten corporations and generated in excess of $350 million US, while TOP IV (1997–2000), with eleven corporations, generated in excess of $550 million US. The TOP V (2001–2004) marketing program encompassed the Salt Lake City Olympic Winter Games and the Athens Olympic Games. Its proposed sponsorship fee of $55 million US was intended to "yield a 22%

increase from the base amount charged during TOP IV."[30] The program had the participation of ten worldwide Olympic partners, and at its conclusion in 2004 was expected to generate approximately $600 million US for the Olympic movement.

Despite the obvious financial success of the first three TOP programs, the USOC's growing dissatisfaction with the competence of ISL's executives in dealing with major U.S. companies, and the IOC's own reservations concerning ISL's operational efficiency due to a string of personnel changes, prompted Samaranch to end the IOC/ISL relationship in 1996. According to Richard Pound, the link provided by the TOP program to the Olympic movement "should have been a wonderful opportunity for an agency to be present at the highest levels of international business." As he continued: "In the most objective view, the TOP program had got to where it was because of the value of the 'property' and not because of the agency involved."[31] In its place, the IOC established—while also assuming stockholder status in—a new company called Meridian Management (now IOC Television & Marketing Services SA). Meridian Management's task, as had been the case with ISL, was to lead the IOC's efforts in the generation of corporate sponsorship dollars. With the emergence of Meridian Management, Samaranch took yet another giant step towards the IOC's transformation into a corporate entity.[32] Although some question the commercialization of the modern Olympic movement, for Juan Antonio Samaranch, the seventh president of the IOC, the "Olympic Partners enhance the Olympic Games experience for all, while they promote the Olympic ideals of peace, friendship, and solidarity."[33]

Conclusions

In an attempt to assess Samaranch's presidency on matters concerning revenue generation, we first need to establish some context for our comments. When Samaranch arrived in Lausanne, the IOC was wrestling with the means to maintain its activities on the world's stage, given geopolitical issues of the 1970s and its own financial problems. Tense relations between the IOC and OCOGs concerning the management of television negotiations and the distribution of television revenue in the 1970s, when coupled with the IOC's sole dependence on this revenue stream for its administrative existence, as well as the growing demands for Olympic revenue from the IOC's partners (the ISFs and NOCs), warranted a new organizational philosophy concerning financial matters. Central to this new philosophy, given the many questions raised about the relevance of the Olympic movement in the global community, was the complementary desire to elevate the status of the IOC's principal product, the Olympic Games.

This chapter addressed Samaranch's philosophy concerning the management of the IOC's television and corporate sponsorship portfolios. First, the corporate environment that emerged in Lausanne during his presidency was successful, beyond all expectations, in generating the necessary wealth to execute and in fact expand the IOC's mandate. The IOC's partner organizations also benefited greatly from the increased Olympic revenues. With close to $9.5 billion US in television fees accrued during his tenure in Lausanne, and in excess of $1.7 billion US generated through TOP, financial security was no longer a pressing, day-to-day concern for the Olympic movement at the time of his departure. Second, new energies in television negotiations aimed at securing maximum reach for Olympic broadcasts, and promotional benefits emanating from the international marketing program, greatly advanced the profile of the Olympic Games. Further enhancing the profile of the Olympic Games, especially in a North American context, was Samaranch's decision to open the Games to professional athletes. There is little doubt that this agenda paid enormous dividends in fostering increased exposure of the Olympic movement to a worldwide audience. Yet these successes must be contrasted with the commensurate challenges and failings engendered by this new financial philosophy.

Samaranch's failure to manage accelerating changes in the Olympic movement brought about by the new-found wealth resulted in damage to the Olympic movement's image. First, the new financial package available to prospective host cities encouraged increasing numbers to chase the Olympic rings. While this increased interest was a positive development, the new wealth compromised the bid process by fuelling a "win at all costs" mentality. Well before Salt Lake City's bid scandal revelations, bid committees exploited the existing gift-giving culture as a means of securing IOC members' support. Within this bloated bid process, a number of IOC members sought personal benefit in exchange for pledging their support to particular bid cities. Despite obvious warning signals concerning the conduct of some IOC members, as well as runaway largesse on the part of bid committees, Samaranch made no tangible effort to rein in those engaged in these activities. His failure to intervene in stemming this conduct resulted in the public relations disaster of 1998 and 1999. Second, his success in promoting the status of Olympic competition attracted a significant degree of interest from ISF leaders who desired a place on the

Olympic program for their sports, and encouraged intense jockeying on the part of ISF officials whose sports were already part of the Olympic program, but who desired an expanded place. While his effort to increase the number of events open to female athletes was admirable, he demonstrated little ability to control the overall growth in the size of the Olympic program. When combined with the desire of successive organizing committees to construct more grandiose facilities, the prospect for hosting an Olympic festival (especially a Summer Games) was pushed well beyond the means of countless cities around the world. Having inherited Samaranch's legacy of gigantism, Jacques Rogge is left with the unenviable task of engaging ISF leaders in a meaningful dialogue aimed at establishing an Olympic program that is manageable for communities entrusted with host privileges. Last, the enhanced profile of the Olympic spectacle increased the opportunities for financial rewards associated with success in certain sports. Samaranch's financial agenda did not invite the first use of performance enhancing drugs in Olympic competition. An historical analysis of doping in Olympic competition provides many examples well in advance of Samaranch's presidential tenure; however, an increasing number of athletes, consumed by a desire to excel, pursued competitive advantages possible through the use of performance enhancing drugs in the 1980s and 1990s. Samaranch's token response to the proliferation of doping in the Olympics was regrettable. His failure, until 1999, to generate a consensus within the Olympic family aimed at tackling the problem aggressively merits criticism.

When he stepped down from the presidency of the IOC, Samaranch commented that the "Olympic world" had changed greatly during his tenure.[34] He is, of course, correct. The IOC's corporate transformation, a process involving baby steps under Lord Killanin, was completed. Lawyers and marketing experts roamed the halls of Lausanne's Château de Vidy. Television viewer numbers exploded, and the private sector considered a sponsorship link with the Olympic movement as an effective conduit to advertise its products to the consumer public. Even Samaranch must have been startled by the success of the money-making machine he created. However, Samaranch was much more successful in enhancing the Olympic movement's revenue generating potential than he was in managing the results of his success. Many Olympic observers wonder aloud today who the Games are for—the athletes or the business community. Doping, gigantism, and bid scandals—collectively, these represent the less flattering elements of Samaranch's presidential legacy, and central issues that will consume Jacques Rogge's time and energies.

Notes

1 This extensive story is addressed in Barney, Wenn, and Martyn 2002, 151–273. Pound now heads the World Anti-Doping Agency (WADA), and Payne has moved on (as of August 2004) to work with Formula One automobile racing.

2 Brundage decided that the bulk of the money from the 1964 and 1968 television contracts would flow to the organizing committees. The ISFs did receive small shares of the money, but leaders of these organizations—as well as NOC officials, who believed their claim for money as valid as those offered by their ISF counterparts—lobbied him aggressively to develop a distribution formula that would provide more substantial sums to members of the Olympic tripartite group. His efforts to secure television money from the 1960 Rome and Squaw Valley organizing committees (the first time that Olympic television rights were actively marketed) had failed to pay significant dividends in the wake of the IOC's establishment of its first formal definition of "television rights" in 1958. Squaw Valley refused to turn over any television money, and Rome officials turned aside Brundage's demands for IOC control of the allocation of the money, eventually ceding approximately $53,000 to the IOC (a sum that Brundage deemed too small to be shared with the ISFs). Squaw Valley and Rome officials dismissed Brundage's demand that the IOC control distribution of the money (according to its new television policy, Rule 49 of the Olympic Charter) because Rule 49 was passed in 1958, three years after the respective communities had been entrusted with staging the 1960 Olympic festivals. See Barney, Wenn, and Martyn 2002, 68–77.

3 *Minutes of the Meeting of the IOC Executive Board,* Rome, 22–24 April 1966, 8–9, International Olympic Committee (hereafter cited as IOCA), Lausanne, Switzerland; and *Minutes of the 65th Session of the International Olympic Committee,* Rome, 25–29 April 1966, 4–5, Avery Brundage Collection (hereafter cited as ABC), Box 93, Reel 51, International Centre for Olympic Studies, University of Western Ontario.

4 While the IOC would not approve a policy that would place IOC officials at the negotiations table until 1977 (in advance of negotiations for the 1984 Olympic festivals), Killanin mused as early as 1973 that increasing aggravation as a result of the actions of organizing committee officials, who schemed for ways to reduce the shares of money allotted to the IOC and its affiliated organizations, might necessitate such a move. Lord Killanin to Monique Berlioux (IOC Director), 21 March 1973, "N.1, Droits de TV Montréal du 4.12.69 au 30.6.76," Binder, IOCA.

5 Miller 1992, 33–35.

6 *Minutes of the 79th Session of the International Olympic Committee,* Prague, 15–18 June 1977, p. 35; and Annex #33, 98–102, IOCA.

7 *Minutes of the Meeting of the IOC Executive Board,* Lausanne, 10–11 October 1986, 40, IOCA. The change was made known to candidate cities for the 1992 festivals in December 1985.

8 *Minutes of the Meeting of the Commission of New Sources of Financing,* Lausanne, 9 October 1986, 5, IOCA. However, Samaranch's concern can be traced back to 1982.

9 For sample discussions of the Goodwill Games project at the IOC Executive Board level, see *Minutes of the Meeting of the IOC Executive Board,* Lausanne, 11–12 February 1986, 37–40; *Minutes of the Meeting of the IOC Executive Board,* Seoul, 22–24 April 1986, 37–38.

10 In 1986, the Olympic Charter, which stipulated that Winter and Summer Games be held in the same year, was changed by the IOC. The Winter and Summer Olympics would now be held alternately every two years. To adjust to this new schedule, the Winter Games in Lillehammer, Norway, were held in 1994.

11 For insightful commentary on Arledge's career, consider his own words in Arledge 2003.

12 Spence, with Diles, 1988, 36–42.

13 Richard Pound understood, but did not accept, Samaranch's approach. See *Minutes of the Meeting of the IOC Executive Board,* Seoul, 22–24 April 1986, Annex #10, 81, IOCA.

14 Alan Abrahamson and Randy Harvey, "How NBC Got the Gold," *Los Angeles Times,* 13 August 2000; and *Minutes of the Meeting of the IOC Executive Board,* Lausanne, 24–26 September 1995, 3; 20, IOCA.

15 Richard Pound to Dick Ebersol, 2 October 1995, IOC Sunset File, Personal Computer Files of Richard Pound (hereafter cited as PCFRP), Montreal, Canada; and "Notes for the Remarks by Richard W. Pound: Olympic Television Announcement re: 2004, 2006, 2008: New York, December 12, 1995," IOC Sunset File, PCFRP.

16 "Report to the Finance Commission Paris 6th June 1986," 6, "Seoul 1988 TV General août-décembre 1986," File, IOCA.

17 Juan Antonio Samaranch to Richard Pound, 1 October 1985, "Seoul 1988 TV-General 1985 II" File, IOCA; and Minutes of the Meeting of the IOC Executive Board, Lausanne, 11–12 February 1986, 5, IOCA.

18 *Congressional Record—Extension of Remarks, 101st Congress, 2nd Session (136 Cong. Rec. E 3452), vol. 136, no. 148, Thursday October 25, 1990; Minutes of the Meeting of the IOC Executive Board,* Puerto Rico, 27–29 August 1989, 31, IOCA; *Minutes of the Meeting of the IOC Executive Board,* Belgrade, 24–26 April 1990, 49, IOCA; and "Notes of a Meeting with Congressman Tom McMillen, Washington, D.C., 17 January 1991, IOC-USOC File, PCFRP.

19 *Minutes of the Meeting of the IOC Executive Board,* Lausanne, 4–6 March 1996, 33; "Marketing Report to the IOC Executive Board, Atlanta, July 11–13 1996," in *Minutes of the Meeting of the IOC Executive Board,* 11–13 July 1996, Atlanta, Annex #9, 106, IOCA; and "Briefing Memorandum: IOC-USOC Meeting October 8, 1996," IOC-USOC File, PCFRP.

20 *Minutes of the Meeting of the IOC Executive Board,* Lausanne, 8–10 October 1996, 15–16, IOCA.

21 Attempting to recoup monies expended for the 1976 Olympic festival, the Montreal OCOG, having designed and purchased a number of trademark emblems, asked Stanley R. Shefler, president of Intelicense Corp. SA, to establish a licensing program for the Olympic pictograms. Upon learning of the Intelicense initiative, IOC director Monique Berlioux wrote a letter to all NOCs, instructing them not to do business with Intelicense. In her letter, Berlioux reminded the NOCs that the Montreal OCOG was constituted for a limited period of time surrounding the Games of the Twenty-first Olympiad, and, according to the Olympic Charter, would soon be liquidated. Responding to Berlioux's letter, Shefler informed the IOC that he intended to take legal action against the organization. However, prior to the initiation of formal proceedings in the Swiss courts, Shefler agreed to a meeting between the two parties. As the meeting progressed, the IOC agreed to purchase the pictograms from the Montreal OCOG for the purpose of establishing its own international marketing program. Despite an auspicious beginning for the Intelicense initiative, conflicts emerged between the IOC and Intelicense that resulted in prolonged litigation. See Barney, Wenn, and Martyn, 2002, 164–68.

22 Klaus Jürgen Hempel to Juan Antonio Samaranch, November 1982, ISL Marketing File, IOCA. Klaus Jürgen Hempel was the managing director and director of the board for ISL.

23 Juan Antonio Samaranch to Klaus Hempel, 17 December 1982, ISL Marketing File, IOCA.

24 Klaus Jürgen Hempel to Juan Antonio Samaranch, November 1982, ISL Marketing File, IOCA.

25 ISL, A Presentation to the International Olympic Committee (New Delhi, 1983), 1, IOCA.

26 ISL, A Presentation to the International Olympic Committee (New Delhi, 1983), 1, IOCA.

27 *See Minutes of the Meeting of the Commission of New Sources of Financing,* Lausanne, 9 October 1986, 5, IOCA. Samaranch had been concerned about this IOC budgetary fact for quite some time—as early as 1982, in fact, when it became apparent that approximately 95 per cent of IOC revenue was derived from the sale of television rights.

28 At the fourth meeting of the Commission of New Sources of Financing in Berlin on 1 June 1985, chairman Louis Guirandou-N'Diaye provided members with a brief overview of the commission's history, including an account of the "IOC's activities in the field of commercialism," which focused on the impact of the worldwide sponsorship program approved by the commission in New Delhi in late March 1983. See *Minutes of the Meeting of the Commission of New Sources of Financing,* Berlin, 1 June 1985, 1, IOCA.

29 *Minutes of the Meeting of the IOC Executive Board,* Lausanne, 28 May 1985, 177–78, IOCA.

30 Meridian Management SA, "'Double-Nickels': The Theory of TOP V Pricing," TOP V Programme File, 1997, 1, IOCA. The proposed TOP V sponsorship fee of $55 million was established by adding a "ten percent premium or multiplier" to the "benchmark" fee of $45 million charged during TOP IV. The adjusted figure ($49.5 million) was then increased by a "three percent inflation factor from the start of TOP-IV until the start of TOP-V (4 years)." The final number was "then rounded to arrive at a suggested price of $55 million."

31 *Minutes of the Marketing Liaison Committee for TOP IV,* Karuizawa, 1995, 4, IOCA.

32 For an extended discussion of the rise of Meridian Management, see Barney, Wenn, and Martyn 2002, 231–42.

33 See IOC Marketing Department, 2000, 1.

34 Alan Abrahamson, "Passing the Torch," *Los Angeles Times,* 9 July 2001.

❧

Olympic Ideals: Pragmatic Method and the Future of the Games

Tim Elcombe

In his 1992 book, *Future of the Olympic Games*, John Lucas assessed the current state of this international sport festival, and the implications for future Games. In an early paragraph, Lucas wrote:

> Only a few have written on contemporary Olympic history, and none have addressed the implications of today's political and sporting events on the future of the Olympic Games. In taking on this challenge, I'm not abandoning my role as historian; rather, because history is an unending continuum, I'm extending my historical concern for the past into the present and on to the remaining years of the 20th century—the future.[1]

A second passage, found on the last page of the text, similarly deserves highlighting:

> I have abiding faith in the *idea* of a near-perfect Olympic Games as a festival of elite sport, as a peace-filled gathering of the human race in a grand union of the beginning and end of life "through the endurance of affection, of trust, of friendship, and of love." The convergence of the Olympic laurel with Olympic gold need not be traumatic, but rather wholly natural. After all, idealism and pragmatism are not necessarily antithetical, just different. I've said throughout this book that balance is the key, the path to Olympian harmony and progress.[2]

The goal of this chapter is not to weave an Olympic narrative, nor to suggest all-encompassing solutions to the current and future crises of the Olympic Games. Instead, I seek to offer a brief overview of a powerful philosophical conception of ideals embedded in the tradition of classic pragmatism—a philosophy that may contribute to the scholarly and existential methods *and* attitudes of all those with a vested interest in the future of the Olympics. By doing so, I believe I will further justify and possibly enhance Lucas's own project—a project that must be implicit in all our work as administrators, historians, and philosophers of sport.

I will comment on how pragmatic notions of ideals offer rich possibilities for Olympic studies. Classic pragmatism's concept of ideals suggests that Lucas (and the rest of us) need not seek a *balance* between ideals and pragmatism. Instead, our projects must tacitly embrace a *thoroughgoing pragmatism*. This brief discussion on pragmatic ideals will also embody descriptions of the role of inquiry, as well as the democratic conditions necessary for pragmatism and the Olympic Games to flourish. First, however, I must begin with a few words on pragmatism in the larger context of modern culture and philosophy.

Philosophy and Pragmatism in the Twenty-First Century

Popular opinion delegates philosophy to a second-class status. Most conceive philosophy as pompous and abstract, or overly simplistic and not worthy of attention. This marginalized condition emerges from the ivory tower abstract game playing engaged in by many professional philosophers, leaving room for the "Chicken Soup for the Soul" franchise to remain the only public engagement with philosophy. Yet the role of philosophy can genuinely contribute to our lives, our institutions, and the future of everything we cherish. John Dewey, facing these same issues of abstractness and triviality, wrote in 1917 that philosophy could recover itself only if "it ceases to be a device for dealing with the problems of philosophers and becomes a method, cultivated by philosophers, for dealing with the problems of men."[3] Dewey, along with his predecessors Charles Peirce and William James, sought to explore new questions arising from the *experienced* plight of humanity, and desired philosophy to become practical, critical, and reconstructive.[4]

Unfortunately, contemporary usage of the term "pragmatism" represents an oversimplified and completely erroneous "whatever works" perspective. Peirce, the father of pragmatism, quickly grew tired of the misuse of his philosophic method and eventually renamed it pragmaticism, a term he described as "ugly enough to be safe from kidnappers."[5] Pragmatism, as envisioned by Peirce, James, and Dewey, stands not as a purely subjective and relative methodology, but as a careful experimental method of inquiry into the conditions of humanity. I believe this revision of philosophical thought holds great potential for the critical analysis of our social institutions—including the Olympic Games. Subsequently, this chapter will briefly introduce how the working power of pragmatic conceptions of ideals can offer the basis of a method beneficial to all interlocutors vested in the flourishing of the Olympics.

Pragmatic Ideals and the Olympics

What are the Olympic ideals? Are they reflected in the Olympic motto— *citius, altius, fortius*? When discussing Olympic ideals, Kofi Annan, Secretary General of the United Nations, lists tolerance, equality, fair play, and peace. An educational website catalogues vision, commitment, discipline, focus, and persistence as the five Olympic ideals. Perhaps an Olympic ideal is reducible to Pierre de Coubertin's statement that "the most important thing in the Olympic Games is not winning but taking part."

To pragmatists, fixed conceptions of Olympic ideals are functionally unimportant and uninteresting. These notions of ideals treat ends or purposes as "objects in themselves"[6]—frozen and isolated as "literally ends to action."[7] Viewed as fixed, eternal, and "out there," one cannot imagine these ideals being actualized.[8] Consequently, this Platonic conception of fixed ideals, as a *telos* (or drive) towards unattainable perfect states, fails to motivate action or to be operational in any sense.

In contrast, many contemporary thinkers completely reject teleological accounts of action or the notion of ideals—instead submitting to pure contingency and the power of "strong poets" in our culture. Nothing outside ourselves, these philosophical theorists contend, motivates our actions or drives us forward to some determined endpoint. Consequently, they would argue that the ideals promoted by the Olympics simply stand as rhetoric, while the direction of the Games must constantly be revised and open to radically new possibilities.

Pragmatic theories carve out a middle ground between the fixed, mechanical teleological conception of ideals and the contrasting purely random, capricious rejection of ends. For a pragmatic thinker, operative ideals—as "active means" or "ends-in-view"—stand as the *means* to provide direction of our activities. Dewey turned to sport to explain his notion of ideals:

Men shoot and throw. At first this is done as an "instinctive" or natural reaction to some situation. The result when it is observed gives a new meaning to the activity. Henceforth, men in throwing and shooting think of it in terms of its outcome; they act intelligently or have an end. Liking the activity in its acquired meaning, they not only "take aim" when they throw instead of throwing at random, but they find or make targets at which to aim. This is the origin and nature of "goals" of action. They are ways of defining and deepening the meaning of activity.

Dewey further wrote:

Having an end or aim is thus a characteristic of *present* activity. It is the means by which an activity becomes adapted when otherwise it would be blind and disorderly, or by which it gets meaning when otherwise it would be mechanical. In a strict sense an end-in-view is a *means* in present action; present action is not a means to a remote end. Men do not shoot because targets exist, but they set up targets in order that throwing and shooting may be more effective and significant.[9]

In contrast to Platonic conceptions of ideals, Dewey's conception of aims cannot be fixed and eternal. Instead, they must be constantly revised, moving us in different directions to live more fully in our ever-changing interactions with the environment. Ideals for Dewey, and pragmatists in general, have real power; they serve as ends-in-view to shape our values and propel us into the future.[10]

The Olympic Games exemplify Dewey's earlier description of the power of operative ideals. Coubertin recognized the value and meaning structures available in racing, throwing, jumping, and kicking. Fittingly, he established a modern festival to engage men (and eventually women) in the ideals of sport and international competition. But, like any social institution, the original ideals need not be the force of today, as social and cultural institutions like the Olympic Games must continuously invent new traditions.[11] Rather than pure randomness or a fixed teleology, Peirce forwards a *developmental teleology*—as growth occurs, it creates and expands future growth.[12] Peirce's developmental teleology concurs with Dewey's notion that ends, in addition to providing meaning to our activity, also direct our future courses—serving as "redirecting pivots *in* action."[13]

Yet classic pragmatists recognize continuity and shared experience as central aspects of our experienced world. While ideals must be revisable in the ever-changing conditions of society, we cannot dismiss the qualities and historical ideals that draw humans to the Olympic Games. The operative ideals of the past serve as the basis for the Games' durability and attraction. Consequently, any inquiry into the ends-of-view affecting the Olympics must first examine the historical ideals and breathe life into them in a modern context—assuming these ideals foster growth in the twenty-first century.

For ideals to be powerful in an existential and desirable sense, however, requires a method in inquiry. Pragmatism itself grew from the emerging conditions of scientific experimentation. Consequently, pragmatism must be grounded in a careful, systematic method—a method I will now briefly introduce.

The Pragmatic Method and Democracy

Pragmatism relies upon its tridimensional paradigm of inquiry—an *active* inquirer working with a subject-*matter* in light of a particular objective or ideal.[14] Counter to modern notions of experimentation with detached, neutral subjects studying external objects, this paradigm manipulates and wholly *engages* the subject-matter with some end driving the inquiry. Consequently, the pragmatic method requires ideals to be operational to determine possible consequences and to invest the project with meaning. Without ends-in-view, the inquiry is meaningless; failure to fully engage the subject-matter renders the conclusions impotent.

Let me offer a commonplace Olympic example to demonstrate the pragmatic method—and its potential for the future of the Olympic Games. The use of performance enhancing substances such as steroids elicits a plurality of arguments and final conclusions. To reach a pragmatic solution, however, we must first ask what ideals currently inform our position about the status of steroid use. Some may argue that fair play ideals justify bans on steroids. However, careful inquiry into actual conditions of elite sport calls into question the genuine equality available to athletes lacking the access to high-level coaches, training methodologies, facilities, and nutritional options. In fact, they may conclude, lifting bans on steroids may afford *more* equality in the Olympics.

Others may contend that the long-term health of athletes solely validates steroid bans. Again, a closer look may point to secretive and subsequent ill-monitored abuse of steroids. Or, opponents may point to the inherent danger in sports such as boxing, pole-vaulting, or platform diving. A third counter to the healthy competitors argument could invoke the life-threatening training regimens tolerated and indirectly encouraged by judges and weight classifications in sports such as figure skating, gymnastics, weightlifting, and boxing.

But do the logic and aesthetic qualities of sport offer operative ideals that may account for several desired ends when considering the experiential consequences of performance enhancing substances? The modern Olympic Games exist as a *sport* festival—thus the cherished qualities of sport must stand as active means. There seem to be durable elements of sport's internal logic that draw participants, spectators, and theorists to the Olympics. Perhaps most central to sport is the construction of artificial barriers that biologically constrained humans must find ways to surmount. A marathoner may not take a shortcut or catch a subway ride to complete the course, although both are more efficient ways to get from Point A to Point B. Why can these artificial barriers not extend into the means of preparation? The drama of track events includes not only how humans function against the constraints of biology and gravity, but also the limitations experienced by an athlete's functional capacity to train.

Decisions on performance enhancement can therefore be informed by a powerful ideal of sport—an ideal that can also encompass ideals of equality and health. Further, this inquiry, driven forward by an operative ideal, offers the Olympics conditions for growth and durability. Since the Games continue to be grounded in a sport context, the attraction will remain—and therefore continue to draw spectators and participants—as well as maintain an event worthy of economic interest. Even the major financial sponsors have a vested interest in the aesthetic quality of sport, as evidenced in the corporate logos found on Olympic posters. Under the bold print inviting the entire world to "Celebrate Humanity," for example, sit the brand marks of McDonalds, Kodak, Panasonic, and others.[15] These financial enterprises invest in a festival that can celebrate the possibilities of humanity. They need the national morale-boosting quality that nation-versus-nation sport events offer. Most invested in the Olympics desire the durability of the national sentiment created in Canadian households in 2000 when Simon Whitfield headed into the final stages of the triathlon trailing the leader, who held a seemingly insurmountable advantage—then put on a tremendous finishing kick to win. Clearly, we all want the Olympic Games to continue to offer examples of human frailty and compassion—exemplified by the scene of Derek Redmond's father breaking through security to carry his son across the finish line after the British runner tore his hamstring in the Olympic 400-metre semifinal in 1992. Few likely want the future of the Olympics to be exemplified by the scene of four American sprinters celebrating dominance by posing and posturing on the Olympic podium, or to view the Games as a competition between technologically created human machines.

A final necessary condition—only by working towards an ideal of democracy can pragmatism be a fully live option to create an environment for human flourishing. Without empowering the numerous polycentric collectives that make up the Olympic Games, notions of operative ideals constructed and reconstructed through pragmatic inquiry cannot be a reality. Communication becomes a crucial element in pushing the bounds of sport while maintaining conditions of durability. Building genuine communities that may ultimately become a great Olympic community thus serves as a powerful ideal and project for the future of the Games.

Philosophers, Historians, and Administrators

With this conception of ideals, inquiry, and community at work, what ends operate in an existential sense emerges as the interesting and important question to pragmatists. What *can* the Olympic ideals be? This replaces the question of what the Olympic ideals *are* in a fixed metaphysical sense. The functional role of the philosopher, historian, and administrator (among others) then takes shape. Philosophers must examine the practical consequences, criticize, and forward reconstructions to the operative Olympic ideals. For example, what role should financial ideals play in the future of the Olympic Games? Should the Olympics be walled off from a pure economic market structure? As a cultural practice, how can the Olympics serve the educational role that Dewey contends is a responsibility of all social institutions that create habits of mind and character? What balance between pushing the limits of human possibility and the moral narratives embodied in Olympic competition do we seek? How true to Coubertin's vision should the Games remain?

From a different perspective, historians must also inquire into these and other questions. They should delve into the meaning structures embedded in the Olympics' historical markers. The historical narratives they reconstruct tell us the moral and aesthetic road we traverse, and flesh out the force of traditional ends. History reveals the sources of durability that inform our current, operative ideals, offering another set of possibilities for the future within an ever-changing, contingent world. The works of Olympic historians provide opportunities to explore shared and contested reservoirs of meanings constructed within this international sport festival.

Administrators must also foster a conscious awareness of the operative Olympic ideals. The International Olympic Committee (IOC), politicians, national and international sport governing bodies, media outlets, and others put Olympic ideals into motion. Unfortunately, it appears as though this large mass singlehandedly defines the current ends of the Olympic Games—unfortunately, since narrow market and political ideals seem to supersede any experiential qualities and meaning structures the Games may provide. Administrators must be informed by pragmatic philosophy and history to make decisions about the future of the Olympic Games. This international institution rests in their hands, for only they currently hold the functional power to operationalize and/or mute the ends-in-view that drive the Olympic Games forward in the twenty-first century.

It seems, experientially, that we can come to a *working* consensus about what operative ideals should take precedence over others to create Olympic growth and durability. All with a vested interest can be involved in dialogue to determine the pragmatic ends that will drive the future of the Olympics. This pragmatic method also requires constant inquiries into the relevance, power, and quality of ends-in-view that shape the Games' current and future conditions. But conclusions reached can never be perceived as fixed and final. New information about steroids—or other ethical dilemmas—may change their status. Or perhaps a new aesthetic will emerge as the primary operative ideal of the Games. The Olympics must also be prepared to face future issues, including genetic technology, the ethical controversies arising in disabled sports, the intrusiveness of market models, the selection and deselection of sports, the host city bidding process, and unforeseen dilemmas that will undoubtedly arise.

Conclusion

In conclusion, I would once again like to return to the work of John Lucas. His vision of the future engaged the potential of what the Olympic Games can be. The Olympics historically existed as an educational institution, a medium for telling moral stories about the limits and possibilities of humanity, and served as a rallying force for national pride. Lucas also recognized the fluidity of our modern landscape. Consequently, we must take up his challenge to see history as "an unending continuum" that accounts for the ever-changing contingencies informing our culture, social institutions, and humanity as a whole. If not, our cherished institutions, including the Olympic Games, may change in ways that challenge their durability and narrative appeal. If this occurs, we will lose an important cultural site for meaning and value.

Based on the work of pragmatism, I must end with one final plea. All theoreticians—including philosophers, sport managers, historians, social scientists and exercise scientists—must seek not to merely be academics who speak to each other in isolation, but professionals enacting real change for real human experience. Consequently, we must all be pragmatists and see our role as Olympic theoreticians in the larger sphere of life. Lucas's formal project must be all of our projects. Our work must always be about expanding the experiential quality, continued relevance, and rich possibilities of institutions such as the Olympics as we move forward in the twenty-first century.

Notes

1 Lucas 1992, xi.
2 Lucas 1992, 215. Emphasis in original.
3 Boydston 1985, 46–47. Dewey most likely would revise this statement in current conditions to eliminate the sexist connotation. It seems fair that the term "men" is used here in a generic sense to encompass all humanity. For a further examination of Dewey's larger claim in a modern context, see Campbell 2003.
4 Peirce, James, and Dewey rejected modern philosophy's propensity for false dualisms, old metaphysical claims, and raging debates over "dead" questions. See Stuhr 2000, 1–9.
5 Peirce 1998b, 335.
6 Dewey 1922, 229.
7 Dewey 1922, 227.
8 Rorty 1998, 102.
9 Dewey 1922, 225–26. Emphasis in original.
10 For a description of Dewey's conception of ideals as "directive means" or "ends-in-view," see Dewey 1922, especially 223–37.
11 This point is attributable to William J. Morgan's response to a question at the 2003 International Association of the Philosophy of Sport Conference, 19 September 2003, University of Gloucestershire, Cheltenham, England.
12 Peirce (1998a) describes the conception of developmental teleology in several places, including within this essay.
13 Dewey 1922, 225. Emphasis in original.
14 Boisvert 1998, 35.
15 The poster can be accessed on the Web at http://multimedia.olympic.org/pdf/en_report_266.pdf.

"To Construct a Better and More Peaceful World" or "War Minus the Shooting"?: The Olympic Movement's Second Century

Mark Dyreson

When I saw the program for this conference and realized that one of the founding fathers of modern Olympic studies, who had devoted an entire volume to the *Future of the Olympic Games*,[1] would be in attendance, I felt very much like a rookie whose inexperience was in great danger of being exposed. With apologies to John Lucas and a brief caveat, I offer my own predictions on what the second century of the modern Olympic Games may hold. Wager on my speculations at your own risk, remembering that I have long pursued the historian's craft, which requires one's vision to be firmly fixed on the past—a position which makes it sometimes difficult to see the future. In my other forays into professional prognostication, I guaranteed in 1991 that the Cold War would continue for many more decades, speculated in 1994 that Utah would never get the Winter Olympic Games, predicted in 1998 that no American presidential candidate during my lifetime would lose the popular vote but win the electoral college, and prophesied in 2000 that the legendary football coach at the great university that signs my paycheque would retire to a Happy Valley pasture by 2001, or by 2002 at the outside. Still, I dare to foresee.

In 1894, as Baron Pierre de Coubertin launched the modern revival of the Olympic Games, he proclaimed that "the aims of the Olympic

Movement are to promote the development of those fine physical and moral qualities which are the basis of amateur sport and to bring together the athletes of the world in a great quadrennial festival of sports thereby creating international respect and goodwill and thus helping to construct a better and more peaceful world."[2] A few decades later, one of the most celebrated novelists of the twentieth century, famous for his indictments of human folly and his warnings about the seductions of totalitarianism, offered a very different view of sports. In his essay "The Sporting Spirit," George Orwell condemned "serious sport" as being "bound up with hatred, jealousy, boastfulness, disregard of all rules and sadistic pleasure in witnessing violence: in other words it is war minus the shooting."[3]

The juxtaposition of the baron's uninhibited idealism and the novelist's unvarnished cynicism has for the first century of modern Olympic history characterized most scholarly estimates of the revived Games. Indeed, Coubertin's and Orwell's quotations serve as an epigraph for sport sociologist Richard Lapchick's 1975 call for continuing the ban against South African participation in Olympic sport as the most effective weapon in the struggle to dismantle apartheid. Lapchick's ironic conjunction of the two polar views of the modern Olympics was strangely reproduced in his own argument. As one of the leaders of the movement to banish South Africa from international athletics, he considered sport as both an instrument of global politics, as "war minus the shooting," and as a utopian balm that could aid humankind "to construct a better and more peaceful world." Lapchick wanted it both ways. Sport was politics. And sport could transcend politics and dissolve the most insidious forms of racial oppression.[4]

Curiously, Lapchick borrowed his ironic conjunction of Orwell and Coubertin from a 1959 essay by the English Olympic middle-distance runner Christopher Chataway, who also served as one of Roger Bannister's "rabbits" in the quest to break the four-minute mile. Ironically, Chataway used Coubertin's and Orwell's competing views of the Olympics to argue against the exclusion of South Africa from the 1960 Olympic Games in Rome.[5]

Although they ended on opposite sides of the South Africa question, both Chataway and Lapchick recognized what I think is the central paradox of the modern Olympic Games. The Games exist simultaneously as a global *lingua franca*[6] and as a staging ground for all manner of political chauvinism. This central paradox led Chataway and Lapchick to follow the same logic to different political conclusions. So powerful are the Olympic Games, believed Chataway, that to exclude South Africa would embitter the defenders of apartheid and increase their determination to maintain racial segregation. Let the hardliners come to Games, counselled Chataway, and breathe the egalitarian air of Olympism. The intoxicating vapours would convert even the most recalcitrant segregationists, and they would return to their homeland to rid South Africa of the racism.[7] So powerful are the Olympic Games, believed Lapchick, that to exclude South Africa would force the defenders of apartheid to surrender their determination to maintain racial segregation. Keep the hardliners away from the Games, promised Lapchick, and in their desperation to gulp the intoxicating air of Olympism, they would give up apartheid and rejoin the civilized world.[8]

The power of the Olympic Games in the twentieth century to capture popular imagination resided ultimately in this paradox. The Olympic movement both held out hope for the creation of a better world and served as war minus the shooting—and sadly, in Munich in 1972, as war *with* the shooting. These contradictory but strangely bound realities made the Olympic Games into the most unique sporting drama of the twentieth century. Other international athletic events such as World Cup soccer tournaments embrace the sport as surrogate for war paradigm without bothering to spend much time wallowing in pious schemes devoted to utopian quests for global harmony. Other international movements devoted to humanitarian uplift—the International Red Cross or Doctors Without Borders or Oxfam, to name a few—manage to work for a better world without also reserving space for regular rounds of war minus the shooting.

I make this claim not as a criticism of the Olympics but as an explanation of its power as a dramatic spectacle that draws enormous audiences. We watch because they are not *just* another sporting contest wrapped in zealous jingoism. We watch because they are not *just* another utopian scheme calling us to live by the whisperings of the angels of our better natures. My personal history with the Olympic Games reflects this paradox. While I have spent a great deal of my scholarly career studying the Olympic Games, I am not particularly an Olympic fan, preferring the parochial American troika of basketball, baseball, and football in which to invest my zeal. But the Olympics do have a strange hold on me, as I once was quadrennially and now am biennially reminded. Some of my fondest childhood memories are wrapped in both the transcendently human and the portentously political moments of the Games. I remember 1968, when my brothers and I fought in the backyard over which one of us got to be Kip Keino in our re-enactment of the 1500-metre final. I also remember black-gloved lessons in the realities of American race relations from

Mexico City. I recall 1972, when my brothers and I fought in the backyard over which one of us got to be Dave Wottle—though we used a baseball cap for our version of his uniform rather than Wottle's signature golf cap, since we lacked the latter and had plenty of the former—in our re-enactment of the 800-metre final. I remember too, the black-ski-masked lessons in the realties of global terrorism from Munich.

I confess to wanting it both ways, as well, in many of my writings on the Olympics. I have consistently sought to demystify Olympism and to expose the frequently tawdry political uses of modern sport. I have at the same time hoped, perhaps naively, that sport could transcend the grubby realities of human politics, and make the world a better and more pacific place.[9] I think I am in good company in my illogic. Certainly Allen Guttmann's writings seem gripped by the same paradox, as do the works of John Lucas, Robert Barney, Stephen Wenn, and Scott Martyn, and Alfred Senn.[10] John MacAloon captures the essence of the paradox as well as anyone in the conclusion of his famous essay on Olympic spectacles. MacAloon argues that the Olympic Games function sometimes as "a theater of self-delusion" and at other times as a drama "full of events that make us notice the moral and social boundaries that have become blurred and banal in daily life."[11]

The embrace of this incongruity seems to me to be strangely loyal to the classical Greek embrace of the Olympic Games. The ancient Olympics were also confounded by the struggles of city-states to fight their rivalries on the sacred grounds of Olympia, conjoined with dreams that the Games could usher in a golden age of pacific Panhellenism.[12] The hubris of nationalism combined with the romance of utopianism make the modern Olympic Games a fascinating revival of classical Greek tragedy. In historical terms, this fundamental conflict made the modern Games the most dramatic sporting events of the twentieth century.

The notion of the Olympic Games as a drama captures something essential about their role in modern history.[13] C.L.R. James, the brilliant West Indian historian, labelled sport as the grand democratic art of the twentieth century, a dramatic struggle that reveals the hopes and foibles of peoples and nations.[14] The usual litany of "problems" identified by those who seek to cure Olympic maladies—gigantism, commercialism, nationalism, corruption, rampant drug usage, murky philosophical principles, and a host of other afflictions—do not threaten the heart of the Olympic drama.[15] In fact, bid scandals, bribery scandals, performance-enhancing chemical scandals, sex scandals, cheating scandals, organized crime scandals, citizenship scandals, tire-iron to the kneecap scandals—in combination with regular bouts of hypocrisy and boorishness from athletes, coaches, judges, spectators, the media, NOC officials, IOC officials, host nation officials, and visiting nation officials—indisputably add to the dramatic appeal of Olympian spectacles. The many troubles besetting the modern Games may reveal the yawning gulf between Olympism's professed ideals and the standard practices of highly competitive athletics, they might inflame national rancour, expand commercial influence, and provide mountains of material for the many critics of the Olympics, but they will not destroy the Games. Indeed, they are, in combination with sterling athletic performances, the lifeblood of modern Olympic tragedies, reminding us of the gap between what is and what ought to be.

In their first century, the modern Olympics provided the most important international stage for epic performances of popular drama. A myriad of difficulties, from world wars to figure skating fixes, could not kill the Games. Will the Olympic Games remain the central venue for modern dramas during their next century? My speculations about the future of the Olympic Games in the twenty-first century are grounded in an historical interpretation of the rise and fall of an older site where the world's consuming masses looked for mechanisms to create a better and more peaceful globe, and for methods to engage in intense national struggles without resorting to combat. The world's fair movement, beginning with the original international exposition at the Crystal Palace in London in 1851, was wrapped around the same dramatic paradox as the modern Olympic Games. In their "golden age," the late nineteenth and early twentieth centuries, world's fairs drew millions and millions of customers to see exhibitions of technological wizardry, to be inculcated into Western notions of progress, to marvel at the contrasts of primitive and modern civilizations, and to revel in the cornucopia of ice cream cones, Ferris wheels, and other consumer culture kitsch that overflowed the fair grounds.[16] Like the later Olympic Games, world's fairs served as beacons of boosterism to advertise cities, regions, and nations. Like the later Olympic Games, world's fairs provoked intense bidding wars for hosting privileges. Like the later Olympic Games, the international exhibitions claimed to be global events but were invented and dominated by the Western industrial powers. Like the later Olympic Games, the international exhibitions were designed and built by elites but drew huge mass audiences. Like the later Olympic Games, the international exhibitions were wrapped in a dysfunctional marriage between national chauvinism and woolly-headed utopianism.[17] Like the later Olympic Games, the international exhibitions offered audiences "symbolic universes" that reaffirmed national and international ideologies.[18] Like the later Olympic Games, the international exhibitions allowed for simplistic comparisons of cultures—so-called primitive and modern, Eastern and Western, industrializing and developing, liberal and totalitarian, exotic and familiar—which captured public fancy.

Before the Olympic Games were revived, world's fairs served as the globe's most significant locations for unarmed combat between nations. The historian Wilbur Zelinsky observed that not only did world's fairs exhibit modern industrial progress, but "the major expositions were also playing fields on which the leading states of the Western world tussled for symbolic power and prestige."[19] If we could magically transport ourselves ninety-nine years into the past, we would find that the Louisiana Purchase Exposition rather than the 1904 Olympic Games commanded the attention of millions of eager fans who flocked to St. Louis. In fact, the 1904 Olympic Games were a sideshow at the St. Louis World's Fair, just one of the many events under the big top at Missouri's cultural circus.[20] My choice of the history of international exhibitions as a source of clues to speculate about the future of the Olympic movement is deliberate and calculated. The modern Olympic movement is in part based on the structure of world's fairs, and three of the first four modern Games, at Paris in 1900, at St. Louis in 1904, and at London in 1908, were embedded in expositions. In 1940 Tokyo planned both an Olympic Games and a world's fair. Each became casualties of the Second World War.[21] Surely the history of international expositions should provide some clues as to what might lie ahead for the Olympic Games.

If a century ago world's fairs were wildly popular events with an enormous fan base, they are today merely curiosities doomed to loiter at the edges of popular consciousness as they crumble into the ash heap of history. The precipitous decline of international expositions should warn the lords of the International Olympic Committee (IOC) that unforeseen changes in media technologies and consumer tastes can have enormous consequences that lead to a swift fall from public favour. What happened to international exhibitions? The last great exposition was the 1939 World's Fair in New York City, where Olympians Johnny Weissmuller and Eleanor Holm starred in Billy Rose's *Aquacade*, the carnival's most popular show.[22] How, after the New York extravaganza, did the world's fair movement disintegrate so quickly and so completely? Why did international expositions become "cultural dinosaurs"—as some of the leading historians of the world's fair movement lament?[23]

A variety of factors combined to extinguish public fascination with world's fairs. Perhaps most significantly, the expositions lost their position as "war minus the shooting," as the leading site for measuring national prowess. Anthropologist Burton Benedict claims that the decline began when "the national competition element in world's fairs was siphoned off by the Olympic Games."[24] Olympic medal counts ultimately proved more alluring as national measuring sticks than comparisons of electric dynamos or the myriad other stultifying details of industrial production housed at fairs.[25] The expositions also lost their position as the major showcases for popular cross-cultural comparisons, especially to sporting events such as the Olympic Games, but also to a growing infrastructure of museums and a thriving mass media devoted to depicting exotic peoples, a genre that stretched in the United States from the glossy pages of *National Geographic* to the glossy cinematography of *National Geographic* movies. The emergence of an international travel industry made trekking affordable to at least the developed world's masses, and allowed common folk to mount personal expeditions to human-made and natural wonders that they had in the past depended on world's fairs to bring to them.[26]

If the allegedly educational elements of the world's fairs lost their power to other venues such as museums, cheap travel junkets, and documentary films, the entertainment possibilities of expositions were also eclipsed. The rise of theme and amusement parks, from local "fun factories" to destination resorts such as Disneyland, destroyed the novelty and even the gigantism of exposition midways. Finally, television made graphic depictions of the world's marvels easily accessible and amazingly affordable to consumers. Images of the world had been available in books for centuries, but immediate visual experiences that did not require high levels of literacy, once the province of world's fairs, found a new outlet in television. No longer did the curious have to battle the hordes of visitors at fairs. Beginning in the middle of the twentieth century they could sit in the comfort of their own homes and consume the world's wonders via their television sets.[27]

It is no coincidence that the media technology which drove expositions into near extinction made the Olympic Games into a major global phenomenon. Television, the bane of world's fairs, was the boon of Olympic growth. Television transformed the Games and made them into the newly wired global village's leading theatre. Nurtured initially under the protective canopy of expositions, the Olympic Games broke away and developed structures that fit well with the new electronic medium. The expositions crumbled, and the Olympic Games were built on their ruins. As historians Robert Barney, Stephen Wenn, and Scott Martyn have asserted in their insightful new history of Olympic commercialism, the Olympic

Games, at the beginning of the twenty-first century, provide transnational corporations with "the opportunity to advertise products to a global audience unmatched in size by any other sport audience in the world."[28] Since the 1960s, television has been the most important advertising medium in the global economy. The marriage of the Olympic Games and television, as Barney, Wenn, and Martyn demonstrate, has made the five-ring symbol of the Olympic Games one of the most powerful icons in the world. Television turned international exhibitions into "cultural dinosaurs," but it transformed the former sideshows at world's fairs, the Olympic Games, into events that drew billions and billions of viewers.[29]

As the twenty-first century begins, the Olympic Games stand in the same position that world's fairs occupied a century earlier. Are there new methods for transmitting cultural products, and new sensational spectaculars, that might steal away the enormous audience that now tunes in to the Olympic Games to witness dramatic clashes of utopian internationalism and passionate patriotism? Lurking in the folds of the Olympic tent, much as the Olympic Games once hid quietly amidst the immense displays of international expositions, are several suspects. They combine the possibility of using new television techniques with new sports. They are cropping up at the fringes of both the Winter and Summer Games. Among the leading contenders are new Olympic events such as beach volleyball, snowboarding, mountain biking, triathlon, and the most recent addition, BMX stunt biking.[30]

The lords of the IOC clearly recognize that these so-called extreme sports are transforming the marketplace. In adding these new events, which appeal directly to the affluent demographics of the North American and European consumers that television corporations lust after, the Olympic leadership signals that it desperately wants to remain in front of this new wave of dramatic spectacles. During their first century, the Olympic Games have created what British historians such as Benedict Anderson and E.J. Hobsbawm label "imagined communities"—the basic social building blocks of modern nations.[31] The appeal of the Olympic Games is that it also holds out the possibility for the creation of an international "imagined community"—a universal human *communitas*, in the lingo of Olympic historian Allen Guttmann.[32] The marriage of television and the Olympic Games has created a different version of "imagined community." Television has made the Olympic Games an ideal site on which to build communities united by the consumption of the products of corporate capitalism. The older national and transnational visions of social unity promoted at the Olympics now compete for space with the burgeoning global community of consumers linked by their desires to purchase the goods and enjoy the lifestyles advertised in Olympic telecasts.

Recent media coverage of Olympic spectacles hits precisely the "imagined community" that television moguls and corporate sponsors seek. Televised Olympic sport imagines a "community" that reflects elite notions of the ideal class, racial, and gender dynamics of post-modern societies. The IOC has co-operated with the television networks in giving birth to visions of a brave new Olympic world. This brave new Olympic world seems to have settled into a North American or Australian or Brazilian resort community where temperate breezes cool post-industrial economies in which everyone has abundant leisure time to ride mountain bikes to work and play beach volleyball at lunchtime. On winter weekends, consumers head to snow-gilded destination resorts for some half-piping. This is a world where class disappears from view because no one ever sees the working class in beach-volleyball land. Here, everyone shares the same suburban values and springs from the same multi-ethnic mélange of cultures. Certainly women seem, at least on the surface, to be empowered by these suburban sporting dreams, competing in growing numbers in these new events. Including more women as players and watchers certainly expands Olympic markets.[33]

In a brilliant updating of the traditional Olympic gilding of internationalism over nationalism, these new sports are promoted as transnational pastimes that link the youth of the world in a rosy harmonic glow. In the brave new Olympic world, the nation-state is initially submerged under the romantic prospect of a universal human quest for extreme thrills. Like an iceberg, the nation-state lurks under the surface, shaping the athletic sea around it. Extreme sport competitions pit national teams against one another. Snowboarding and its fellow disciplines now figure prominently in the national medal counts that remain staples of televised Olympic dramas. Extreme sports have another connection to nationalism as well. Each of these new games—beach volleyball, mountain and BMX biking, triathlon and snowboarding—morphed into the modern consciousness from Southern California, the imperial capital of contemporary American civilization. They are American-invented and designed products, marketing themselves as transnational bulwarks of a global youth culture.[34]

As extreme sports capture gigantic market segments, what will happen to traditional Olympic events such as the hammer throw, the modern pentathlon, and even the marathon? My prediction is that if the Olympic Games want to thrive in the twenty-first century, many of the traditional competitions will gradually fade from the scene as extreme sports increasingly move to the centre of Olympian dramas. The ceaseless "Californication" of popular culture,[35] so familiar to those who live inside or on the borders of the United States, will reshape the Olympic program. If the Olympic movement can keep control of these made-for-television extreme dramas, it has a chance to continue to dominate the global sporting marketplace.

In order to stay relevant, the IOC needs to maintain extreme vigilance, for just outside of the Olympic tent lurk other contenders among the mushrooming market for extreme sports. The IOC needs to capture some of these sports in order to maintain control of the evolving television and sporting trends. The biggest threat to Olympic hegemony in international extreme-sporting dramas are the grand-races-through-exotic-landscapes series, the original *Raid Gauloises* (1989 to the present) and its imitators, the *Eco-Challenge* races (1995–2002), and the *Primal Quest* challenges (2002 to the present). The now defunct *Eco-Challenge* races—the former British paratrooper Mark Burnett's brilliant mixture of ultra-endurance athletics, exotic landscapes, and made-for-television human turmoil—drew enormous numbers of television viewers. Some estimates claimed a billion households tuned in to the endurance dramas.[36] The *Eco-Challenge* franchise incorporated the dramatic structure of the Olympic movement by matching national teams against one another in intense rivalries. Cobbled over the patriotic core rested a veneer crafted from romantic allusions to the kindred spirits of all humankind competing against the awesome forces of nature and the limits of the human species. Like the Olympic Games, the *Eco-Challenge* series moved around the world. In an update of the Olympic format, the *Eco-Challenge* plopped down not in urban centres but in exotic wildernesses. These spectacular landscapes shared top billing with the athletes as the stars of the show. The focus on competition with nature as well as with other humans branded the *Eco-Challenge* as part of the twenty-first century's thriving transnational environmental movement, in spite of the fact that some hardcore environmentalists condemned the damage that the game does to pristine terrain.[37]

Another *Eco-Challenge* innovation, the creation of co-ed teams, represented a crucial new development that—outside of an occasional mixed-gender equestrian team—is unknown in Olympic sport. Having men and women compete both together and against one another fuelled one of the central dramatic features of *Eco-Challenges*. Carefully filmed and edited, and fed to increasingly large audiences, *Eco-Challenges* are intentionally and intensely voyeuristic. *Eco-Challenges* overwhelmed viewers with copious doses of supposedly candid displays of teammates engaged in intense social and psychological conflict. The *Eco-Challenge* method captured human reactions to extreme stress as well as human performances under extreme conditions. *Eco-Challenges* allowed viewers to witness competitors as they suffered emotional and physical breakdowns, to see teams unravel into bitter recriminations as their chances at victory evaporated, to behold the entire human spectrum from the thrill of victory to the agony of defeat. The all-seeing television eye provided views from the outside of the game, offering gorgeous helicopter shots of teams toiling through magnificent landscapes. Simultaneously, television cameras beamed data from inside the game—candid, up-close and personal vignettes of the stress-frayed antics of squabbling competitors. All of the images were carefully edited for maximum dramatic effect. *Eco-Challenge* was not live television, but it was cleverly manufactured to feel more "alive" than traditional live sporting broadcasts.[38]

In the twenty-first century, the *Raid Gauloises*, *Primal Quest*, and new versions of *Eco-Challenge* will become major competitors to the Olympic Games in the global sports marketplace. The 1997 installment of the *Eco-Challenge* series in Australia served as pre-game show for the 2000 Sydney Olympic Games.[39] Like the Olympic Games, these events have begun to draw major corporate sponsors. Advertising industry insiders labelled *Eco-Challenge* as a "growing international sports event."[40] The IOC would do well to incorporate an *Eco-Challenge*-inspired competition into the Olympic franchise.

An evolutionary leap down the sports-entertainment continuum is Burnett's other major pop culture production, *Survivor*. *Survivor*'s twisted mélange of physical, psychological, and social games has become a major television phenomenon. *Survivor*'s genius is that it combines the temporary deprivation of affluent people with semi-athletic competitions. In this game, ostensibly common folk strive for prowess and engage in vicious, juvenile political strife. To guarantee vigorous competition, the players battle for a winner-takes-all prize of $1 million. Although some commentators have claimed the game was inspired by that adolescent fantasy *The Swiss Family Robinson*, I think its origins rest in the dark cynicism of *Lord of the Flies*. The omnipresent television cameras capture every moment of faux hardship and mean-spirited manipulation that it takes to win the game, making *Survivor* a nearly perfect contemporary amalgam of sport and soap opera for the emerging age of voyeurism we increasingly inhabit.[41] The original version of the game—aired in the summer of 2000, just before the Sydney Olympics—drew enormous numbers of viewers in North America, ranking it with the 1996 Summer Olympic Games from Atlanta as the highest-rated summertime television program in history.[42] Television critics argue that *Survivor* has changed the basic nature of the medium. In an industry in which plagiarism is a governing principle, a host of imitations have popped up on the airwaves. *Survivor* has been hailed as the future of television.[43] A leading industry source, *AdWeek*, asserts that *Survivor* has become "the experiential template against which all kinds of phenomena are measured."[44]

Those measurements include comparisons to the Olympic Games. Canadian triathlete Joanne Kay has observed that Burnett's game shows have begun to change the way in which television networks cover Olympic sport. She asserts that the U.S.-based National Broadcasting Corporation's telecast of the 2000 Olympic triathlon at Sydney used *Survivor's* secrets to beam her event to North America. "NBC certainly has a grasp on what animates *Survivor's* success—reality framed by the narrative of fiction, packaged conveniently in pre-digested bite-sized accounts," Kay argues. She also links Burnett to Pierre de Coubertin, saying that the baron "is most certainly the mastermind behind...*Survivor*, the ratings phenomenon so widely credited to Mark Burnett." Alluding to the 2000 Olympic Games in Sydney, she continues: "Indeed, the Baron foresaw this day when 11,000 athletes would come to an island, willingly divided into 199 tribes. He even anticipated an audience made up of the modern world that could watch the struggle for supremacy as it unfolds. They would come not only for the drama—the thrill of victory and the agony of defeat—but also from being voyeurs, privy to the secrets of the human spirit that, to the outsider, are otherwise left untold."[45]

This, I fear, is the Olympic future. The new levels of voyeurism that *Survivor* is spreading through television will change the nature of twenty-first-century sporting spectacles. Increasingly, audiences are going to demand that they get the "inside scoop" on competitors and teams. Viewers will insist that they witness the psychological and social conflicts that have heretofore remained relatively obscured in the sports world. The Olympic Games will have to adjust to this new paradigm in which fans want to know instantaneously not only who won the race but who is sleeping with whom, who is trying to sabotage a coach, and who is working on a teammate's personal frailties in order to maximize a competitive advantage. Sport and soap opera will merge into athletic "Real Worlds," MTV's much-imitated and allegedly reality-based programs. The Olympic Games will either evolve or they will join the "cultural dinosaurs" that a century ago hatched them, the international expositions, on the scrap heap of outdated popular culture.

Lest John Lucas now find himself too depressed by my prognostications to make his way back to the Happy Valley that we both inhabit, let me conclude by reminding him of two salient facts. First, he should remember that my career as a seer of the future has been less than stellar. And second, the future scenario that I have sketched is not the darkest possibility clouding the Olympic horizon. A story emanating from "Around the Rings," a news agency that touts itself as "your independent source of world sport news since 1992," reported in the spring of 2003 that French scientists had nearly finished the process of cloning Pierre de Coubertin from cells preserved in a lock of the baron's hair. Working in ultra-secrecy, the genetic experts at the Laboratoire de Rien were apparently using a "fast-growth method of cell-division" that will bring to life a forty-three-year-old version of Coubertin. The fact that the baron was born in 1863, and was apparently thirty-three in 1896, did not deter the intrepid reporter for "Around the Rings" from continuing the tale. Since I was recently chastised by a colleague that Internet research will soon render scholarly searches in dusty archives extinct, who am I to doubt a Web source headlined "First Ever Human Clone May Be Olympic Founder"?[46]

The news release revealed that the Coubertin clone would be an authentic copy complete with the baron's experiences and sensibilities as well as his hair colour and height. "Fast-track teaching methods that have been developed by the laboratory's fast-growth cell division have given Coubertin wide range of contemporary knowledge, including the Olympics," the reporter explained. The story disclosed that the mayor of Paris was negotiating to retain the cloned Coubertin as a consultant in the Parisian bid for the 2012 Games (which the city later lost to London). The international federation for modern pentathlon was apparently also seeking the reconstituted baron's help in saving what was once the baron's favourite event from plans to replace it with another extreme sport.[47]

Perhaps the reanimated baron might be able to save the Olympic Games from the clutches of Mark Burnett. Certainly the quick-cloning and rapid programming techniques that were purportedly under development in a French lab might offer an alternative to the extreme sports Olympic future. Imagine a cloned Paavo Nurmi running against a reconstituted Emil Zátopek in the 10,000-metre race. Picture a restored Jim Thorpe against a reanimated Bruce Jenner in the decathlon. Think of the television ratings for an Olympic "classic" featuring a cloned team of Olympic all-stars from 1920s and 1930s vying against current Olympians. How many viewers would tune in to see the clones of ancient Greek champions battle the champion clones of the modern era? With these genetically engineered match-ups on the broadcast schedule, the Olympic Games would certainly be in no danger of becoming a "cultural dinosaur" any time soon.

Notes

1 Lucas 1992.
2 Monique Berlioux, ed., *Olympism* (Lausanne: International Olympic Committee, 1972), 1, as cited in Lapchick 1975, xv.
3 Orwell 1998, 442.
4 Lapchick, 1975 cites Coubertin and Orwell in his study of sport and politics in South Africa (p. xv).
5 Christopher Chataway, "An Olympian Appraises the Olympics," *New York Times Sunday Magazine,* 4 October 1959, 50–58.
6 One of the earliest uses of the phrase "the common language of sport" in regard to the Olympic Games is Tunis 1928, 81.
7 Chataway, "An Olympian Appraises the Olympics," 58.
8 Lapchick 1975.
9 See, for instance, Dyreson 1998a; 1998b; 2001; 2003a; 2003b.
10 See the ironic analyses of Guttmann, 1984, as well as Guttmann 1992 and 1994. Other scholars who take ironic positions include Lucas 1980 and 1992; Barney, Wenn, and Martyn 2002; and Senn 1999.
11 MacAloon 1984, 273.
12 The ancient Greeks, according to a recent interpretation by classicist Mark Golden, both established and disputed political and social hierarchies in their Olympic Games. See Golden 1998. As Nigel Crowther's essay in this volume demonstrates, the Panhellenic claims are closer to modern fables than classical realities.
13 MacAloon 1984, 241–80.
14 James 1993 [1963], 195–211.
15 Lucas, 1992, provides an excellent litany of these Olympic problems. See also Guttmann 1992; Senn 1999; Toohey and Veal 2000; Schaffer and Smith 2000.
16 For general overviews of fairs see Allwood 1977; Rydell, Findling, and Pelle 2000; Rydell 1984; and Rydell 1993. On specific connections between fairs and the Olympic Games, see Roche 2000.
17 Rydell, Findling, and Pelle, 2000; Rydell 1984.
18 Rydell 1984.
19 Zelinsky 1988, 85–89.
20 Dyreson 1993, 4–23.
21 Allwood 1977, 176. For an overview of preparations for the Tokyo Games, see Constable 1996, 108–11.
22 Larson 1990, 298.
23 Rydell, Findling, and Pelle 2000, 131–40.
24 Benedict 1983, 60; Rydell, Findling, and Pelle 2000, 131.
25 The details of dynamos might have fascinated Henry Adams at the beginning of the twentieth century, but mass audiences quickly became enamoured with playing fields rather than assembly lines. In fact, the lack of popular interest in the inner workings of technology greatly disturbed Adams. See Adams 1999 [1918].
26 Aron 1999.
27 Rydell 1993, 213–16; Rydell, Findling, and Pelle 2000, 131–40; Roche 2000, 159–61.
28 Barney, Wenn, and Martyn 2002, xii.
29 The Summer Games at Sydney in 2000 drew 3.7 billion television viewers. See Barney, Wenn, and Martyn 2002, 278.

30   Paul 2001, 16–17; Emily Badger, "From Underground to the Mainstream," *Washington Post*, 30 August 2003, sec. D, p. 6; Jessica Halloran, "BMX Bandits Out to Take Gold," *Sydney Morning Herald*, 2 July 2003, sec. 1, p. 5; Mike Breshnahan, "Olympic Spotlight to Shine on BMX," *Los Angeles Times,* 16 August 2003, sec. 4, p. 7; Simon 2002, 177–208; Rinehart and Grenfell 2002, 302–14; Nelson 2002, 8–14; Gordon and Gegax 2002, 48–51; Streisand 2002, 53; Barrand 2002, 18–22; Rinehart 1999, 8–9.

31   Anderson 1991, 1–7; Hobsbawm 1992, 141–43.

32   Guttmann 1994, 188.

33   Pope et al. 1997, 63–73; Barney, Wenn, and Martyn 2002, 243–65.

34   Rinehart and Sydnor 2003.

35   The term "Californication" emerged in idiomatic American English in the 1970s in Western states where the migrations of Californians and California culture created animosity. The term has since broadened to denote the spread of American mass culture around the world. The Red Hot Chili Peppers' *Californication* album (1999) cemented the term in the contemporary lexicon.

36   For popular and scholarly accounts of *Eco-Challenge* and other "adventure races," see Ballard 2002; Anderson 2002; "Reversal of Fortune: The Inaugural Primal Quest Adventure Race Featured the Usual Blackouts and Sleep Deprivation," 2002; Hoffer 2000; Schneider 2002; Kay and Laberge 2002a; Kay and Laberge, 2002b; Siff and Caldwell 2001; Mann and Schaad 2001. The *Eco-Challenge* went on what may well be a permanent hiatus in 2002. The other two races continue to thrive. Both the *Raid Gauloises* and *Primal Quest* have websites to promote their products.

37   Mestel 1995, 55.

38   *Eco-Challenge: Morocco,* Unapix, 1999; *Eco-Challenge: Australia,* Unapix, 1999; *Eco-Challenge: British Columbia,* Unapix, 1998; *Eco-Challenge: The Prize,* Unapix, 1998; *Eco-Challenge: Gathering Fire and Ice,* Unapix, 1998; *Eco-Challenge: Breaking Point/The Storm,* Unapix, 1998.

39   Andrew Horney, "Eco-Challenge Will Bring Us $50 Million of Free Publicity," *Sydney Morning Herald,* 6 February 1997, sec. Business, p. 32.

40   "Advil Sponsorship-Venue Mix So Effective It Hurts," 2002, 14.

41   *Survivor: Season One,* Paramount, 2001; *Survivor: Season Two—The Australian Outback,* Paramount, 2001. See Burnett 2001a, 2001b.

42   Kate Jaimet, "Who Will Survive?" *Ottawa Citizen,* 22 August 2000, sec. E, p. 6.

43   Sigesmund 2001.

44   Goldman 2001, 20.

45   Joanne Kay, "Survival of the Chattiest: Will Somebody Please Vote NBC and CBC Off the Island?," *Ottawa Citizen,* 23 September 2000, sec. A, p. 17.

46   "First-Ever Human Clone May Be Olympic Founder," 15 April 2003, *Around the Rings*, <http://www.aroundtherings.com/other/2003/04/01/decoubertin.clone/index.html>. Accessed 15 September 2003.

47   "First-Ever Human Clone May Be Olympic Founder."

WORKS CITED IN PART II

∼

Adams, Henry. 1999. *The Education of Henry Adams*. Edited by Ira B. Nadel. New York: Oxford University Press.

"Advil Sponsorship-Venue Mix So Effective It Hurts." 2002. *Strategy*, April 8, 14.

Allwood, John. 1977. *The Great Exhibitions*. London: Studio Vista.

American Olympic Committee. 1936. *Report of the American Olympic Committee, Games of the XIth Olympiad, Berlin, Germany*. New York: AOC.

Anderson, Benedict. 1991. *Imagined Communities: Reflections on the Origin and Spread of Nationalism*. Rev. ed. London: Verso.

Anderson, Kelli. 2002. "Eco Boost." *Sports Illustrated*, September 23, A18–A19.

Arledge, Roone. 2003. *Roone: A Memoir*. New York: HarperCollins.

Aron, Cindy. 1999. *Working at Play: A History of Vacations in the United States*. New York: Oxford University Press.

Ballard, Chris. 2002. "Full Tilt through Fiji." *Sports Illustrated*, November 18, A14–A17.

Barney, Robert K., Stephen R. Wenn, and Scott G. Martyn. 2002. *Selling the Five Rings: The International Olympic Committee and the Rise of Olympic Commercialism*. Salt Lake City: University of Utah Press.

Barrand, Drew. 2002. "Television Captures Extremists: The Worldwide Growth in Popularity of Extreme Sports Has Seen a Change in Attitude from Broadcasters." *Sport Business International*, October, 18–22.

Benedict, Burton. 1983. *The Anthropology of World's Fairs: San Francisco's Panama Pacific International Exposition of 1915*. Berkeley, CA: Lowie Museum of Anthropology and Scholar Press.

Berlioux, Monique, ed. 1972. *Olympism*. Lausanne: International Olympic Committee.

Boisvert, Raymond. 1998. *John Dewey: Rethinking Our Time*. Albany: NY: State University of New York Press.

Booth, Douglas. 1990. "South Africa's 'Autonomous Sport' Strategy: Desegregation Apartheid Style." *Sporting Traditions* 6(2):155–79.

———. 1998. *The Race Game: Sport and Politics in South Africa*. London: Frank Cass Publishers.

Borgers, Walter. 1996. *The Olympic Torch Relays, 1936–1994*. Kassel: AGON-Sportverlag.

Boydston, Ann, ed. 1985. *John Dewey: The Middle Works, 1899–1924*. Vol. 10. Carbondale: Southern Illinois University Press.

Brennan, Joseph L. 1994. *Duke: The Life Story of Hawai`i's Duke Kahanamoku*. Honolulu: Ku Pa`a Publishing.

Burnett, Mark, executive producer. 1998–1999. *Eco-Challenge* series: *Breaking Point/The Storm* (1998); *British Columbia* (1998); *Gathering Fire and Ice* (1998); *The Prize* (1998); *Australia* (1999); *Morocco* (1999). New York: Unapix Home Video.

———, executive producer. 2001a. *Survivor: Season One*. Los Angeles: Paramount Home Video.

———. 2001b. Survivor: *Season Two—The Australian Outback*. Los Angeles: Paramount Home Video.

Camp, Walter. 1912. "The Olympic Games of 1912." *Colliers*, 49, 6 July, 22–26.

Campbell, James. 2003. "Advancing American Philosophy: Pragmatism and Philosophical Scholarship." In *In Dewey's Wake: Unfinished Work of Pragmatic Reconstruction*, ed. William J. Gavin, 9–23. Albany, NY: State University of New York Press.

Connell, R.W. 1995. *Masculinities*. Los Angeles: University of California Press.

Constable, George. 1998. *The XI, XII, and XIII Olympiads*. Los Angeles: World Sports Research.

Coubertin, Pierre de. 1966. "Closing words, Stockholm 1912." In *The Olympic Idea: Discourses and Essays*, 39. Schorndorf, Germany: Carl Diem Institute.

———. 2000. *Olympism: Selected Writings*, ed. Norbert Müller. Lausanne: International Olympic Committee.

De Olympiade. 1926. *Newsletter of the Dutch Organizing Committee for the 1928 Olympic Games*. February and May.

Dewey, John. 1922. *Human Nature and Conduct: An Introduction to Social Psychology*. New York: Carlton House.

Dyreson, Mark. 1992. "America's Athletic Missionaries: Political Performance, Olympic Spectacle and the Quest for an American National Culture, 1896–1912." *Olympika: The International Journal of Olympic Studies* 1:70–91.

———. 1993. "The Playing Fields of Progress: American Athletic Nationalism and the St. Louis Olympics of 1904." *Gateway Heritage* 14(fall):4–23.

———. 1998a. *Making the American Team: Sport, Culture, and the Olympic Experience.* Urbana and Chicago: University of Illinois Press.

———. 1998b. "Olympic Games and Historical Imagination: Notes from the Fault Line of Tradition and Modernity." *Olympika: The International Journal of Olympic Studies* 7:25–41.

———. 2001. "Maybe It's Better to Bowl Alone: Sport, Community, and Democracy in American Thought." *Culture, Society, Sport* 4(spring):19–30.

———. 2003a. "Return to the Melting Pot: An Old American Olympic Story." *Olympika: The International Journal of Olympic Studies* 12:1–22.

———. 2003b. "Globalizing the Nation-Making Process: Modern Sport in World History." *International Journal of the History of Sport* 20(March):91–106.

Fatton, Robert, Jr. 1986. *Black Consciousness in South Africa.* Albany: State University of New York Press.

Fea, John. 1996. "Lake Placid 1932: The Third Winter Olympics." In *Historical Dictionary of the Olympic Movement,* ed. John E. Findling and Kimberly D. Pelle, 232–36. Westport, CT: Greenwood.

Fearon, Peter. 1979. *The Origins and Nature of the Great Slump, 1929–1932.* London: Macmillan.

Golden, Mark. 1998. *Sport and Society in Ancient Greece.* Cambridge: Cambridge University Press.

Goldman, Debra. 2001. "Debra Goldman's Consumer Republic." *AdWeek,* March 5, 20.

Gordon, Devin, and T. Trent Gegax. 2002. "Dudes and Dinner Rolls: Once the Obnoxious Kid Brother, Extreme Sports Are Suddenly the Backbone of a U.S. Medal Machine." *Newsweek,* February 25, 48–51.

Gratton, Reg. 1999. "The Media." In *Staging the Olympics: The Event and Its Impact,* ed. Richard Cashman and Anthony Hughes, 121–31. Sydney: University of New South Wales Press.

Gregson, Ian. 1999. *Irresistible Force: Disability Sport in Canada.* Victoria, BC: Polestar.

Guttmann, Allen. 1984. *The Games Must Go On: Avery Brundage and the Olympic Movement.* New York: Columbia University Press.

———. 1992. *The Olympics: A History of the Modern Games.* Urbana: University of Illinois Press.

———. 1994. *Games and Empires: Modern Sports and Cultural Imperialism.* New York: Columbia University Press.

Guttmann, Sir Ludwig. 1976. "Reflection on the 1976 Toronto Olympiad for the Physically Disabled." *Paraplegia* 14(3):225–40.

———. 1976. *Sport for the Physically Handicapped.* Paris: UNESCO.

Hall, Sandra Kimberley, and Greg Ambrose. 1995. *Memories of Duke: The Legend Comes to Life.* Honolulu: Bess Press.

Hobsbawm, E.J. 1992. *Nations and Nationalism since 1780: Programme, Myth, Reality.* 2nd ed. Cambridge: Cambridge University Press.

Hoffer, Richard. 2000. "The Real Real World—Forget Survivor: Sports Is the Best Reality Television Around." *Sports Illustrated,* July 17, 25.

"How Does the Media Cover the Games?" 1996. Olympic Review, June–July, 60.

IOC Marketing Department. 2000. "Sydney 2000: Marketing Summary." *Marketing Matters* 17, September, 1.

Jackson, Robert W., and Alix Fredrickson. 1979. "Sports for the Physically Disabled: The 1976 Olympiad (Toronto)." *American Journal of Sports Medicine* 7(5): 293–96.

Jackson, Roger. 1977. "What Did We Learn from the Torontolympiad?" *Canadian Family Physician* 23(586):66–69.

James, C.L.R. 1993. *Beyond a Boundary*. 1963. Reprint, Durham, NC: Duke University Press.

Jennings, Andrew. 1996. *The New Lords of the Rings*. Sydney: Simon and Schuster.

Kanin, David B. 1981. *A Political History of the Olympic Games*. Boulder, CO: Westview Press.

Kay, Joanne, and Suzanne Laberge. 2002a. "Mapping the Field of 'AR': Adventure Racing and Bourdieu's Concept of Field." *Sociology of Sport Journal* 19:25–46.

———. 2002b. "The 'New' Corporate Habitus in Adventure Racing." *International Review for the Sociology of Sport* 37(March):17–36.

Kidd, Bruce. 1992. "Cultural Wars of the Montreal Olympics." *International Review for the Sociology of Sport* 27(2):151–64.

Lapchick, Richard E. 1975. *The Politics of Race and International Sport: The Case of South Africa*. Westport, CT: Greenwood.

Larson, Donald G. 1990. "New York, 1939–1940." In *Historical Dictionary of World's Fairs and Expositions, 1851–1988*, ed. John E. Findling and Kimberly D. Pelle, 293–300. Westport, CT: Greenwood.

Legg, David F.H. 2000. "Organizational Strategy Formation in the Canadian Wheelchair Sports Association (1967–1997): A Comparison to Leavy and Wilson (1994)." Ph.D. diss., University of Alberta.

Lenskyj, Helen Jefferson. 2000. *Inside the Olympic Industry: Power, Politics, and Activism*. Albany: State University of New York Press.

Loiselle, Richard T. 1973. "Wheelchair Sports: Development in Canada and Its Impact on the Rehabilitation of the Physically Disabled." Unpublished master's thesis, Dalhousie University, Halifax, NS.

Lucas, John. 1980. *The Modern Olympic Games*. South Brunswick, NJ: A.S. Barnes.

———. 1992. *Future of the Olympic Games*. Champaign, IL: Human Kinetics Books.

Lyberg, Wolf. 1996. *Fabulous Years of the IOC*. Lausanne: International Olympic Committee.

MacAloon, John J. 1984. "Olympic Games and the Theory of Spectacle in Modern Societies." In *Rite, Drama, Festival, Spectacle: Rehearsals toward a Theory of Cultural Performance*, ed. John J. MacAloon, 241–80. Philadelphia: Institute for the Study of Human Issues.

Macintosh, Donald, and Michael Hawes. 1994. *Sport and Canadian Diplomacy*. Montreal: McGill-Queen's University Press.

Macintosh, Donald, Hart Cantelon, and Lisa McDermott. 1993. "The IOC and South Africa: A Lesson in Transnational Relations." *International Review for the Sociology of Sport* 28(4):373–95.

Macintosh, Donald, Donna Greenhorn, and David Black. 1992. "Canadian Diplomacy and the 1978 Edmonton Commonwealth Games." *Journal of Sport History* 19(spring):26–55.

Mallon, Bill, and Ture Widlund. 2002. *The 1912 Olympic Games.* Jefferson, NC: McFarland and Company.

Mann, Don, and Kara Schaad. 2001. *The Complete Guide to Adventure Racing.* New York: Hatherleigh Press.

Merrett, Christopher. 2003. "Sport and Nationalism in Post-Liberation South Africa in the 1990s: Transcendental Euphoria or Nation Building?" *Sport History Review* 34(spring):33–59.

Mestel, Rosie. 1995. "Will Wilderness Survive the Eco-Athletes?" *New Scientist,* February 11, 55.

Miller, David. 1992. *Olympic Revolution: The Biography of Juan Antonio Samaranch.* London: Pavilion Books.

Morrow, Don. 1987. "Sweetheart Sport, Barbara Ann Scott and the Post–World War II Image of the Female Athlete in Canada." *Canadian Journal of History of Sport* 18(1):36–54.

Morrow, Don, and Kevin B. Wamsley. 2005. *Sport in Canada: A History.* Toronto: Oxford University Press.

Morrow, Don, and Janice Waters. 1982. "Method in Sport History: A Content Analysis Approach." *Canadian Journal of History of Sport* 13(2):30–37.

Moss, B. 1912. "America's Olympic Argonauts." *Harper's Weekly* 56, 6 July, 11–12.

Nauright, John. 1991. "Sport, Manhood and Empire: British Responses to the 1905 Rugby Tour." *International Journal of the History of Sport* 8(summer):239–55.

———. 1993. "'Like Fleas on a Dog': Emerging National and International Conflict over New Zealand Rugby Ties with South Africa, 1965–1974." *Sporting Traditions* 10(November):55–77.

Nauright, John, and David Black. 1999. "New Zealand and International Sport: The Case of All Black-Springbok Rugby, Sanctions and Protest against Apartheid 1959–1992." In *Sport, Power and Society in New Zealand: Historical and Contemporary Perspectives,* ed. John Nauright, *ASSH Studies in Sport History* 11, 67–93.

Neame, L.E. 1962. *A History of Apartheid.* London: Pall Mall Press.

Nelson, K. 2002. "Going to Extremes: Lifestyle Sports Events and Festivals Mature into Viable Competitors in the World of Sports Marketing." *Sports Travel* 6 (July/August):8–14.

Official Report of the Organising Committee for the XIV Olympiad. 1951. London: British Olympic Association.

Organizing Committee for the Olympic Winter Games. 1932. *Official Report for the III Winter Olympic Games.* Lake Placid, NY: The Committee.

Organizing Committee, Torontolympiad 1976. 1977. *A Time to Be Together.* Toronto: Organizing Committee.

Oriard, Michael. 1997. "Muhammad Ali: The Hero in the Age of Mass Media." In *Major Problems in American Sport History*, ed. Steven A. Reiss, 390–99. Boston: Houghton Mifflin.

Orwell, George. 1998. "The Sporting Spirit." In *I Belong to the Left*, Vol. 17 of *The Complete Works of George Orwell*, ed. Peter Davison, 440–43. London: Secker and Warburg. Originally published in the *Tribune* (London), 14 December 1945.

Paddock, Charles W. 1932. *The Fastest Human*. New York: Thomas Nelson and Sons.

"Passings." [Obituary of Duke Kahanamoku.] 1968. *Time*, 2 February, 8.

Paul, Pamela. 2001. "Good Sports." *American Demographics* 23(October):16–17.

Peirce, Charles. 1998a. "Evolutionary Love." In *The Essential Peirce: Selected Philosophical Writings, Volume 1 (1867–1893)*, ed. Nathan Houser and Christian Kloesel, 352–71. Bloomington: Indiana University Press.

———. 1998b. "What Pragmatism Is." In *The Essential Peirce: Selected Philosophical Writings, Volume 2 (1893–1913)*, ed. Nathan Houser and Christian Kloesel, 341–45. Bloomington: Indiana University Press.

Pope, S.W., et al. 1997. "Virtual Games: The Media Coverage of the 1996 Olympics." *Journal of Sport History* 24(spring):63–73.

Poulin, Kristen, Christina Flaxel, and Stan Swartz. 2002. *Trail Running: From Novice to Master*. Seattle: Mountaineers Books.

Pound, Richard. 2001. Panel Presentation, Olympic Round Table, Wilfrid Laurier University.

Pukui, Mary Kawena, and Samuel H. Elbert, with Ester T. Mookini and Yu Mapuana Nishizawa. 1992. *New Pocket Hawaiian Dictionary*. Honolulu: University of Hawaii Press.

Quick, Shayne P. 1990. "Black Knight Checks White King: The Conflict between Avery Brundage and the African Nations over South African Membership in the IOC." *Canadian Journal of History of Sport* 21(2):20–29.

"Reversal of Fortune. The Inaugural Primal Quest Adventure Race Featured the Usual Blackouts and Sleep Deprivation." 2002. *Sports Illustrated*, August 5, A14–A17.

Riess, Steven A. 1981. "Power without Authority: Los Angeles' Elites and the Construction of the Coliseum." *Journal of Sport History* 8(spring):50–65.

Riggin, Aileen. 2000. "An Olympian's Oral History: Aileen Riggin." Interview by Dr. Margaret Costa, 11 November 1994. Los Angeles: Amateur Athletic Foundation of Los Angeles. Accessed online at http://www.aafla.org.

Rinehart, Robert. 1999. "Extreme Sports: Grass Roots or Electronic Sport?" *Business of Sport* 4(May):8–9.

Rinehart, Robert, and Christopher C. Grenfell. 2002. "BMX Spaces: Children's Grass Roots' Courses and Corporate-Sponsored Tracks." *Sociology of Sport Journal* 19:302–14.

Rinehart, Robert E., and Synthia Sydnor, eds. 2003. *To the Extreme: Alternative Sports, Inside and Out*. Albany: State University of New York Press.

Roche, Maurice. 2000. *Mega-Events and Modernity: Olympics and Expos in the Growth of Global Culture*. London: Routledge.

Rorty, Richard. 1998. *Achieving Our Country: Leftist Thought in Twentieth-Century America*. Cambridge, MA: Harvard University Press.

Ryan, Allan J. 1976. "Another Olympics, Another Flame; Different Athletes, Different Game." *Physician and Sports Medicine* 4(10):133, 135, 137.

Ryan, Joan. 1995. *Little Girls in Pretty Boxes: The Making and Breaking of Elite Gymnasts and Figure Skaters*. New York: Doubleday.

Rydell, Robert W. 1984. *All the World's a Fair: Visions of Empire at American International Expositions, 1876–1916*. Chicago: University of Chicago Press.

———. 1993. *World of Fairs: The Century-of-Progress Expositions*. Chicago: University of Chicago Press.

Rydell, Robert W., John E. Findling, and Kimberly Pelle. 2000. *Fair America: World's Fairs in the United States*. Washington: Smithsonian Institution Press.

Schaffer, Kay, and Sidonie Smith, ed. 2000. *The Olympics at the Millennium: Power, Politics, and the Games*. New Brunswick, NJ: Rutgers University Press.

Schneider, T. 2002. "Mark Burnett: The Creator of 'Survivor' and the Eco-Challenge Shares His Thoughts on Building Phenomenal Name-Brand Events and the Value of Seeking Out Personal Challenges." *Sports Travel* 6(June):42–43.

Schweinbenz, Amanda. 2001. "All Dressed Up and Nowhere to Run: Women's Uniforms and Clothing in the Olympic Games from 1900 to 1932." Unpublished master's thesis, University of Western Ontario, London, ON.

Schweinbenz, Amanda, and Kevin B Wamsley. 2001. "Lilies, Pixies, Mermaids, and Sweethearts: The Feminization of Olympic Female Athletes in the Popular Media." Unpublished paper, International Society for Comparative Physical Education and Sport conference, Windsor, ON.

Senn, Alfred E. 1999. *Power, Politics, and the Olympic Games*. Champaign, IL: Human Kinetics.

Shearman, Mark. 1977. "The 1976 Olympic Games: A Close-Up Look at Track and Field Events." *Runners' World Magazine* 13(7):218–31.

Siff, Barry, and Liz Caldwell. 2001. *Adventure Racing: The Ultimate Guide*. Boulder, CO: Velo Press.

Sigesmund, B.J. 2001. "The Tribe Has Spoken." *Newsweek Web Exclusive*, September 6.

Simon, Jonathan. 2002. "Taking Risks: Extreme Sports and the Embrace of Risk in Advanced Liberal Societies." In *Embracing Risk: The Changing Culture of Insurance and Responsibility*, ed. Tom Baker and Jonathan Simon, 177–208. Chicago: University of Chicago Press.

Simri, Uriel. 1977. *A Historical Analysis of the Role of Women in the Modern Olympic Games*. Netanya, Israel: Wingate Institute for Physical Education and Sport.

Simson, Vyv, and Andrew Jennings. 1992. *The Lords of the Rings*. Sydney: Simon and Schuster.

Spence, James, with Dave Diles. 1988. *Up Close and Personal: The Inside Story of Network Television Sports*. New York: Atheneum Publishers.

Stanton, Richard. 2000. *The Forgotten Olympic Art Competitions*. Victoria, BC: Trafford.

Streisand, Betsy. 2002. "Must-Ski TV: Sappy Profiles Are Out; Extreme Sports Are In." *U.S. News and World Report*, January 28–February 4, 53.

Stuhr, John J. "Introduction." 2000. In *Pragmatism and Classical American Philosophy: Essential Readings and Interpretive Essays*, ed. John J. Stuhr, 2nd ed., 1–9. New York: Oxford University Press.

Toohey, Kristine, and A.J. Veal. 2000. *The Olympic Games: A Social Science Approach*. Wallingford, England: CABI.

Trask, Haunani-Kay. 1993. *From a Native Daughter: Colonialism and Sovereignty in Hawai`i*. Honolulu: University of Hawaii Press.

Tunis, John R. 1928. *$port$: Heroics and Hysterics*. New York: John Day.

Wamsley, Kevin B. 1997. "Power and Privilege in Historiography: Constructing Percy Page." *Sport History Review* 28(2):146–55.

———. 2000a. "Symbolic Body Practices: Gender Configurations in the Early Olympic Games." *Proceedings, North American Society for Sport History*, Banff, AB, May.

———. 2000b. "Organizing Gender in the Modern Olympic Games." Keynote address to the Singapore Olympic Academy, 2000.

———. 2002. "The Global Sport Monopoly: A Synopsis of 20th-Century Olympic Politics." *International Journal* 57(3):395–411.

Wamsley, Kevin B., and Guy Schultz. 2000. "Rogues and Bedfellows: The IOC and the Incorporation of the FSFI." In *Bridging Three Centuries: Intellectual Crossroads and the Modern Olympic Movement*, ed. Kevin B. Wamsley, Scott G. Martyn, Gordon H. MacDonald, and Robert K. Barney, 113–18. London, ON: International Centre for Olympic Studies, University of Western Ontario.

Wenn, Stephen R. 1991. "Give Me the Keys Please: Avery Brundage, Canadian Journalists, and the Barbara Scott Phaeton Affair." *Journal of Sport History* 18 (summer):241–54.

White, Jeremy. 2002. "'The Los Angeles Way of Doing Things': The Olympic Village and the Practice of Boosterism in 1932." *Olympika: The International Journal of Olympic Studies* II:79–116.

Wiggins, David K. 1989. "Great Speed but Little Stamina: The Historical Debate over Black Athletic Superiority." *Journal of Sport History* 16(summer):158–85.

Young, Michael. 1988. "The Melbourne Press and the 1980 Moscow Olympic Boycott Controversy." *Sporting Traditions* 4(2):184–200.

Zelinsky, Wilbur. 1988. *Nation into State: The Shifting Symbolic Foundations of American Nationalism*. Chapel Hill, NC: University of North Carolina Press.

GLOSSARY OF TERMS

agon	contest, struggle, or gathering
agonothetes	sponsors of the games (or contests)
akon	light spear or javelin
akontist	javelin thrower
alytarch	an official who acted as a "policeman" at Olympia
Altis	the grove of wild olive trees in the Sanctuary area at Olympia; a term used for the Sanctuary grounds as a whole
anolympiad	a non-Olympiad, where victors' names are removed from official records by the Eleans
apene	a chariot race for two mules rather than horses, held at Olympia between 500 and 444 BC
aporoi	poor Greek citizens, ones "without means"
Arcteia	an initiation festival to honour Artemis in Attica in which young girls took part in foot races or ritual chases
athloi	heroic deeds or struggles, whether in battle or elsewhere, including athletic contests
athlon	the prize for a victor in a contest
athlos	a struggle or contest normally with a prize to the victor
athlothetes	the prize giver, often synonymous with agonothetes

balbis	starting line for foot races; also an area to mark the line (bater) for jumping, and the release of the discus and javelin in the pentathlon
basileus (pl. basileis)	chief, king
bater	stone sill from which jumpers must leap, and discus and javelin throwers must release their throws in the pentathlon; generally also a starting line
chiton	a Greek dress of finer material, often falling to the ankles
chôra	region or territory
commensality	eating or drinking in a group
crown games	Panhellenic games; victors at these games were crowned with wreaths (stephanai) of olive, laurel, pine or celery branches
Curetes	another name for the Dactyls of Crete
Dactyls	mythical metal workers on Crete with magical powers who helped protect Zeus as a baby
demos	people of a city-state, the public
demosion	belonging to the "demos" or public
dendrophoria	bringing or bearing a tree or branch from one place to another
diaitetai	an earlier name for the judges (Hellanodikai) at Olympia, "umpires" or "arbitrators"
diaulus	a foot race of two stades, from one end of the stadium, around a post (kampter) and back again
Dioscuri	the twins, Castor and Pollux, heroes of Sparta
discobolus	discus throwing event in the pentathlon
ekecheiria	Sacred Truce for the games, literally "holding of hands"
epichoric	local, pertaining to a region
epinician ode	a poem written to honour an athletic victor; performed by a chorus dancing and singing to music
eros	an erotic form of love, desire
euporoi	wealthy Greeks, ones "well provided for"
exomis	a sleeveless shirt worn by men normally
gymnasiarch	an official in charge of the gymnasium
halma	the jumping event in the pentathlon
halteres	weights of metal or stone carried by jumpers in the pentathlon
Hellanodikai	nobles chosen every four years at Elis to organize and run the Olympic Games, including the judging of events
Heraion	temple of Hera
Heraea	a festival with races for virgin girls in honour of Hera at Olympia

himantes	thongs of ox-hide wrapped around the hands and wrists to protect boxers' hands
hippodrome	track for equestrian events
hippotrophy	horse raising, training
hoplitodromos	race in armour, with runners carrying a shield, and sometimes wearing a helmet and greaves
hydria	a large three-handled vessel for carrying water
Hyperboreans	mythical people from the extreme north
interiores et reconditas litteras	"more erudite and profound writings"
kampter	a turning post in the stadium and hippodrome, also used to mark the bater in the pentathlon
kleros	a lot or marker used to draw lanes in races or match competitors in combat events
kourotrophic	child nurturing, an epithet of several goddesses
Linear B	the writing script of the Myceneans
logos	story or tale
mastigophoros	"whip-bearer"
Metroon	temple for the mother of the gods, Rhea
Olympic court	a body at Olympia active after the Persian Wars in resolving disputes between Greek city-states
paideia	education, up-bringing
Panhellenic	"all Greek," describing things which included Greeks from all parts of the Aegean, Mediterranean and Black Seas
pankration	a combat sport which combines boxing and wrestling techniques
Pelopion	shrine to the hero, Pelops
penētes	workers, labourers
pentathlon	an athletic contest with five individual events: discus, jump, javelin, foot race and wrestling
periodonikes	a victor in all four of the Panhellenic Games–Olympic, Pythian (Delphic), Isthmian and Nemean
periodos	a circuit of four Panhellenic Games held over a four-year span
philotimia	literally "a love or desire for honour," seeking distinction
plousioi	the rich; wealthy citizens, aristocracy
politeia	constitution of the poleis or city-states
polis (pl. poleis)	Greek city-state, e.g. Elis or Laconia
ptôchoi	poor Greek citizens
Pythia	the priestess of Apollo Pythias at Delphi

rhyton	tall conical drinking vessel
sarcophagus	coffin
Selloi	original inhabitants of Dodona in northwest Greece
spondophoroi	heralds who bring notice of the Sacred Truce of Olympia to the Greek city-states
stade (or stadion)	a distance of 600 local feet, and so a term given to the race course, and the foot race of this distance
synoecism	amalgamation of local villages into a larger town or city
theoroi	ambassadors or a mission from a city state to a festival
Titans	an earlier race of divine giants, led by Cronos
zans or zanes	bronze statues of Zeus erected outside the stadium by athletes caught cheating at the Olympic Games

Some Common Terms for Periods of Time

Bronze Age	ca. 3000–1050 BC
Early Helladic	ca. 3000–2100 BC Greek Mainland
Middle Helladic	ca. 2100–1700 BC Greek Mainland
Minoan	ca. 3000–1050 BC on Crete
Mycenean	ca. 1700–1050 BC mainly Greek Mainland
Dark Age	ca. 1050–900 BC
Iron Age (early)	ca. 1050–700 BC
Archaic	ca. 700–480 BC
Classical	480–323 BC
Hellenistic	323–31 BC
Roman Imperial (early)	31 BC–AD 312

INDEX

Page numbers in italics refer to illustrations.
Abbreviations: IOC (International Olympic Committee); "Olympics" (Olympic Games)